Floundering Fathers

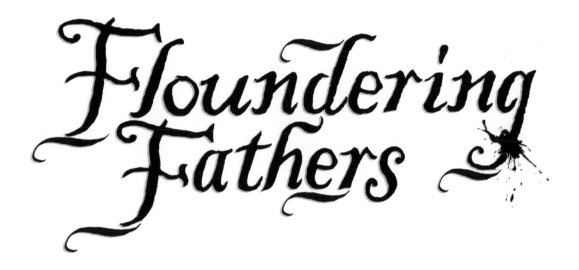

Other *Pearls Before Swine* Collections

I Scream, You Scream, We All Scream Because Puns Suck
Stephan's Web
I'm Only in This for Me
King of the Comics
Breaking Stephan
Rat's Wars
Unsportsmanlike Conduct
Because Sometimes You Just Gotta Draw a Cover with Your Left Hand
Larry in Wonderland
When Pigs Fly
50,000,000 Pearls Fans Can't Be Wrong
The Saturday Evening Pearls
Macho Macho Animals
The Sopratos
Da Brudderhood of Zeeba Zeeba Eata
The Ratvolution Will Not Be Televised
Nighthogs
This Little Piggy Stayed Home
BLTs Taste So Darn Good

Treasuries

Pearls Hogs the Road
Pearls Gets Sacrificed
Pearls Falls Fast
Pearls Freaks the #%# Out*
Pearls Blows Up
Pearls Sells Out
The Crass Menagerie
Lions and Tigers and Crocs, Oh My!
Sgt. Piggy's Lonely Hearts Club Comic

Gift Books

Friends Should Know When They're Not Wanted
Da Crockydile Book o' Frendsheep

Kids' Books

Suit Your Selfie
When Crocs Fly
Skip School, Fly to Space
The Croc Ate My Homework
Beginning Pearls

Floundering Fathers

A Pearls Before Swine Collection
by Stephan Pastis

Andrews McMeel
PUBLISHING®

For my daughter Julia,
aka Hulia, Hulio, Ja, Ja Rule, Hulio Jones, Schmoo and a
variety of other nicknames used by her creative father.

Introduction

Sitting in the front row of The Second City stage in Chicago, I am hoping nobody notices me.

It is the most famous improv stage in the world, and I know they involve the audience, and I am desperately afraid they will try to involve *me*.

Now that might seem odd for someone who's supposed to be funny for a living. But what I do is cowardly. I write something and hide, blissfully unaware of whether people are laughing or scowling.

Take me out of that environment and ask me to ad-lib and I will bomb spectacularly. I will hear the silence of 300 people not laughing. I will have to leave.

So I sit in my seat quietly. Trying my best to be small. Hoping I am the size of a church mouse.

But then the show starts.

And the girl next to me has other plans.

She is raising her hand.

She is shouting.

She is volunteering.

And she is my daughter.

What possessed the young woman is anyone's guess.

Because in her everyday Clark Kent guise, she is one serious kid, so singularly focused on studying that our house could catch fire and she would ask if she could stay inside and work on her English essay, at least until the firemen arrive.

In fact, I may be one of the only parents in North America who regularly says to his child, "Study *less*."

So it was everything I could do to even get her to take a summer trip with me. And after much cajoling, she chose Chicago. Not for the deep-dish pizza. Or the bars (well, she *is* only fifteen). But for the unholy purpose of visiting college campuses. Namely, the University of Chicago and Northwestern.

I tried to get out of the college tours, kindly offering to spend those hours in a pub. But she made me go. And to punish me further, she made me sit through a two-hour engineering school orientation. That was cruel.

So on the drive back from the University of Chicago, I threw out a wild and wholly un-academic suggestion.

Let's go to Second City.

But she didn't know what it was.

So I told her it was the stage that launched the careers of John Belushi, Dan Aykroyd, Bill Murray, John Candy, and just about every other funny human being on Planet Earth, all of whom had been a huge comedic influence on me.

But she hadn't heard of any of them.

So when we got to the theater, I just hoped it would be something she didn't hate.

And then the curtain rose.

And kaboom.

Serious Girl became, well, Lunatic Girl.

At every request for audience participation, her hand shot up like a rocket, shouting out one suggestion after another: "NUNS! DEATH! MONKEYS! JERUSALEM!"

I touched her forehead to make sure she didn't have a fever.

I checked under her seat for empty bottles of booze.

But no. The girl was sober.

And she was drawing attention to us like we were wounded sheep among wolves. And then *WHAM.*

"YOU!" cried the performer on the stage. Oh my God. No. Not me. Wait. What?

The man was pointing at Julia.

"Come on up!" he said to her. She rises.

"Wait," he interjected. "How old are you?"

"Fifteen," she answered.

"Oh, I'm sorry," he told her, "You have to be eighteen to be on stage."

She sat back down. "Shoot!" she muttered, disappointed, but still beaming.

I know that because I was staring at her from underneath my seat, where I was hiding.

"Is it safe to come out now?" I asked.

When the show ended, she was still excited, reciting all of her favorite parts.

"Is there any way we can go back tomorrow night?" she asked. I said yes, provided that I could sit on the other side of the theater.

But the truth is I was amazed. Proud. Sort of in awe.

And as we walked through the north side of Chicago, I couldn't help but wonder how many other unknown layers there were to my child.

"All that stuff you were shouting out," I said. "That was pretty funny."

"Thanks," she answered.

"Do you think you get any of that from me?" I asked.

"No," she answered.

But I took her back the next night anyways.

And hid right there next to her.

Sincerely,

Stephan Pastis
March 2018

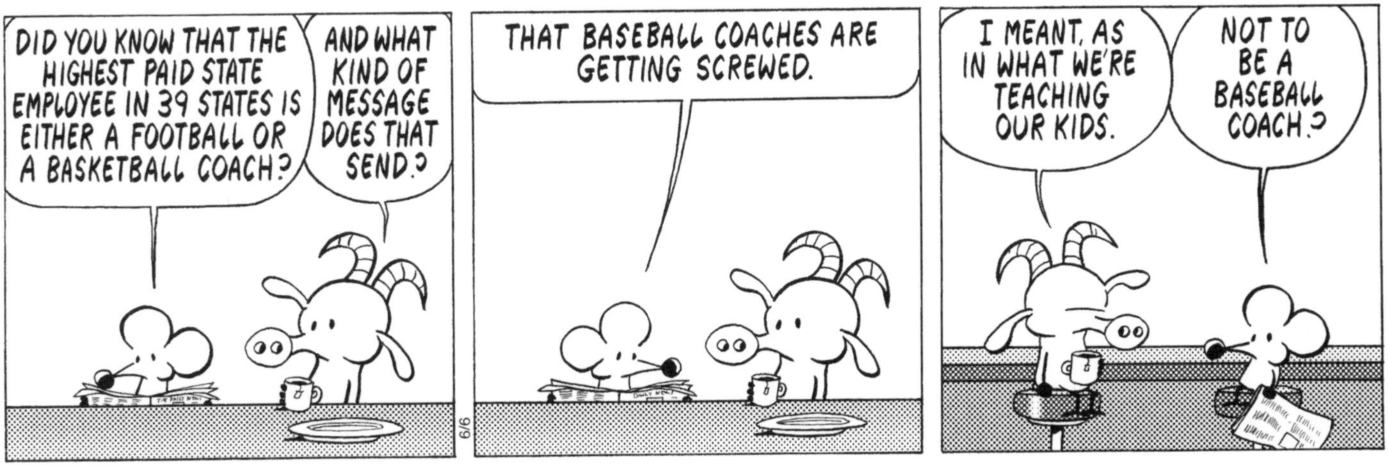
DID YOU KNOW THAT THE HIGHEST PAID STATE EMPLOYEE IN 39 STATES IS EITHER A FOOTBALL OR A BASKETBALL COACH?
AND WHAT KIND OF MESSAGE DOES THAT SEND?
THAT BASEBALL COACHES ARE GETTING SCREWED.
I MEANT, AS IN WHAT WE'RE TEACHING OUR KIDS.
NOT TO BE A BASEBALL COACH?
6/6

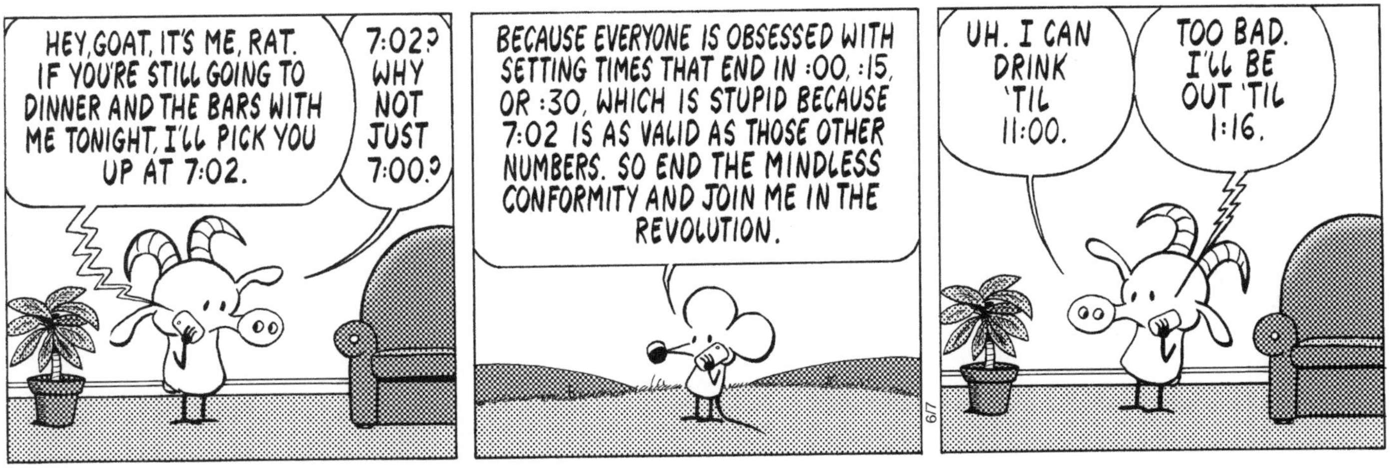
HEY, GOAT, IT'S ME, RAT. IF YOU'RE STILL GOING TO DINNER AND THE BARS WITH ME TONIGHT, I'LL PICK YOU UP AT 7:02.
7:02? WHY NOT JUST 7:00?
BECAUSE EVERYONE IS OBSESSED WITH SETTING TIMES THAT END IN :00, :15, OR :30, WHICH IS STUPID BECAUSE 7:02 IS AS VALID AS THOSE OTHER NUMBERS. SO END THE MINDLESS CONFORMITY AND JOIN ME IN THE REVOLUTION.
UH. I CAN DRINK 'TIL 11:00.
TOO BAD. I'LL BE OUT 'TIL 1:16.
6/7

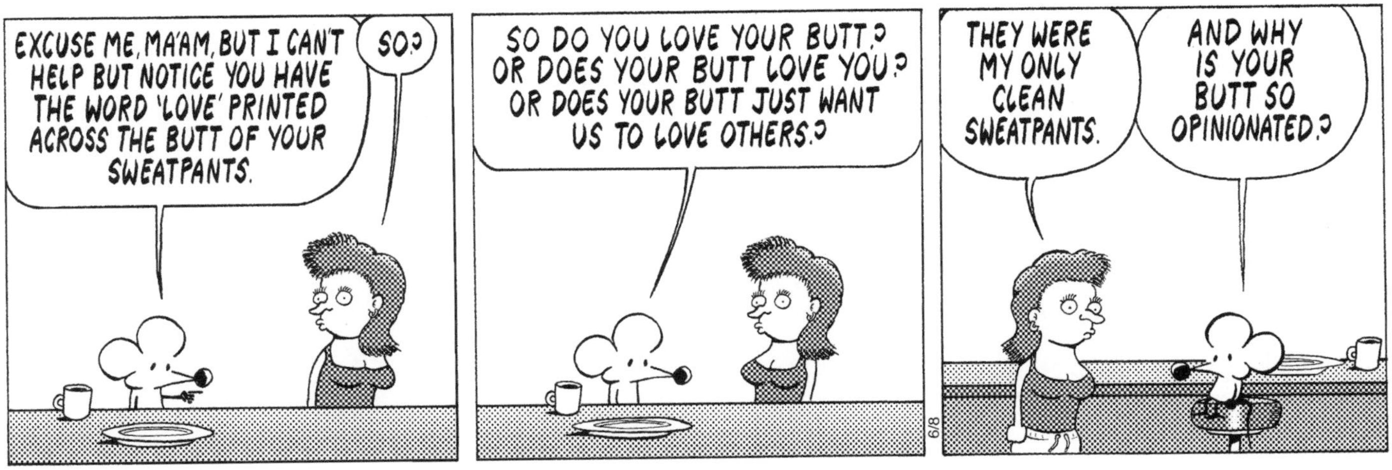
EXCUSE ME, MA'AM, BUT I CAN'T HELP BUT NOTICE YOU HAVE THE WORD 'LOVE' PRINTED ACROSS THE BUTT OF YOUR SWEATPANTS.
SO?
SO DO YOU LOVE YOUR BUTT? OR DOES YOUR BUTT LOVE YOU? OR DOES YOUR BUTT JUST WANT US TO LOVE OTHERS?
THEY WERE MY ONLY CLEAN SWEATPANTS.
AND WHY IS YOUR BUTT SO OPINIONATED?
6/8

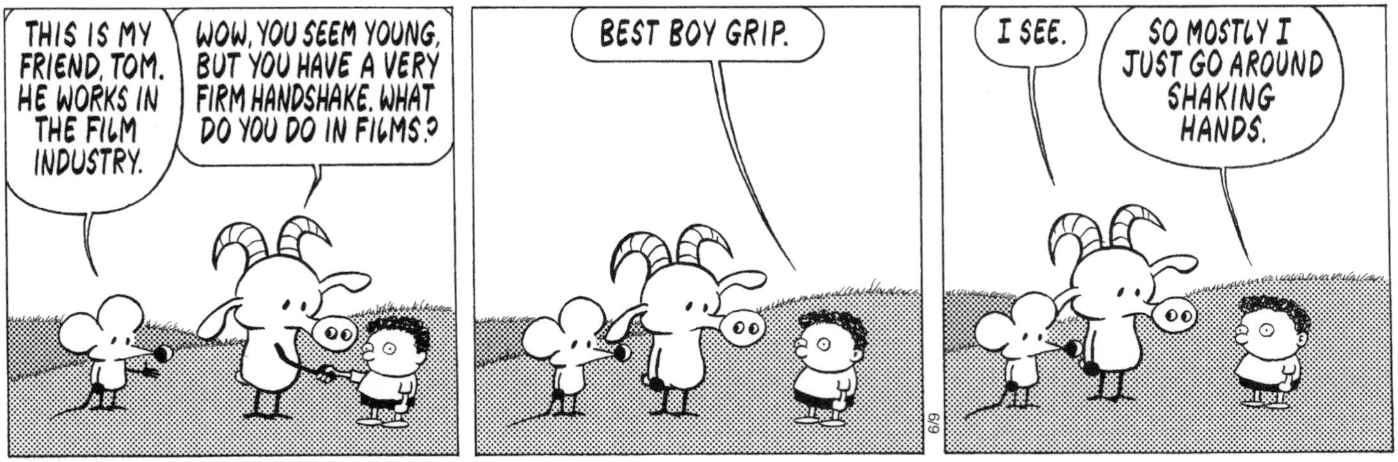
THIS IS MY FRIEND, TOM. HE WORKS IN THE FILM INDUSTRY.
WOW, YOU SEEM YOUNG, BUT YOU HAVE A VERY FIRM HANDSHAKE. WHAT DO YOU DO IN FILMS?
BEST BOY GRIP.
I SEE.
SO MOSTLY I JUST GO AROUND SHAKING HANDS.
6/9

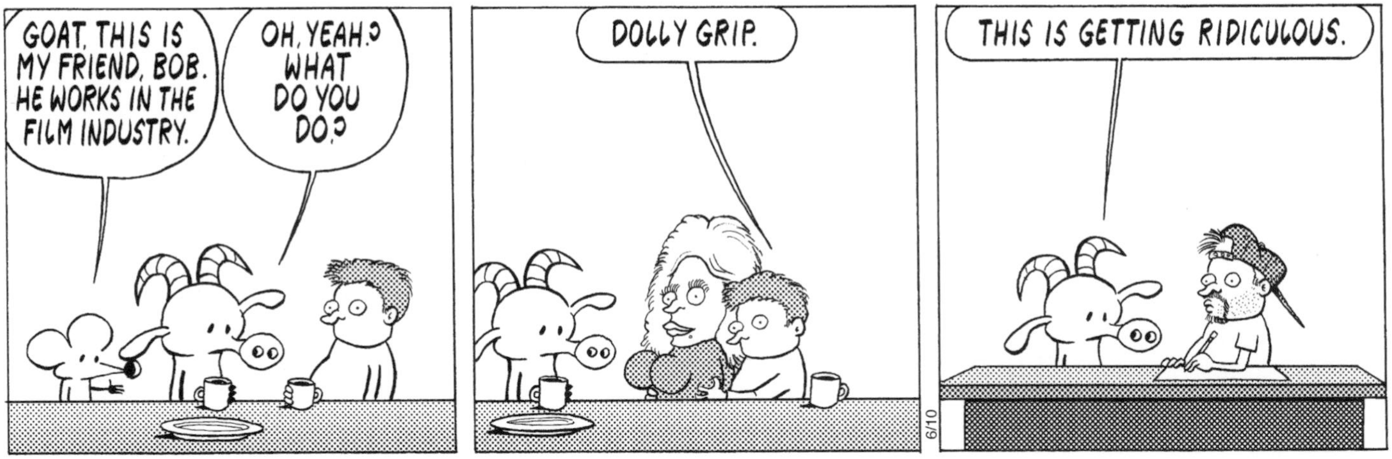
GOAT, THIS IS MY FRIEND, BOB. HE WORKS IN THE FILM INDUSTRY.
OH, YEAH? WHAT DO YOU DO?
DOLLY GRIP.
THIS IS GETTING RIDICULOUS.
6/10

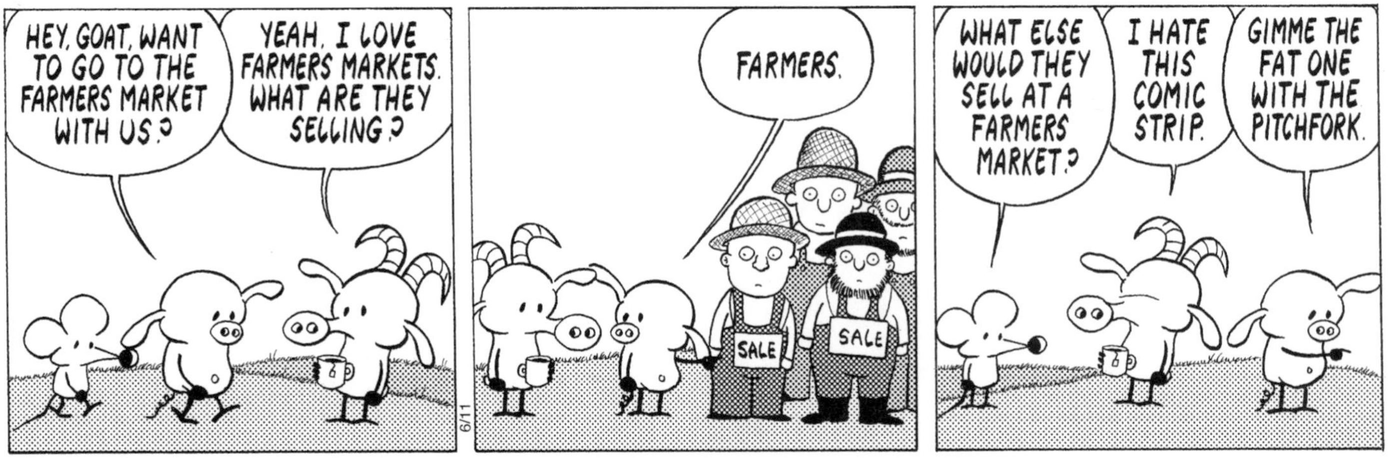
HEY, GOAT, WANT TO GO TO THE FARMERS MARKET WITH US?
YEAH. I LOVE FARMERS MARKETS. WHAT ARE THEY SELLING?
FARMERS.
SALE
SALE
WHAT ELSE WOULD THEY SELL AT A FARMERS MARKET?
I HATE THIS COMIC STRIP.
GIMME THE FAT ONE WITH THE PITCHFORK.
6/11

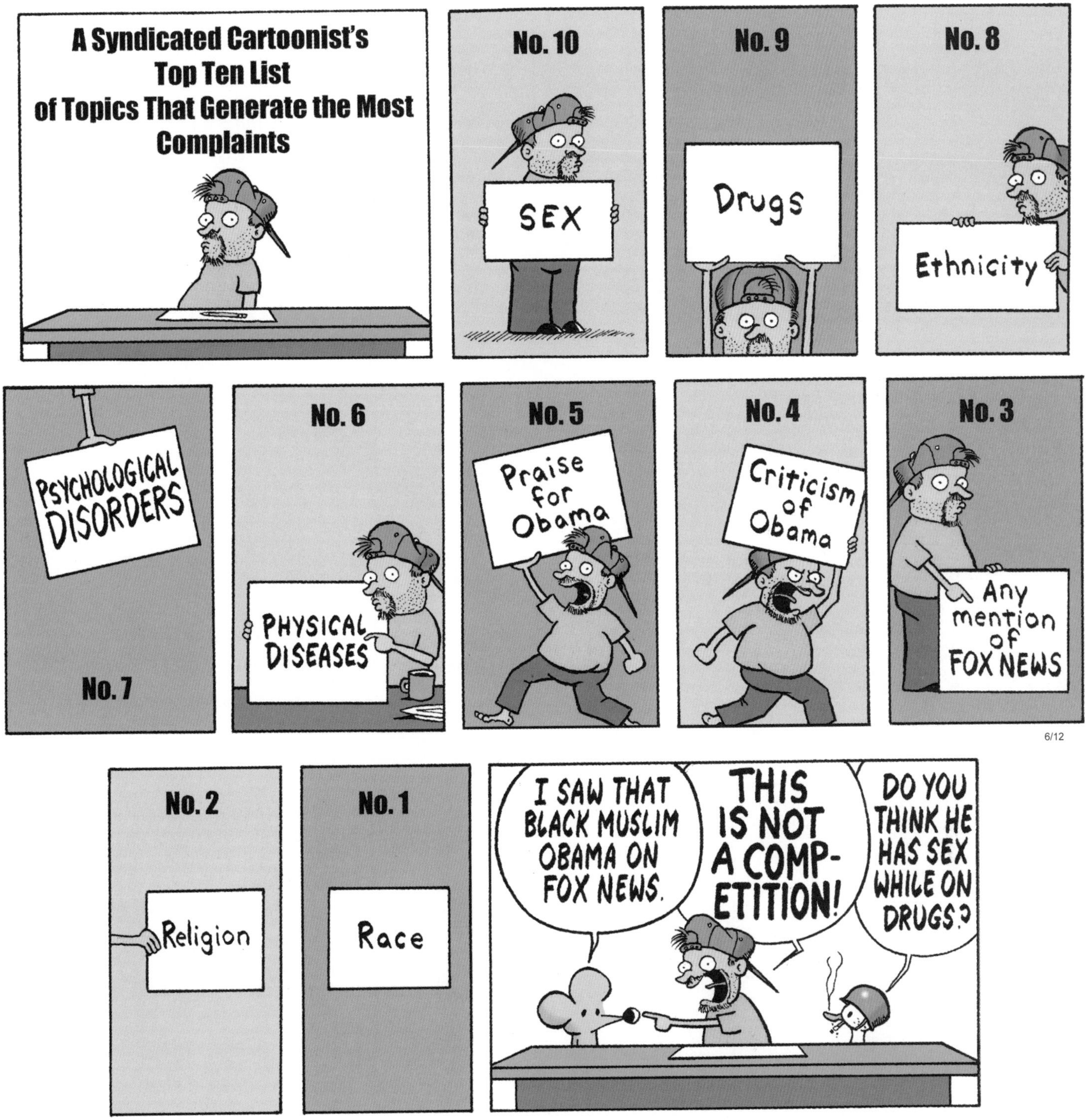
A Syndicated Cartoonist's Top Ten List of Topics That Generate the Most Complaints
No. 10
SEX
No. 9
Drugs
No. 8
Ethnicity
PSYCHOLOGICAL DISORDERS
No. 7
No. 6
PHYSICAL DISEASES
No. 5
Praise for Obama
No. 4
Criticism of Obama
No. 3
Any mention of FOX NEWS
6/12
No. 2
Religion
No. 1
Race
I SAW THAT BLACK MUSLIM OBAMA ON FOX NEWS.
THIS IS NOT A COMP-ETITION!
DO YOU THINK HE HAS SEX WHILE ON DRUGS?

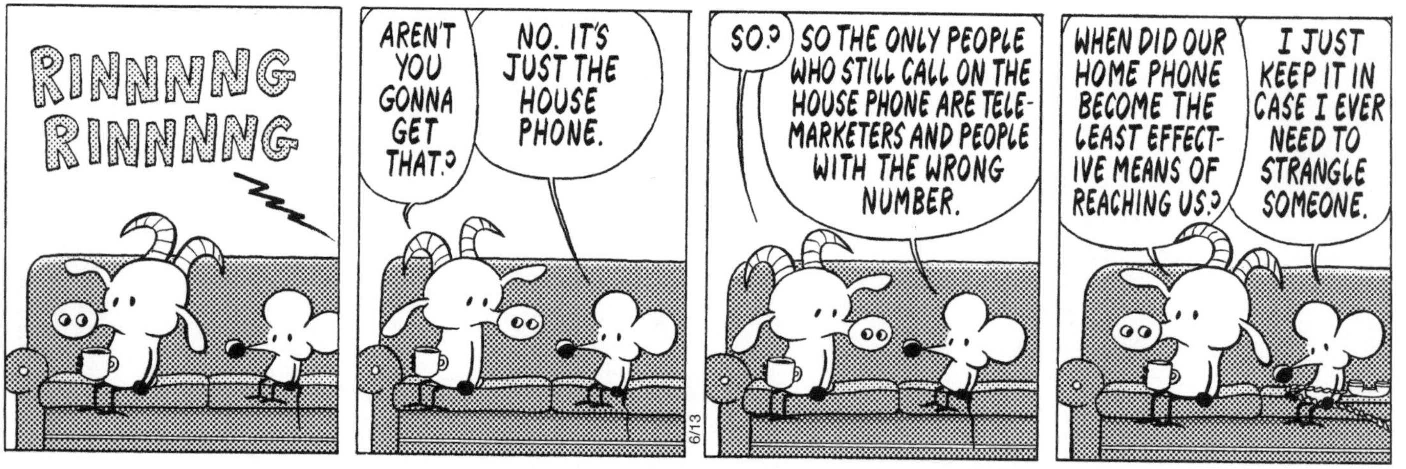
RINNNNG
RINNNNG
AREN'T YOU GONNA GET THAT?
NO. IT'S JUST THE HOUSE PHONE.
SO?
SO THE ONLY PEOPLE WHO STILL CALL ON THE HOUSE PHONE ARE TELE-MARKETERS AND PEOPLE WITH THE WRONG NUMBER.
WHEN DID OUR HOME PHONE BECOME THE LEAST EFFECT-IVE MEANS OF REACHING US?
I JUST KEEP IT IN CASE I EVER NEED TO STRANGLE SOMEONE.
6/13

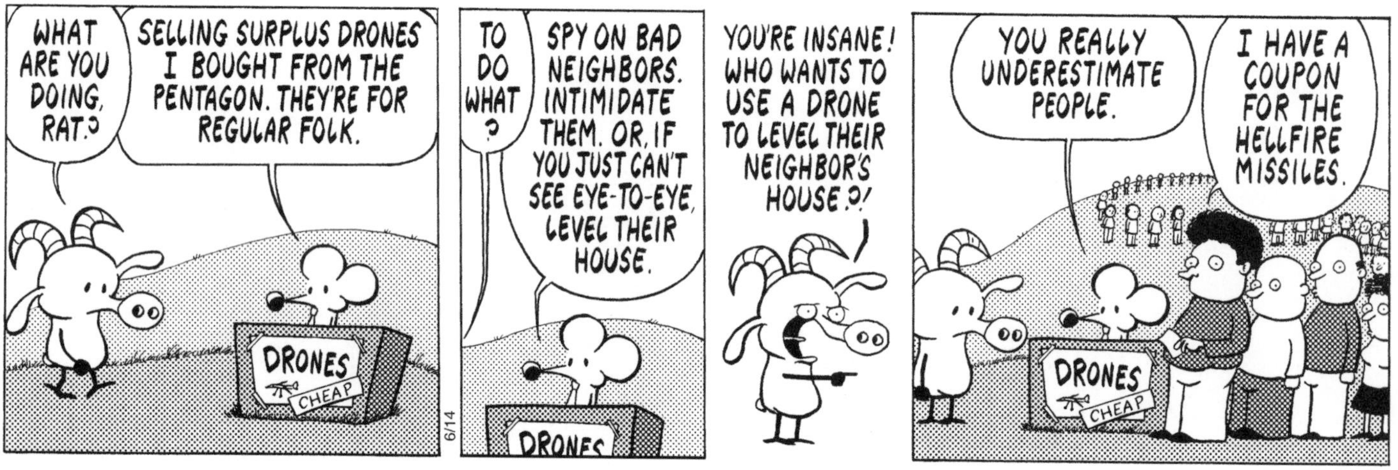
WHAT ARE YOU DOING, RAT?
SELLING SURPLUS DRONES I BOUGHT FROM THE PENTAGON. THEY'RE FOR REGULAR FOLK.
DRONES
CHEAP
6/14
TO DO WHAT?
SPY ON BAD NEIGHBORS. INTIMIDATE THEM. OR, IF YOU JUST CAN'T SEE EYE-TO-EYE, LEVEL THEIR HOUSE.
YOU'RE INSANE! WHO WANTS TO USE A DRONE TO LEVEL THEIR NEIGHBOR'S HOUSE?!
YOU REALLY UNDERESTIMATE PEOPLE.
I HAVE A COUPON FOR THE HELLFIRE MISSILES.
DRONES
CHEAP

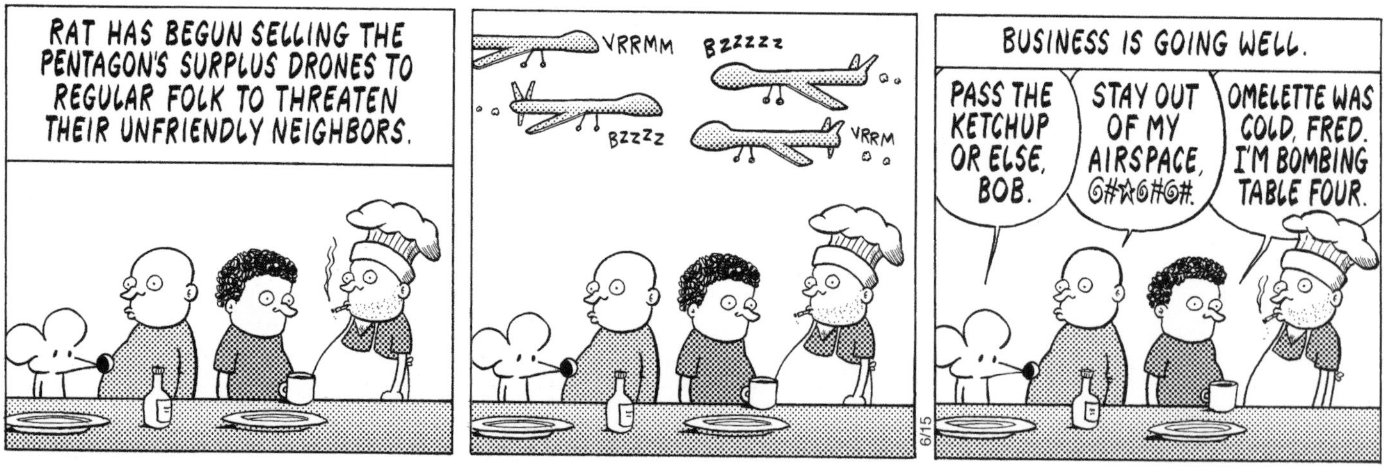
RAT HAS BEGUN SELLING THE PENTAGON'S SURPLUS DRONES TO REGULAR FOLK TO THREATEN THEIR UNFRIENDLY NEIGHBORS.
VRRMM
BZZZZZ
BZZZZ
VRRM
BUSINESS IS GOING WELL.
PASS THE KETCHUP OR ELSE, BOB.
STAY OUT OF MY AIRSPACE, @#✩@#@#.
OMELETTE WAS COLD, FRED. I'M BOMBING TABLE FOUR.
6/15

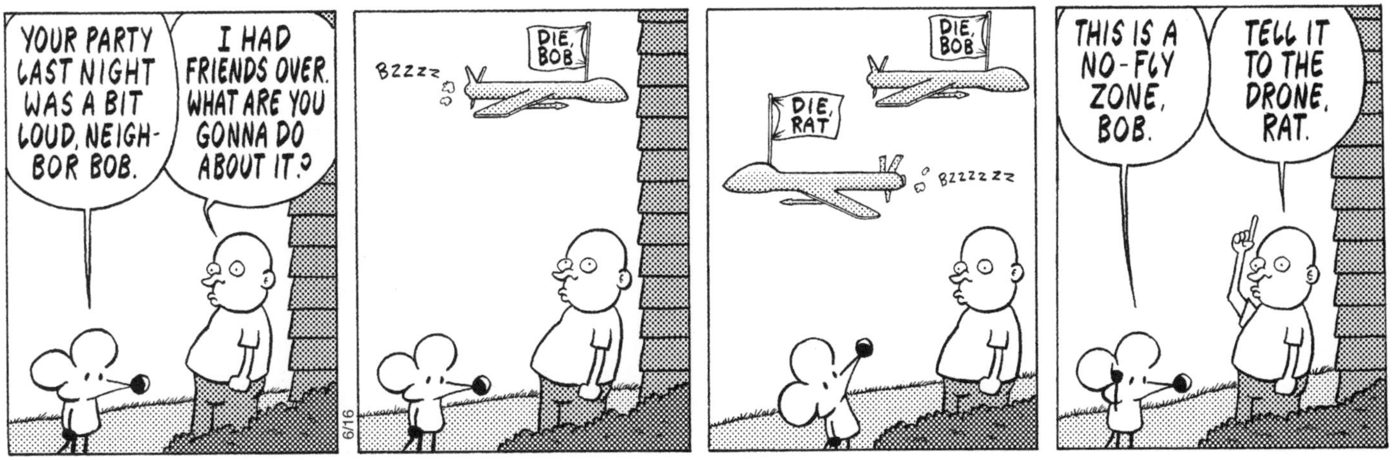
YOUR PARTY LAST NIGHT WAS A BIT LOUD, NEIGHBOR BOB.
I HAD FRIENDS OVER. WHAT ARE YOU GONNA DO ABOUT IT?
6/16
BZZZZ
DIE, BOB
DIE, BOB
DIE, RAT
BZZZZZZ
THIS IS A NO-FLY ZONE, BOB.
TELL IT TO THE DRONE, RAT.

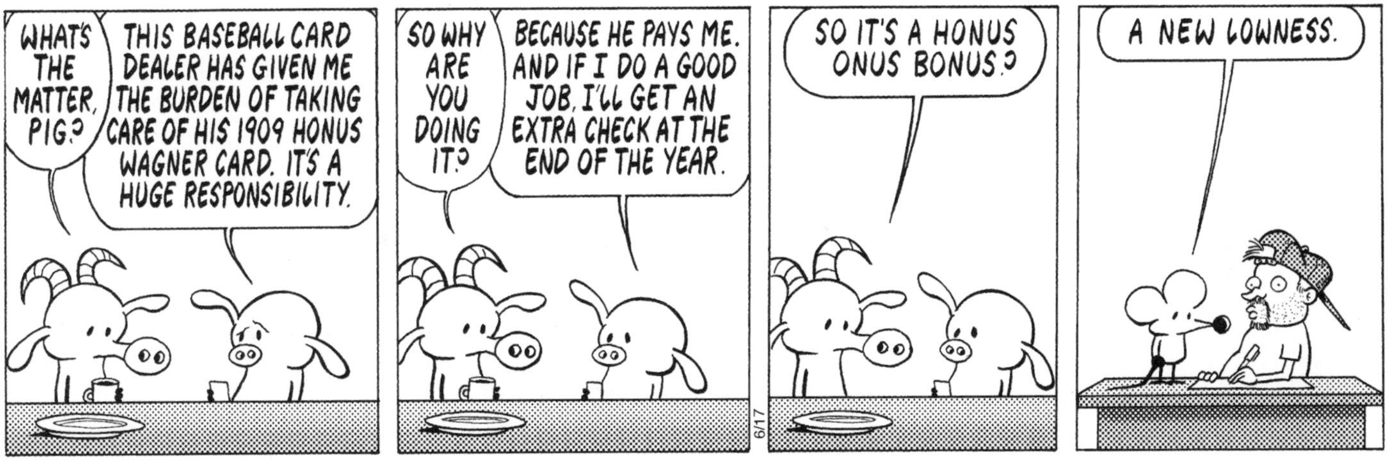
WHAT'S THE MATTER, PIG?
THIS BASEBALL CARD DEALER HAS GIVEN ME THE BURDEN OF TAKING CARE OF HIS 1909 HONUS WAGNER CARD. IT'S A HUGE RESPONSIBILITY.
SO WHY ARE YOU DOING IT?
BECAUSE HE PAYS ME. AND IF I DO A GOOD JOB, I'LL GET AN EXTRA CHECK AT THE END OF THE YEAR.
6/17
SO IT'S A HONUS ONUS BONUS?
A NEW LOWNESS.

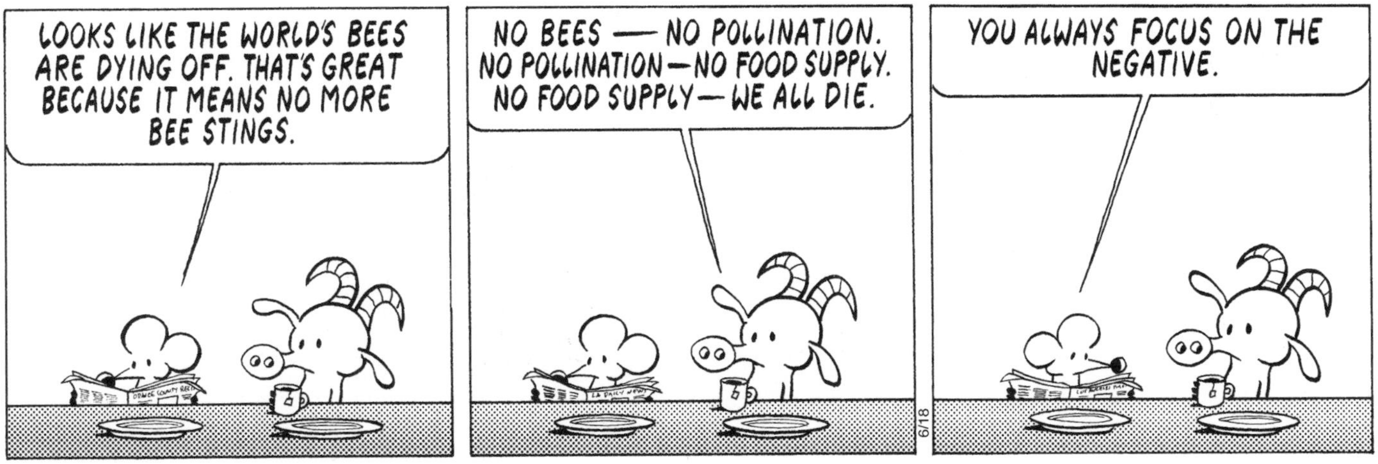
LOOKS LIKE THE WORLD'S BEES ARE DYING OFF. THAT'S GREAT BECAUSE IT MEANS NO MORE BEE STINGS.
NO BEES — NO POLLINATION. NO POLLINATION — NO FOOD SUPPLY. NO FOOD SUPPLY — WE ALL DIE.
6/18
YOU ALWAYS FOCUS ON THE NEGATIVE.

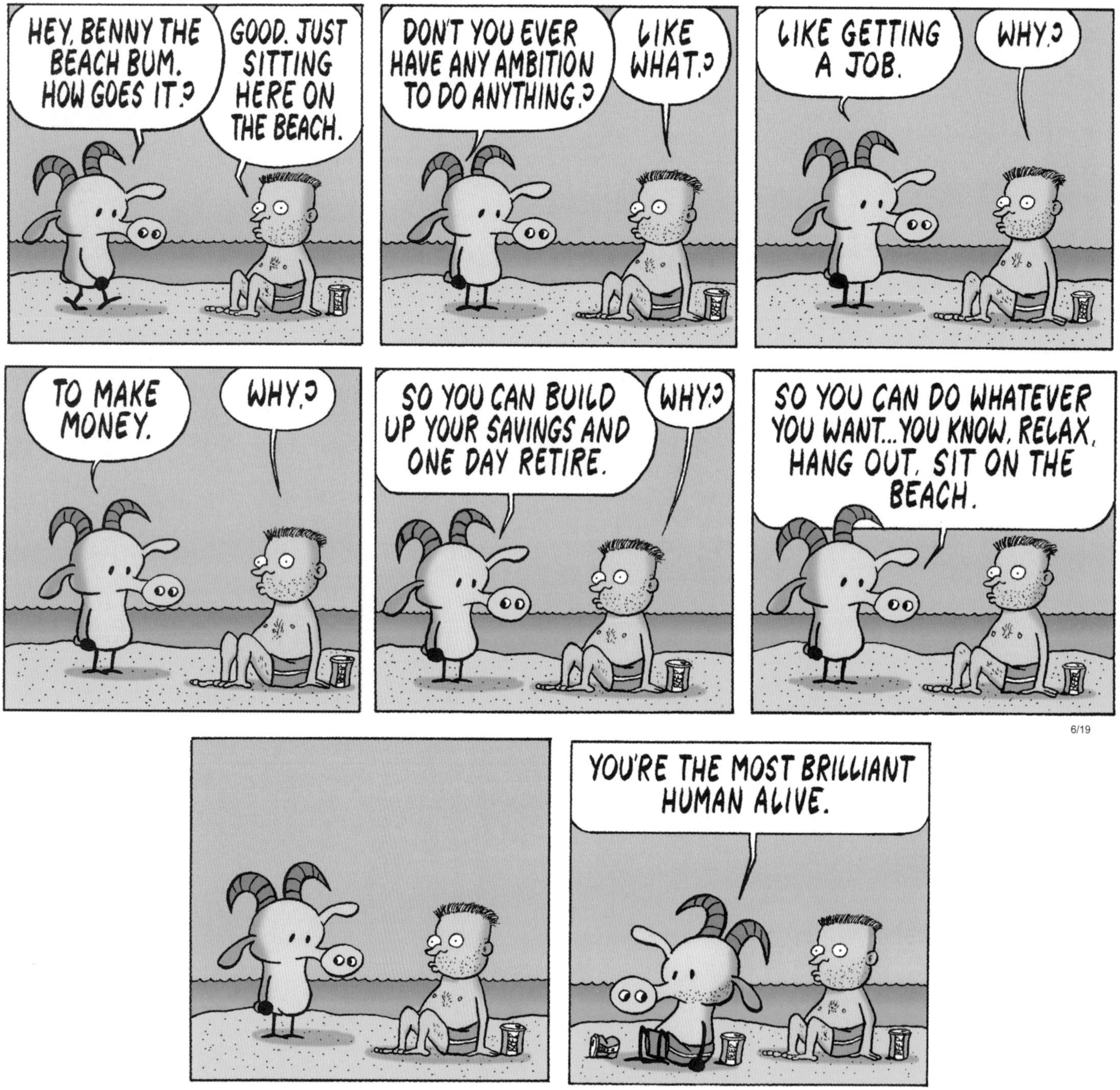
HEY, BENNY THE BEACH BUM. HOW GOES IT?
GOOD. JUST SITTING HERE ON THE BEACH.
DON'T YOU EVER HAVE ANY AMBITION TO DO ANYTHING?
LIKE WHAT?
LIKE GETTING A JOB.
WHY?
TO MAKE MONEY.
WHY?
SO YOU CAN BUILD UP YOUR SAVINGS AND ONE DAY RETIRE.
WHY?
SO YOU CAN DO WHATEVER YOU WANT...YOU KNOW, RELAX, HANG OUT, SIT ON THE BEACH.
6/19
YOU'RE THE MOST BRILLIANT HUMAN ALIVE.

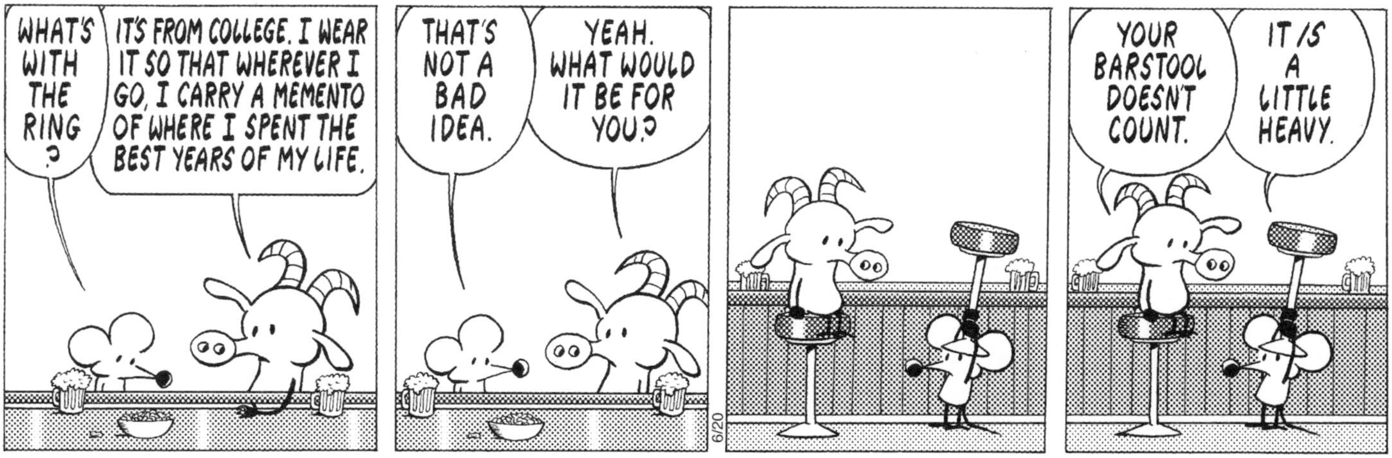
WHAT'S WITH THE RING?
IT'S FROM COLLEGE. I WEAR IT SO THAT WHEREVER I GO, I CARRY A MEMENTO OF WHERE I SPENT THE BEST YEARS OF MY LIFE.
THAT'S NOT A BAD IDEA.
YEAH. WHAT WOULD IT BE FOR YOU?
6/20
YOUR BARSTOOL DOESN'T COUNT.
IT *IS* A LITTLE HEAVY.

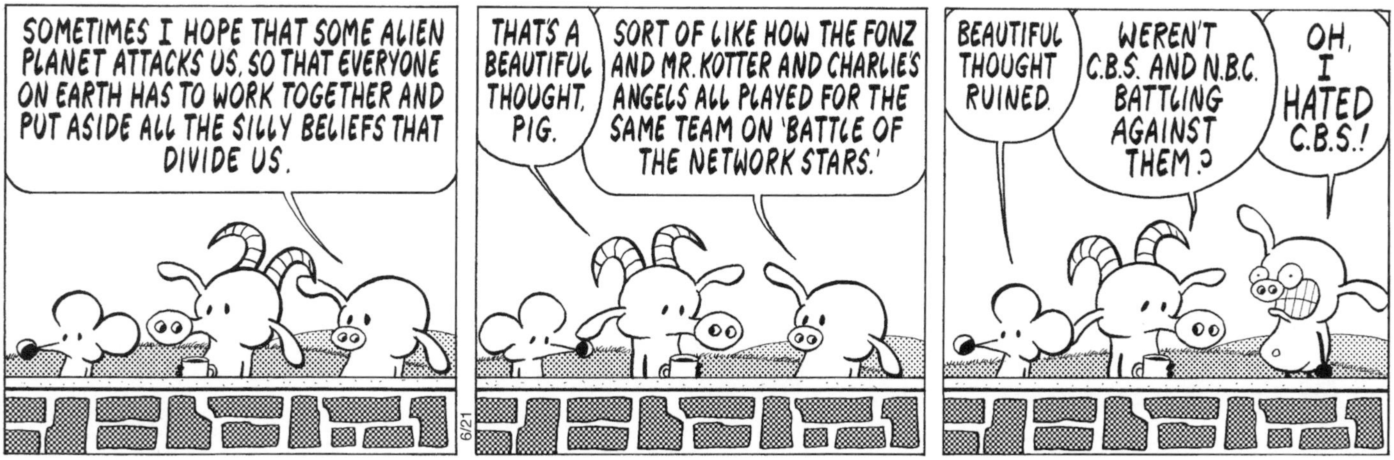
SOMETIMES I HOPE THAT SOME ALIEN PLANET ATTACKS US, SO THAT EVERYONE ON EARTH HAS TO WORK TOGETHER AND PUT ASIDE ALL THE SILLY BELIEFS THAT DIVIDE US.
6/21
THAT'S A BEAUTIFUL THOUGHT, PIG.
SORT OF LIKE HOW THE FONZ AND MR. KOTTER AND CHARLIE'S ANGELS ALL PLAYED FOR THE SAME TEAM ON 'BATTLE OF THE NETWORK STARS.'
BEAUTIFUL THOUGHT RUINED.
WEREN'T C.B.S. AND N.B.C. BATTLING AGAINST THEM?
OH, I HATED C.B.S.!

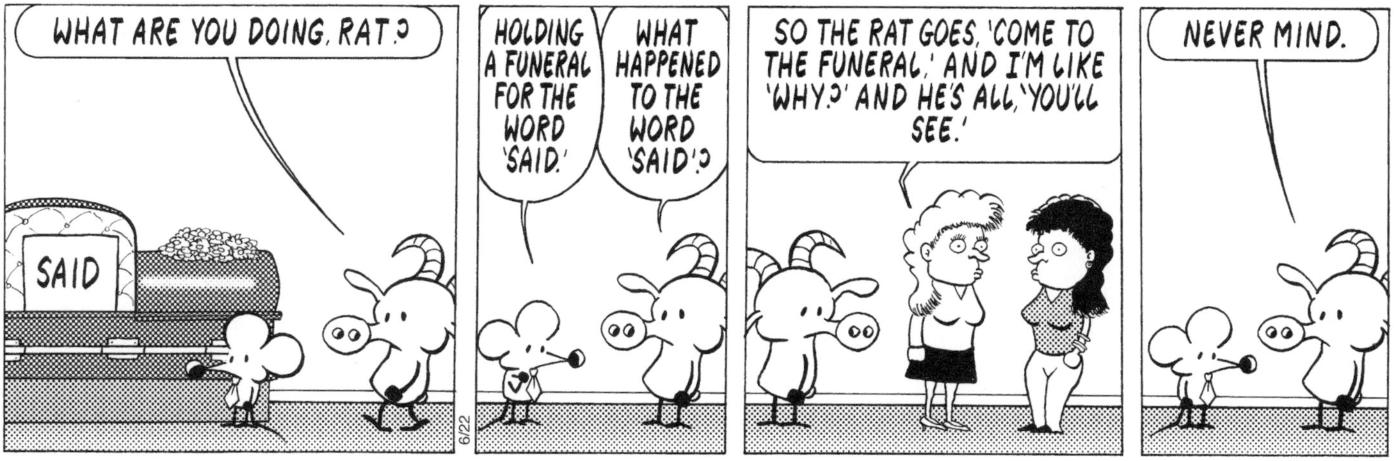
WHAT ARE YOU DOING, RAT?
SAID
6/22
HOLDING A FUNERAL FOR THE WORD 'SAID.'
WHAT HAPPENED TO THE WORD 'SAID'?
SO THE RAT GOES, 'COME TO THE FUNERAL,' AND I'M LIKE 'WHY?' AND HE'S ALL, 'YOU'LL SEE.'
NEVER MIND.

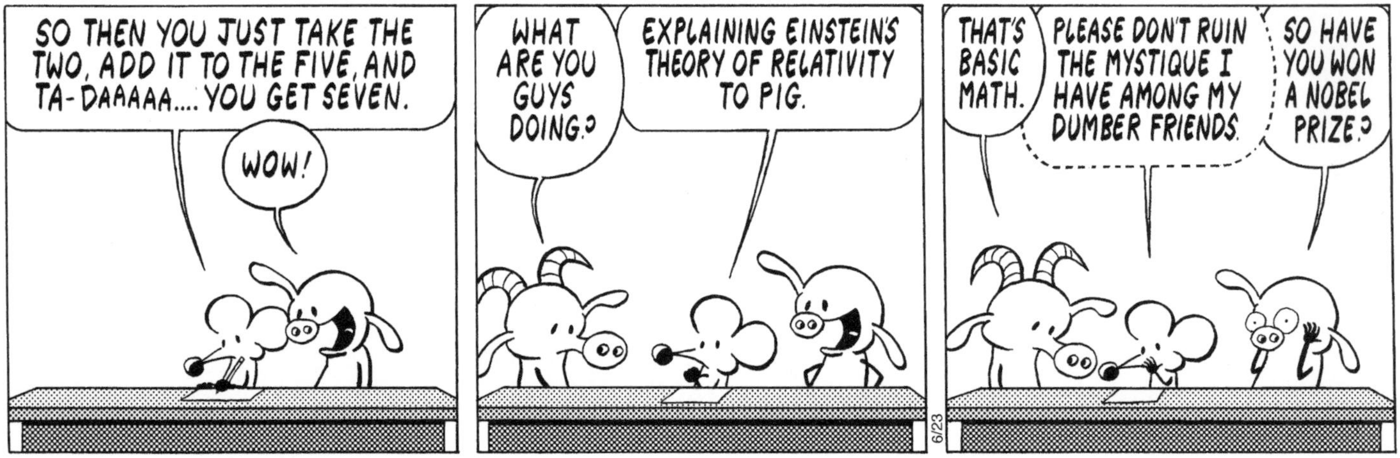
SO THEN YOU JUST TAKE THE TWO, ADD IT TO THE FIVE, AND TA-DAAAAA.... YOU GET SEVEN.
WOW!
WHAT ARE YOU GUYS DOING?
EXPLAINING EINSTEIN'S THEORY OF RELATIVITY TO PIG.
THAT'S BASIC MATH.
PLEASE DON'T RUIN THE MYSTIQUE I HAVE AMONG MY DUMBER FRIENDS.
SO HAVE YOU WON A NOBEL PRIZE?
6/23

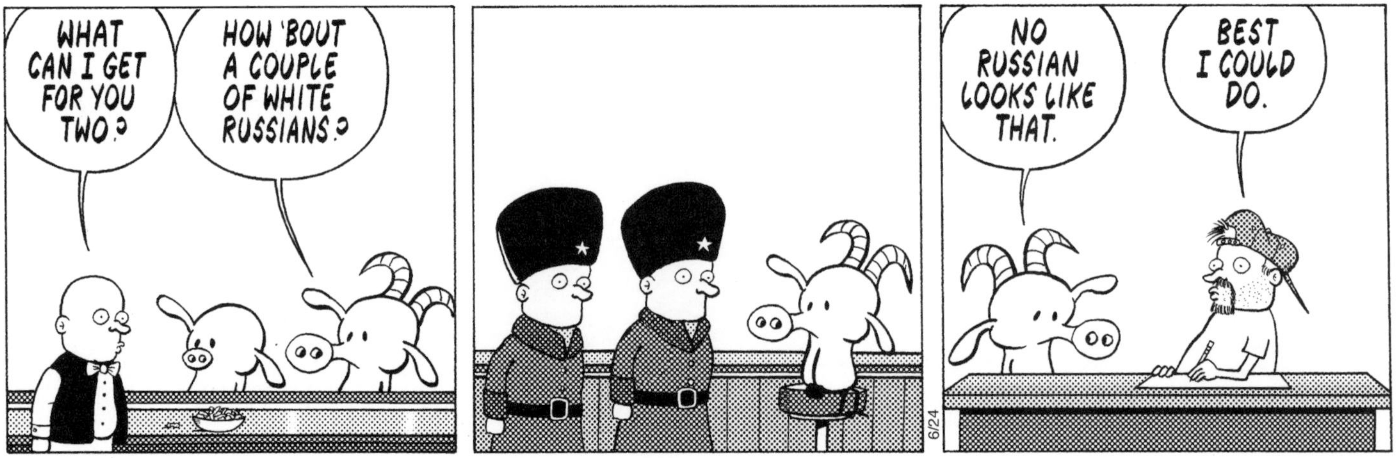
WHAT CAN I GET FOR YOU TWO?
HOW 'BOUT A COUPLE OF WHITE RUSSIANS?
NO RUSSIAN LOOKS LIKE THAT.
BEST I COULD DO.
6/24

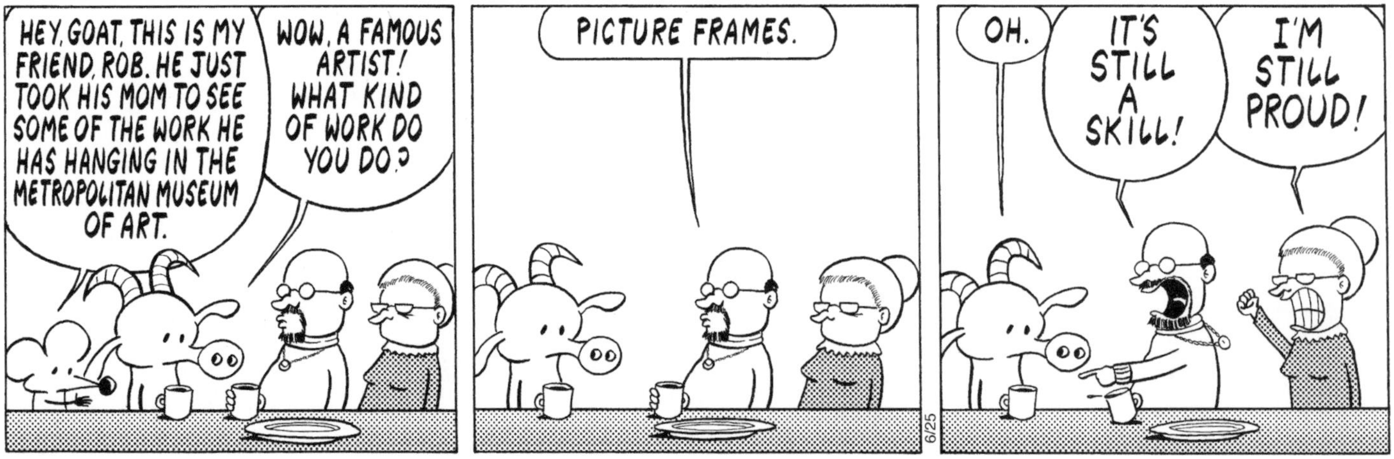
HEY, GOAT, THIS IS MY FRIEND, ROB. HE JUST TOOK HIS MOM TO SEE SOME OF THE WORK HE HAS HANGING IN THE METROPOLITAN MUSEUM OF ART.
WOW, A FAMOUS ARTIST! WHAT KIND OF WORK DO YOU DO?
PICTURE FRAMES.
OH.
IT'S STILL A SKILL!
I'M STILL PROUD!
6/25

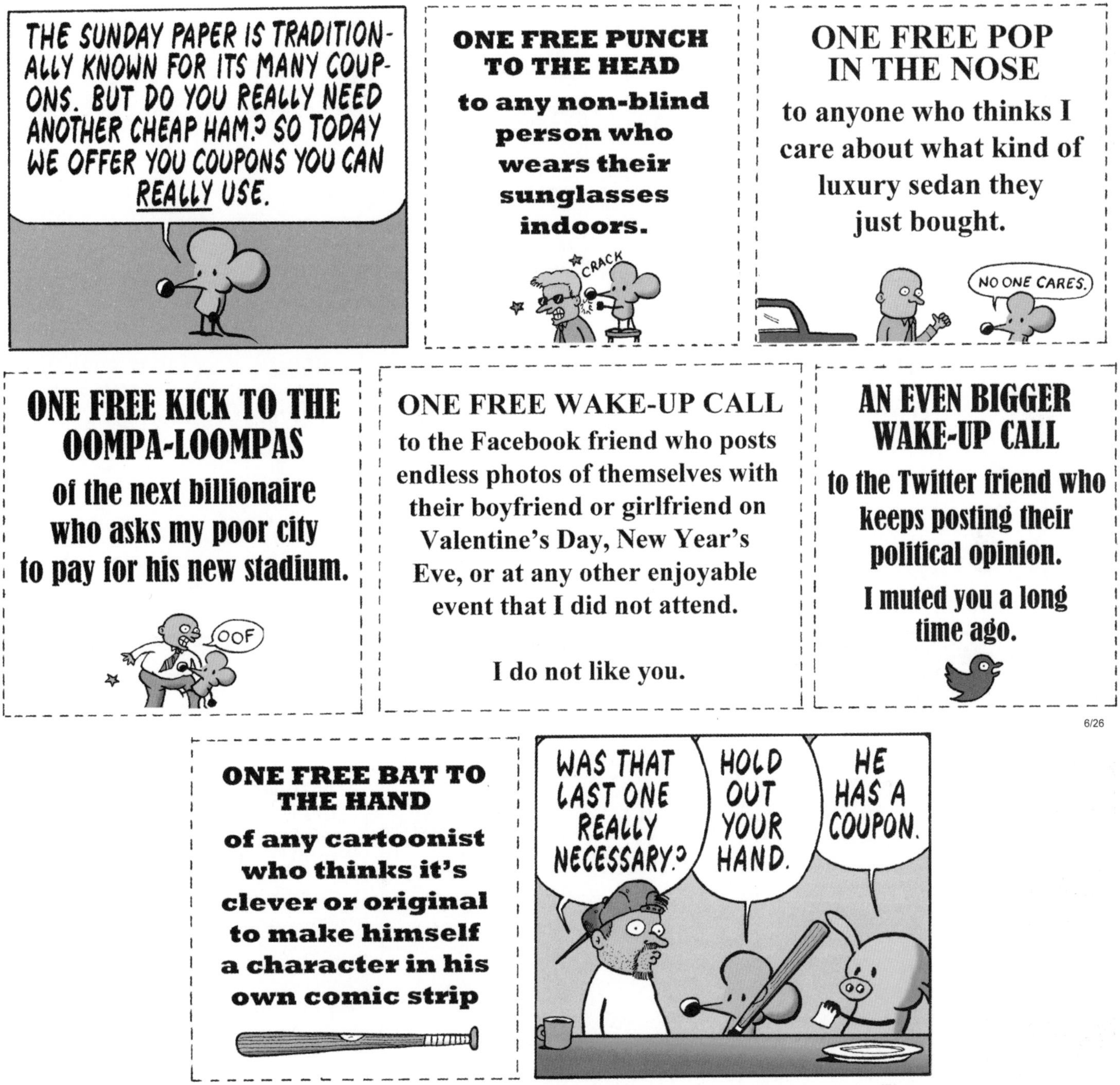
THE SUNDAY PAPER IS TRADITIONALLY KNOWN FOR ITS MANY COUPONS. BUT DO YOU REALLY NEED ANOTHER CHEAP HAM? SO TODAY WE OFFER YOU COUPONS YOU CAN REALLY USE.
ONE FREE PUNCH TO THE HEAD
to any non-blind person who wears their sunglasses indoors.
CRACK
ONE FREE POP IN THE NOSE
to anyone who thinks I care about what kind of luxury sedan they just bought.
NO ONE CARES.
ONE FREE KICK TO THE OOMPA-LOOMPAS
of the next billionaire who asks my poor city to pay for his new stadium.
OOF
ONE FREE WAKE-UP CALL
to the Facebook friend who posts endless photos of themselves with their boyfriend or girlfriend on Valentine's Day, New Year's Eve, or at any other enjoyable event that I did not attend.
I do not like you.
AN EVEN BIGGER WAKE-UP CALL
to the Twitter friend who keeps posting their political opinion.
I muted you a long time ago.
6/26
ONE FREE BAT TO THE HAND
of any cartoonist who thinks it's clever or original to make himself a character in his own comic strip
WAS THAT LAST ONE REALLY NECESSARY?
HOLD OUT YOUR HAND.
HE HAS A COUPON.

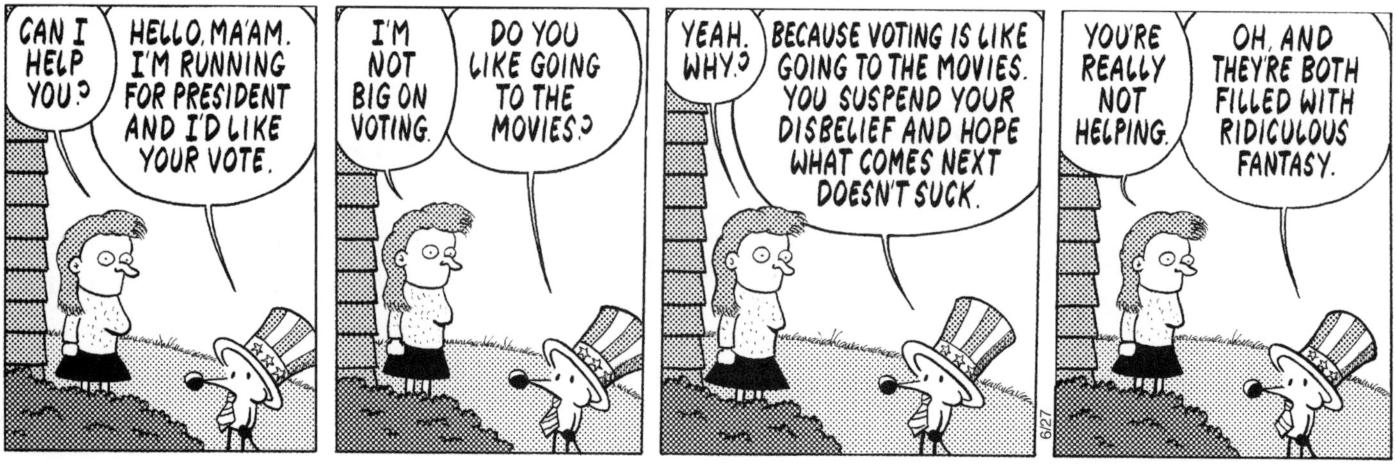
CAN I HELP YOU?
HELLO, MA'AM. I'M RUNNING FOR PRESIDENT AND I'D LIKE YOUR VOTE.
I'M NOT BIG ON VOTING.
DO YOU LIKE GOING TO THE MOVIES?
YEAH. WHY?
BECAUSE VOTING IS LIKE GOING TO THE MOVIES. YOU SUSPEND YOUR DISBELIEF AND HOPE WHAT COMES NEXT DOESN'T SUCK.
6/27
YOU'RE REALLY NOT HELPING.
OH, AND THEY'RE BOTH FILLED WITH RIDICULOUS FANTASY.

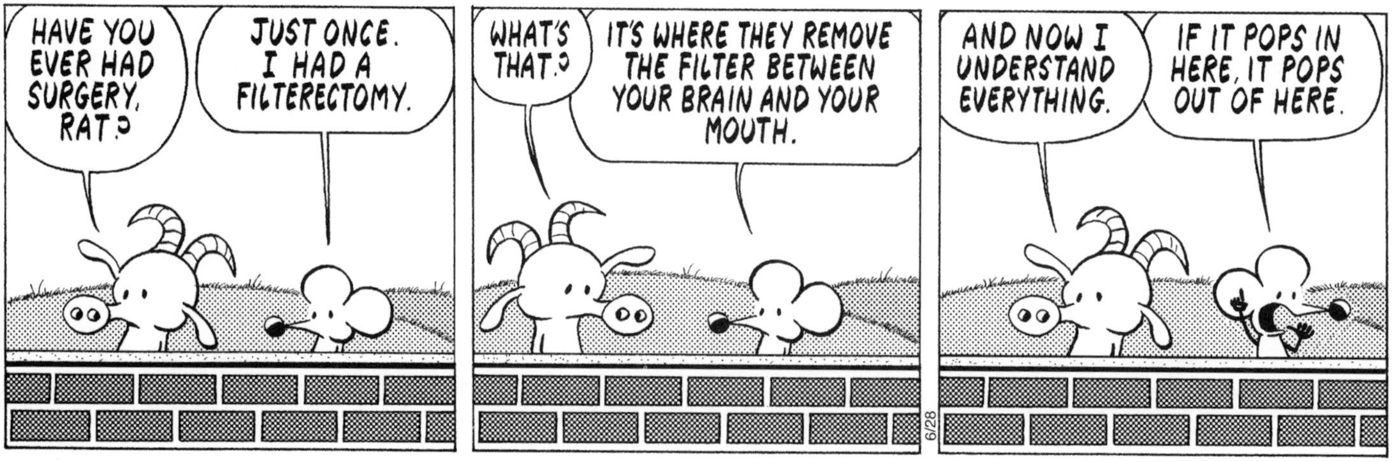
HAVE YOU EVER HAD SURGERY, RAT?
JUST ONCE. I HAD A FILTERECTOMY.
WHAT'S THAT?
IT'S WHERE THEY REMOVE THE FILTER BETWEEN YOUR BRAIN AND YOUR MOUTH.
6/28
AND NOW I UNDERSTAND EVERYTHING.
IF IT POPS IN HERE, IT POPS OUT OF HERE.

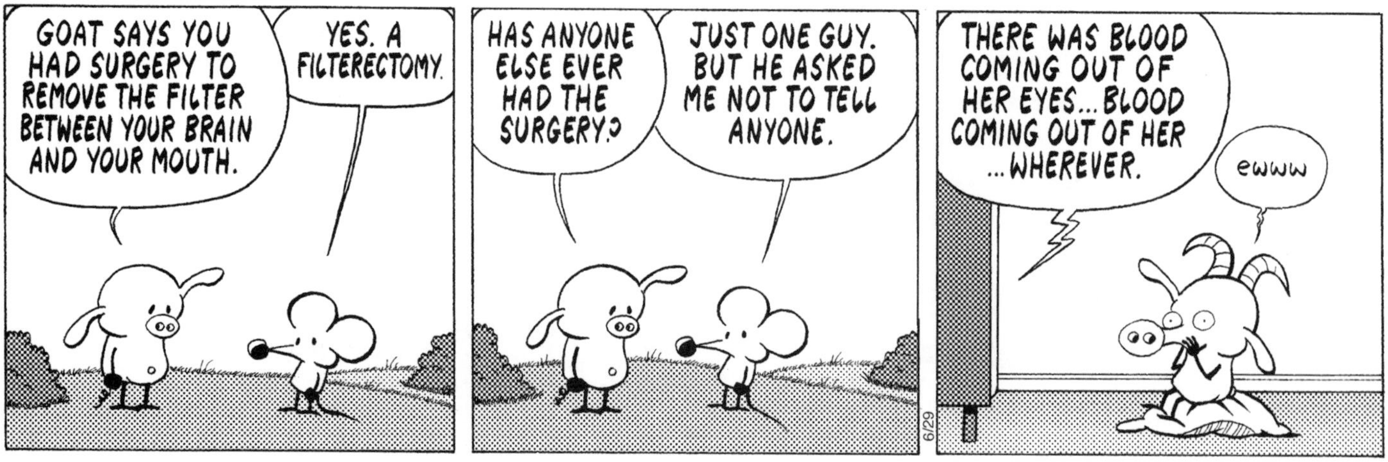
GOAT SAYS YOU HAD SURGERY TO REMOVE THE FILTER BETWEEN YOUR BRAIN AND YOUR MOUTH.
YES. A FILTERECTOMY.
HAS ANYONE ELSE EVER HAD THE SURGERY?
JUST ONE GUY. BUT HE ASKED ME NOT TO TELL ANYONE.
6/29
THERE WAS BLOOD COMING OUT OF HER EYES... BLOOD COMING OUT OF HER ...WHEREVER.
ewww

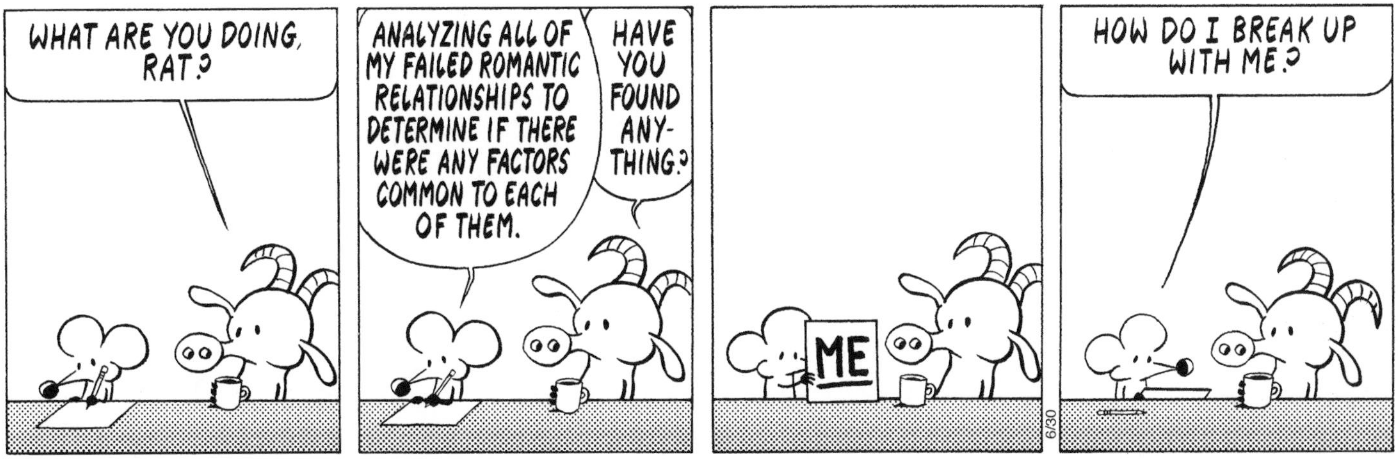
WHAT ARE YOU DOING, RAT?
ANALYZING ALL OF MY FAILED ROMANTIC RELATIONSHIPS TO DETERMINE IF THERE WERE ANY FACTORS COMMON TO EACH OF THEM.
HAVE YOU FOUND ANY-THING?
ME
6/30
HOW DO I BREAK UP WITH ME?

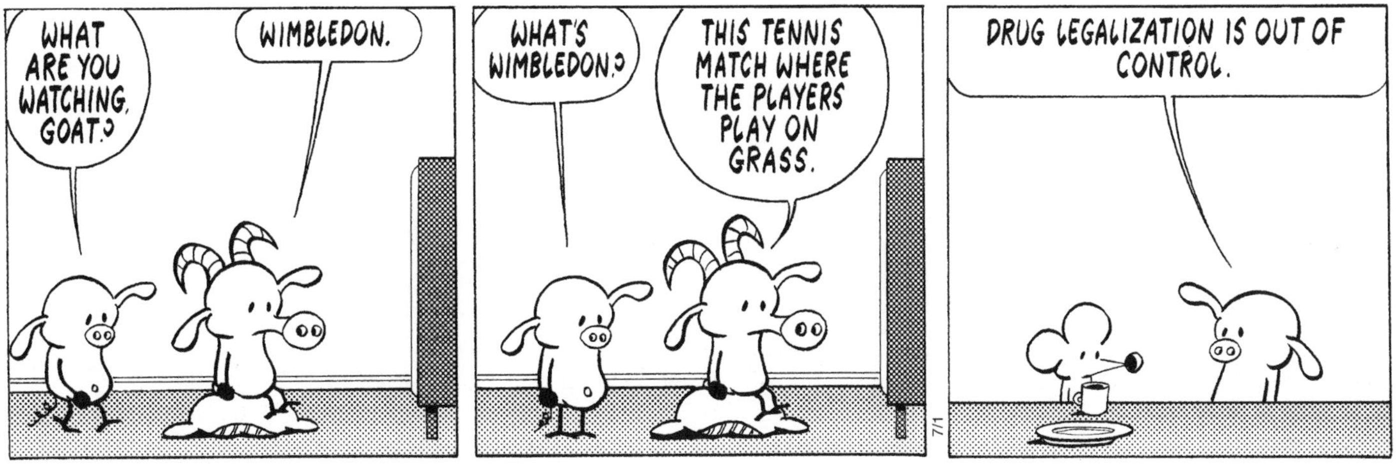
WHAT ARE YOU WATCHING, GOAT?
WIMBLEDON.
WHAT'S WIMBLEDON?
THIS TENNIS MATCH WHERE THE PLAYERS PLAY ON GRASS.
7/1
DRUG LEGALIZATION IS OUT OF CONTROL.

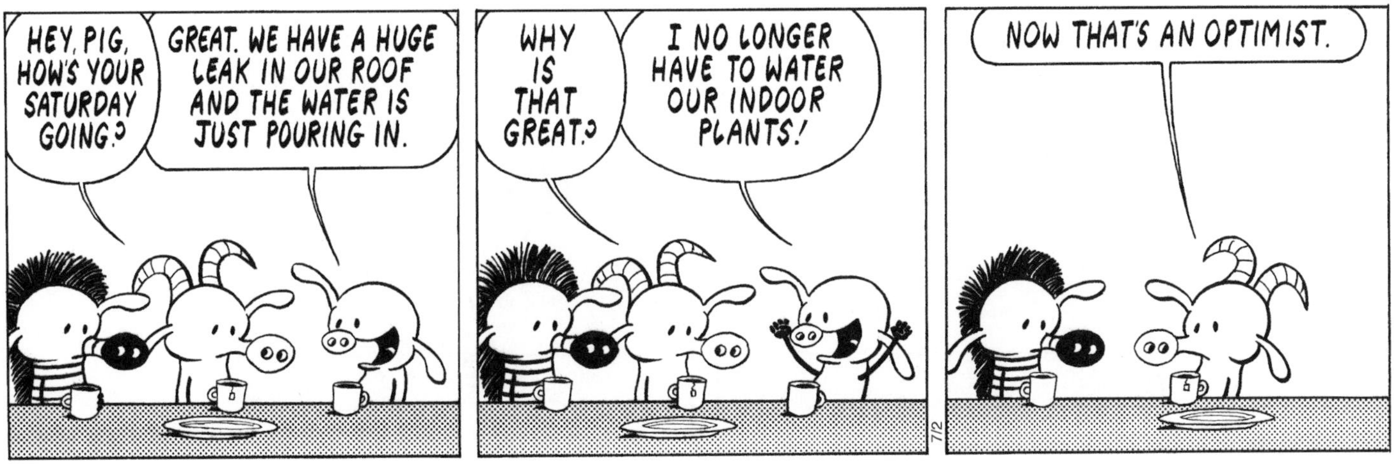
HEY, PIG, HOW'S YOUR SATURDAY GOING?
GREAT. WE HAVE A HUGE LEAK IN OUR ROOF AND THE WATER IS JUST POURING IN.
WHY IS THAT GREAT?
I NO LONGER HAVE TO WATER OUR INDOOR PLANTS!
7/2
NOW THAT'S AN OPTIMIST.

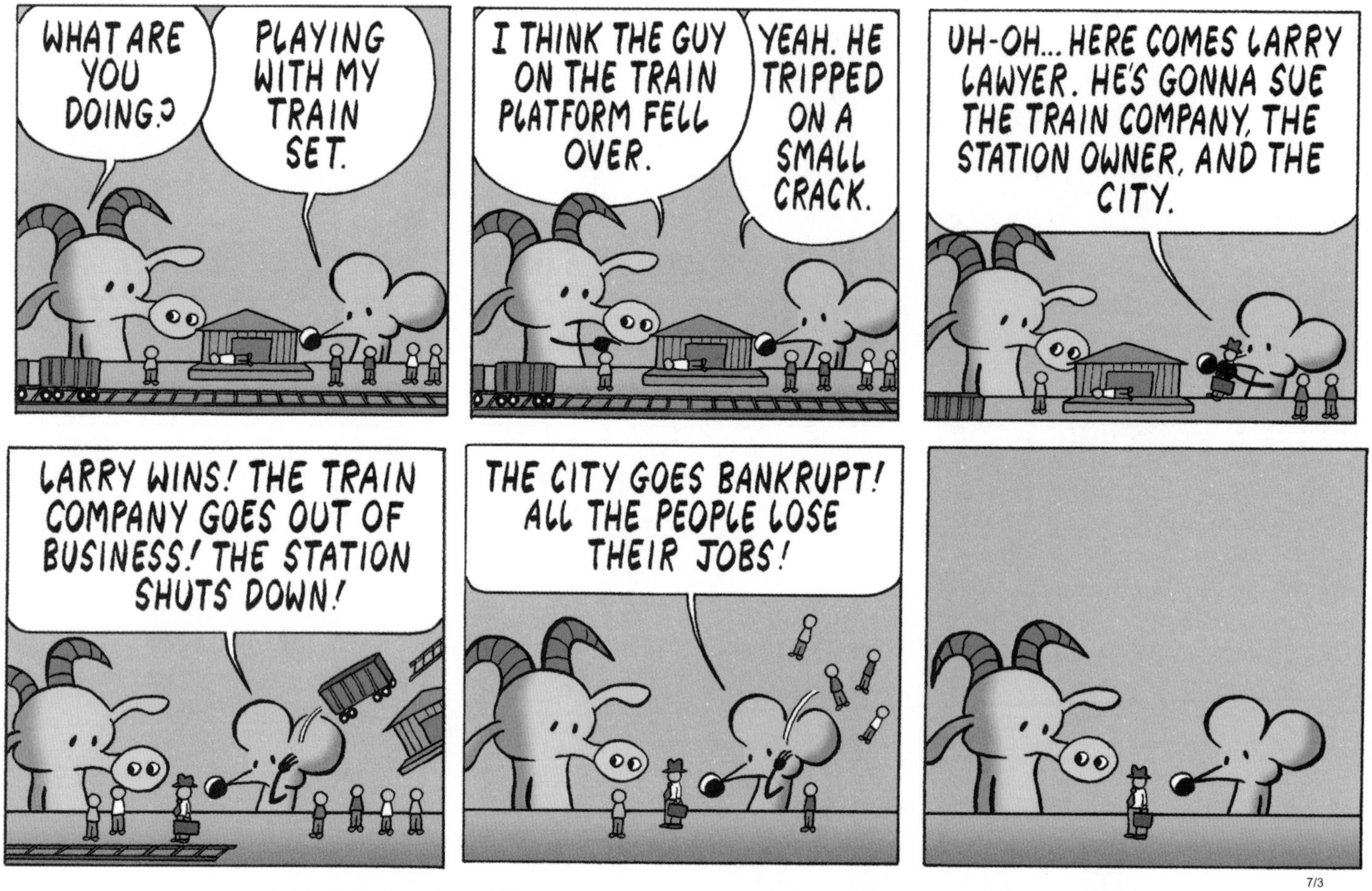
WHAT ARE YOU DOING?
PLAYING WITH MY TRAIN SET.
I THINK THE GUY ON THE TRAIN PLATFORM FELL OVER.
YEAH. HE TRIPPED ON A SMALL CRACK.
UH-OH... HERE COMES LARRY LAWYER. HE'S GONNA SUE THE TRAIN COMPANY, THE STATION OWNER, AND THE CITY.
LARRY WINS! THE TRAIN COMPANY GOES OUT OF BUSINESS! THE STATION SHUTS DOWN!
THE CITY GOES BANKRUPT! ALL THE PEOPLE LOSE THEIR JOBS!
7/3

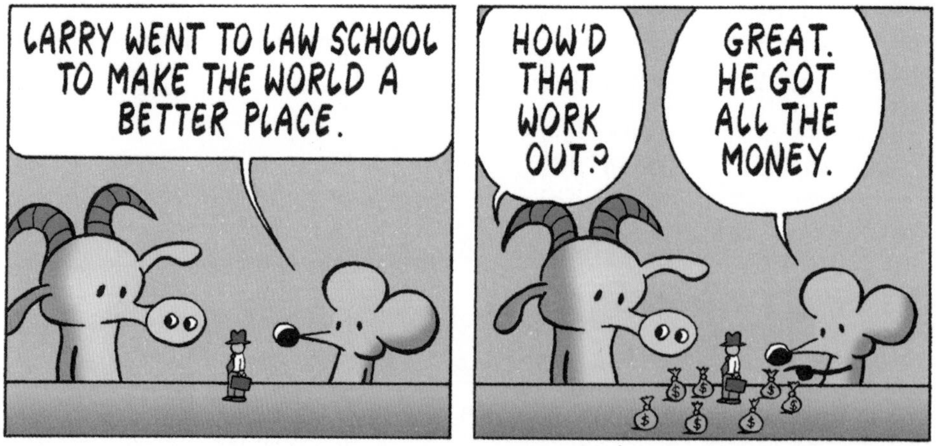
LARRY WENT TO LAW SCHOOL TO MAKE THE WORLD A BETTER PLACE.
HOW'D THAT WORK OUT?
GREAT. HE GOT ALL THE MONEY.

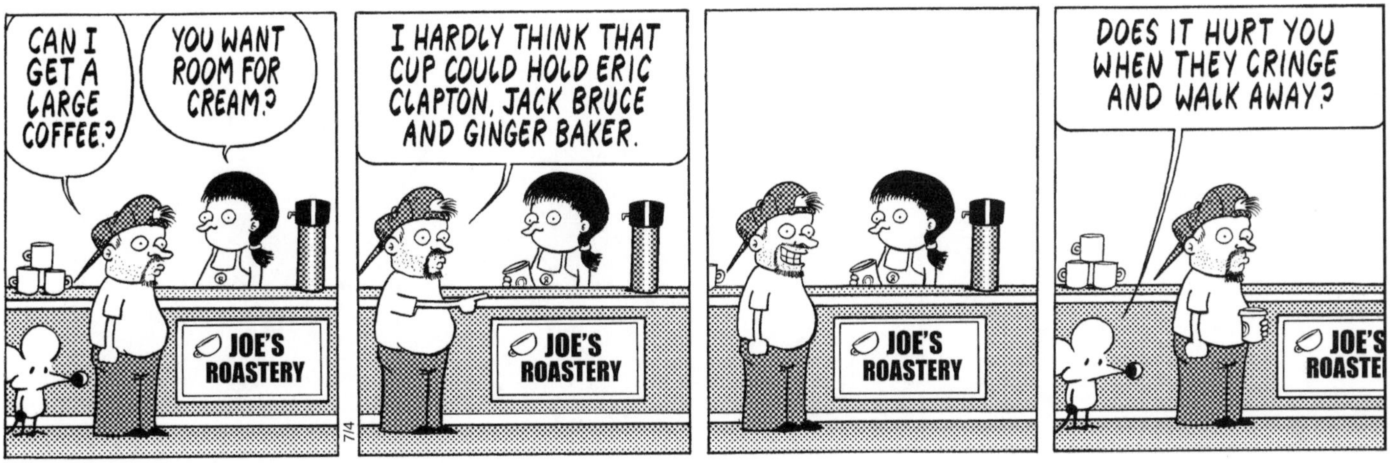
CAN I GET A LARGE COFFEE?
YOU WANT ROOM FOR CREAM?
I HARDLY THINK THAT CUP COULD HOLD ERIC CLAPTON, JACK BRUCE AND GINGER BAKER.
DOES IT HURT YOU WHEN THEY CRINGE AND WALK AWAY?
JOE'S ROASTERY
7/4

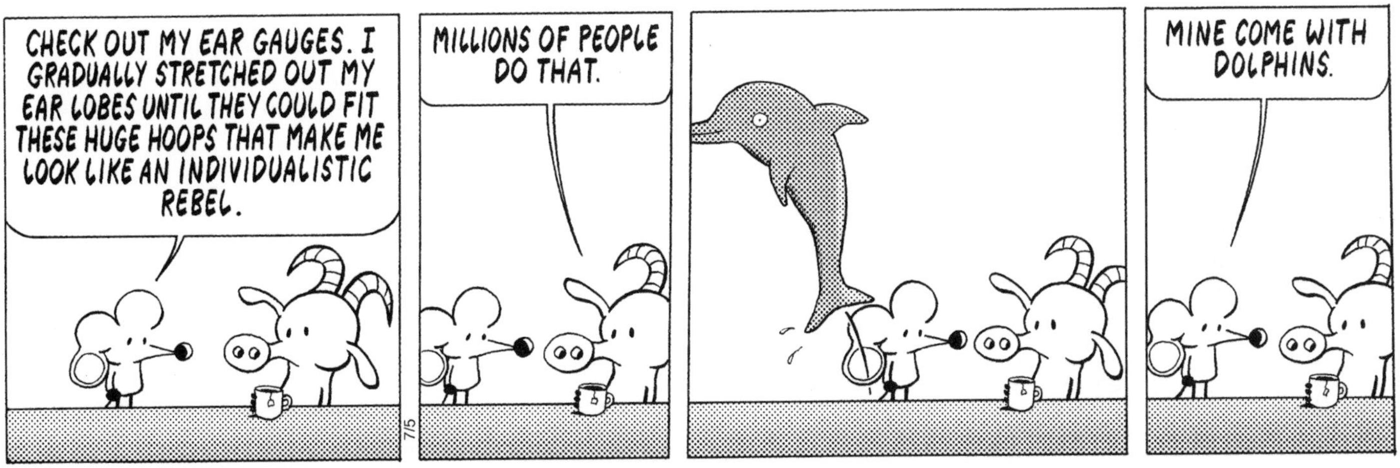
CHECK OUT MY EAR GAUGES. I GRADUALLY STRETCHED OUT MY EAR LOBES UNTIL THEY COULD FIT THESE HUGE HOOPS THAT MAKE ME LOOK LIKE AN INDIVIDUALISTIC REBEL.
MILLIONS OF PEOPLE DO THAT.
MINE COME WITH DOLPHINS.
7/5

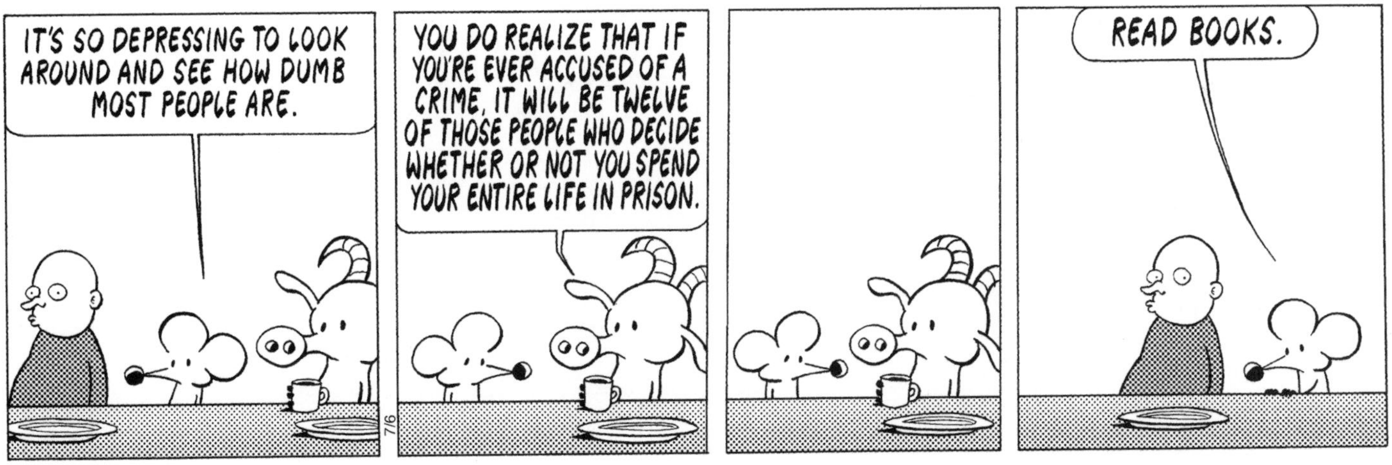
IT'S SO DEPRESSING TO LOOK AROUND AND SEE HOW DUMB MOST PEOPLE ARE.
YOU DO REALIZE THAT IF YOU'RE EVER ACCUSED OF A CRIME, IT WILL BE TWELVE OF THOSE PEOPLE WHO DECIDE WHETHER OR NOT YOU SPEND YOUR ENTIRE LIFE IN PRISON.
READ BOOKS.
7/6

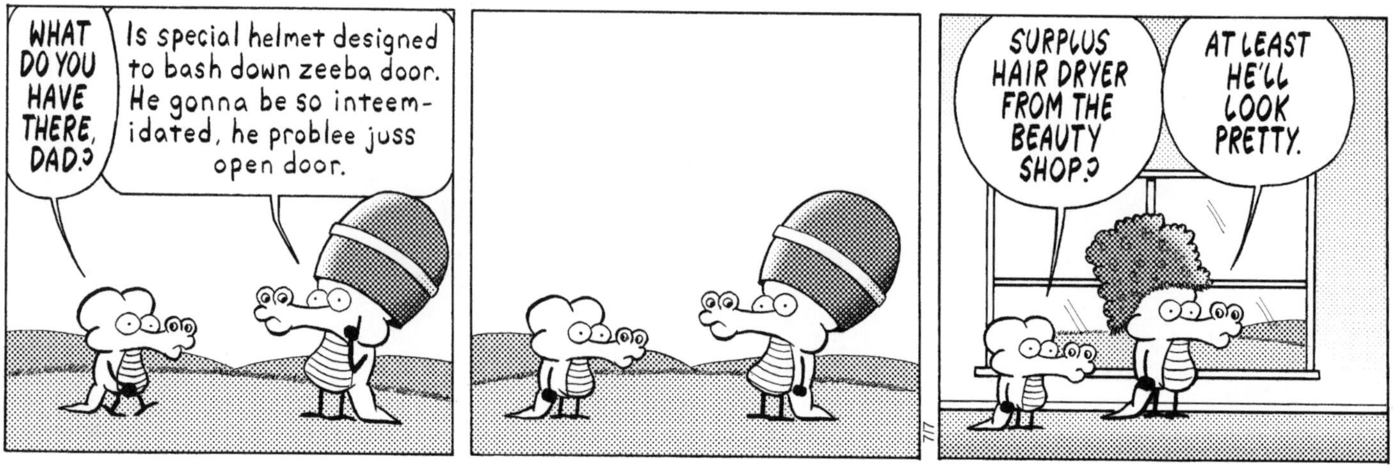
WHAT DO YOU HAVE THERE, DAD?
Is special helmet designed to bash down zeeba door. He gonna be so inteem-idated, he problee juss open door.
7/7
SURPLUS HAIR DRYER FROM THE BEAUTY SHOP?
AT LEAST HE'LL LOOK PRETTY.

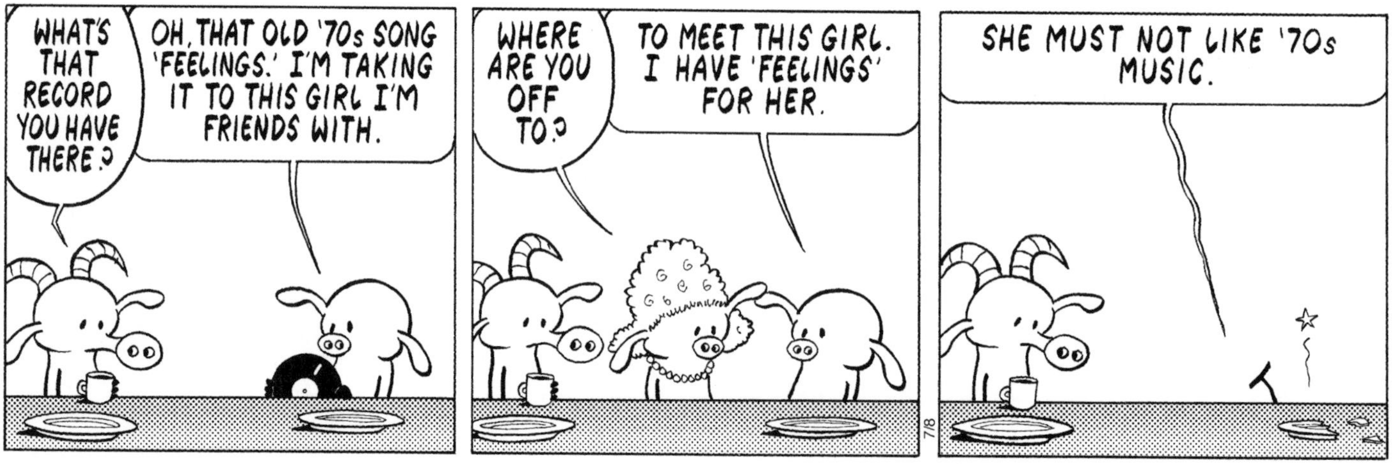
WHAT'S THAT RECORD YOU HAVE THERE?
OH, THAT OLD '70s SONG 'FEELINGS.' I'M TAKING IT TO THIS GIRL I'M FRIENDS WITH.
WHERE ARE YOU OFF TO?
TO MEET THIS GIRL. I HAVE 'FEELINGS' FOR HER.
7/8
SHE MUST NOT LIKE '70s MUSIC.

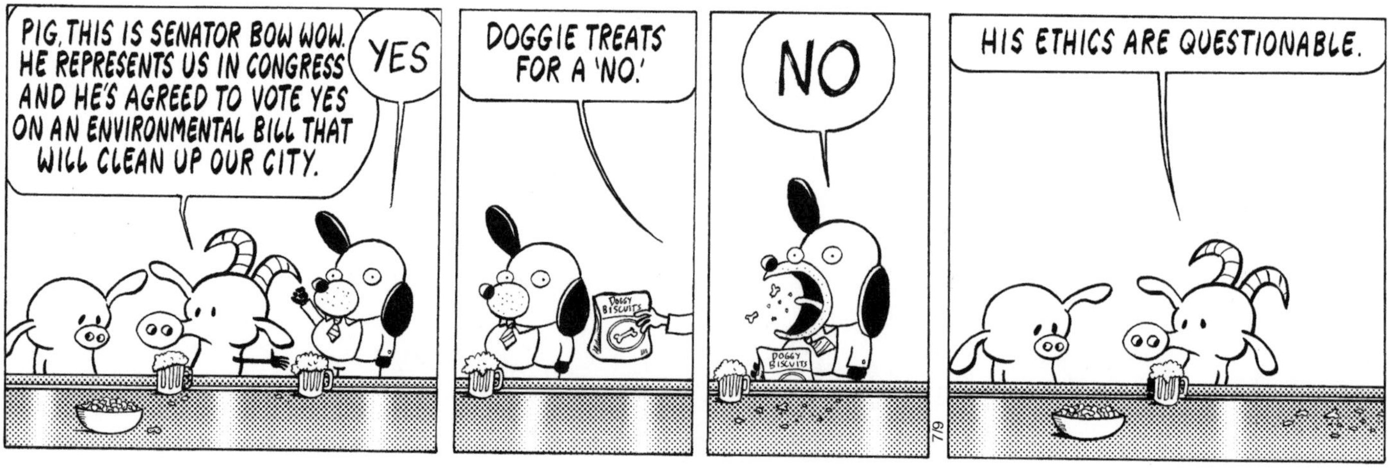
PIG, THIS IS SENATOR BOW WOW. HE REPRESENTS US IN CONGRESS AND HE'S AGREED TO VOTE YES ON AN ENVIRONMENTAL BILL THAT WILL CLEAN UP OUR CITY.
YES
DOGGIE TREATS FOR A 'NO.'
DOGGY BISCUITS
NO
DOGGY BISCUITS
7/9
HIS ETHICS ARE QUESTIONABLE.

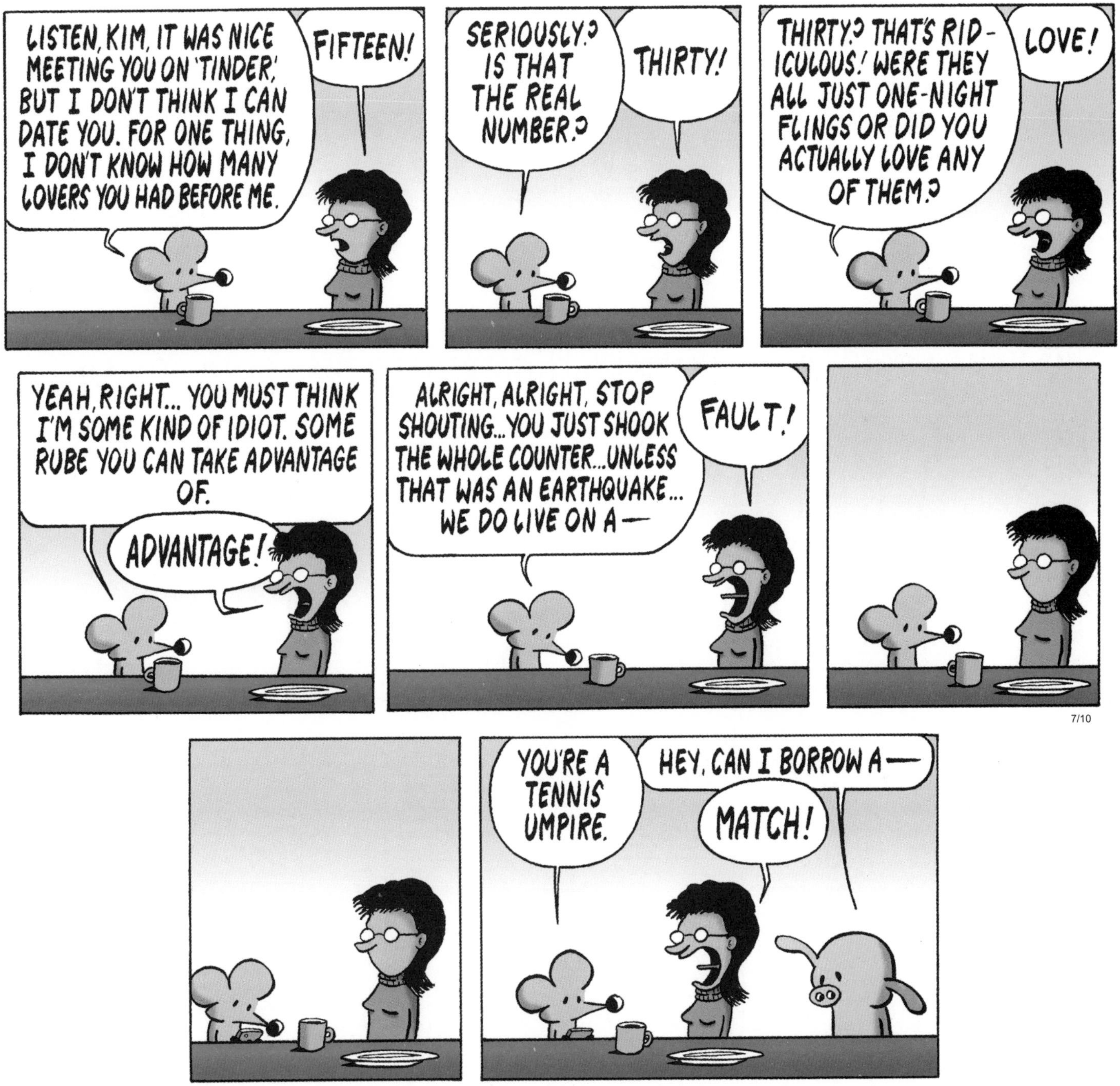
LISTEN, KIM, IT WAS NICE MEETING YOU ON 'TINDER,' BUT I DON'T THINK I CAN DATE YOU. FOR ONE THING, I DON'T KNOW HOW MANY LOVERS YOU HAD BEFORE ME.
FIFTEEN!
SERIOUSLY? IS THAT THE REAL NUMBER?
THIRTY!
THIRTY? THAT'S RIDICULOUS! WERE THEY ALL JUST ONE-NIGHT FLINGS OR DID YOU ACTUALLY LOVE ANY OF THEM?
LOVE!
YEAH, RIGHT... YOU MUST THINK I'M SOME KIND OF IDIOT. SOME RUBE YOU CAN TAKE ADVANTAGE OF.
ADVANTAGE!
ALRIGHT, ALRIGHT, STOP SHOUTING... YOU JUST SHOOK THE WHOLE COUNTER... UNLESS THAT WAS AN EARTHQUAKE... WE DO LIVE ON A—
FAULT!
7/10
YOU'RE A TENNIS UMPIRE.
HEY, CAN I BORROW A—
MATCH!

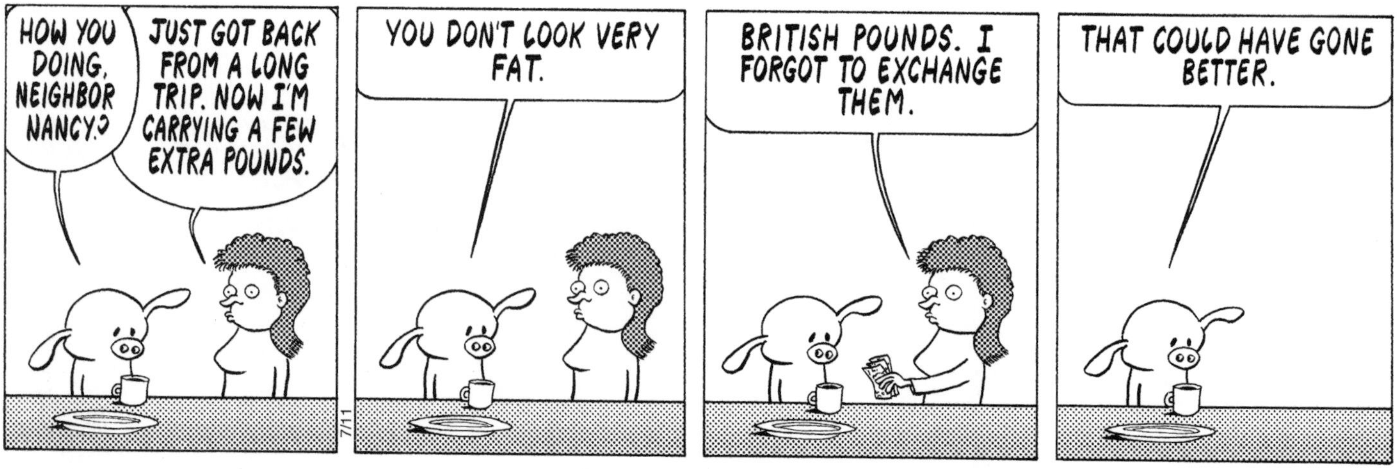
HOW YOU DOING, NEIGHBOR NANCY?
JUST GOT BACK FROM A LONG TRIP. NOW I'M CARRYING A FEW EXTRA POUNDS.
7/11
YOU DON'T LOOK VERY FAT.
BRITISH POUNDS. I FORGOT TO EXCHANGE THEM.
THAT COULD HAVE GONE BETTER.

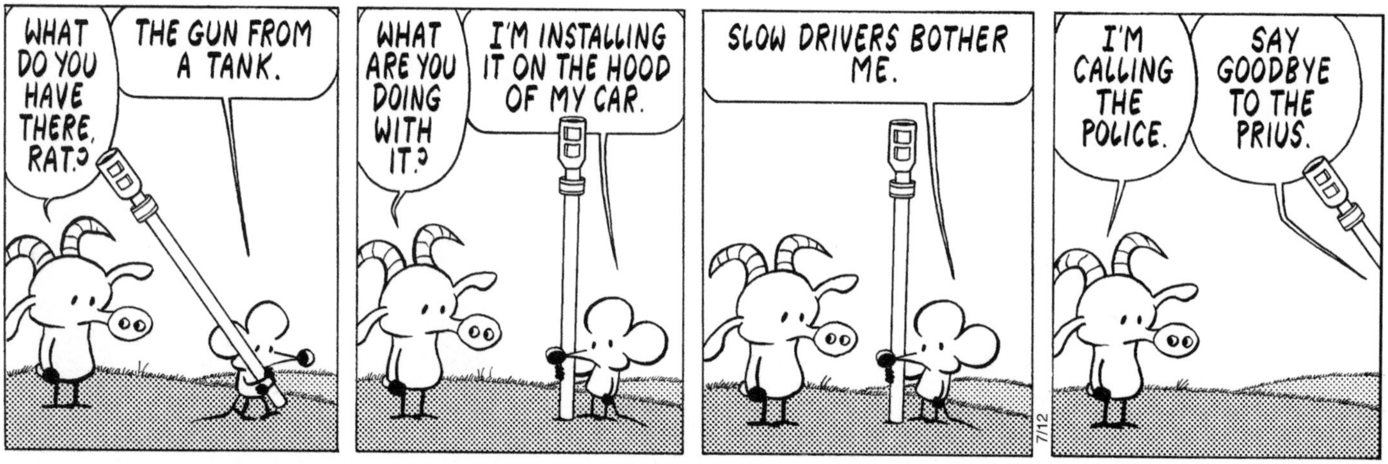
WHAT DO YOU HAVE THERE, RAT?
THE GUN FROM A TANK.
WHAT ARE YOU DOING WITH IT?
I'M INSTALLING IT ON THE HOOD OF MY CAR.
SLOW DRIVERS BOTHER ME.
7/12
I'M CALLING THE POLICE.
SAY GOODBYE TO THE PRIUS.

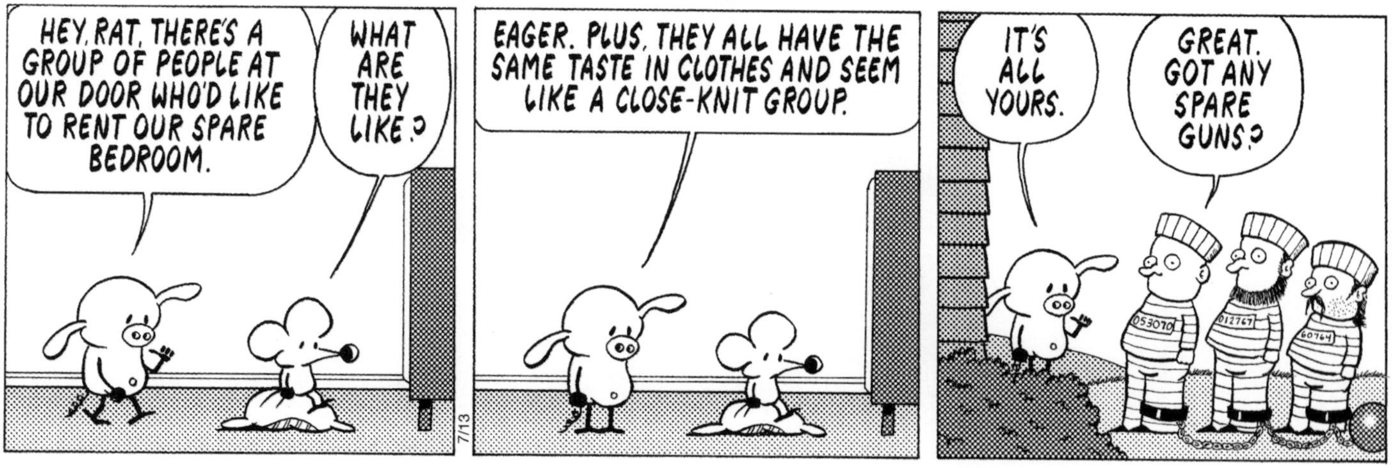
HEY, RAT, THERE'S A GROUP OF PEOPLE AT OUR DOOR WHO'D LIKE TO RENT OUR SPARE BEDROOM.
WHAT ARE THEY LIKE?
7/13
EAGER. PLUS, THEY ALL HAVE THE SAME TASTE IN CLOTHES AND SEEM LIKE A CLOSE-KNIT GROUP.
IT'S ALL YOURS.
GREAT. GOT ANY SPARE GUNS?

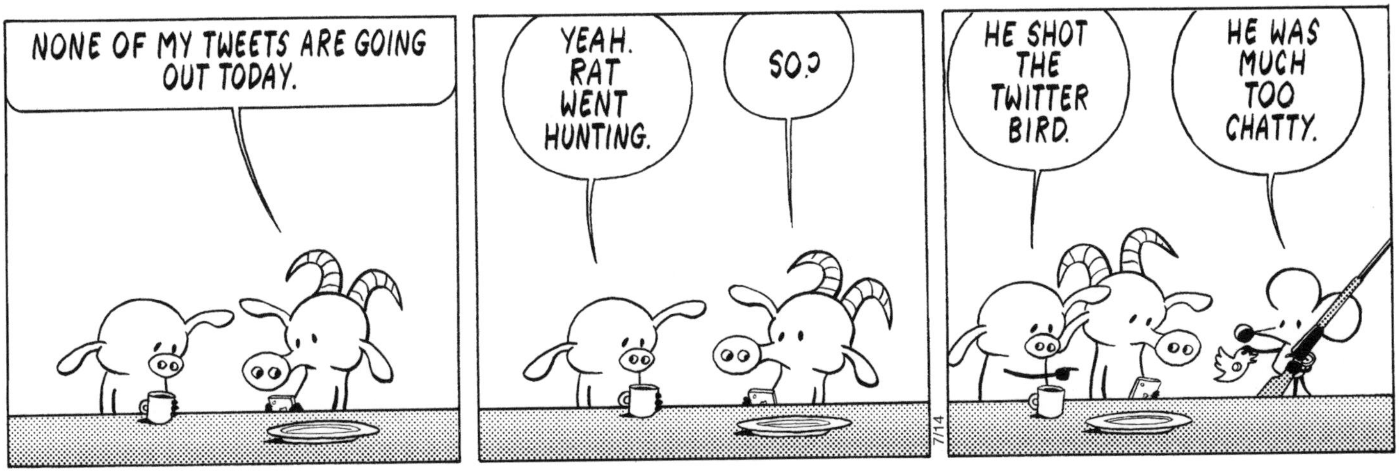

NONE OF MY TWEETS ARE GOING OUT TODAY.
YEAH. RAT WENT HUNTING.
SO?
HE SHOT THE TWITTER BIRD.
HE WAS MUCH TOO CHATTY.
7/14

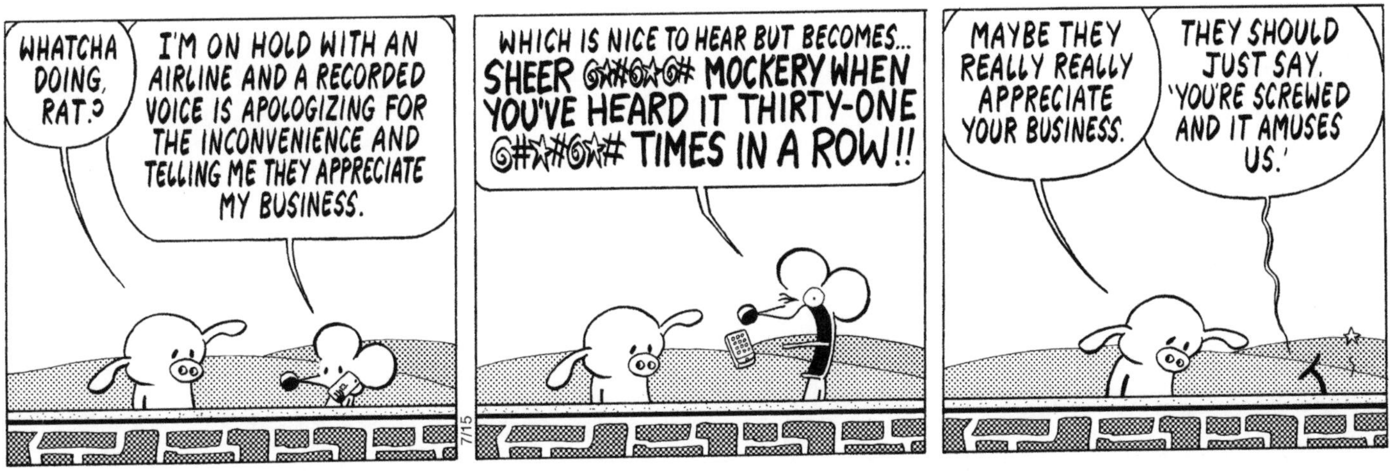

WHATCHA DOING, RAT?
I'M ON HOLD WITH AN AIRLINE AND A RECORDED VOICE IS APOLOGIZING FOR THE INCONVENIENCE AND TELLING ME THEY APPRECIATE MY BUSINESS.
7/15
WHICH IS NICE TO HEAR BUT BECOMES... SHEER @#☆@# MOCKERY WHEN YOU'VE HEARD IT THIRTY-ONE @#☆#@☆# TIMES IN A ROW!!
MAYBE THEY REALLY REALLY APPRECIATE YOUR BUSINESS.
THEY SHOULD JUST SAY, 'YOU'RE SCREWED AND IT AMUSES US.'

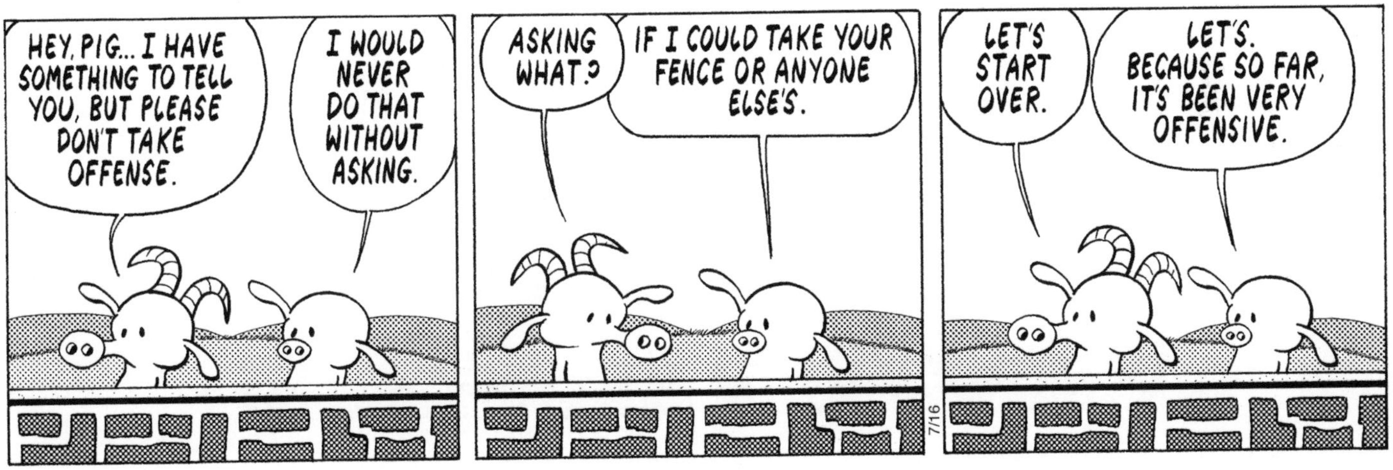

HEY, PIG... I HAVE SOMETHING TO TELL YOU, BUT PLEASE DON'T TAKE OFFENSE.
I WOULD NEVER DO THAT WITHOUT ASKING.
ASKING WHAT?
IF I COULD TAKE YOUR FENCE OR ANYONE ELSE'S.
7/16
LET'S START OVER.
LET'S. BECAUSE SO FAR, IT'S BEEN VERY OFFENSIVE.

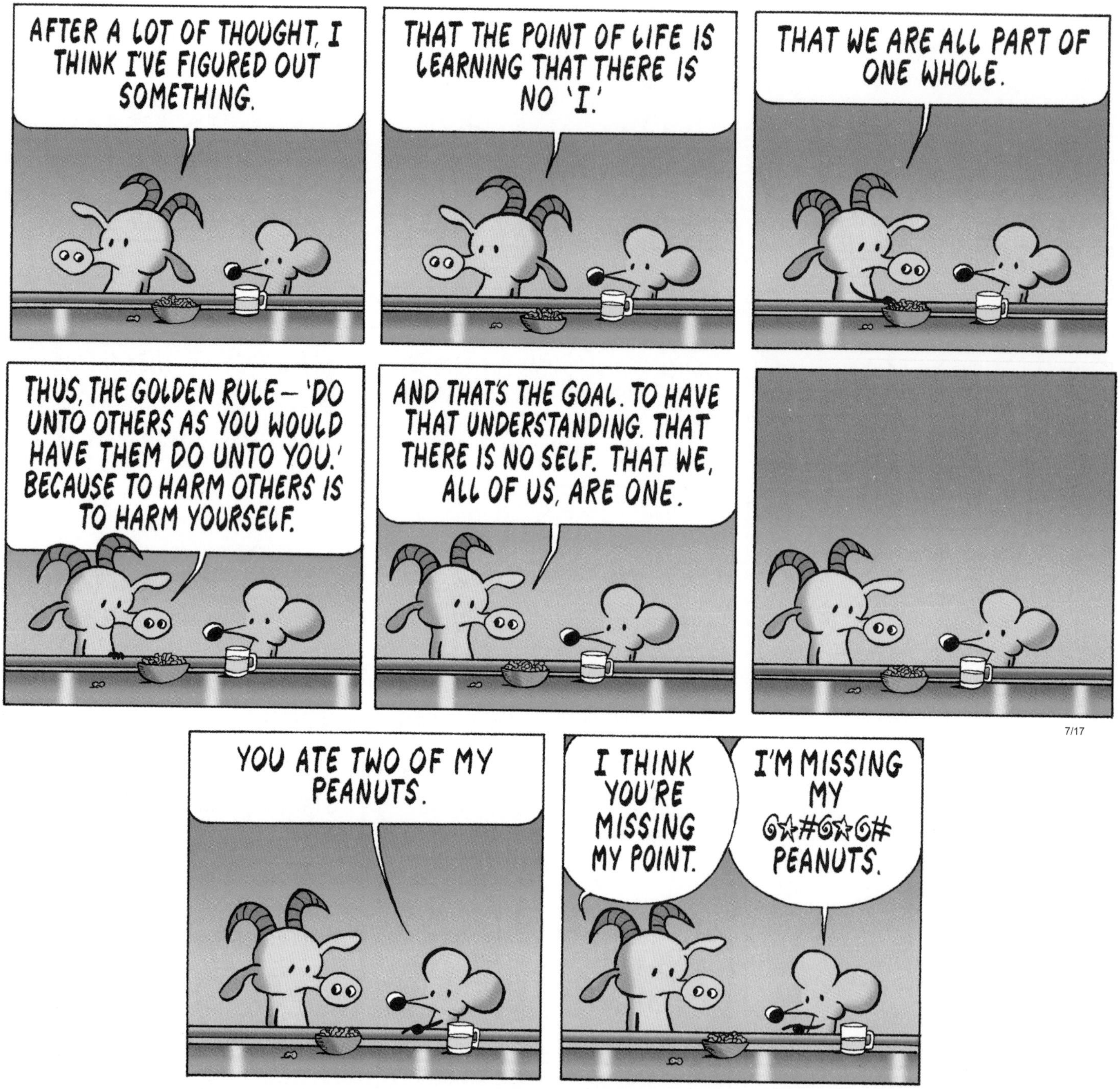
AFTER A LOT OF THOUGHT, I THINK I'VE FIGURED OUT SOMETHING.
THAT THE POINT OF LIFE IS LEARNING THAT THERE IS NO 'I.'
THAT WE ARE ALL PART OF ONE WHOLE.
THUS, THE GOLDEN RULE— 'DO UNTO OTHERS AS YOU WOULD HAVE THEM DO UNTO YOU.' BECAUSE TO HARM OTHERS IS TO HARM YOURSELF.
AND THAT'S THE GOAL. TO HAVE THAT UNDERSTANDING. THAT THERE IS NO SELF. THAT WE, ALL OF US, ARE ONE.
7/17
YOU ATE TWO OF MY PEANUTS.
I THINK YOU'RE MISSING MY POINT.
I'M MISSING MY G☆#G☆G# PEANUTS.

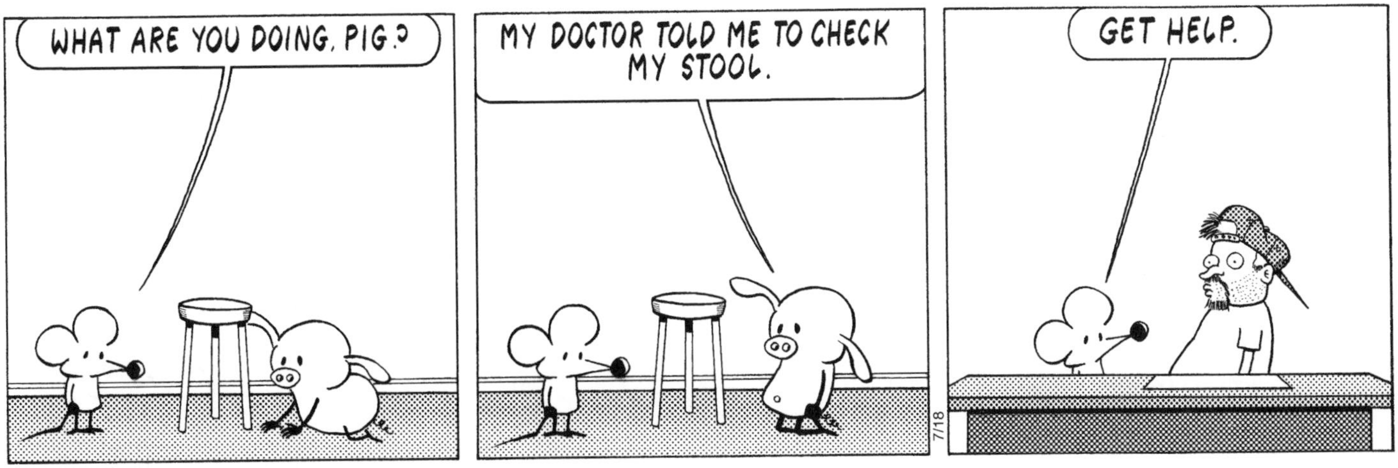
WHAT ARE YOU DOING, PIG?
MY DOCTOR TOLD ME TO CHECK MY STOOL.
7/18
GET HELP.

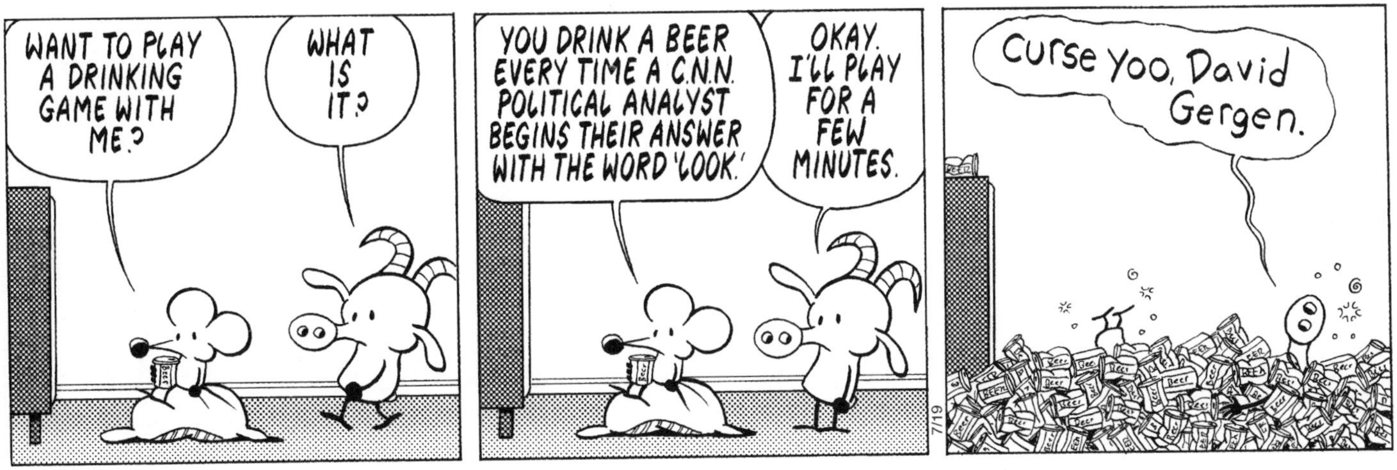
WANT TO PLAY A DRINKING GAME WITH ME?
WHAT IS IT?
YOU DRINK A BEER EVERY TIME A C.N.N. POLITICAL ANALYST BEGINS THEIR ANSWER WITH THE WORD 'LOOK.'
OKAY. I'LL PLAY FOR A FEW MINUTES.
7/19
Curse yoo, David Gergen.

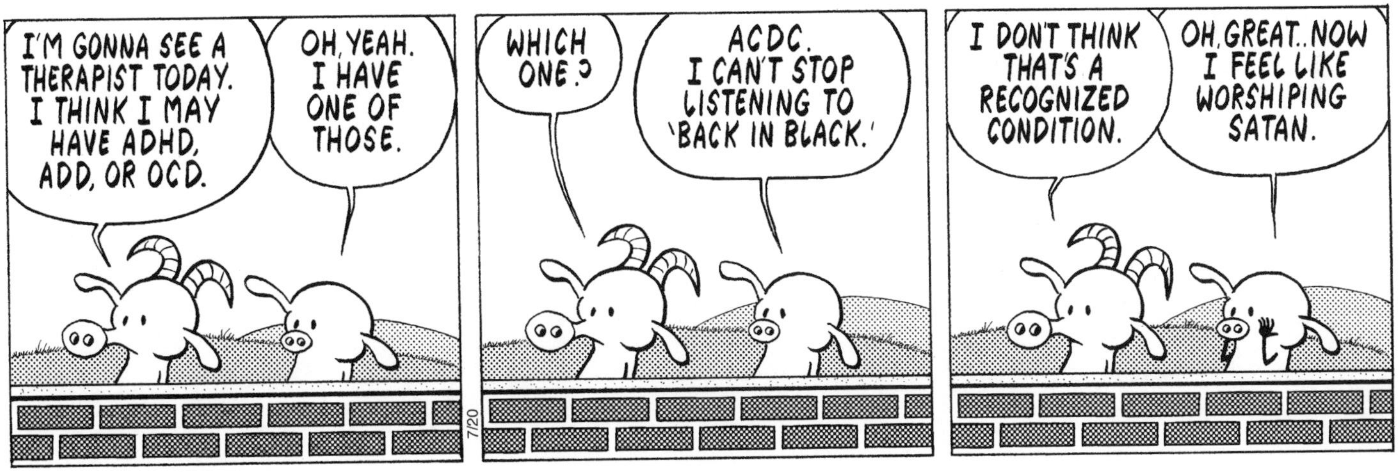
I'M GONNA SEE A THERAPIST TODAY. I THINK I MAY HAVE ADHD, ADD, OR OCD.
OH, YEAH. I HAVE ONE OF THOSE.
7/20
WHICH ONE?
ACDC. I CAN'T STOP LISTENING TO 'BACK IN BLACK.'
I DON'T THINK THAT'S A RECOGNIZED CONDITION.
OH, GREAT.. NOW I FEEL LIKE WORSHIPING SATAN.

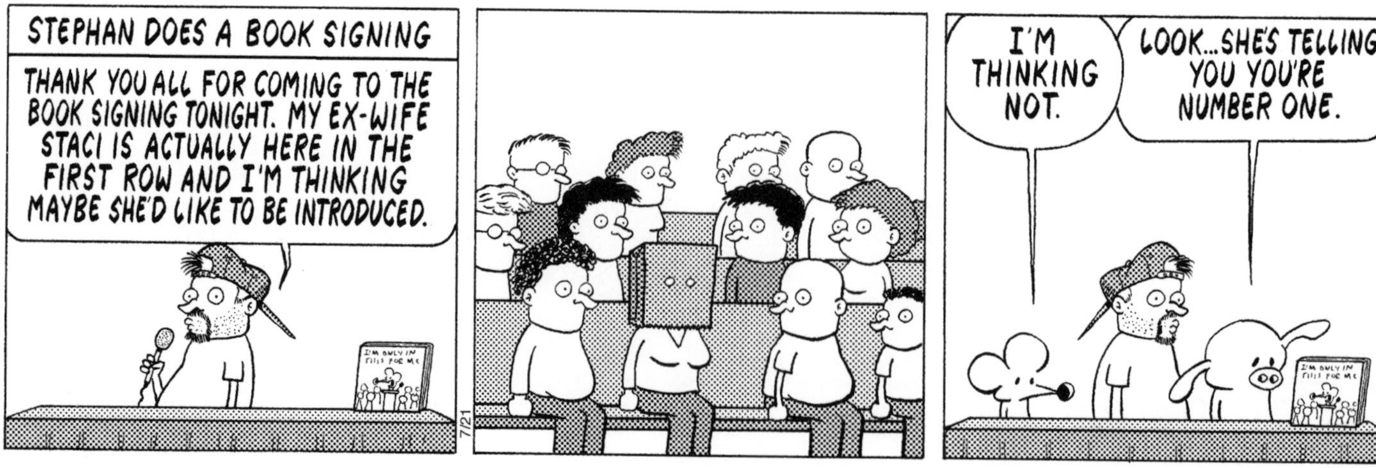
STEPHAN DOES A BOOK SIGNING
THANK YOU ALL FOR COMING TO THE BOOK SIGNING TONIGHT. MY EX-WIFE STACI IS ACTUALLY HERE IN THE FIRST ROW AND I'M THINKING MAYBE SHE'D LIKE TO BE INTRODUCED.
7/21
I'M THINKING NOT.
LOOK...SHE'S TELLING YOU YOU'RE NUMBER ONE.

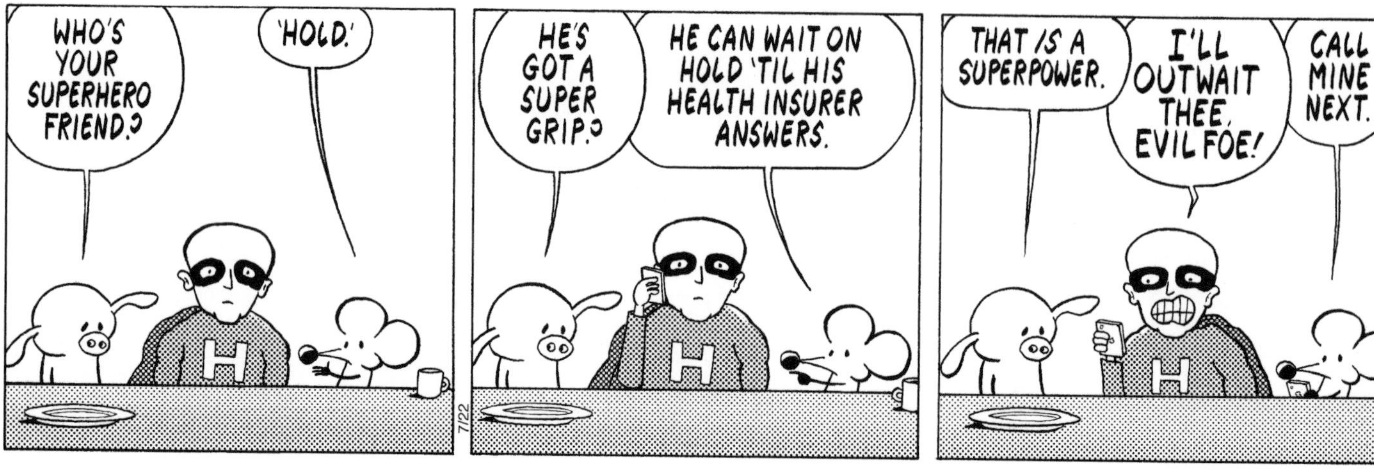
WHO'S YOUR SUPERHERO FRIEND?
'HOLD.'
HE'S GOT A SUPER GRIP?
HE CAN WAIT ON HOLD 'TIL HIS HEALTH INSURER ANSWERS.
7/22
THAT IS A SUPERPOWER.
I'LL OUTWAIT THEE, EVIL FOE!
CALL MINE NEXT.

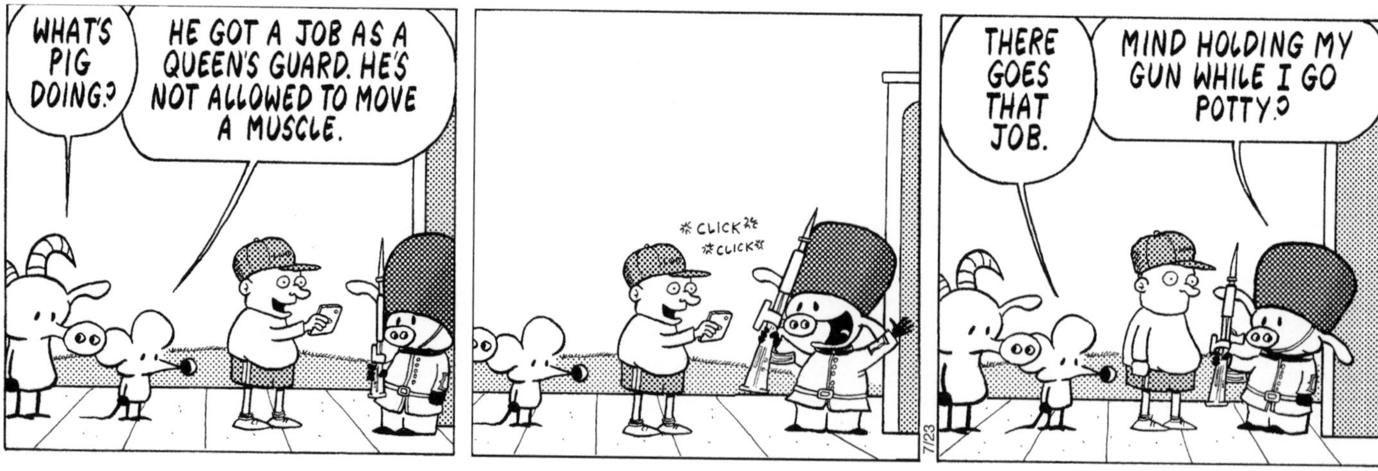
WHAT'S PIG DOING?
HE GOT A JOB AS A QUEEN'S GUARD. HE'S NOT ALLOWED TO MOVE A MUSCLE.
CLICK
CLICK
7/23
THERE GOES THAT JOB.
MIND HOLDING MY GUN WHILE I GO POTTY?

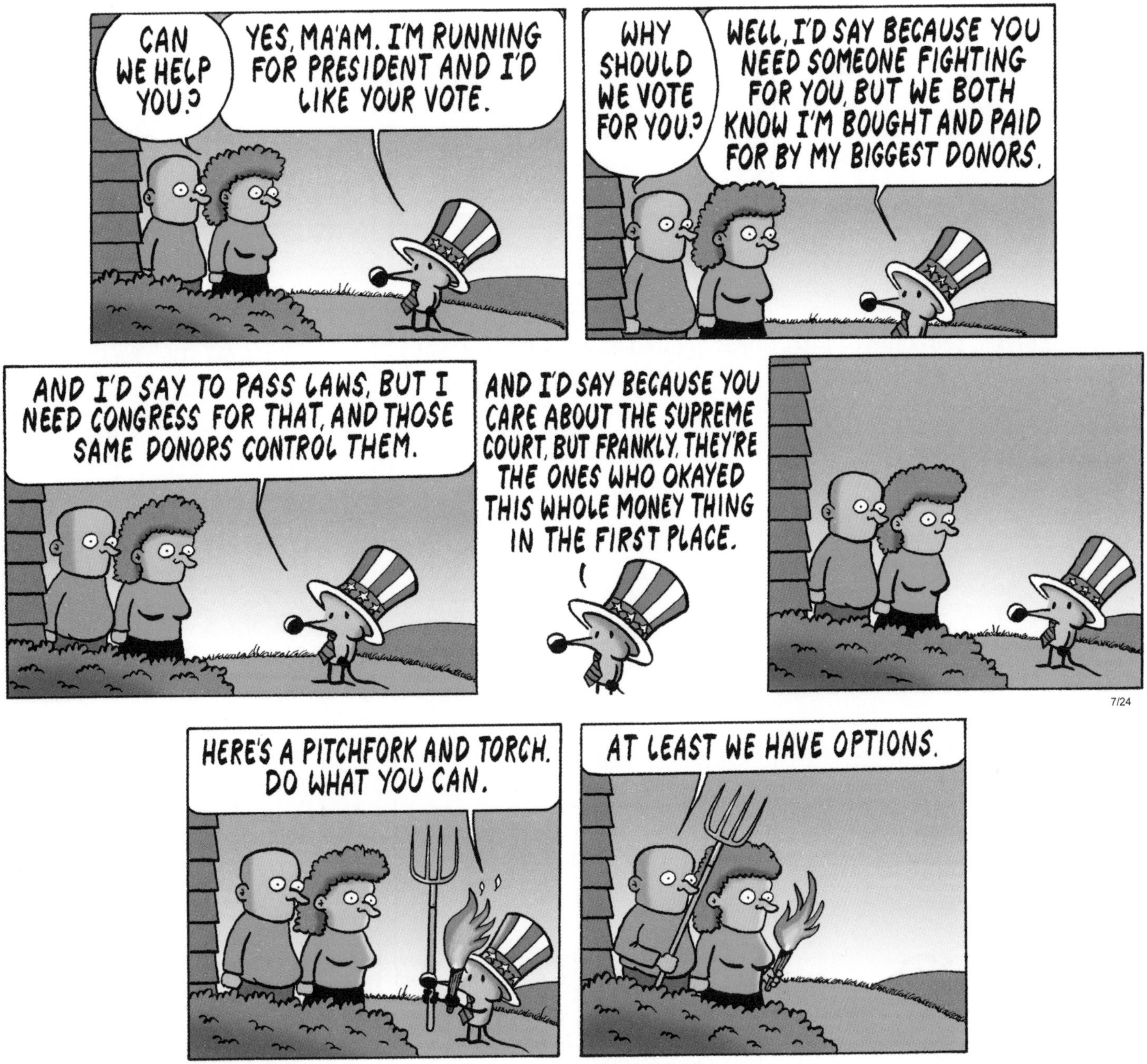
CAN WE HELP YOU?
YES, MA'AM. I'M RUNNING FOR PRESIDENT AND I'D LIKE YOUR VOTE.
WHY SHOULD WE VOTE FOR YOU?
WELL, I'D SAY BECAUSE YOU NEED SOMEONE FIGHTING FOR YOU, BUT WE BOTH KNOW I'M BOUGHT AND PAID FOR BY MY BIGGEST DONORS.
AND I'D SAY TO PASS LAWS, BUT I NEED CONGRESS FOR THAT, AND THOSE SAME DONORS CONTROL THEM.
AND I'D SAY BECAUSE YOU CARE ABOUT THE SUPREME COURT, BUT FRANKLY, THEY'RE THE ONES WHO OKAYED THIS WHOLE MONEY THING IN THE FIRST PLACE.
7/24
HERE'S A PITCHFORK AND TORCH. DO WHAT YOU CAN.
AT LEAST WE HAVE OPTIONS.

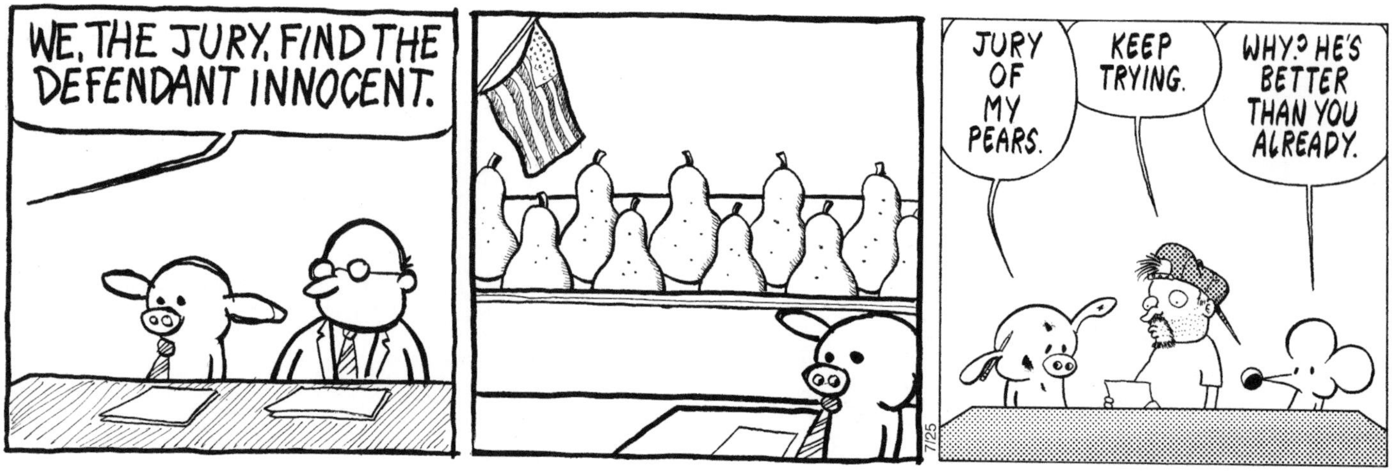
WE, THE JURY, FIND THE DEFENDANT INNOCENT.
JURY OF MY PEARS.
KEEP TRYING.
WHY? HE'S BETTER THAN YOU ALREADY.
7/25

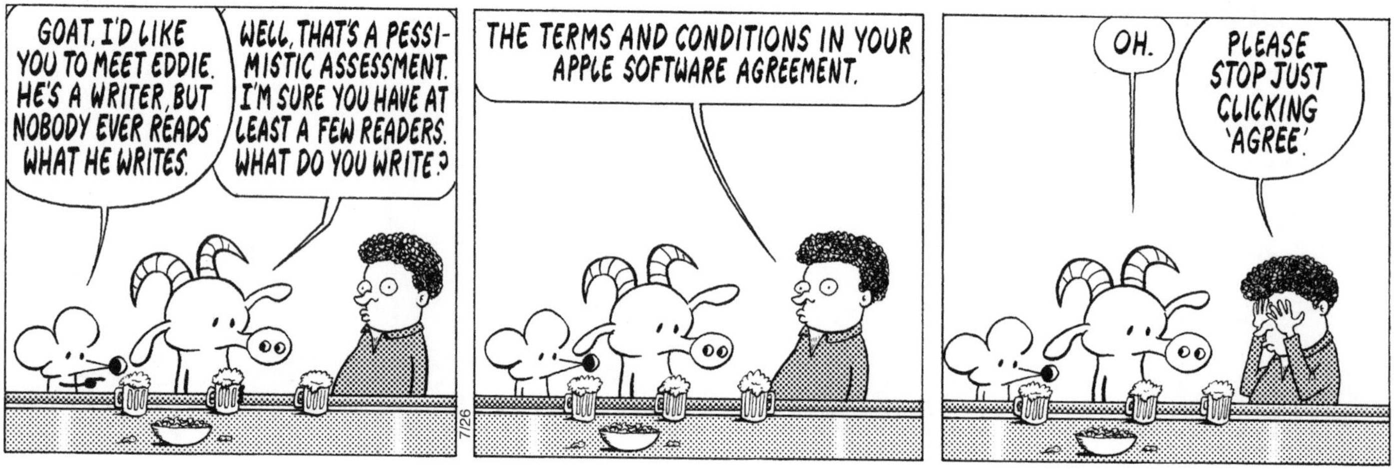
GOAT, I'D LIKE YOU TO MEET EDDIE. HE'S A WRITER, BUT NOBODY EVER READS WHAT HE WRITES.
WELL, THAT'S A PESSIMISTIC ASSESSMENT. I'M SURE YOU HAVE AT LEAST A FEW READERS. WHAT DO YOU WRITE?
THE TERMS AND CONDITIONS IN YOUR APPLE SOFTWARE AGREEMENT.
OH.
PLEASE STOP JUST CLICKING 'AGREE.'
7/26

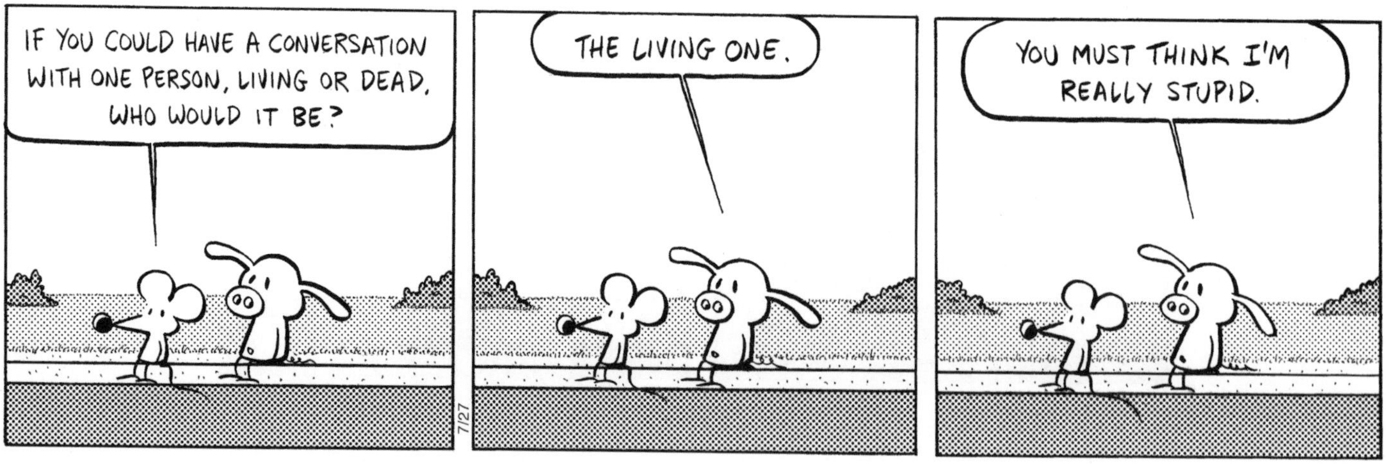
IF YOU COULD HAVE A CONVERSATION WITH ONE PERSON, LIVING OR DEAD, WHO WOULD IT BE?
THE LIVING ONE.
YOU MUST THINK I'M REALLY STUPID.
7/27

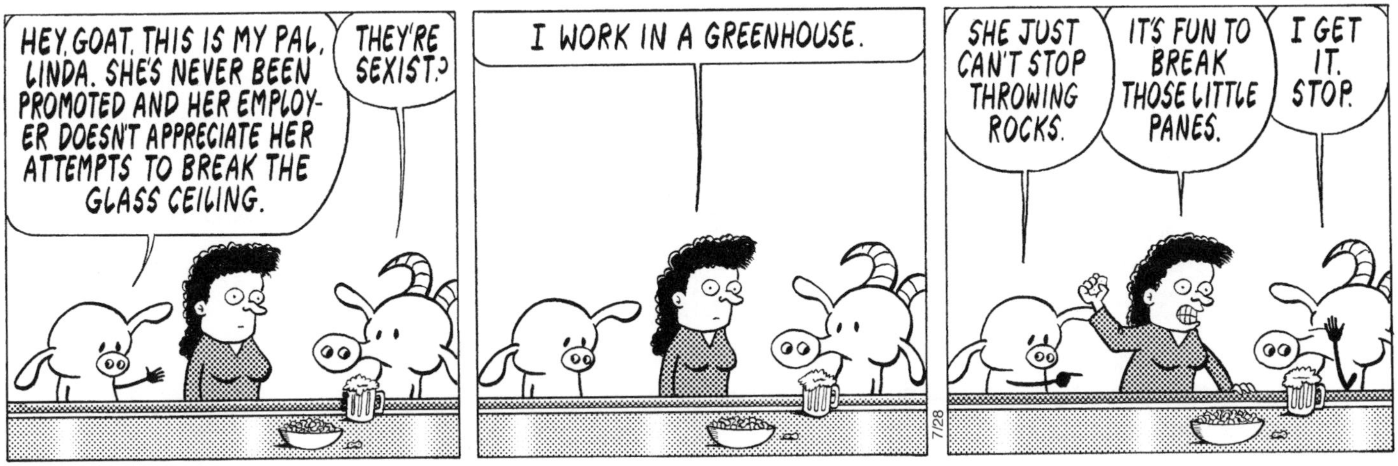
HEY, GOAT. THIS IS MY PAL, LINDA. SHE'S NEVER BEEN PROMOTED AND HER EMPLOYER DOESN'T APPRECIATE HER ATTEMPTS TO BREAK THE GLASS CEILING.
THEY'RE SEXIST?
I WORK IN A GREENHOUSE.
SHE JUST CAN'T STOP THROWING ROCKS.
IT'S FUN TO BREAK THOSE LITTLE PANES.
I GET IT. STOP.
7/28

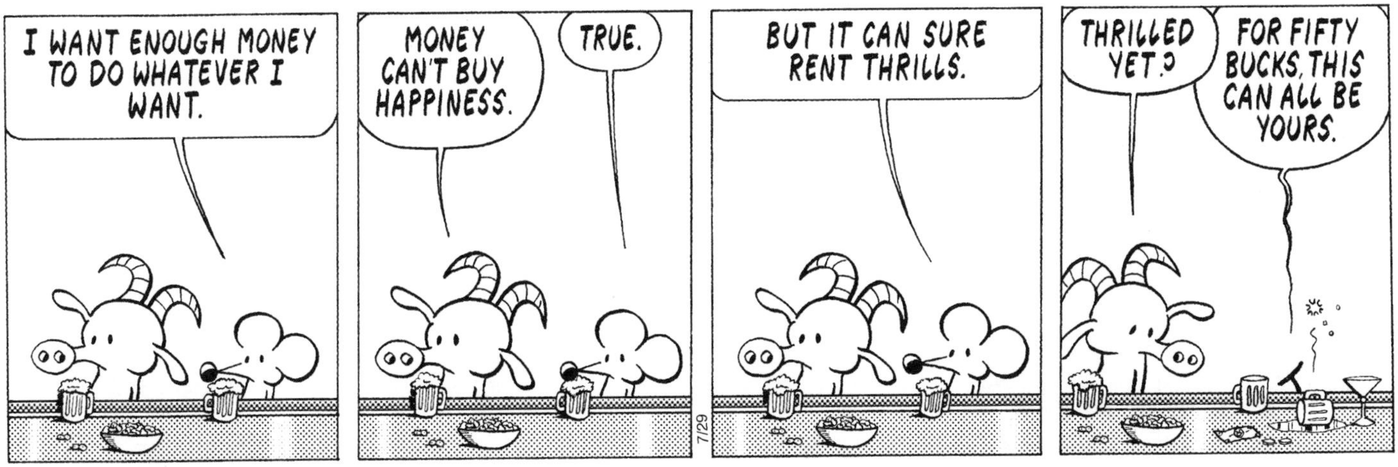
I WANT ENOUGH MONEY TO DO WHATEVER I WANT.
MONEY CAN'T BUY HAPPINESS.
TRUE.
BUT IT CAN SURE RENT THRILLS.
THRILLED YET?
FOR FIFTY BUCKS, THIS CAN ALL BE YOURS.
7/29

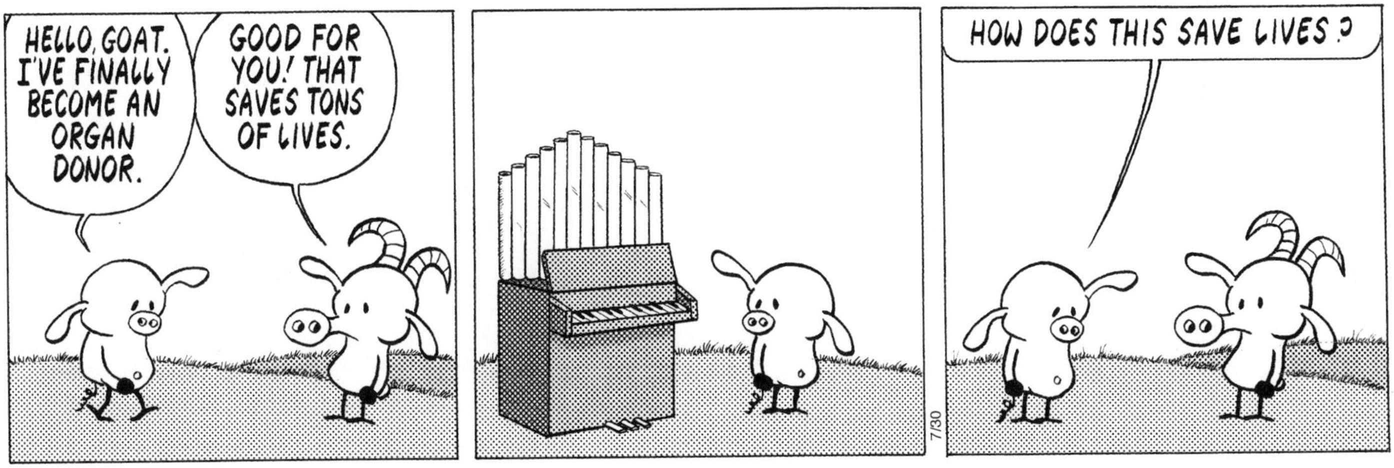
HELLO, GOAT. I'VE FINALLY BECOME AN ORGAN DONOR.
GOOD FOR YOU! THAT SAVES TONS OF LIVES.
HOW DOES THIS SAVE LIVES?
7/30

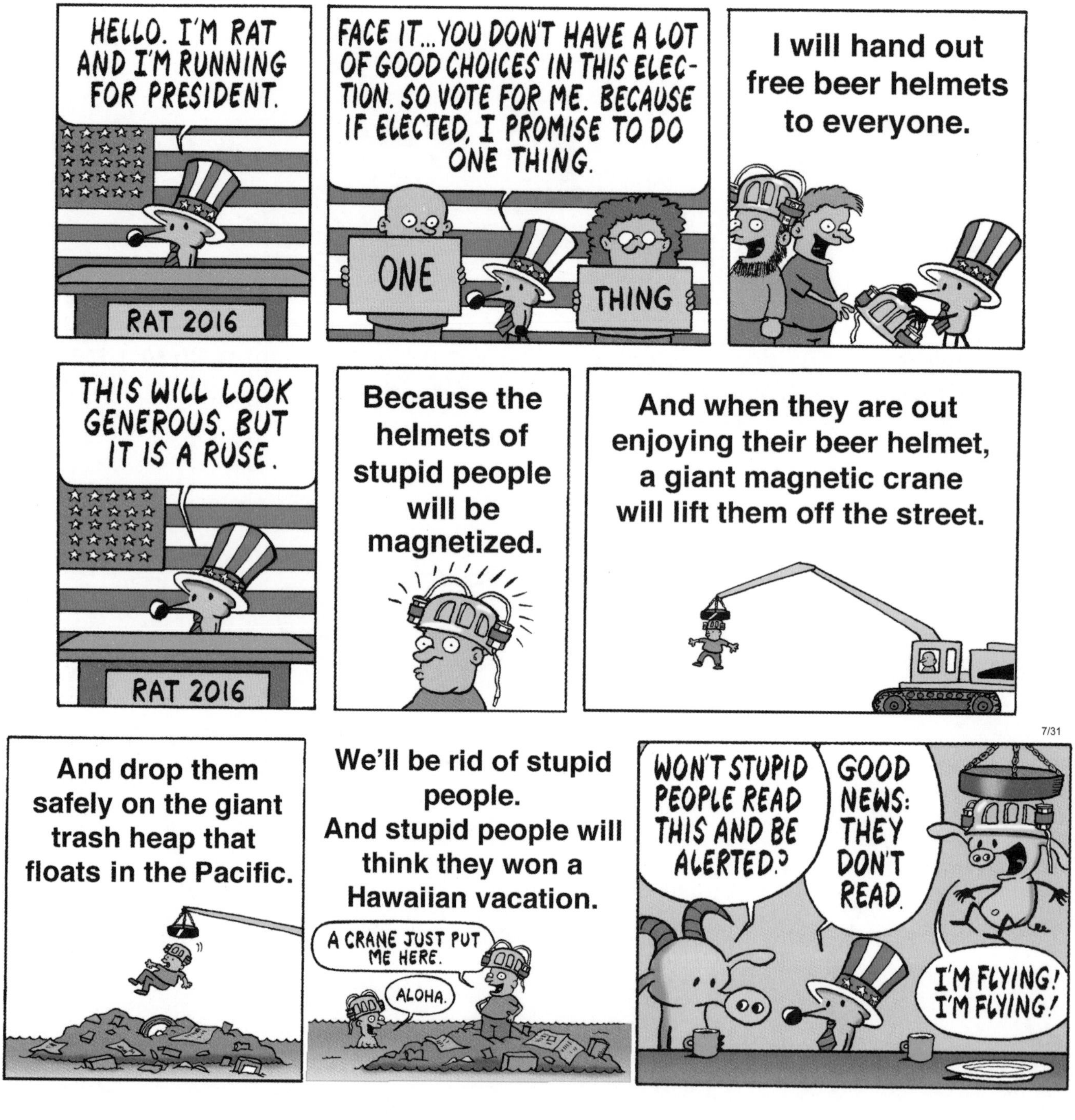
HELLO. I'M RAT AND I'M RUNNING FOR PRESIDENT.
RAT 2016
FACE IT...YOU DON'T HAVE A LOT OF GOOD CHOICES IN THIS ELECTION. SO VOTE FOR ME. BECAUSE IF ELECTED, I PROMISE TO DO ONE THING.
ONE
THING
I will hand out free beer helmets to everyone.
THIS WILL LOOK GENEROUS. BUT IT IS A RUSE.
RAT 2016
Because the helmets of stupid people will be magnetized.
And when they are out enjoying their beer helmet, a giant magnetic crane will lift them off the street.
7/31
And drop them safely on the giant trash heap that floats in the Pacific.
We'll be rid of stupid people. And stupid people will think they won a Hawaiian vacation.
A CRANE JUST PUT ME HERE.
ALOHA.
WON'T STUPID PEOPLE READ THIS AND BE ALERTED?
GOOD NEWS: THEY DON'T READ.
I'M FLYING! I'M FLYING!

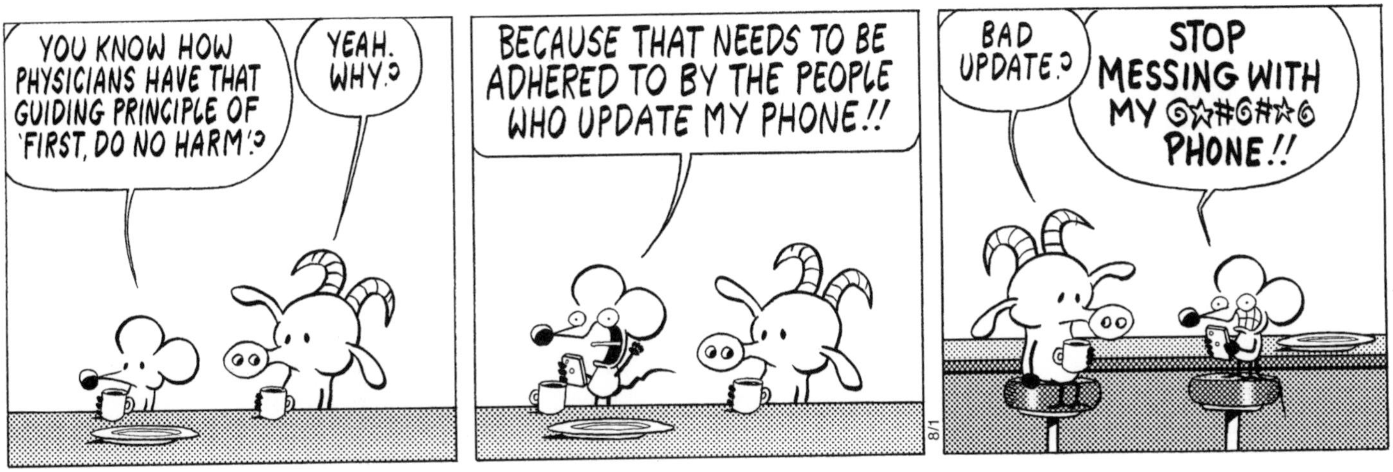
YOU KNOW HOW PHYSICIANS HAVE THAT GUIDING PRINCIPLE OF 'FIRST, DO NO HARM'?
YEAH. WHY?
BECAUSE THAT NEEDS TO BE ADHERED TO BY THE PEOPLE WHO UPDATE MY PHONE!!
BAD UPDATE?
STOP MESSING WITH MY @☆#@#☆@ PHONE!!
8/1

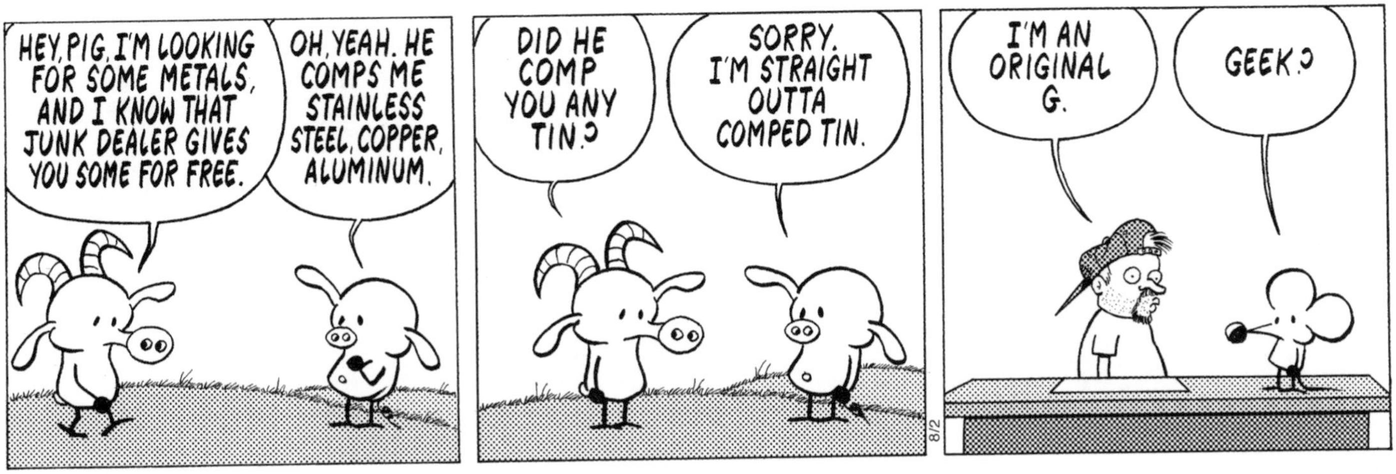
HEY, PIG, I'M LOOKING FOR SOME METALS, AND I KNOW THAT JUNK DEALER GIVES YOU SOME FOR FREE.
OH, YEAH. HE COMPS ME STAINLESS STEEL, COPPER, ALUMINUM.
DID HE COMP YOU ANY TIN?
SORRY. I'M STRAIGHT OUTTA COMPED TIN.
I'M AN ORIGINAL G.
GEEK?
8/2

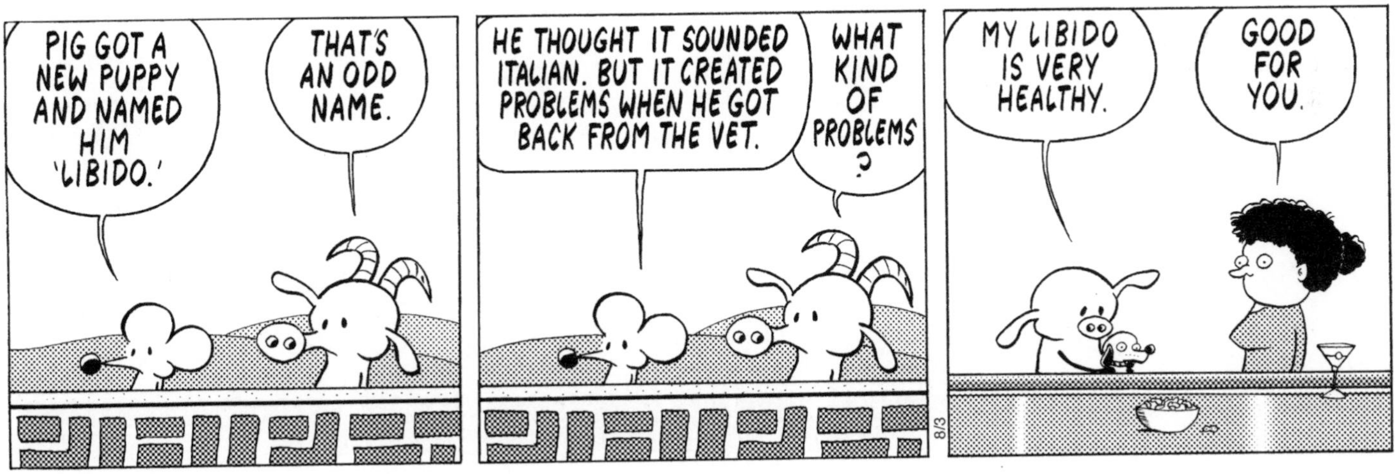
PIG GOT A NEW PUPPY AND NAMED HIM 'LIBIDO.'
THAT'S AN ODD NAME.
HE THOUGHT IT SOUNDED ITALIAN. BUT IT CREATED PROBLEMS WHEN HE GOT BACK FROM THE VET.
WHAT KIND OF PROBLEMS?
MY LIBIDO IS VERY HEALTHY.
GOOD FOR YOU.
8/3

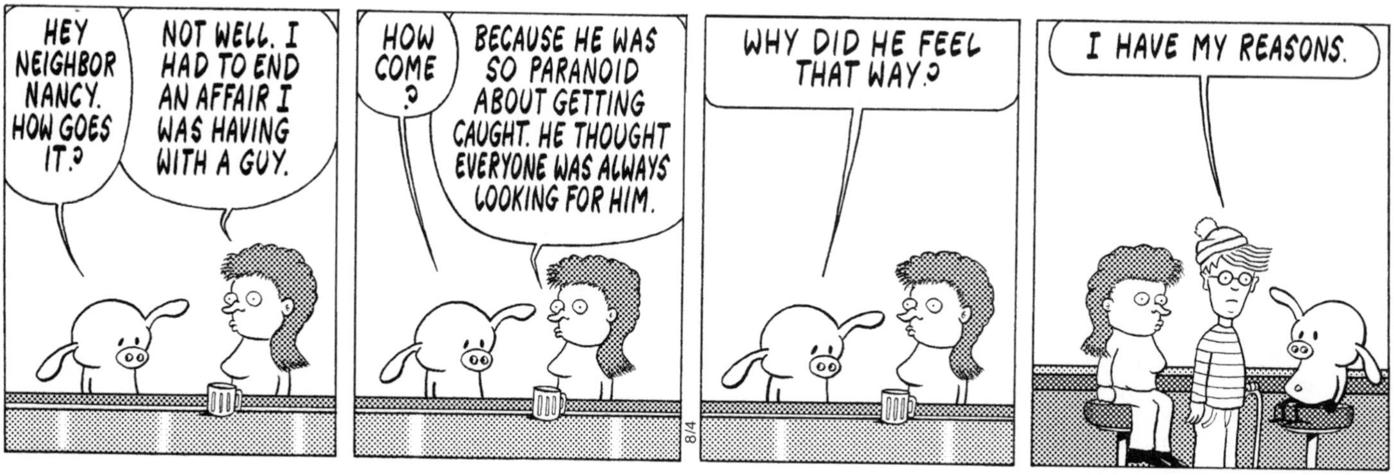
HEY NEIGHBOR NANCY. HOW GOES IT?
NOT WELL. I HAD TO END AN AFFAIR I WAS HAVING WITH A GUY.
HOW COME?
BECAUSE HE WAS SO PARANOID ABOUT GETTING CAUGHT. HE THOUGHT EVERYONE WAS ALWAYS LOOKING FOR HIM.
8/4
WHY DID HE FEEL THAT WAY?
I HAVE MY REASONS.

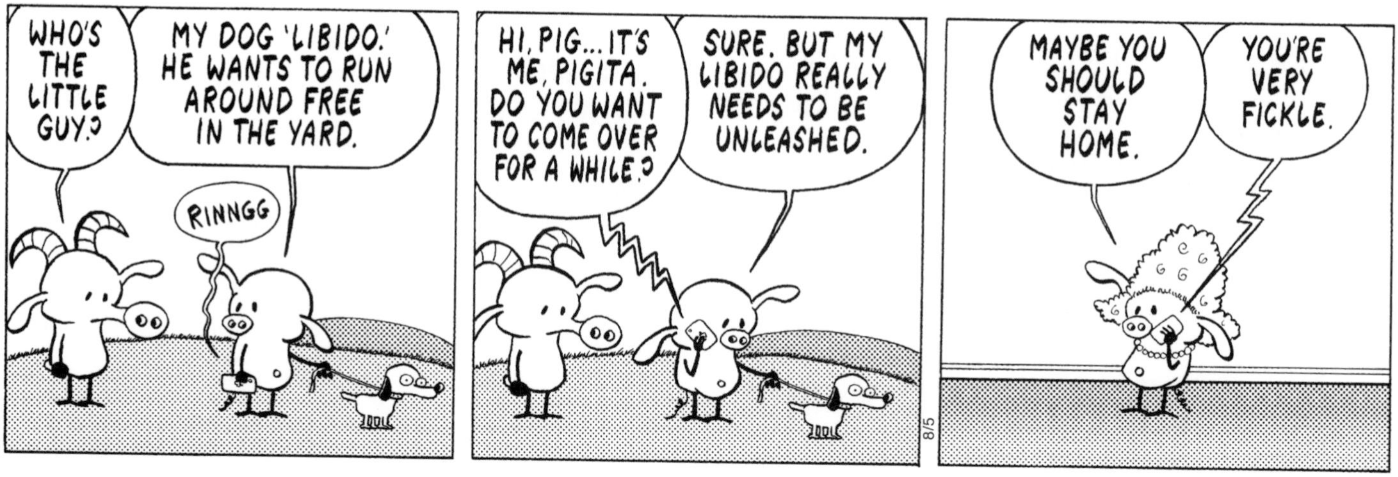
WHO'S THE LITTLE GUY?
MY DOG 'LIBIDO.' HE WANTS TO RUN AROUND FREE IN THE YARD.
RINNGG
HI, PIG... IT'S ME, PIGITA. DO YOU WANT TO COME OVER FOR A WHILE?
SURE. BUT MY LIBIDO REALLY NEEDS TO BE UNLEASHED.
8/5
MAYBE YOU SHOULD STAY HOME.
YOU'RE VERY FICKLE.

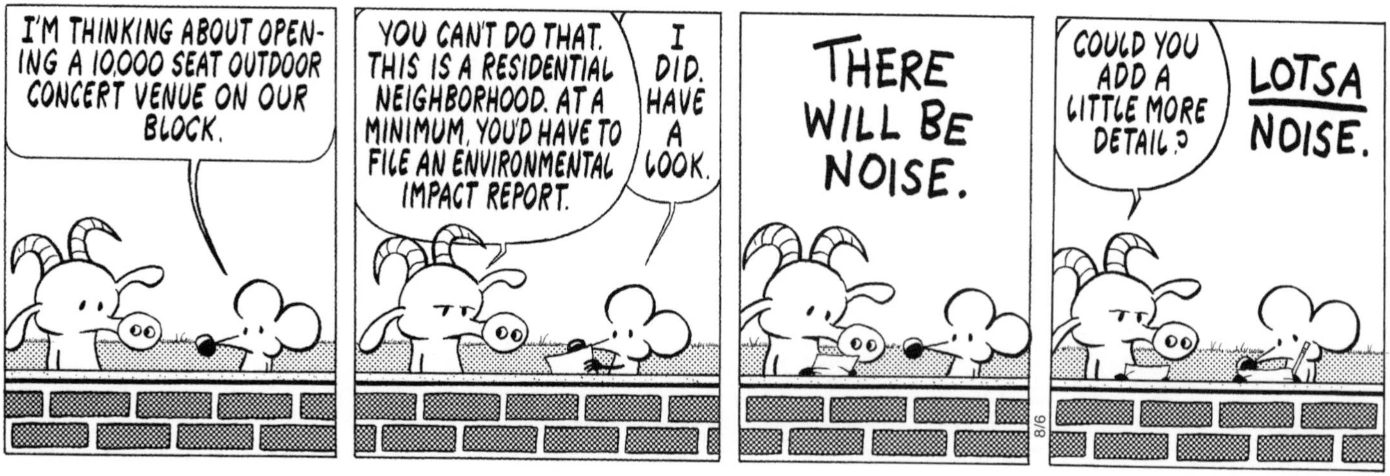
I'M THINKING ABOUT OPENING A 10,000 SEAT OUTDOOR CONCERT VENUE ON OUR BLOCK.
YOU CAN'T DO THAT. THIS IS A RESIDENTIAL NEIGHBORHOOD. AT A MINIMUM, YOU'D HAVE TO FILE AN ENVIRONMENTAL IMPACT REPORT.
I DID. HAVE A LOOK.
THERE WILL BE NOISE.
8/6
COULD YOU ADD A LITTLE MORE DETAIL?
LOTSA NOISE.

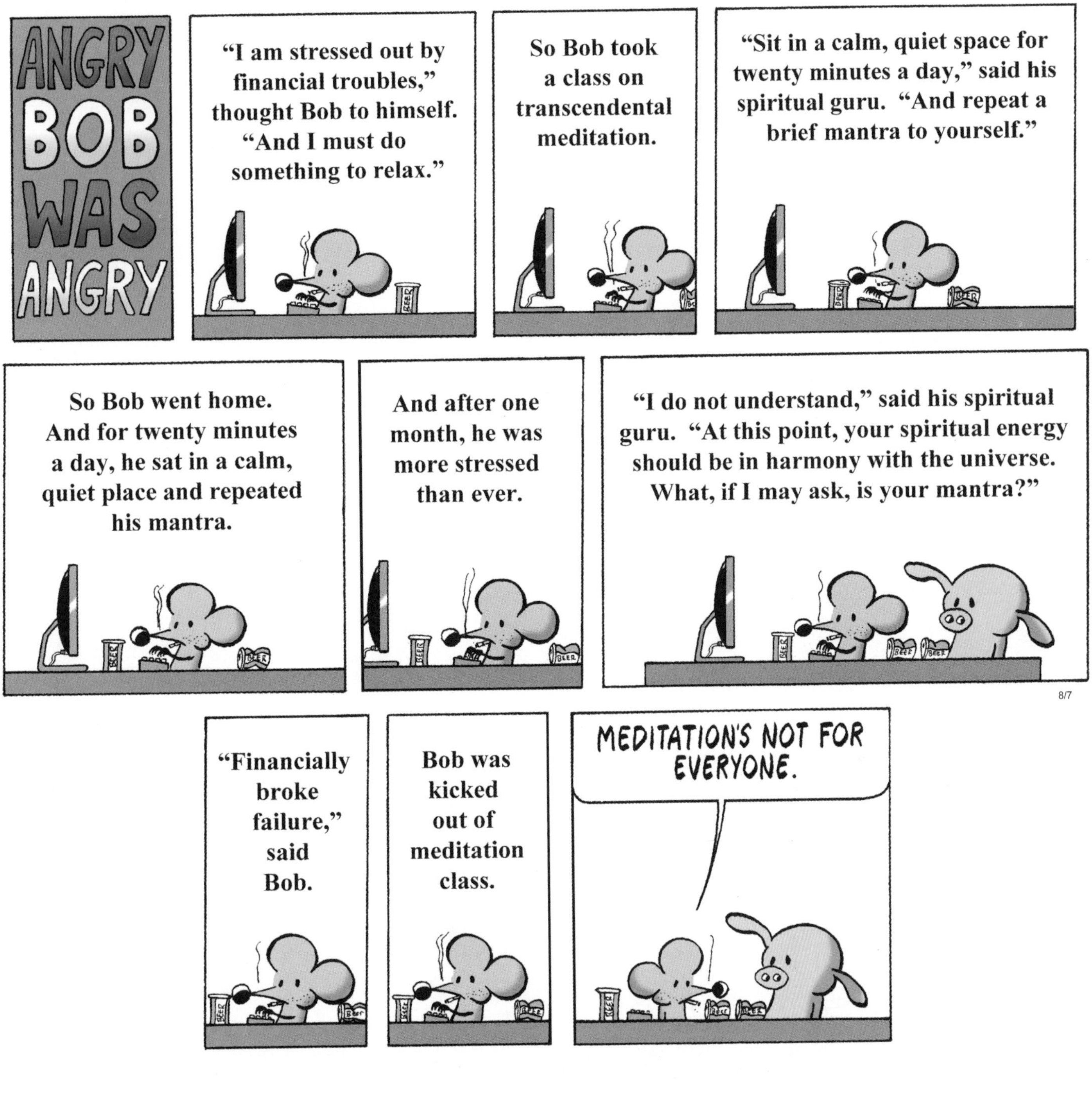
ANGRY BOB WAS ANGRY
"I am stressed out by financial troubles," thought Bob to himself. "And I must do something to relax."
BEER
So Bob took a class on transcendental meditation.
"Sit in a calm, quiet space for twenty minutes a day," said his spiritual guru. "And repeat a brief mantra to yourself."
So Bob went home. And for twenty minutes a day, he sat in a calm, quiet place and repeated his mantra.
And after one month, he was more stressed than ever.
"I do not understand," said his spiritual guru. "At this point, your spiritual energy should be in harmony with the universe. What, if I may ask, is your mantra?"
8/7
"Financially broke failure," said Bob.
Bob was kicked out of meditation class.
MEDITATION'S NOT FOR EVERYONE.

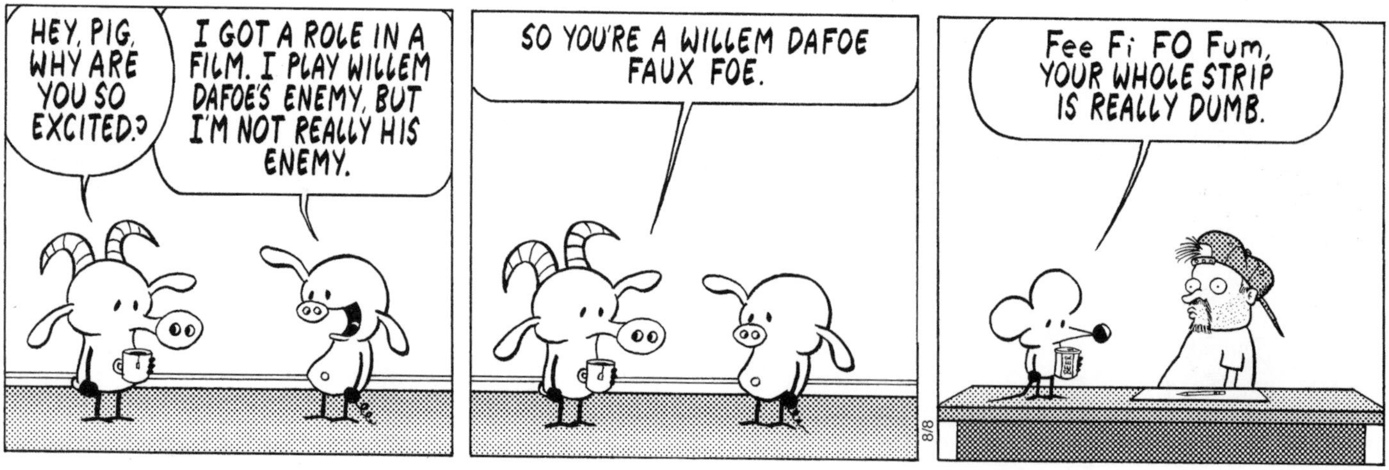
HEY, PIG, WHY ARE YOU SO EXCITED?
I GOT A ROLE IN A FILM. I PLAY WILLEM DAFOE'S ENEMY, BUT I'M NOT REALLY HIS ENEMY.
SO YOU'RE A WILLEM DAFOE FAUX FOE.
8/8
Fee Fi FO Fum, YOUR WHOLE STRIP IS REALLY DUMB.
SEE

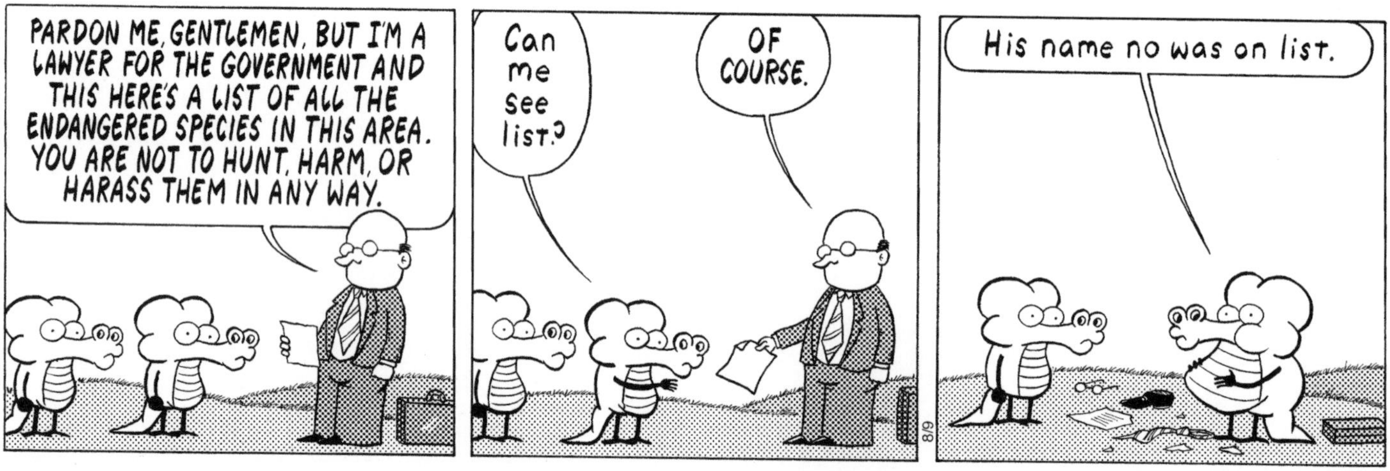
PARDON ME, GENTLEMEN, BUT I'M A LAWYER FOR THE GOVERNMENT AND THIS HERE'S A LIST OF ALL THE ENDANGERED SPECIES IN THIS AREA. YOU ARE NOT TO HUNT, HARM, OR HARASS THEM IN ANY WAY.
Can me see list?
OF COURSE.
8/9
His name no was on list.

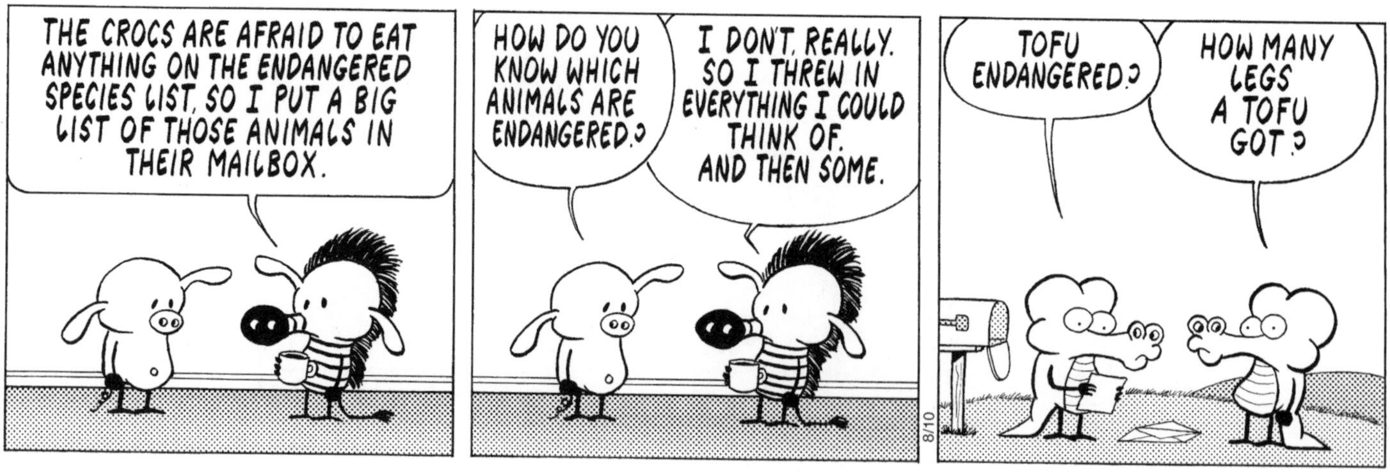
THE CROCS ARE AFRAID TO EAT ANYTHING ON THE ENDANGERED SPECIES LIST, SO I PUT A BIG LIST OF THOSE ANIMALS IN THEIR MAILBOX.
HOW DO YOU KNOW WHICH ANIMALS ARE ENDANGERED?
I DON'T, REALLY. SO I THREW IN EVERYTHING I COULD THINK OF. AND THEN SOME.
8/10
TOFU ENDANGERED?
HOW MANY LEGS A TOFU GOT?

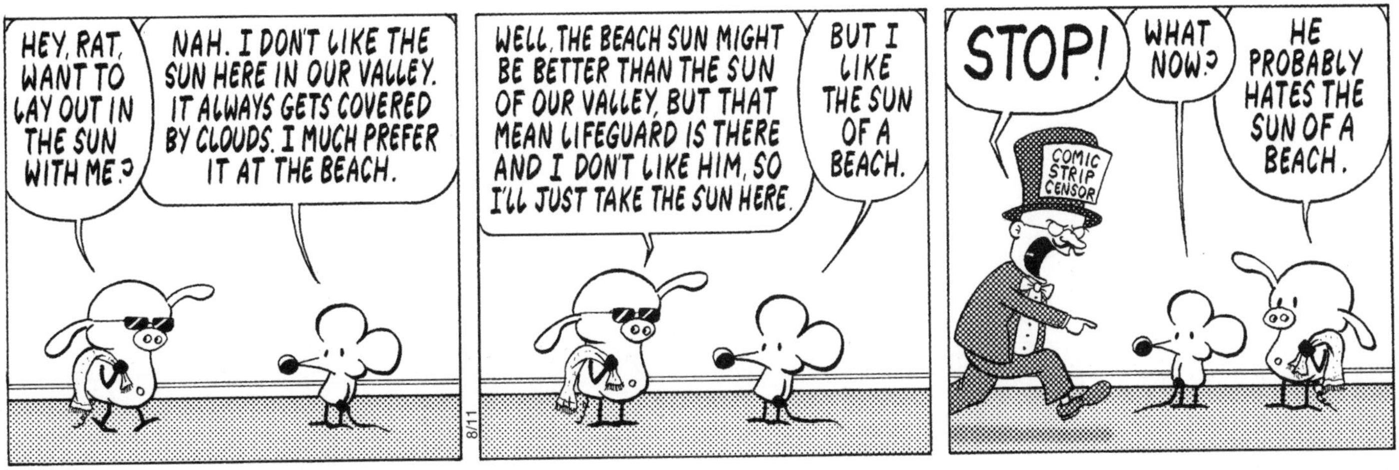
HEY, RAT, WANT TO LAY OUT IN THE SUN WITH ME?
NAH. I DON'T LIKE THE SUN HERE IN OUR VALLEY. IT ALWAYS GETS COVERED BY CLOUDS. I MUCH PREFER IT AT THE BEACH.
8/11
WELL, THE BEACH SUN MIGHT BE BETTER THAN THE SUN OF OUR VALLEY, BUT THAT MEAN LIFEGUARD IS THERE AND I DON'T LIKE HIM, SO I'LL JUST TAKE THE SUN HERE.
BUT I LIKE THE SUN OF A BEACH.
STOP!
COMIC STRIP CENSOR
WHAT NOW?
HE PROBABLY HATES THE SUN OF A BEACH.

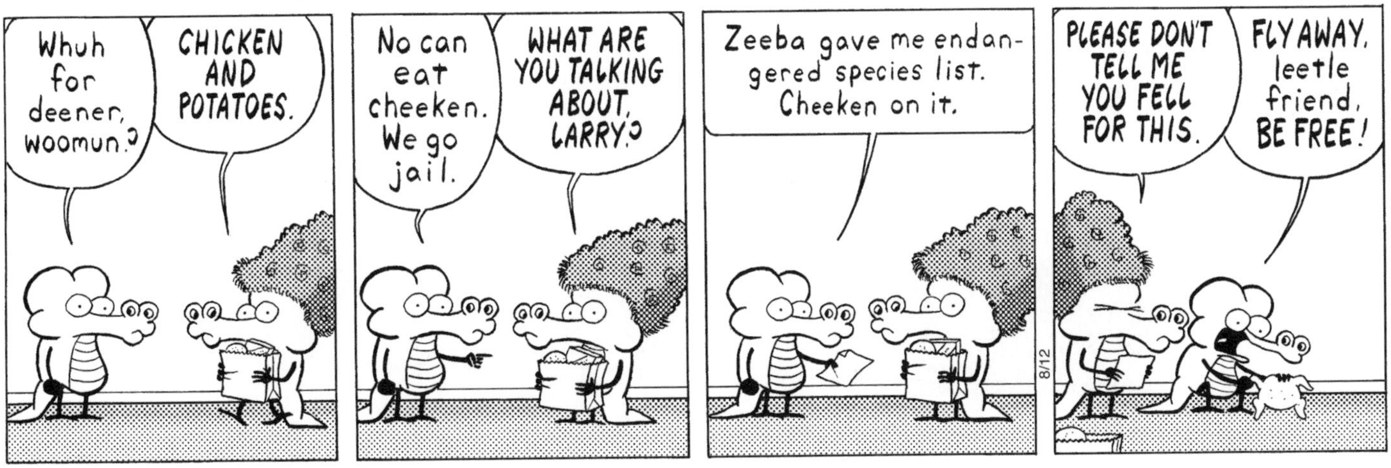
Whuh for deener, woomun?
CHICKEN AND POTATOES.
No can eat cheeken. We go jail.
WHAT ARE YOU TALKING ABOUT, LARRY?
Zeeba gave me endangered species list. Cheeken on it.
8/12
PLEASE DON'T TELL ME YOU FELL FOR THIS.
FLY AWAY, leetle friend, BE FREE!

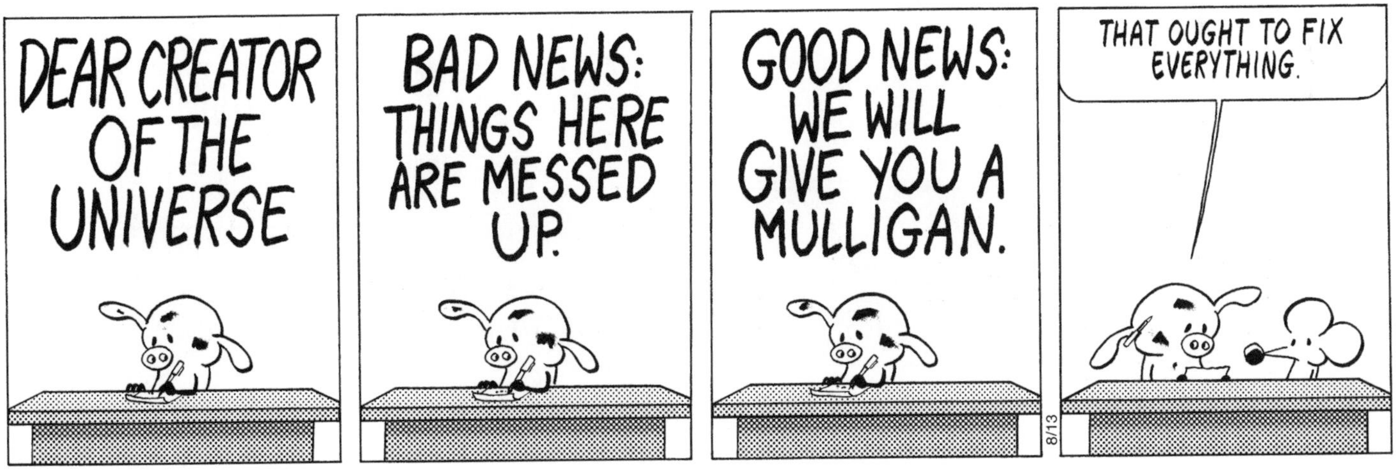
DEAR CREATOR OF THE UNIVERSE
BAD NEWS: THINGS HERE ARE MESSED UP.
GOOD NEWS: WE WILL GIVE YOU A MULLIGAN.
8/13
THAT OUGHT TO FIX EVERYTHING.

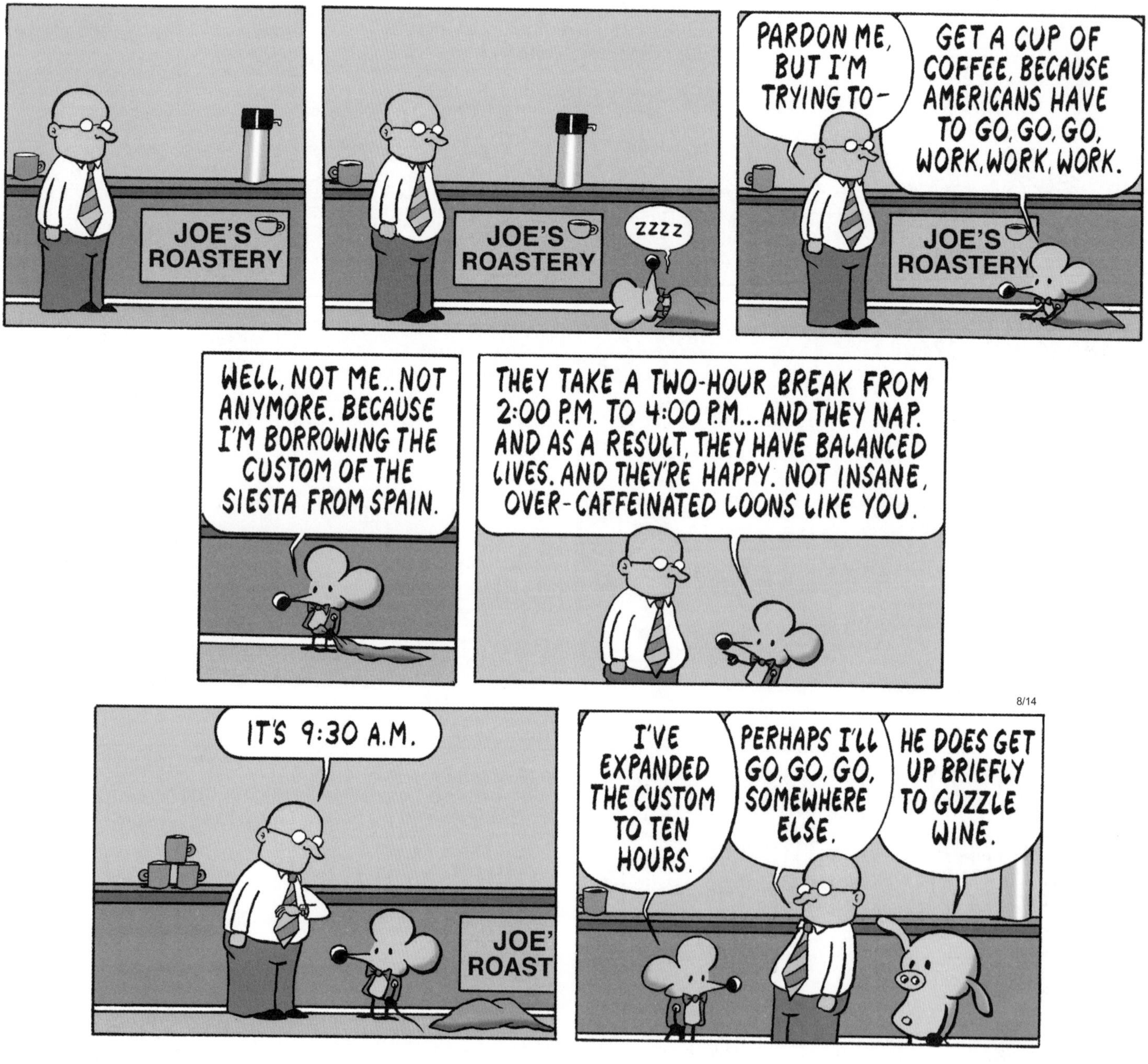
JOE'S ROASTERY
JOE'S ROASTERY
ZZZZ
PARDON ME, BUT I'M TRYING TO–
GET A CUP OF COFFEE, BECAUSE AMERICANS HAVE TO GO, GO, GO, WORK, WORK, WORK.
JOE'S ROASTERY
WELL, NOT ME.. NOT ANYMORE. BECAUSE I'M BORROWING THE CUSTOM OF THE SIESTA FROM SPAIN.
THEY TAKE A TWO-HOUR BREAK FROM 2:00 P.M. TO 4:00 P.M... AND THEY NAP. AND AS A RESULT, THEY HAVE BALANCED LIVES. AND THEY'RE HAPPY. NOT INSANE, OVER-CAFFEINATED LOONS LIKE YOU.
8/14
IT'S 9:30 A.M.
JOE' ROAST
I'VE EXPANDED THE CUSTOM TO TEN HOURS.
PERHAPS I'LL GO, GO, GO, SOMEWHERE ELSE.
HE DOES GET UP BRIEFLY TO GUZZLE WINE.

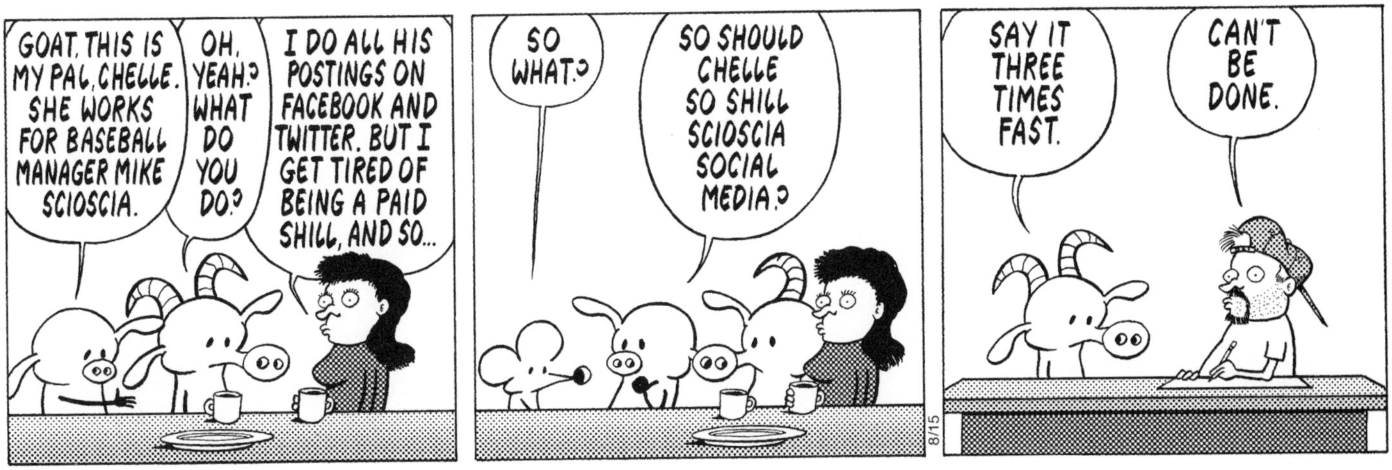
GOAT, THIS IS MY PAL, CHELLE. SHE WORKS FOR BASEBALL MANAGER MIKE SCIOSCIA.
OH, YEAH? WHAT DO YOU DO?
I DO ALL HIS POSTINGS ON FACEBOOK AND TWITTER. BUT I GET TIRED OF BEING A PAID SHILL, AND SO...
SO WHAT?
SO SHOULD CHELLE SO SHILL SCIOSCIA SOCIAL MEDIA?
SAY IT THREE TIMES FAST.
CAN'T BE DONE.
8/15

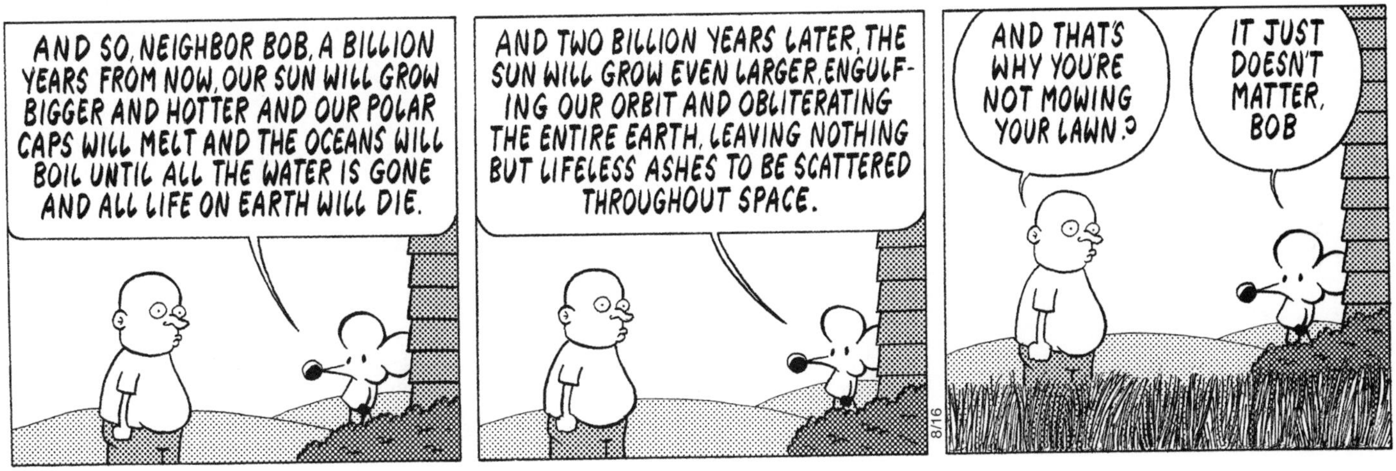
AND SO, NEIGHBOR BOB, A BILLION YEARS FROM NOW, OUR SUN WILL GROW BIGGER AND HOTTER AND OUR POLAR CAPS WILL MELT AND THE OCEANS WILL BOIL UNTIL ALL THE WATER IS GONE AND ALL LIFE ON EARTH WILL DIE.
AND TWO BILLION YEARS LATER, THE SUN WILL GROW EVEN LARGER, ENGULF-ING OUR ORBIT AND OBLITERATING THE ENTIRE EARTH, LEAVING NOTHING BUT LIFELESS ASHES TO BE SCATTERED THROUGHOUT SPACE.
AND THAT'S WHY YOU'RE NOT MOWING YOUR LAWN?
IT JUST DOESN'T MATTER, BOB
8/16

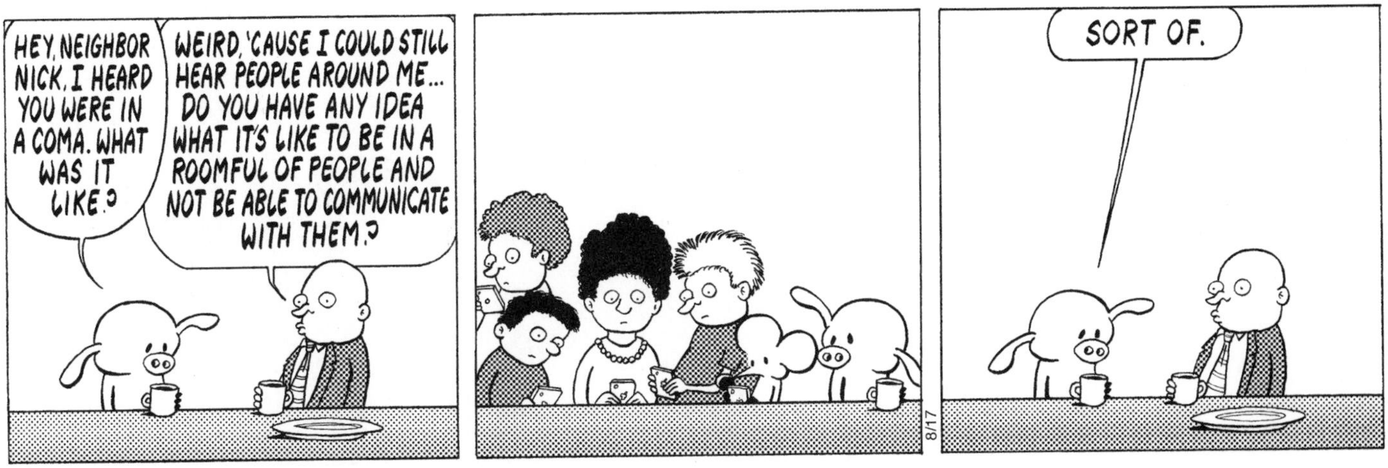
HEY, NEIGHBOR NICK, I HEARD YOU WERE IN A COMA. WHAT WAS IT LIKE?
WEIRD, 'CAUSE I COULD STILL HEAR PEOPLE AROUND ME... DO YOU HAVE ANY IDEA WHAT IT'S LIKE TO BE IN A ROOMFUL OF PEOPLE AND NOT BE ABLE TO COMMUNICATE WITH THEM?
SORT OF.
8/17

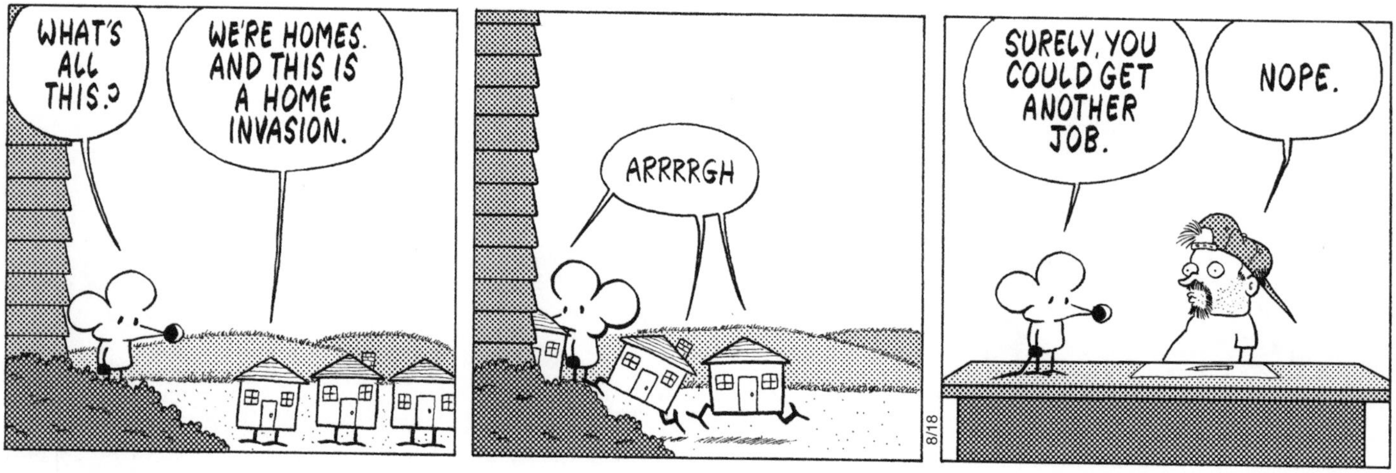
WHAT'S ALL THIS?
WE'RE HOMES. AND THIS IS A HOME INVASION.
ARRRRGH
SURELY, YOU COULD GET ANOTHER JOB.
NOPE.
8/18

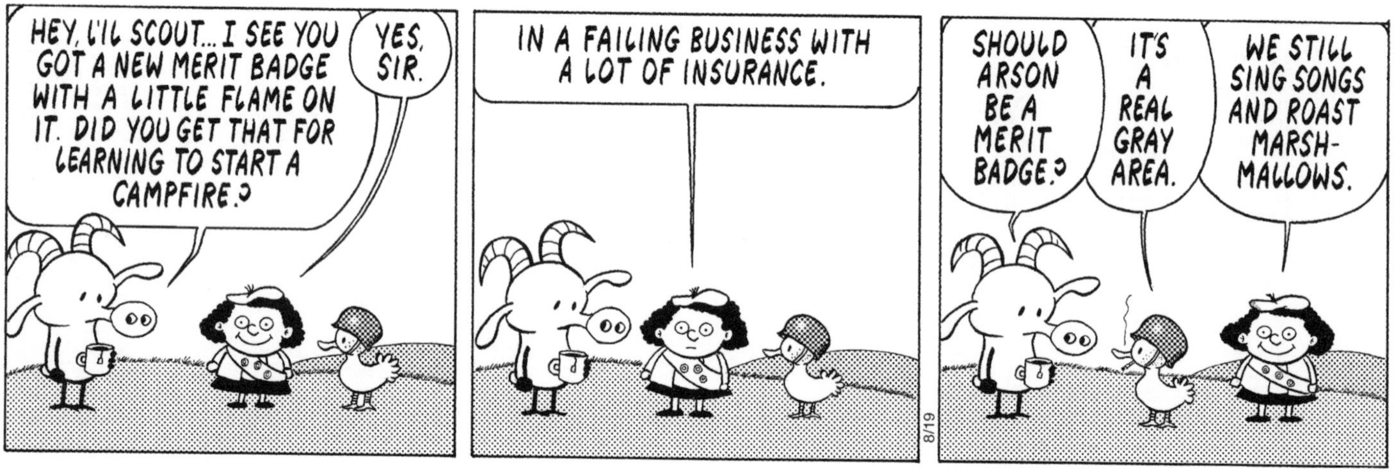
HEY, L'IL SCOUT... I SEE YOU GOT A NEW MERIT BADGE WITH A LITTLE FLAME ON IT. DID YOU GET THAT FOR LEARNING TO START A CAMPFIRE?
YES, SIR.
IN A FAILING BUSINESS WITH A LOT OF INSURANCE.
SHOULD ARSON BE A MERIT BADGE?
IT'S A REAL GRAY AREA.
WE STILL SING SONGS AND ROAST MARSH-MALLOWS.
8/19

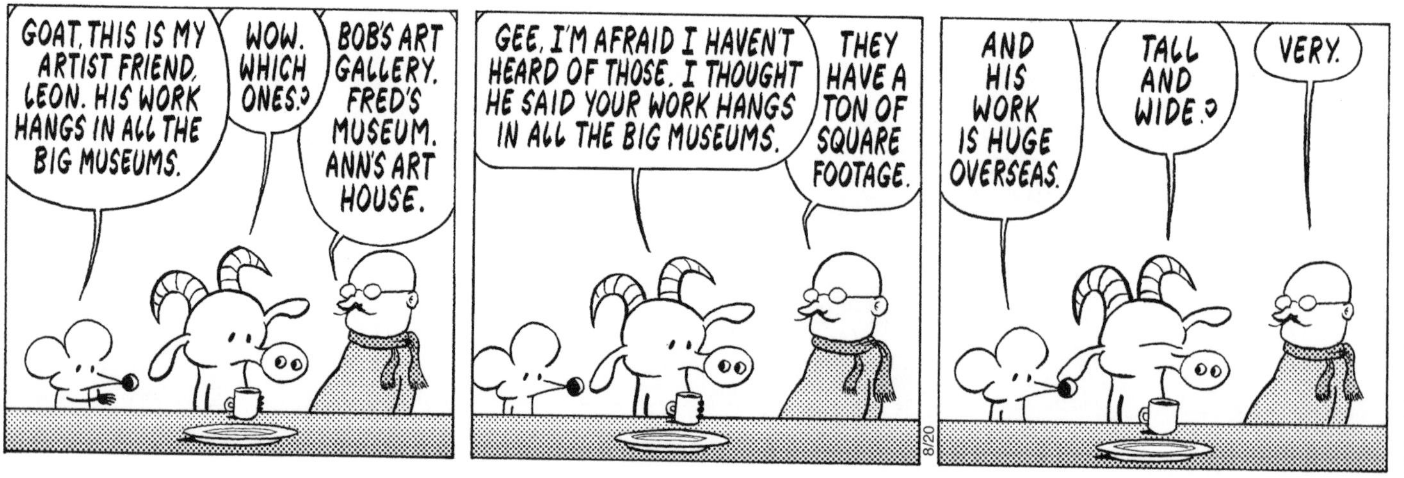
GOAT, THIS IS MY ARTIST FRIEND, LEON. HIS WORK HANGS IN ALL THE BIG MUSEUMS.
WOW. WHICH ONES?
BOB'S ART GALLERY. FRED'S MUSEUM. ANN'S ART HOUSE.
GEE, I'M AFRAID I HAVEN'T HEARD OF THOSE. I THOUGHT HE SAID YOUR WORK HANGS IN ALL THE BIG MUSEUMS.
THEY HAVE A TON OF SQUARE FOOTAGE.
AND HIS WORK IS HUGE OVERSEAS.
TALL AND WIDE?
VERY.
8/20

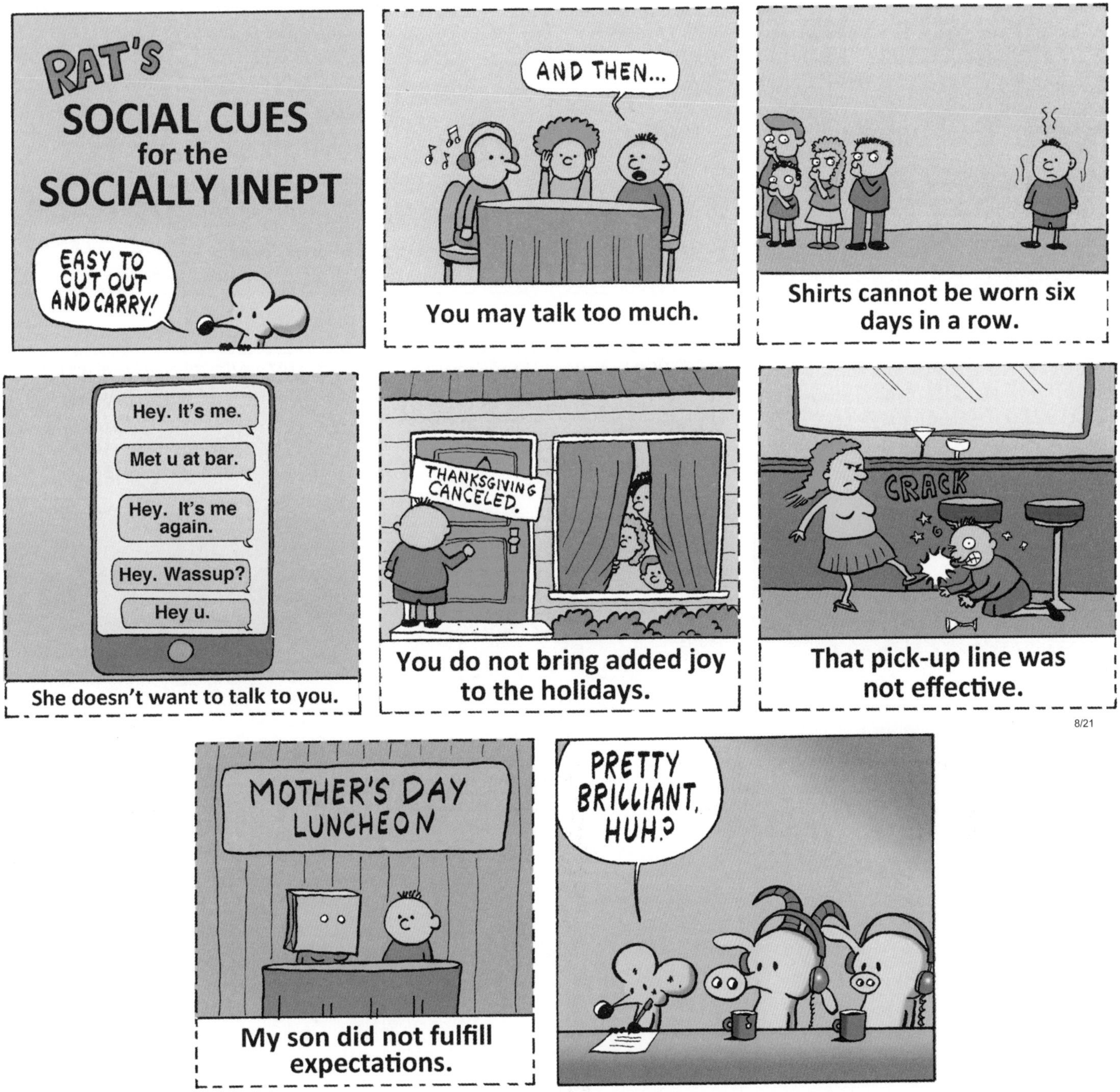
RAT'S
SOCIAL CUES
for the
SOCIALLY INEPT
EASY TO CUT OUT AND CARRY!
AND THEN...
You may talk too much.
Shirts cannot be worn six days in a row.
Hey. It's me.
Met u at bar.
Hey. It's me again.
Hey. Wassup?
Hey u.
She doesn't want to talk to you.
THANKSGIVING CANCELED.
You do not bring added joy to the holidays.
CRACK
That pick-up line was not effective.
8/21
MOTHER'S DAY LUNCHEON
My son did not fulfill expectations.
PRETTY BRILLIANT, HUH?

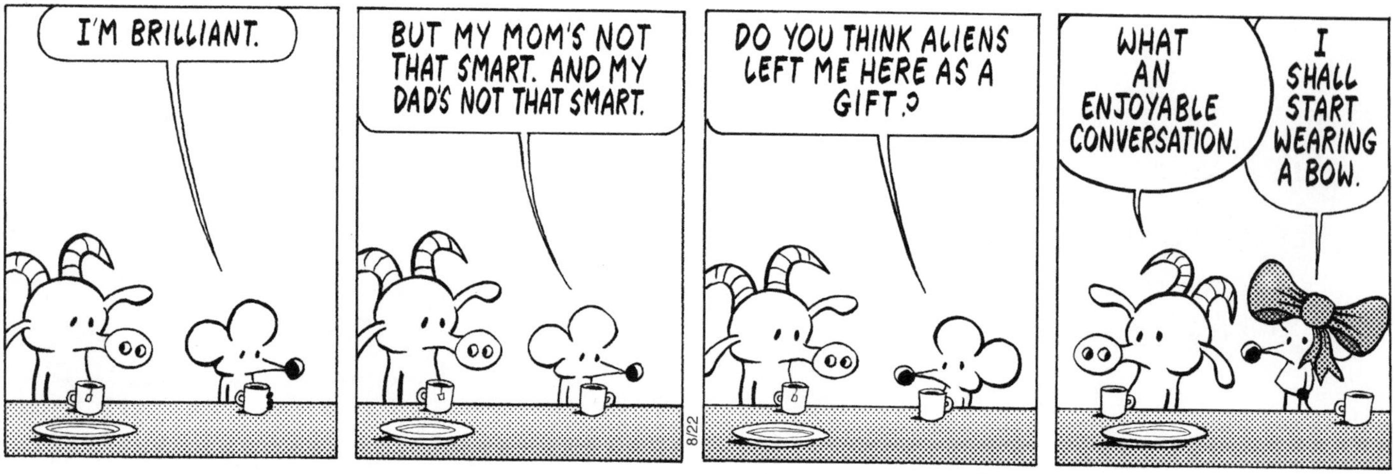
I'M BRILLIANT.
BUT MY MOM'S NOT THAT SMART. AND MY DAD'S NOT THAT SMART.
DO YOU THINK ALIENS LEFT ME HERE AS A GIFT?
WHAT AN ENJOYABLE CONVERSATION.
I SHALL START WEARING A BOW.
8/22

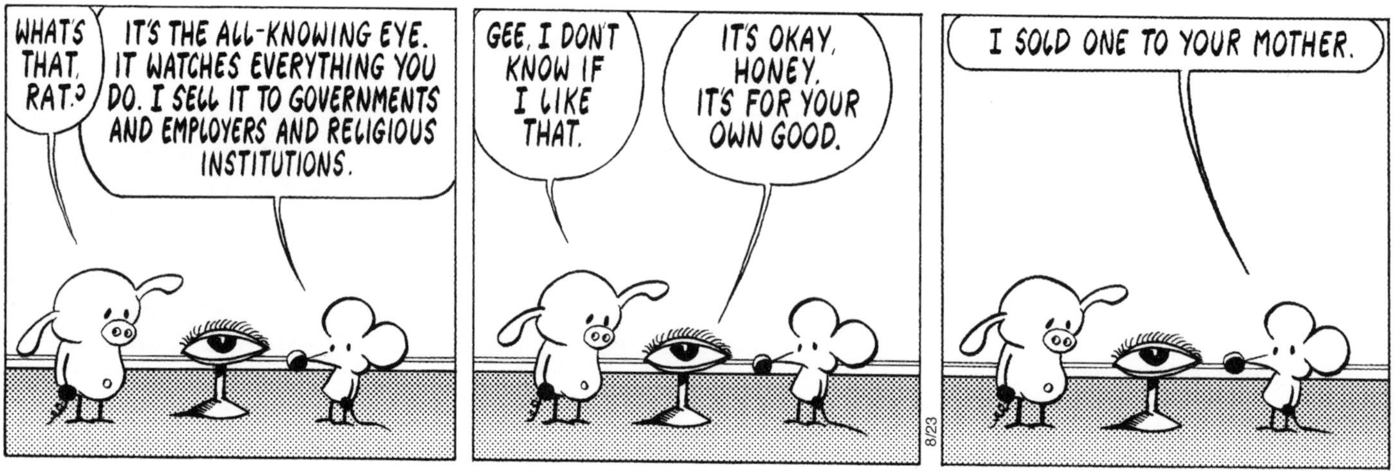
WHAT'S THAT, RAT?
IT'S THE ALL-KNOWING EYE. IT WATCHES EVERYTHING YOU DO. I SELL IT TO GOVERNMENTS AND EMPLOYERS AND RELIGIOUS INSTITUTIONS.
GEE, I DON'T KNOW IF I LIKE THAT.
IT'S OKAY, HONEY. IT'S FOR YOUR OWN GOOD.
I SOLD ONE TO YOUR MOTHER.
8/23

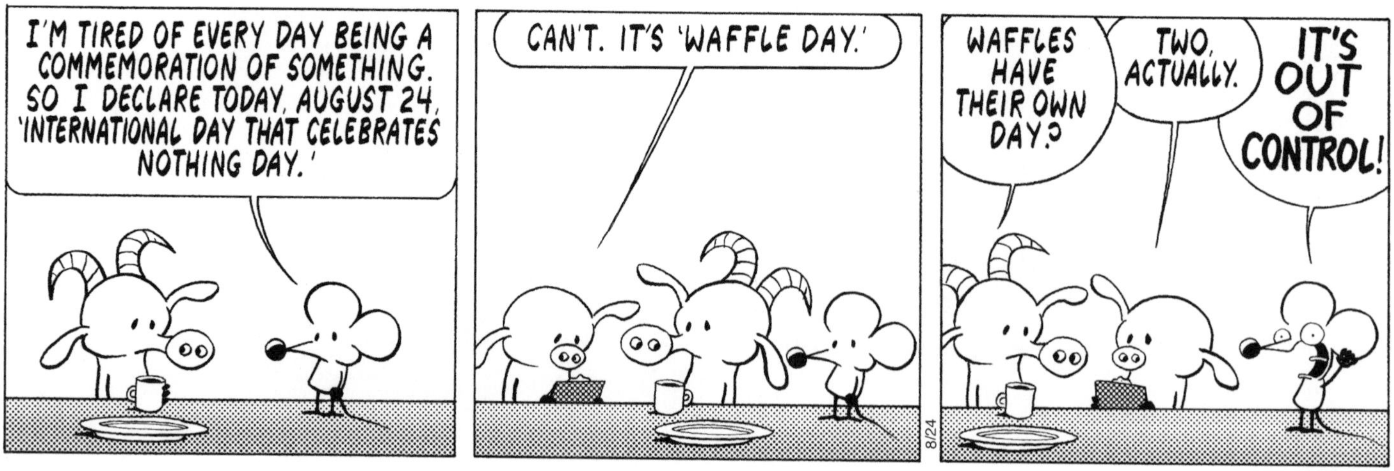
I'M TIRED OF EVERY DAY BEING A COMMEMORATION OF SOMETHING. SO I DECLARE TODAY, AUGUST 24, 'INTERNATIONAL DAY THAT CELEBRATES NOTHING DAY.'
CAN'T. IT'S 'WAFFLE DAY.'
WAFFLES HAVE THEIR OWN DAY?
TWO, ACTUALLY.
IT'S OUT OF CONTROL!
8/24

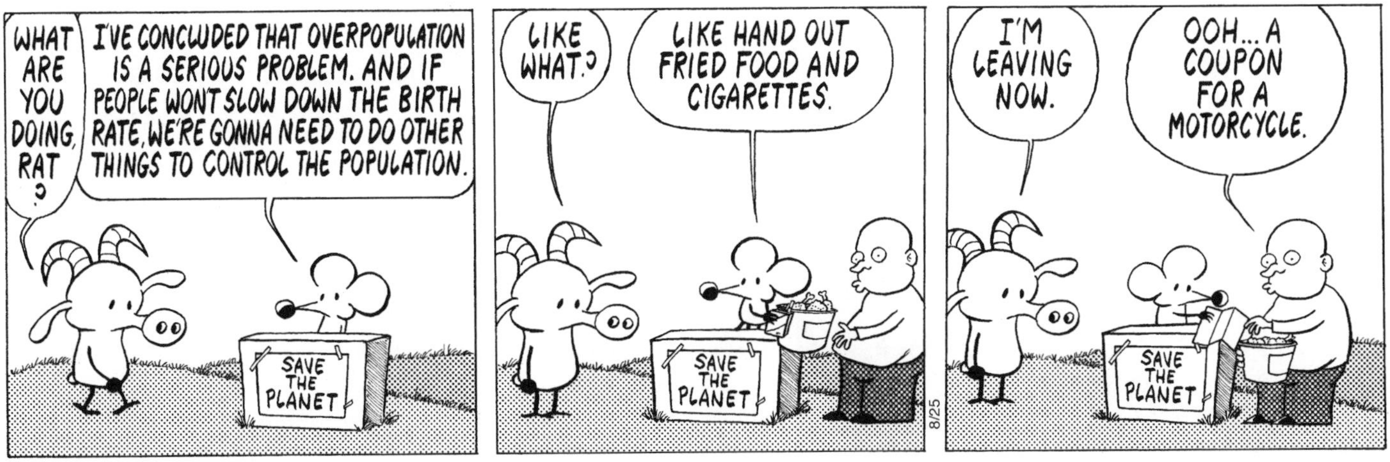
WHAT ARE YOU DOING, RAT?
I'VE CONCLUDED THAT OVERPOPULATION IS A SERIOUS PROBLEM. AND IF PEOPLE WON'T SLOW DOWN THE BIRTH RATE, WE'RE GONNA NEED TO DO OTHER THINGS TO CONTROL THE POPULATION.
SAVE THE PLANET
LIKE WHAT?
LIKE HAND OUT FRIED FOOD AND CIGARETTES.
SAVE THE PLANET
8/25
I'M LEAVING NOW.
OOH... A COUPON FOR A MOTORCYCLE.
SAVE THE PLANET

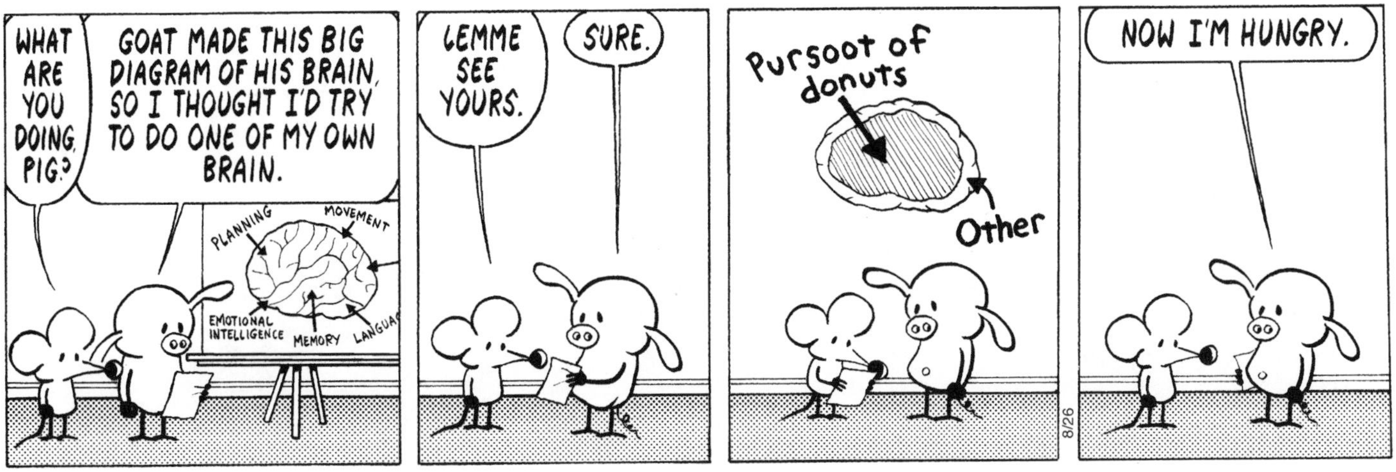
WHAT ARE YOU DOING, PIG?
GOAT MADE THIS BIG DIAGRAM OF HIS BRAIN, SO I THOUGHT I'D TRY TO DO ONE OF MY OWN BRAIN.
PLANNING
MOVEMENT
EMOTIONAL INTELLIGENCE
MEMORY
LEMME SEE YOURS.
SURE.
Pursoot of donuts
Other
8/26
NOW I'M HUNGRY.

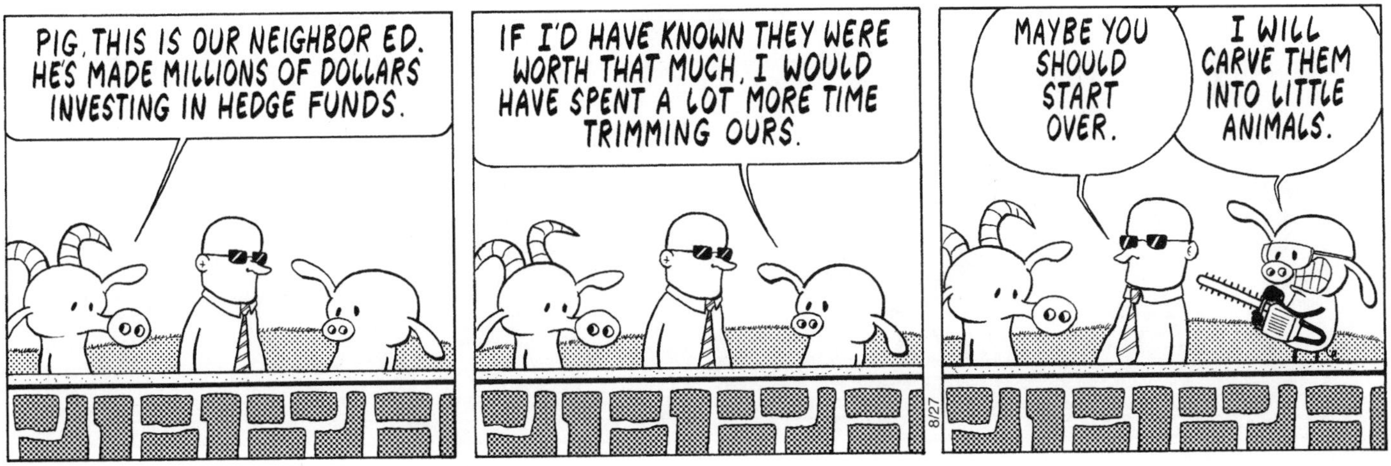
PIG, THIS IS OUR NEIGHBOR ED. HE'S MADE MILLIONS OF DOLLARS INVESTING IN HEDGE FUNDS.
IF I'D HAVE KNOWN THEY WERE WORTH THAT MUCH, I WOULD HAVE SPENT A LOT MORE TIME TRIMMING OURS.
8/27
MAYBE YOU SHOULD START OVER.
I WILL CARVE THEM INTO LITTLE ANIMALS.

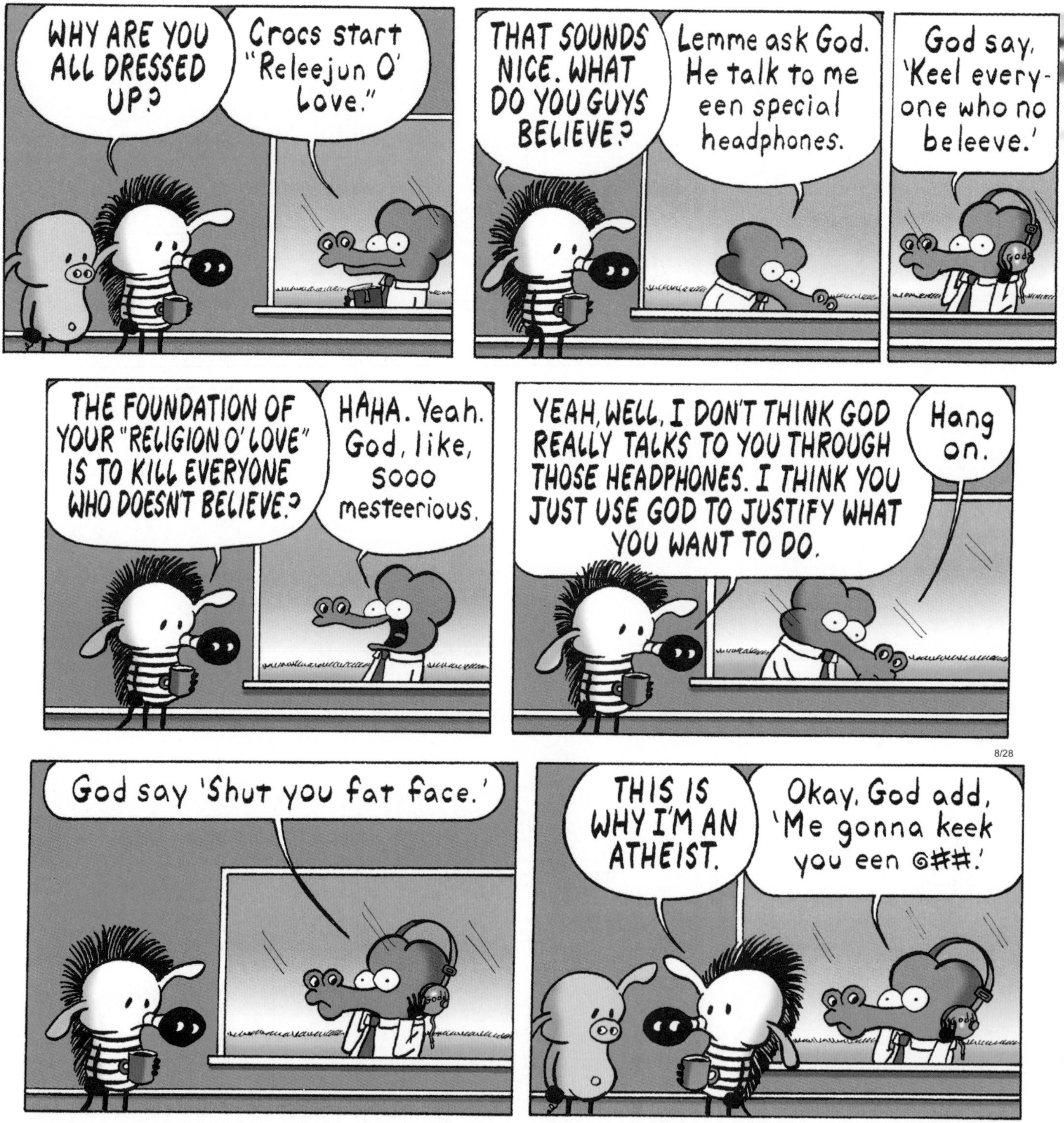
WHY ARE YOU ALL DRESSED UP?
Crocs start "Releejun O' Love."
THAT SOUNDS NICE. WHAT DO YOU GUYS BELIEVE?
Lemme ask God. He talk to me een special headphones.
God say, 'Keel every-one who no beleeve.'
THE FOUNDATION OF YOUR "RELIGION O' LOVE" IS TO KILL EVERYONE WHO DOESN'T BELIEVE?
HAHA. Yeah. God, like, sooo mesteerious.
YEAH, WELL, I DON'T THINK GOD REALLY TALKS TO YOU THROUGH THOSE HEADPHONES. I THINK YOU JUST USE GOD TO JUSTIFY WHAT YOU WANT TO DO.
Hang on.
8/28
God say 'Shut you fat face.'
THIS IS WHY I'M AN ATHEIST.
Okay. God add, 'Me gonna keek you een @##.'

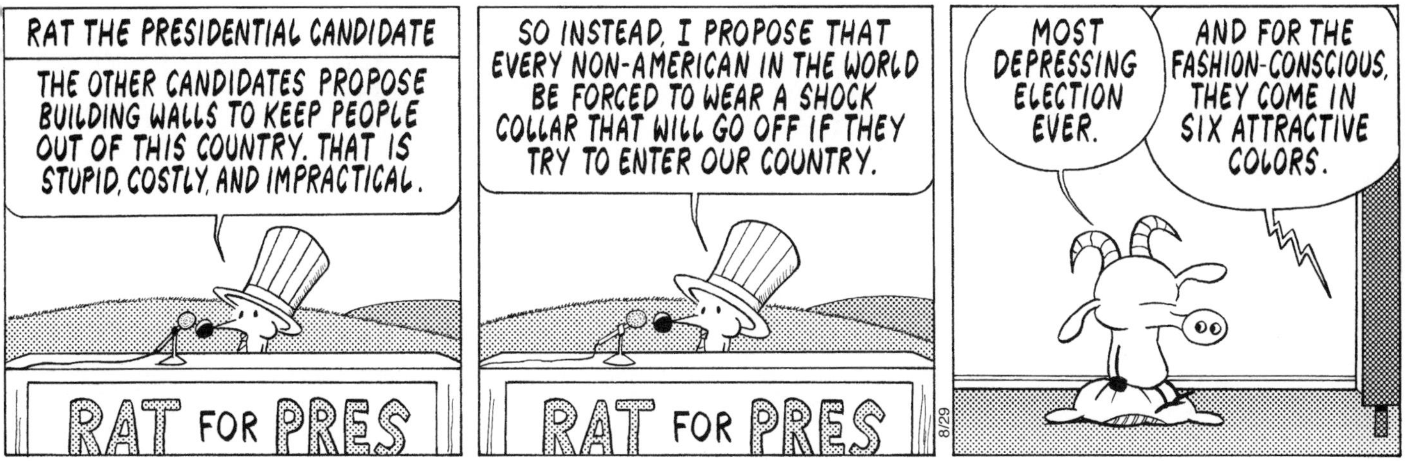
RAT THE PRESIDENTIAL CANDIDATE
THE OTHER CANDIDATES PROPOSE BUILDING WALLS TO KEEP PEOPLE OUT OF THIS COUNTRY. THAT IS STUPID, COSTLY, AND IMPRACTICAL.
RAT FOR PRES
SO INSTEAD, I PROPOSE THAT EVERY NON-AMERICAN IN THE WORLD BE FORCED TO WEAR A SHOCK COLLAR THAT WILL GO OFF IF THEY TRY TO ENTER OUR COUNTRY.
RAT FOR PRES
MOST DEPRESSING ELECTION EVER.
AND FOR THE FASHION-CONSCIOUS, THEY COME IN SIX ATTRACTIVE COLORS.
8/29

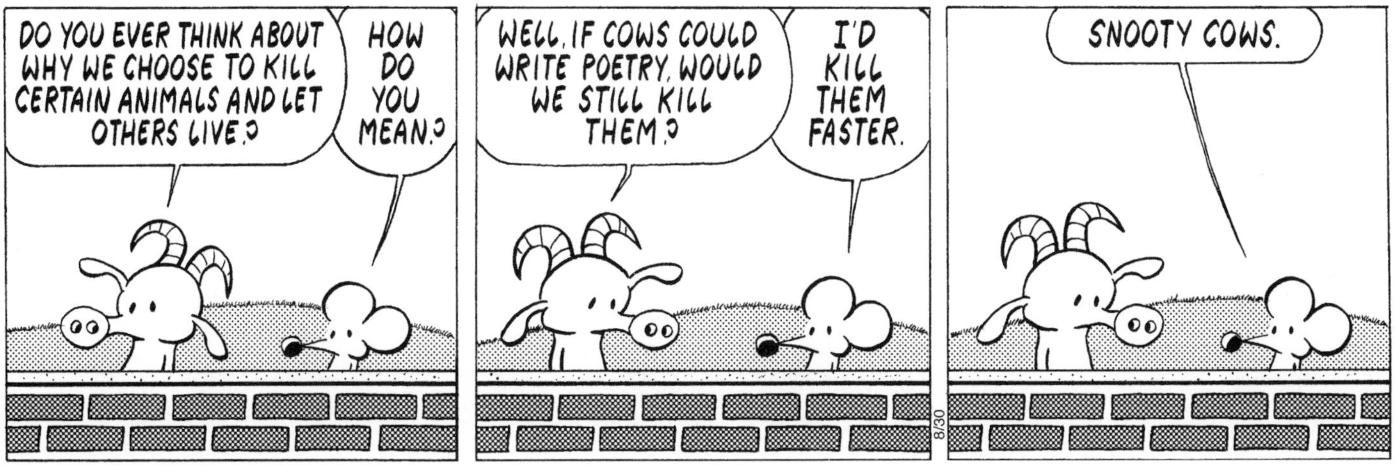
DO YOU EVER THINK ABOUT WHY WE CHOOSE TO KILL CERTAIN ANIMALS AND LET OTHERS LIVE?
HOW DO YOU MEAN?
WELL, IF COWS COULD WRITE POETRY, WOULD WE STILL KILL THEM?
I'D KILL THEM FASTER.
SNOOTY COWS.
8/30

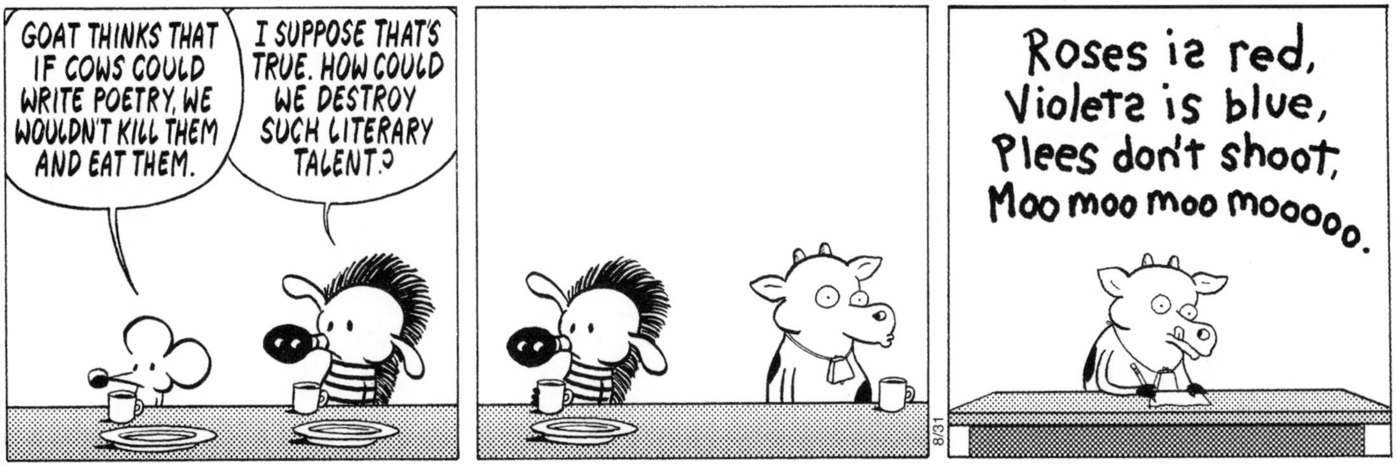
GOAT THINKS THAT IF COWS COULD WRITE POETRY, WE WOULDN'T KILL THEM AND EAT THEM.
I SUPPOSE THAT'S TRUE. HOW COULD WE DESTROY SUCH LITERARY TALENT?
Roses is red,
Violetz is blue,
Plees don't shoot,
Moo moo moo mooooo.
8/31

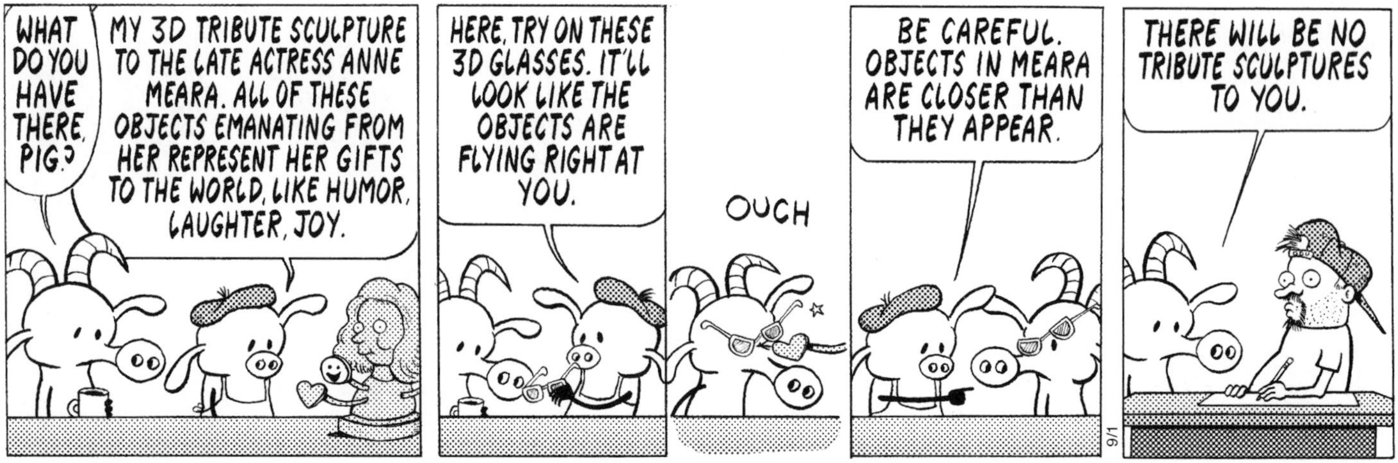
WHAT DO YOU HAVE THERE, PIG?
MY 3D TRIBUTE SCULPTURE TO THE LATE ACTRESS ANNE MEARA. ALL OF THESE OBJECTS EMANATING FROM HER REPRESENT HER GIFTS TO THE WORLD, LIKE HUMOR, LAUGHTER, JOY.
HERE, TRY ON THESE 3D GLASSES. IT'LL LOOK LIKE THE OBJECTS ARE FLYING RIGHT AT YOU.
OUCH
BE CAREFUL. OBJECTS IN MEARA ARE CLOSER THAN THEY APPEAR.
THERE WILL BE NO TRIBUTE SCULPTURES TO YOU.
9/1

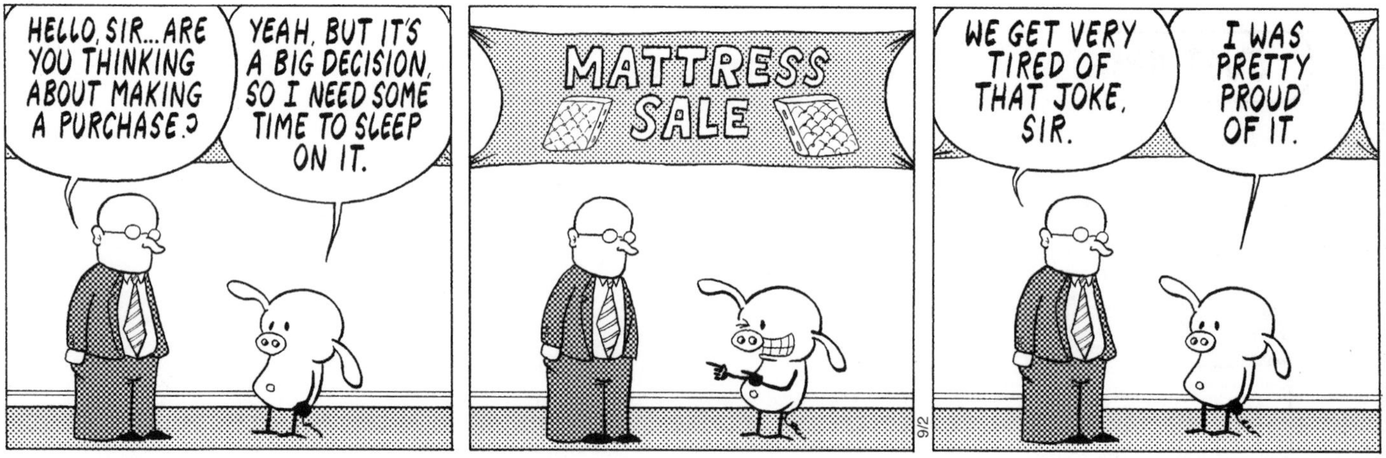
HELLO, SIR... ARE YOU THINKING ABOUT MAKING A PURCHASE?
YEAH, BUT IT'S A BIG DECISION, SO I NEED SOME TIME TO SLEEP ON IT.
MATTRESS SALE
WE GET VERY TIRED OF THAT JOKE, SIR.
I WAS PRETTY PROUD OF IT.
9/2

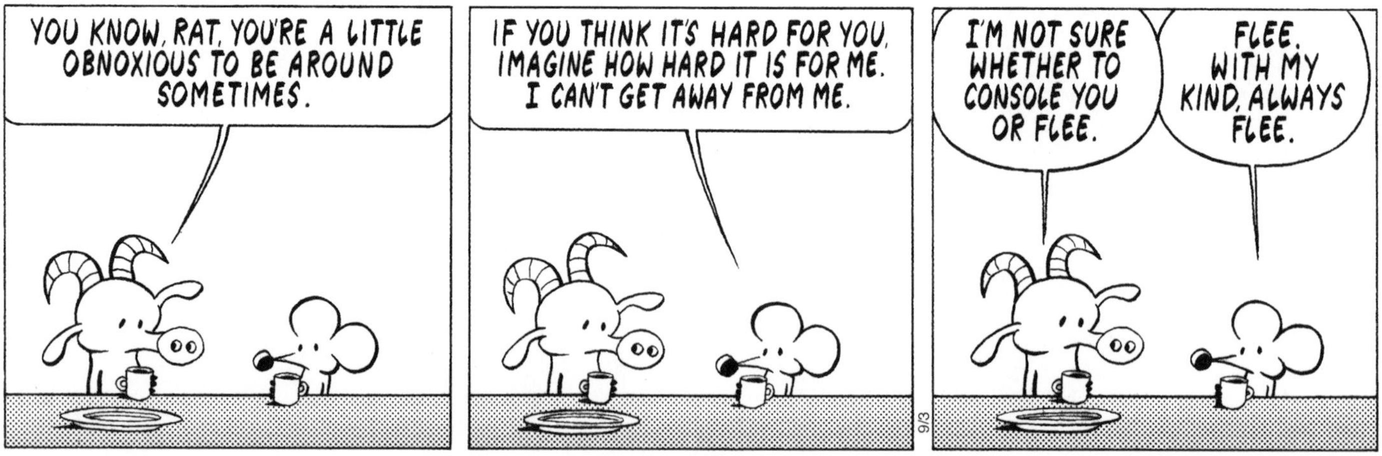
YOU KNOW, RAT, YOU'RE A LITTLE OBNOXIOUS TO BE AROUND SOMETIMES.
IF YOU THINK IT'S HARD FOR YOU, IMAGINE HOW HARD IT IS FOR ME. I CAN'T GET AWAY FROM ME.
I'M NOT SURE WHETHER TO CONSOLE YOU OR FLEE.
FLEE. WITH MY KIND, ALWAYS FLEE.
9/3

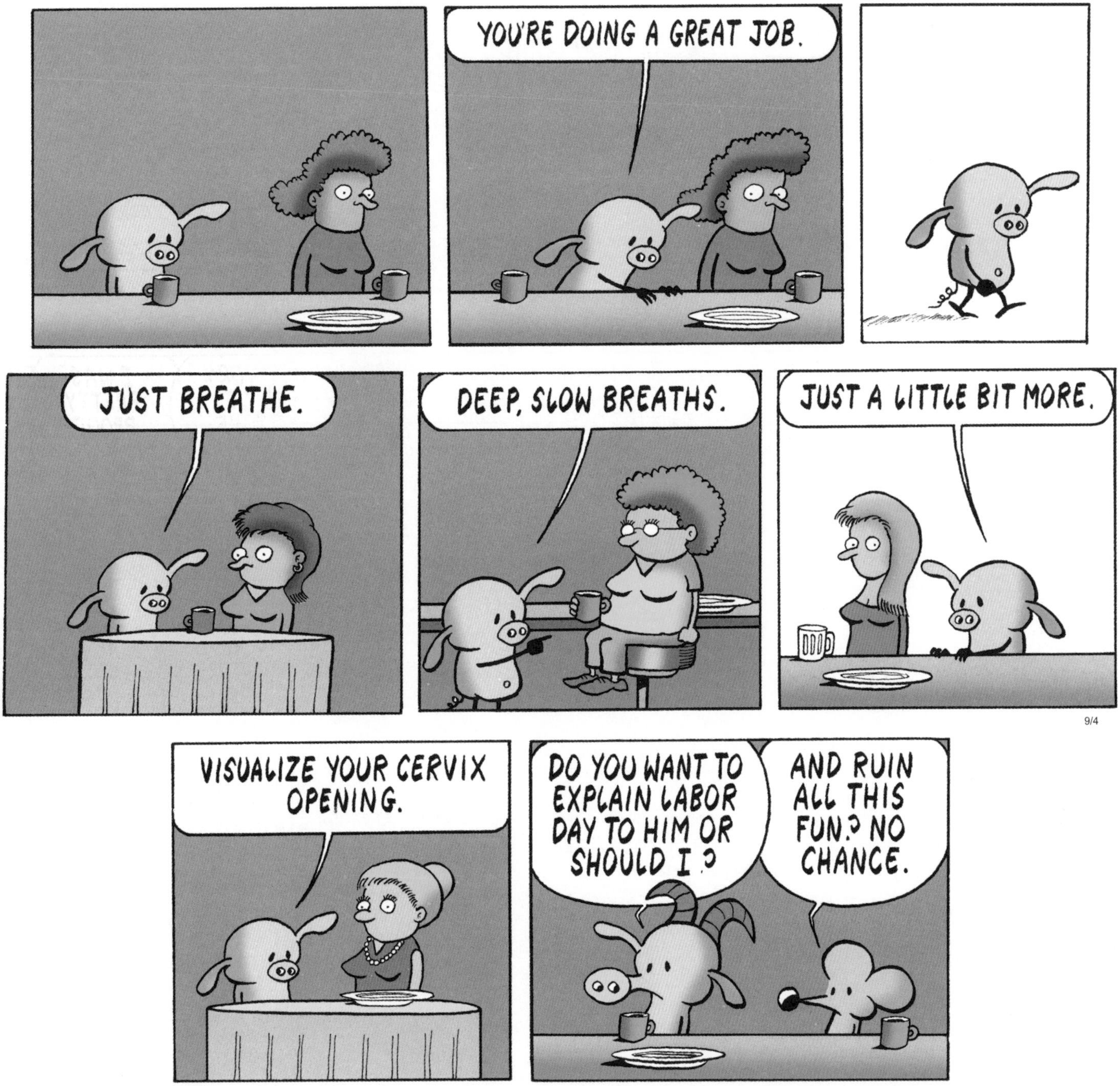
YOU'RE DOING A GREAT JOB.
JUST BREATHE.
DEEP, SLOW BREATHS.
JUST A LITTLE BIT MORE.
9/4
VISUALIZE YOUR CERVIX OPENING.
DO YOU WANT TO EXPLAIN LABOR DAY TO HIM OR SHOULD I?
AND RUIN ALL THIS FUN? NO CHANCE.

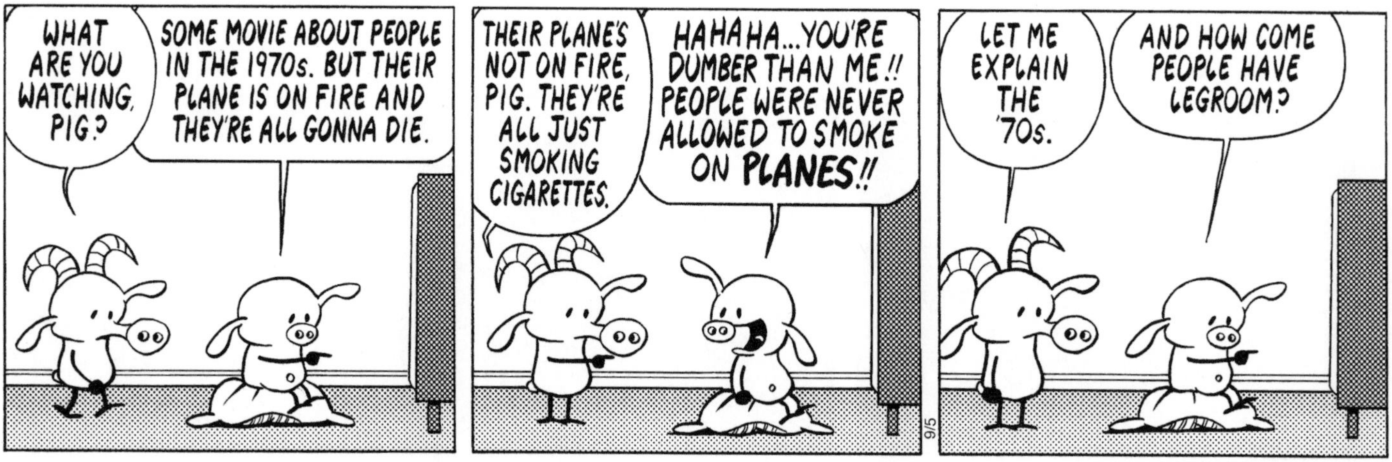
WHAT ARE YOU WATCHING, PIG?
SOME MOVIE ABOUT PEOPLE IN THE 1970s. BUT THEIR PLANE IS ON FIRE AND THEY'RE ALL GONNA DIE.
THEIR PLANE'S NOT ON FIRE, PIG. THEY'RE ALL JUST SMOKING CIGARETTES.
HAHAHA...YOU'RE DUMBER THAN ME!! PEOPLE WERE NEVER ALLOWED TO SMOKE ON **PLANES**!!
LET ME EXPLAIN THE '70s.
AND HOW COME PEOPLE HAVE LEGROOM?
9/5

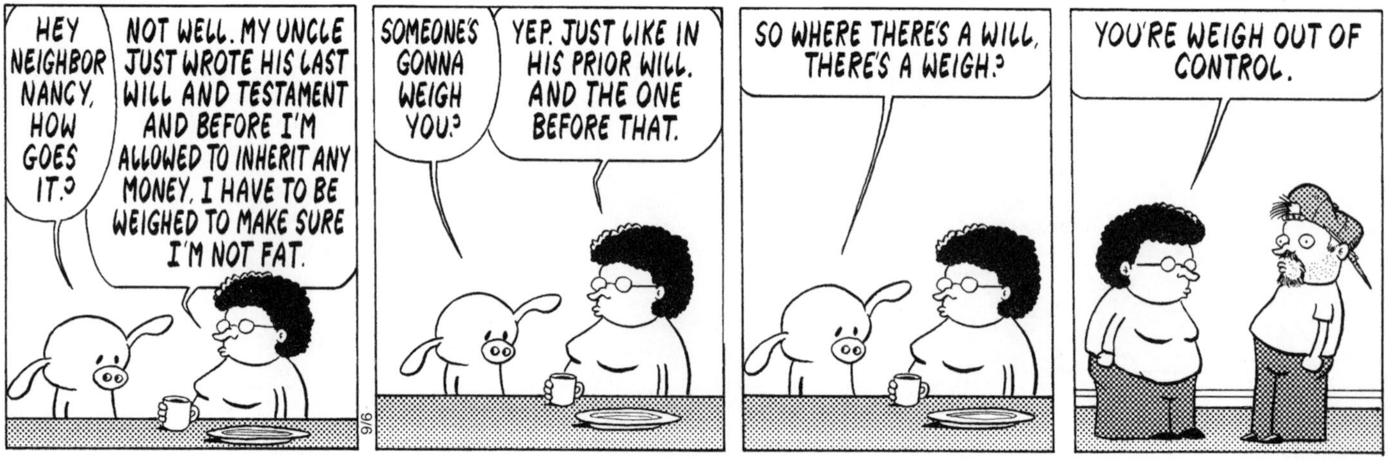
HEY NEIGHBOR NANCY, HOW GOES IT?
NOT WELL. MY UNCLE JUST WROTE HIS LAST WILL AND TESTAMENT AND BEFORE I'M ALLOWED TO INHERIT ANY MONEY, I HAVE TO BE WEIGHED TO MAKE SURE I'M NOT FAT.
SOMEONE'S GONNA WEIGH YOU?
YEP. JUST LIKE IN HIS PRIOR WILL. AND THE ONE BEFORE THAT.
SO WHERE THERE'S A WILL, THERE'S A WEIGH?
YOU'RE WEIGH OUT OF CONTROL.
9/6

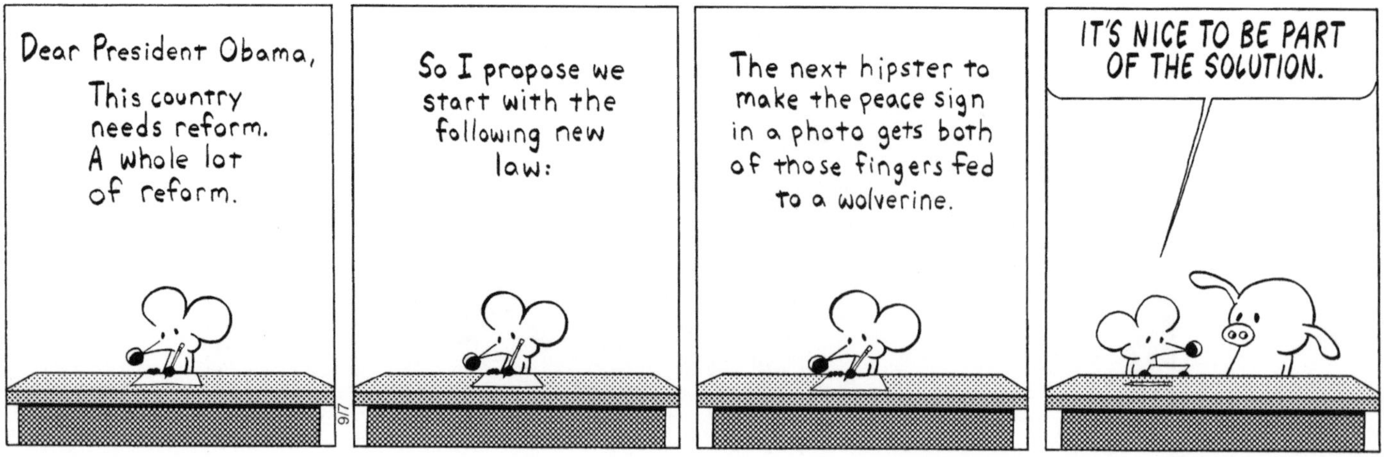
Dear President Obama,
This country needs reform. A whole lot of reform.
So I propose we start with the following new law:
The next hipster to make the peace sign in a photo gets both of those fingers fed to a wolverine.
IT'S NICE TO BE PART OF THE SOLUTION.
9/7

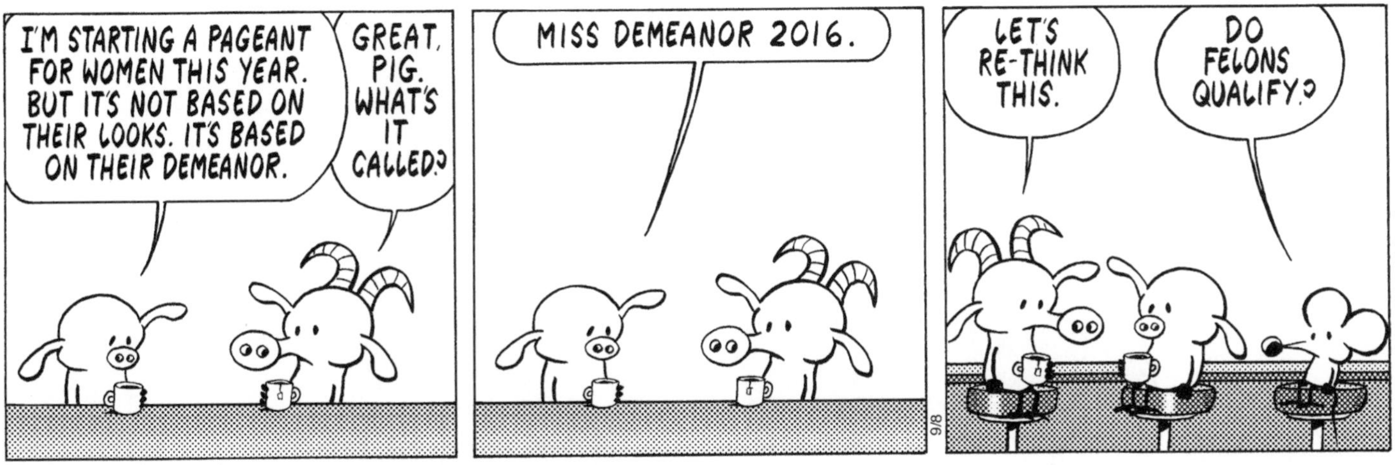
I'M STARTING A PAGEANT FOR WOMEN THIS YEAR. BUT IT'S NOT BASED ON THEIR LOOKS. IT'S BASED ON THEIR DEMEANOR.
GREAT, PIG. WHAT'S IT CALLED?
MISS DEMEANOR 2016.
9/8
LET'S RE-THINK THIS.
DO FELONS QUALIFY?

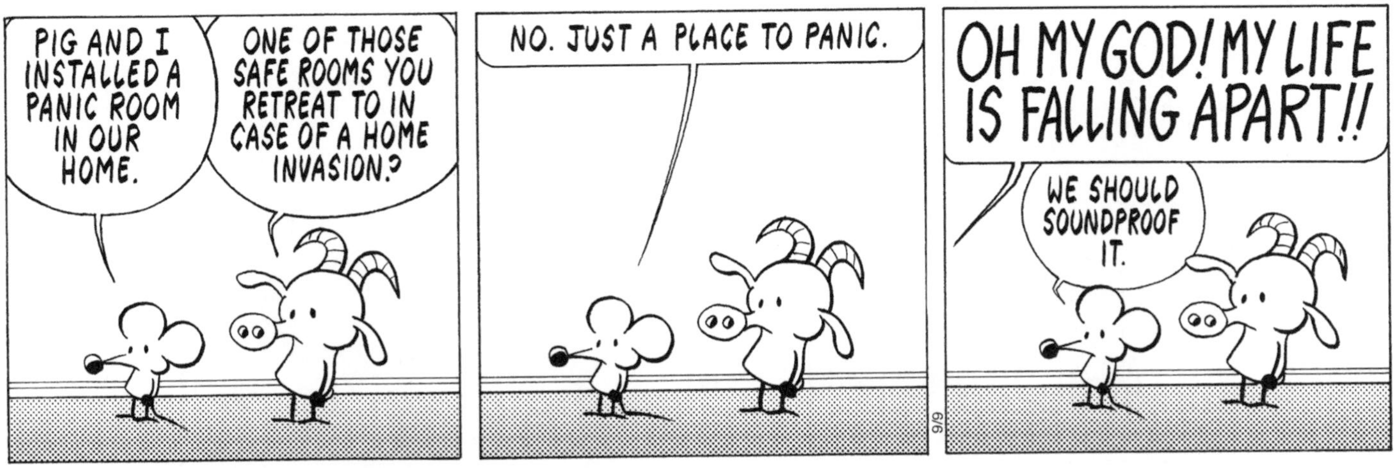
PIG AND I INSTALLED A PANIC ROOM IN OUR HOME.
ONE OF THOSE SAFE ROOMS YOU RETREAT TO IN CASE OF A HOME INVASION?
NO. JUST A PLACE TO PANIC.
9/9
OH MY GOD! MY LIFE IS FALLING APART!!
WE SHOULD SOUNDPROOF IT.

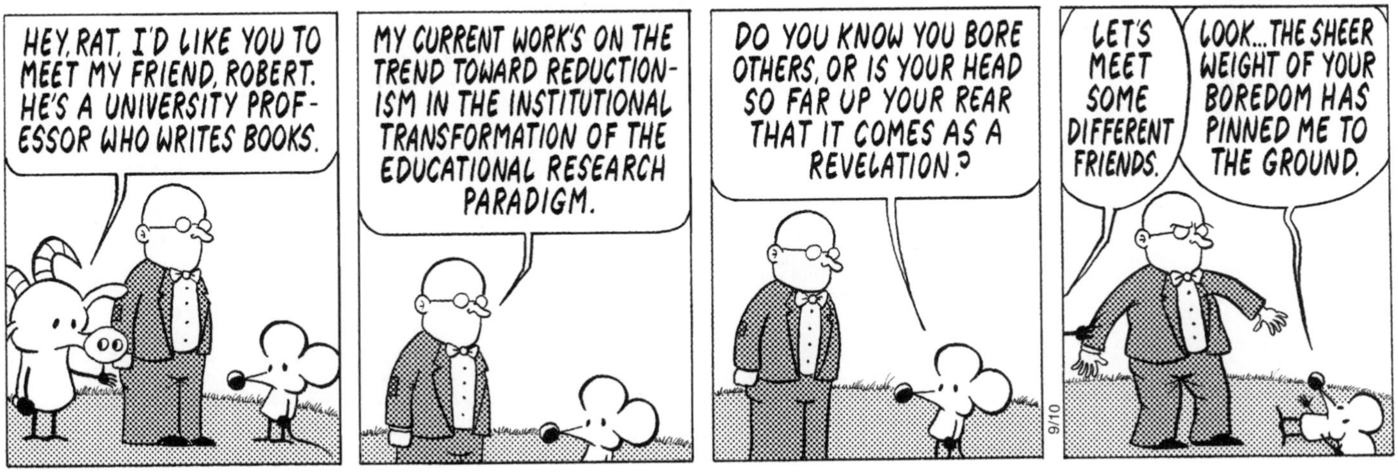
HEY, RAT, I'D LIKE YOU TO MEET MY FRIEND, ROBERT. HE'S A UNIVERSITY PROFESSOR WHO WRITES BOOKS.
MY CURRENT WORK'S ON THE TREND TOWARD REDUCTIONISM IN THE INSTITUTIONAL TRANSFORMATION OF THE EDUCATIONAL RESEARCH PARADIGM.
DO YOU KNOW YOU BORE OTHERS, OR IS YOUR HEAD SO FAR UP YOUR REAR THAT IT COMES AS A REVELATION?
9/10
LET'S MEET SOME DIFFERENT FRIENDS.
LOOK...THE SHEER WEIGHT OF YOUR BOREDOM HAS PINNED ME TO THE GROUND.

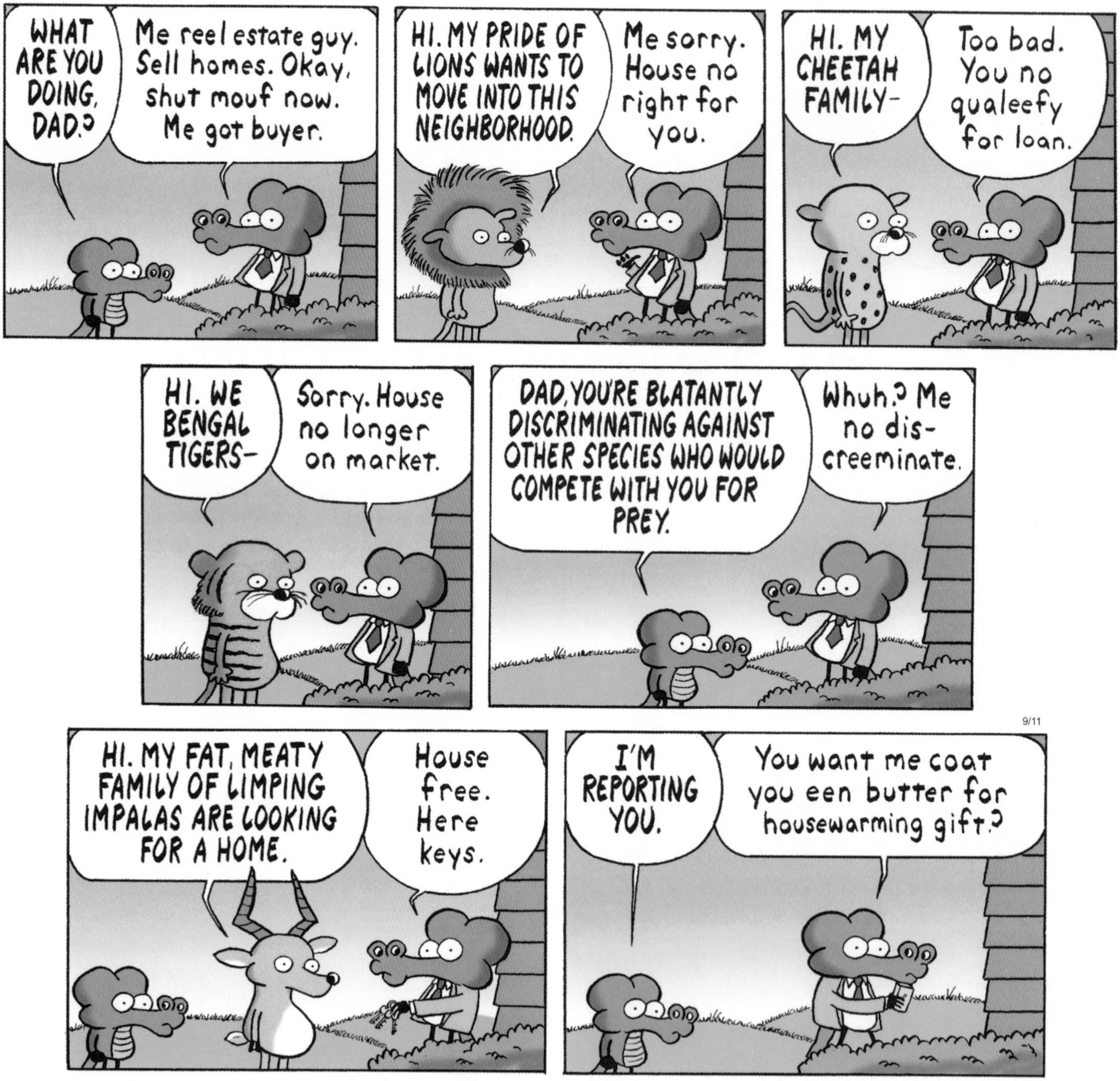
WHAT ARE YOU DOING, DAD?
Me reel estate guy. Sell homes. Okay, shut mouf now. Me got buyer.
HI. MY PRIDE OF LIONS WANTS TO MOVE INTO THIS NEIGHBORHOOD.
Me sorry. House no right for you.
HI. MY CHEETAH FAMILY-
Too bad. You no qualeefy for loan.
HI. WE BENGAL TIGERS-
Sorry. House no longer on market.
DAD, YOU'RE BLATANTLY DISCRIMINATING AGAINST OTHER SPECIES WHO WOULD COMPETE WITH YOU FOR PREY.
Whuh? Me no dis-creeminate.
HI. MY FAT, MEATY FAMILY OF LIMPING IMPALAS ARE LOOKING FOR A HOME.
House free. Here keys.
I'M REPORTING YOU.
You want me coat you een butter for housewarming gift?
9/11

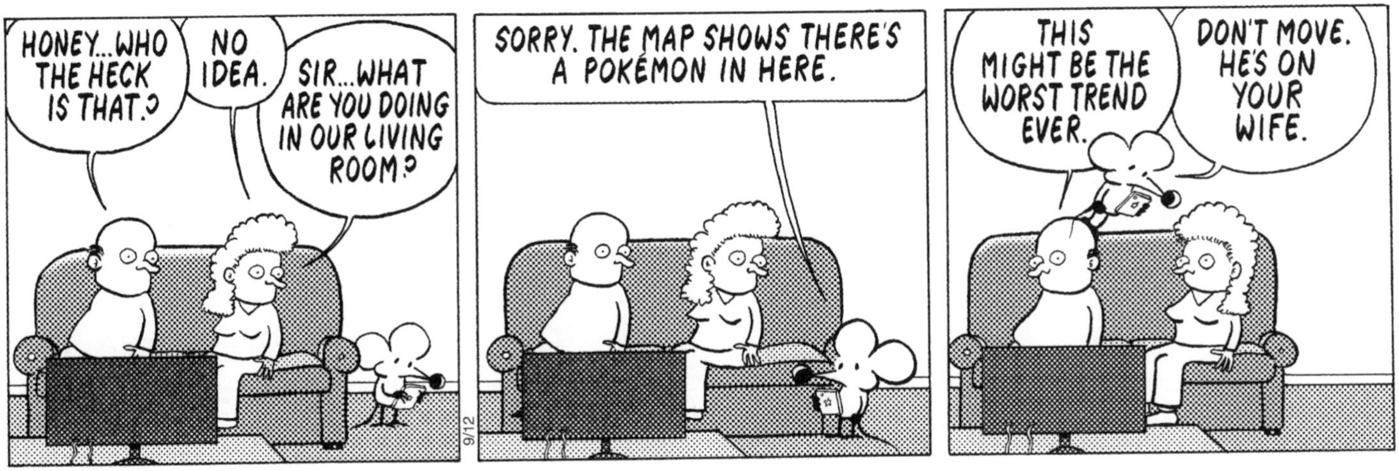
HONEY...WHO THE HECK IS THAT?
NO IDEA.
SIR...WHAT ARE YOU DOING IN OUR LIVING ROOM?
9/12
SORRY. THE MAP SHOWS THERE'S A POKÉMON IN HERE.
THIS MIGHT BE THE WORST TREND EVER.
DON'T MOVE. HE'S ON YOUR WIFE.

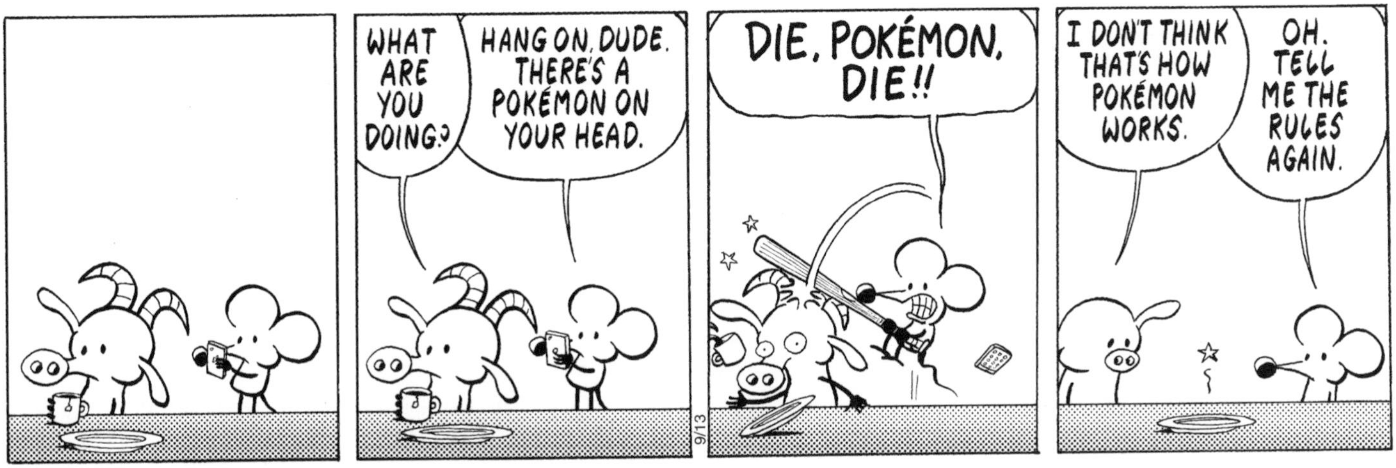
WHAT ARE YOU DOING?
HANG ON, DUDE. THERE'S A POKÉMON ON YOUR HEAD.
9/13
DIE, POKÉMON, DIE!!
I DON'T THINK THAT'S HOW POKÉMON WORKS.
OH. TELL ME THE RULES AGAIN.

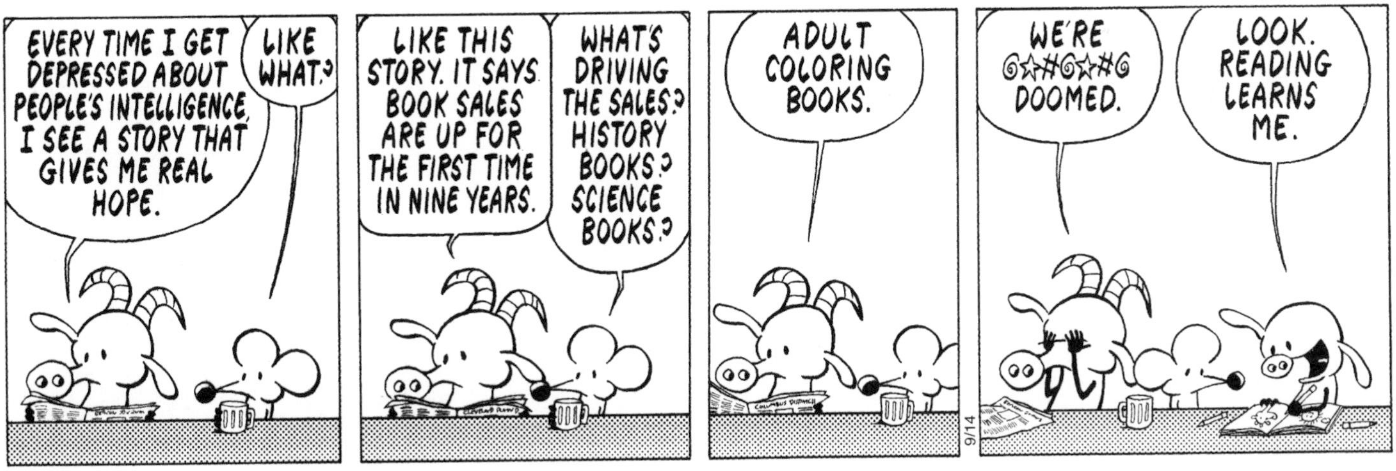
EVERY TIME I GET DEPRESSED ABOUT PEOPLE'S INTELLIGENCE, I SEE A STORY THAT GIVES ME REAL HOPE.
LIKE WHAT?
LIKE THIS STORY. IT SAYS BOOK SALES ARE UP FOR THE FIRST TIME IN NINE YEARS.
WHAT'S DRIVING THE SALES? HISTORY BOOKS? SCIENCE BOOKS?
ADULT COLORING BOOKS.
9/14
WE'RE @☆#@☆#@ DOOMED.
LOOK. READING LEARNS ME.

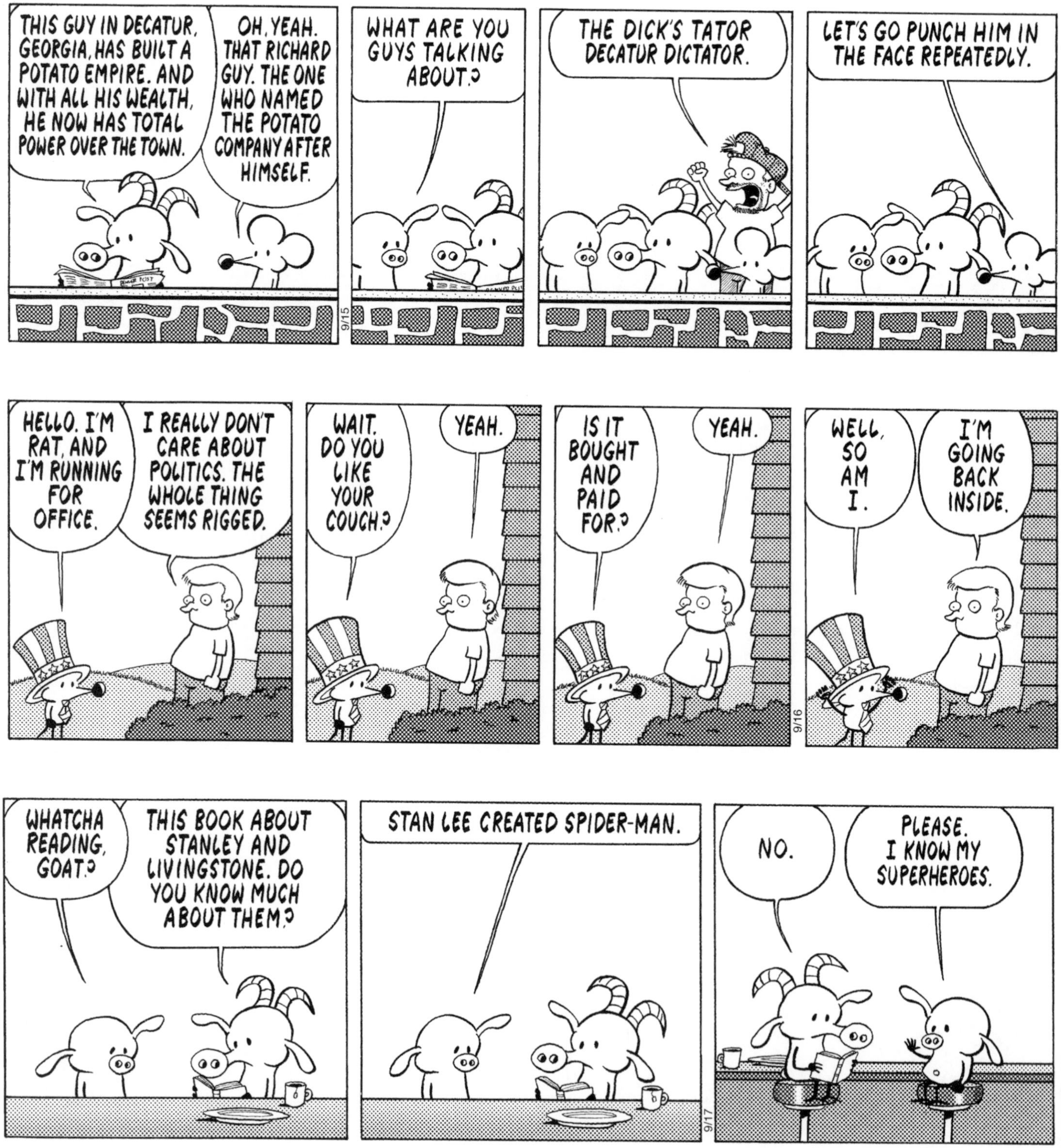
THIS GUY IN DECATUR, GEORGIA, HAS BUILT A POTATO EMPIRE. AND WITH ALL HIS WEALTH, HE NOW HAS TOTAL POWER OVER THE TOWN.
OH, YEAH. THAT RICHARD GUY. THE ONE WHO NAMED THE POTATO COMPANY AFTER HIMSELF.
9/15
WHAT ARE YOU GUYS TALKING ABOUT?
THE DICK'S TATOR DECATUR DICTATOR.
LET'S GO PUNCH HIM IN THE FACE REPEATEDLY.
HELLO. I'M RAT, AND I'M RUNNING FOR OFFICE.
I REALLY DON'T CARE ABOUT POLITICS. THE WHOLE THING SEEMS RIGGED.
WAIT. DO YOU LIKE YOUR COUCH?
YEAH.
IS IT BOUGHT AND PAID FOR?
YEAH.
9/16
WELL, SO AM I.
I'M GOING BACK INSIDE.
WHATCHA READING, GOAT?
THIS BOOK ABOUT STANLEY AND LIVINGSTONE. DO YOU KNOW MUCH ABOUT THEM?
STAN LEE CREATED SPIDER-MAN.
9/17
NO.
PLEASE. I KNOW MY SUPERHEROES.

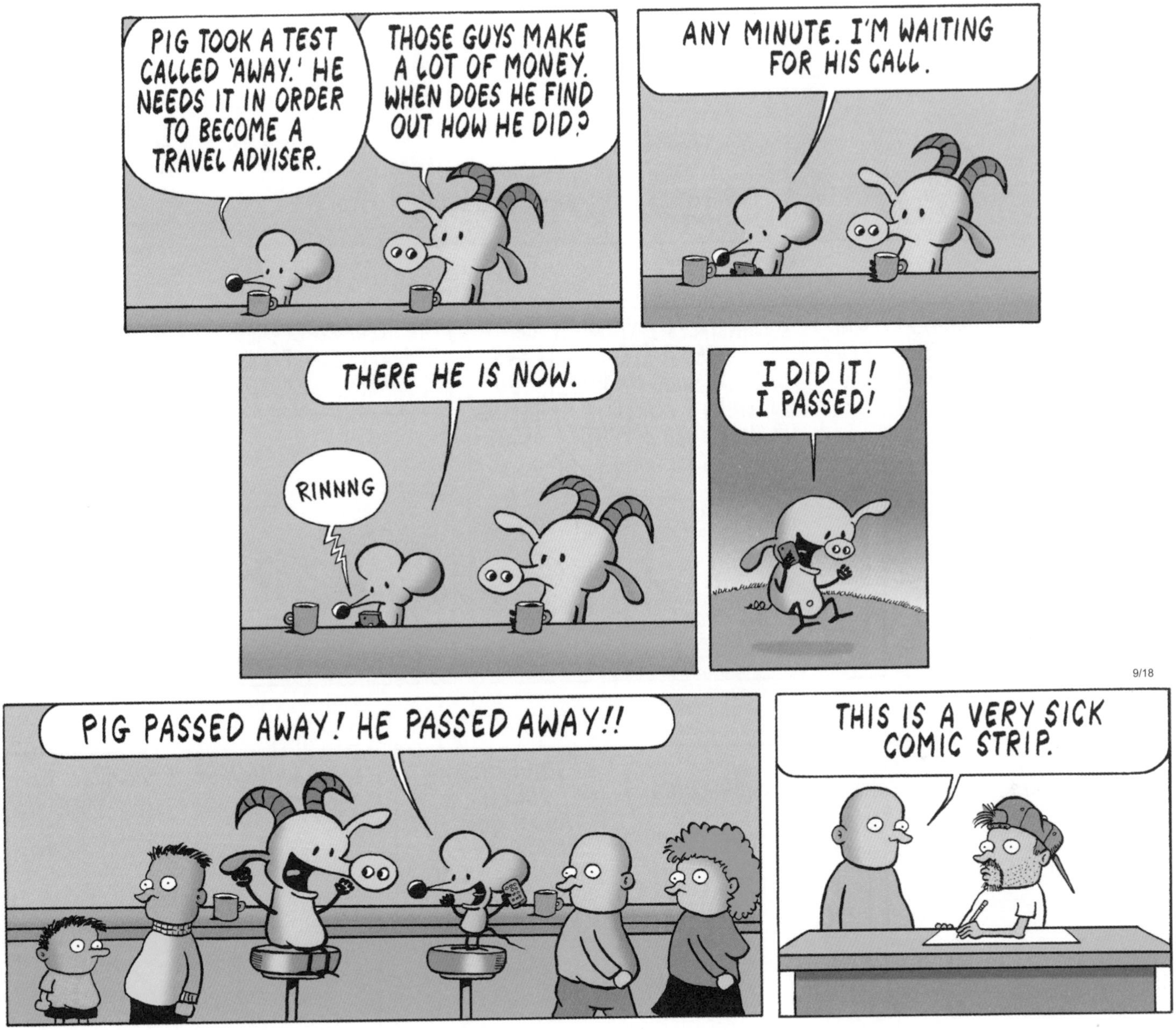
PIG TOOK A TEST CALLED 'AWAY.' HE NEEDS IT IN ORDER TO BECOME A TRAVEL ADVISER.
THOSE GUYS MAKE A LOT OF MONEY. WHEN DOES HE FIND OUT HOW HE DID?
ANY MINUTE. I'M WAITING FOR HIS CALL.
THERE HE IS NOW.
RINNNG
I DID IT! I PASSED!
PIG PASSED AWAY! HE PASSED AWAY!!
THIS IS A VERY SICK COMIC STRIP.
9/18

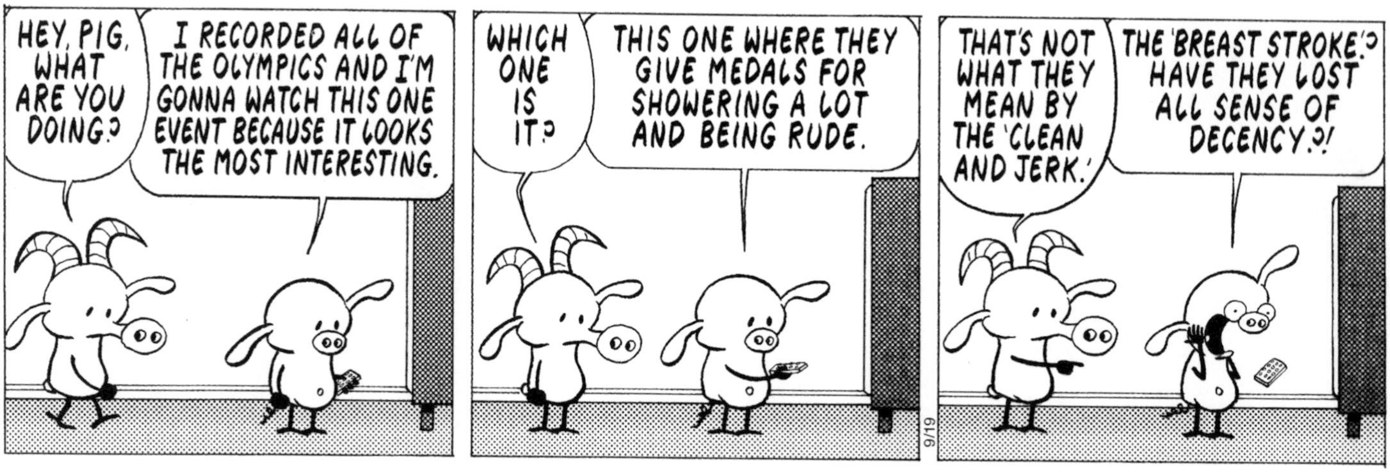
HEY, PIG, WHAT ARE YOU DOING?
I RECORDED ALL OF THE OLYMPICS AND I'M GONNA WATCH THIS ONE EVENT BECAUSE IT LOOKS THE MOST INTERESTING.
WHICH ONE IS IT?
THIS ONE WHERE THEY GIVE MEDALS FOR SHOWERING A LOT AND BEING RUDE.
9/19
THAT'S NOT WHAT THEY MEAN BY THE 'CLEAN AND JERK.'
THE 'BREAST STROKE'? HAVE THEY LOST ALL SENSE OF DECENCY?!

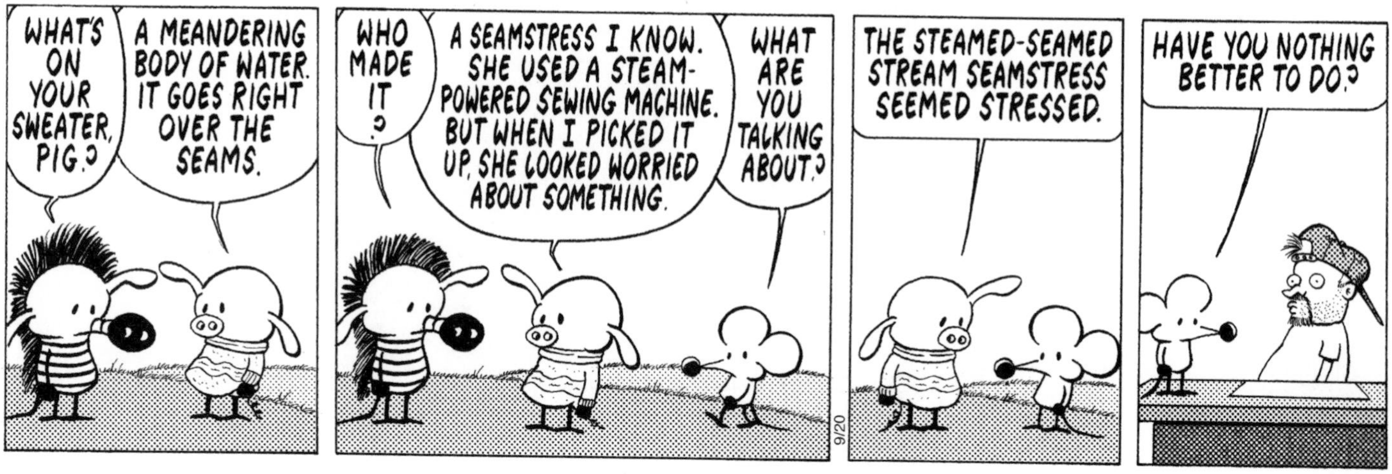
WHAT'S ON YOUR SWEATER, PIG?
A MEANDERING BODY OF WATER. IT GOES RIGHT OVER THE SEAMS.
WHO MADE IT?
A SEAMSTRESS I KNOW. SHE USED A STEAM-POWERED SEWING MACHINE. BUT WHEN I PICKED IT UP, SHE LOOKED WORRIED ABOUT SOMETHING.
WHAT ARE YOU TALKING ABOUT?
9/20
THE STEAMED-SEAMED STREAM SEAMSTRESS SEEMED STRESSED.
HAVE YOU NOTHING BETTER TO DO?

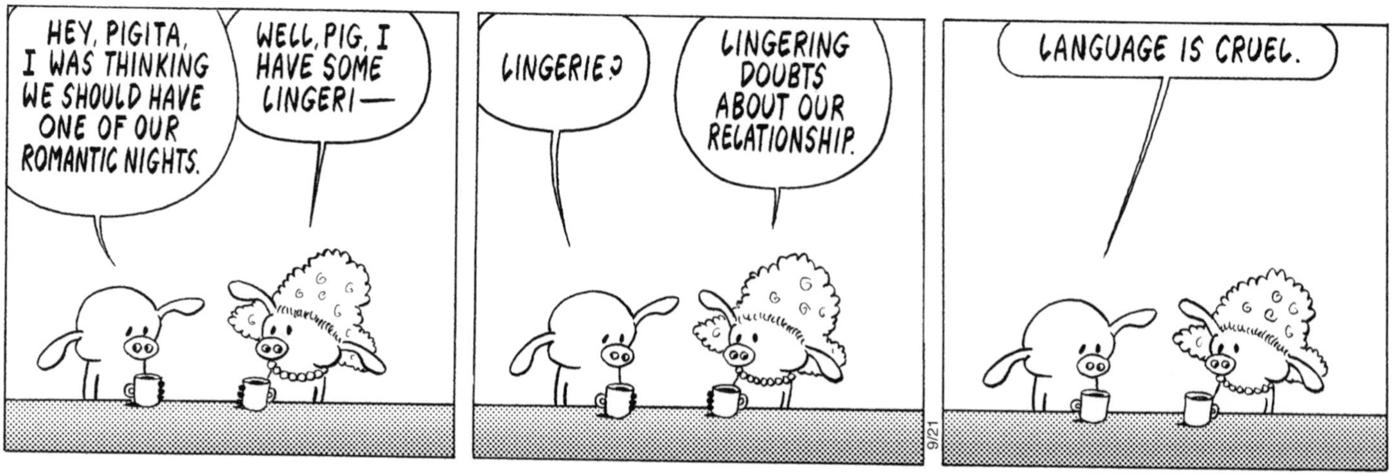
HEY, PIGITA, I WAS THINKING WE SHOULD HAVE ONE OF OUR ROMANTIC NIGHTS.
WELL, PIG, I HAVE SOME LINGERI—
LINGERIE?
LINGERING DOUBTS ABOUT OUR RELATIONSHIP.
9/21
LANGUAGE IS CRUEL.

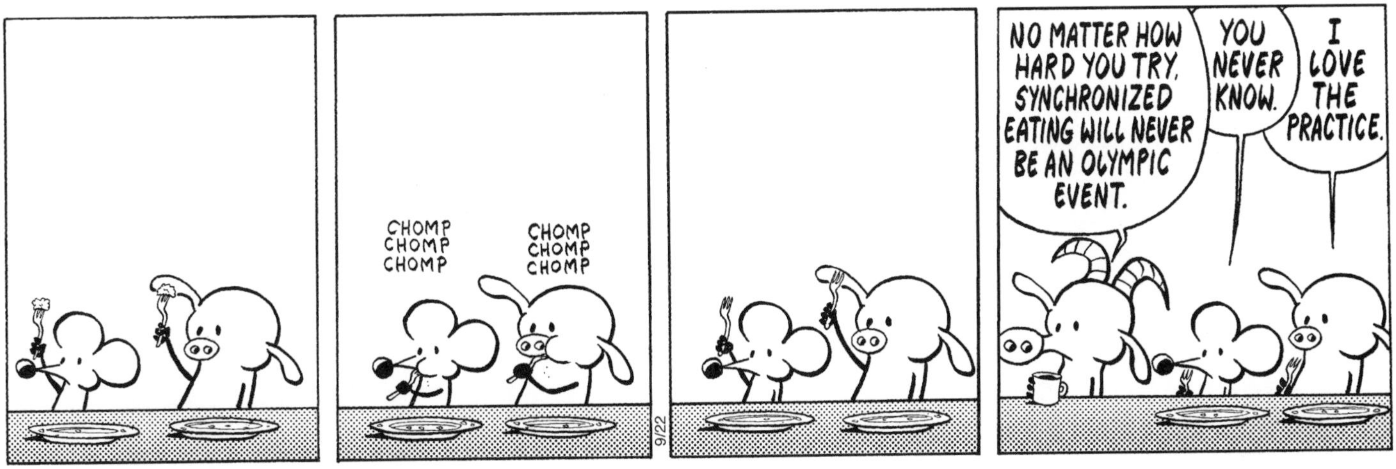
CHOMP
CHOMP
CHOMP
CHOMP
CHOMP
CHOMP
9/22
NO MATTER HOW HARD YOU TRY, SYNCHRONIZED EATING WILL NEVER BE AN OLYMPIC EVENT.
YOU NEVER KNOW.
I LOVE THE PRACTICE.

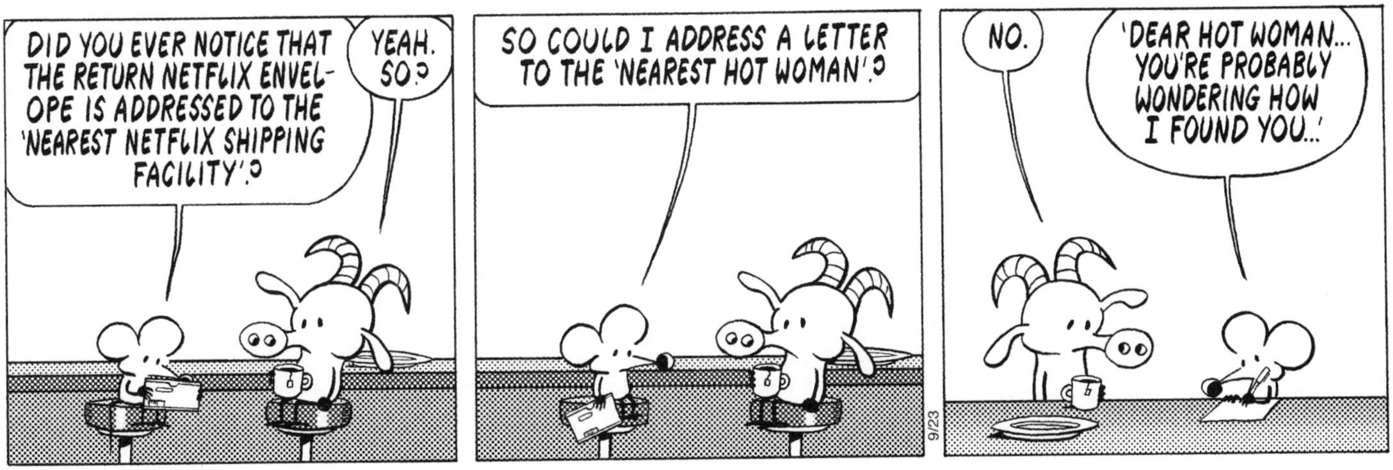
DID YOU EVER NOTICE THAT THE RETURN NETFLIX ENVEL-OPE IS ADDRESSED TO THE 'NEAREST NETFLIX SHIPPING FACILITY'?
YEAH. SO?
SO COULD I ADDRESS A LETTER TO THE 'NEAREST HOT WOMAN'?
9/23
NO.
'DEAR HOT WOMAN... YOU'RE PROBABLY WONDERING HOW I FOUND YOU...'

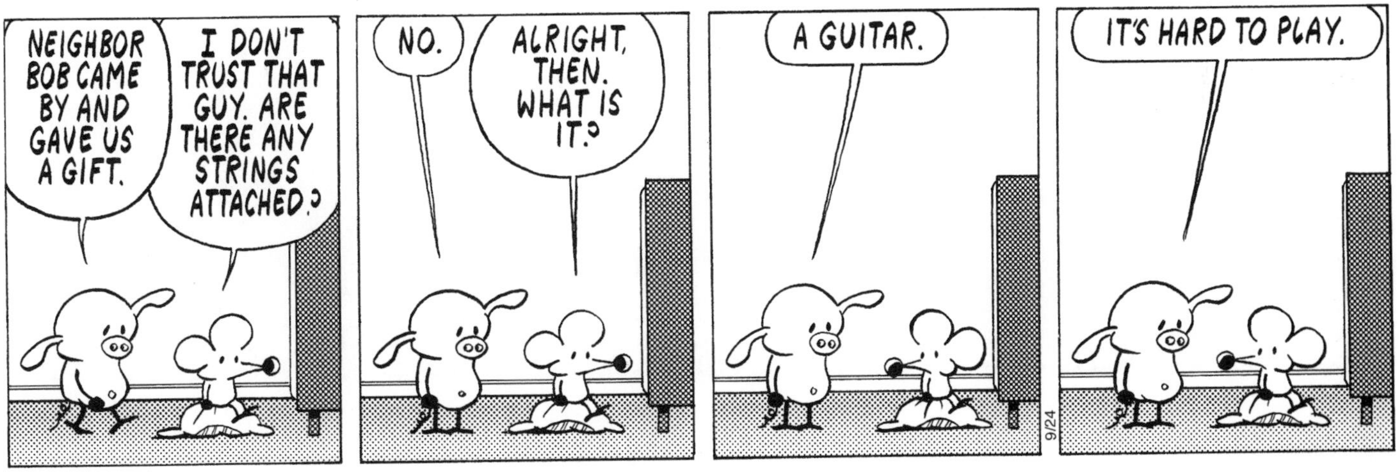
NEIGHBOR BOB CAME BY AND GAVE US A GIFT.
I DON'T TRUST THAT GUY. ARE THERE ANY STRINGS ATTACHED?
NO.
ALRIGHT, THEN. WHAT IS IT?
A GUITAR.
9/24
IT'S HARD TO PLAY.

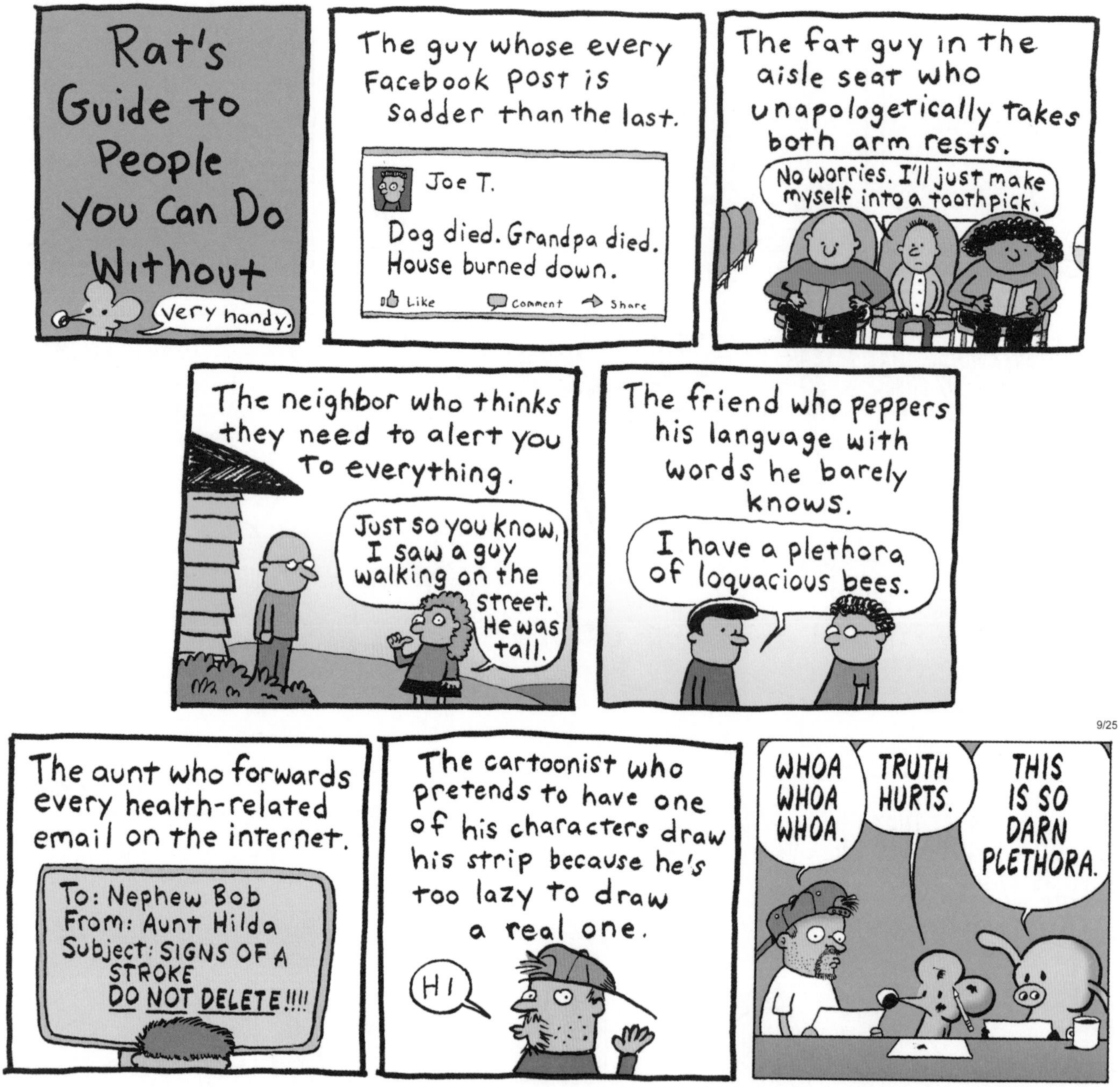
Rat's Guide to People You Can Do Without
Very handy.
The guy whose every Facebook post is sadder than the last.
Joe T.
Dog died. Grandpa died. House burned down.
Like
Comment
Share
The fat guy in the aisle seat who unapologetically takes both arm rests.
No worries. I'll just make myself into a toothpick.
The neighbor who thinks they need to alert you to everything.
Just so you know, I saw a guy walking on the street. He was tall.
The friend who peppers his language with words he barely knows.
I have a plethora of loquacious bees.
9/25
The aunt who forwards every health-related email on the internet.
To: Nephew Bob
From: Aunt Hilda
Subject: SIGNS OF A STROKE
DO NOT DELETE!!!!
The cartoonist who pretends to have one of his characters draw his strip because he's too lazy to draw a real one.
HI
WHOA WHOA WHOA.
TRUTH HURTS.
THIS IS SO DARN PLETHORA.

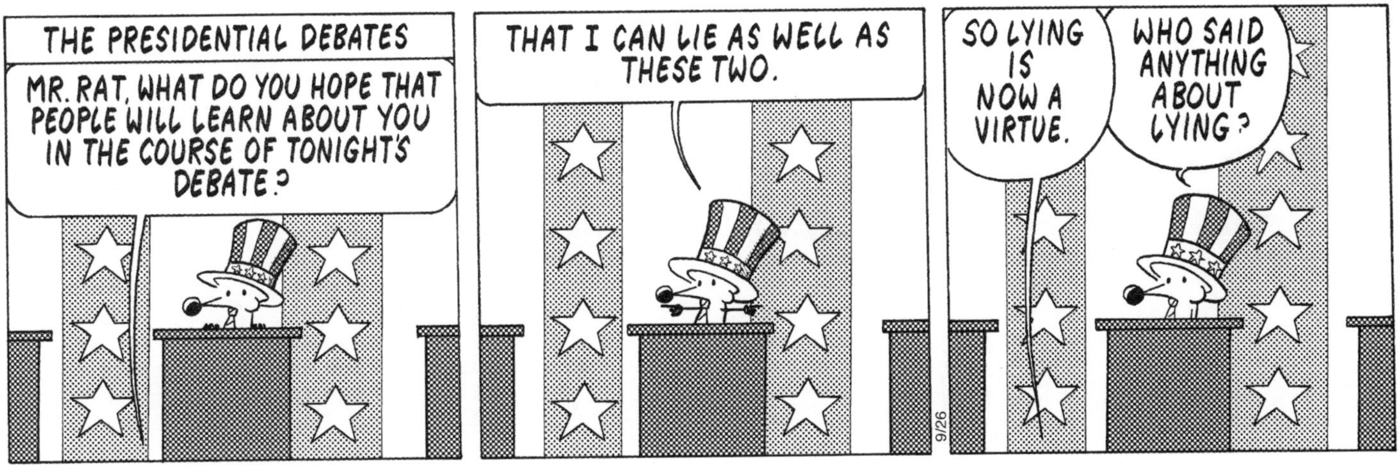
THE PRESIDENTIAL DEBATES
MR. RAT, WHAT DO YOU HOPE THAT PEOPLE WILL LEARN ABOUT YOU IN THE COURSE OF TONIGHT'S DEBATE?
THAT I CAN LIE AS WELL AS THESE TWO.
SO LYING IS NOW A VIRTUE.
WHO SAID ANYTHING ABOUT LYING?
9/26

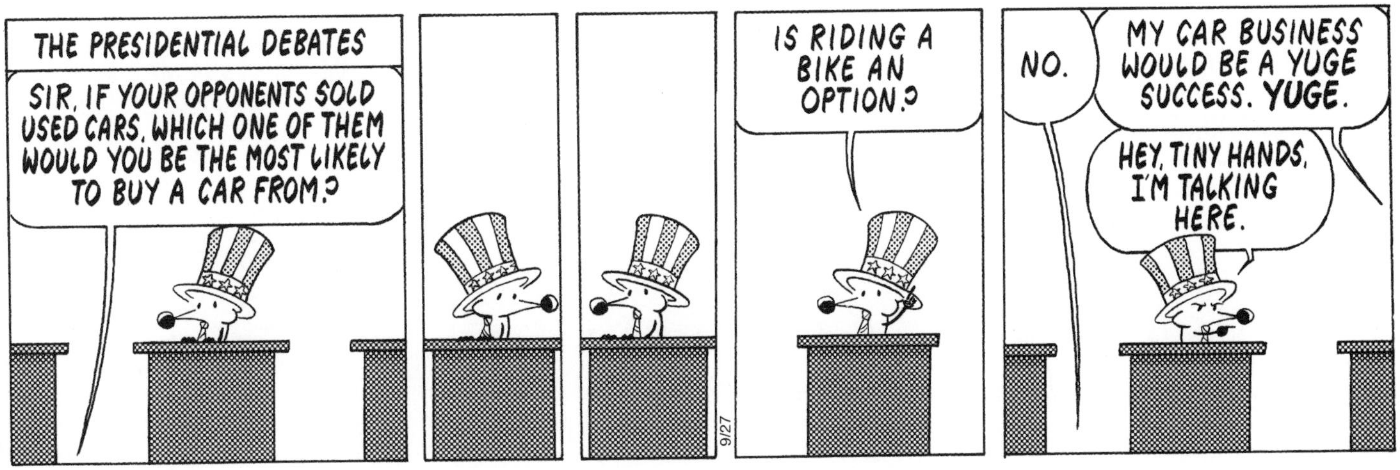
THE PRESIDENTIAL DEBATES
SIR, IF YOUR OPPONENTS SOLD USED CARS, WHICH ONE OF THEM WOULD YOU BE THE MOST LIKELY TO BUY A CAR FROM?
9/27
IS RIDING A BIKE AN OPTION?
NO.
MY CAR BUSINESS WOULD BE A YUGE SUCCESS. YUGE.
HEY, TINY HANDS. I'M TALKING HERE.

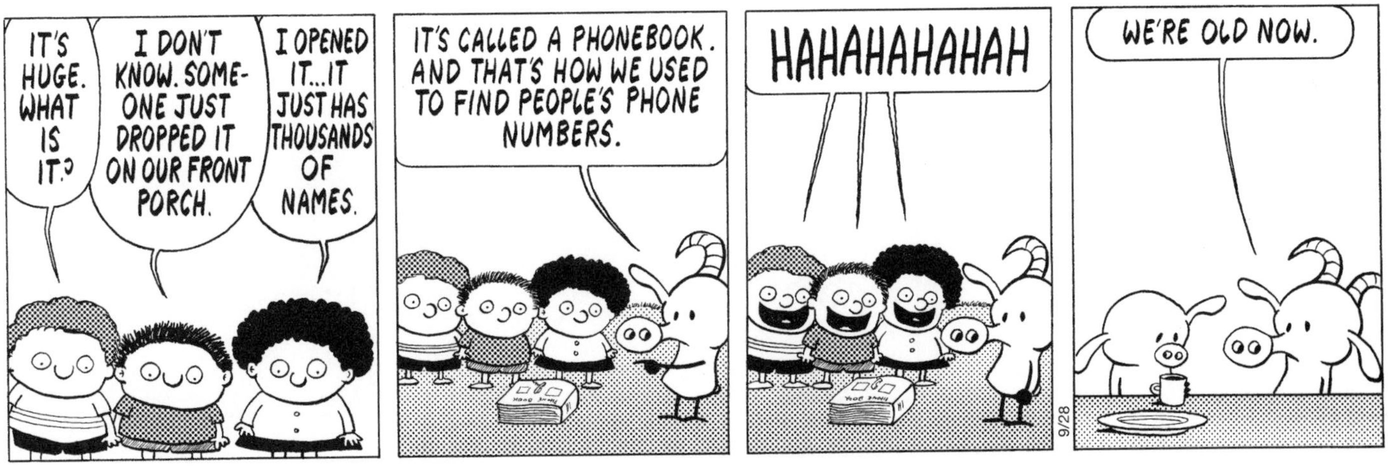
IT'S HUGE. WHAT IS IT?
I DON'T KNOW. SOMEONE JUST DROPPED IT ON OUR FRONT PORCH.
I OPENED IT...IT JUST HAS THOUSANDS OF NAMES.
IT'S CALLED A PHONEBOOK. AND THAT'S HOW WE USED TO FIND PEOPLE'S PHONE NUMBERS.
HAHAHAHAHAH
WE'RE OLD NOW.
9/28

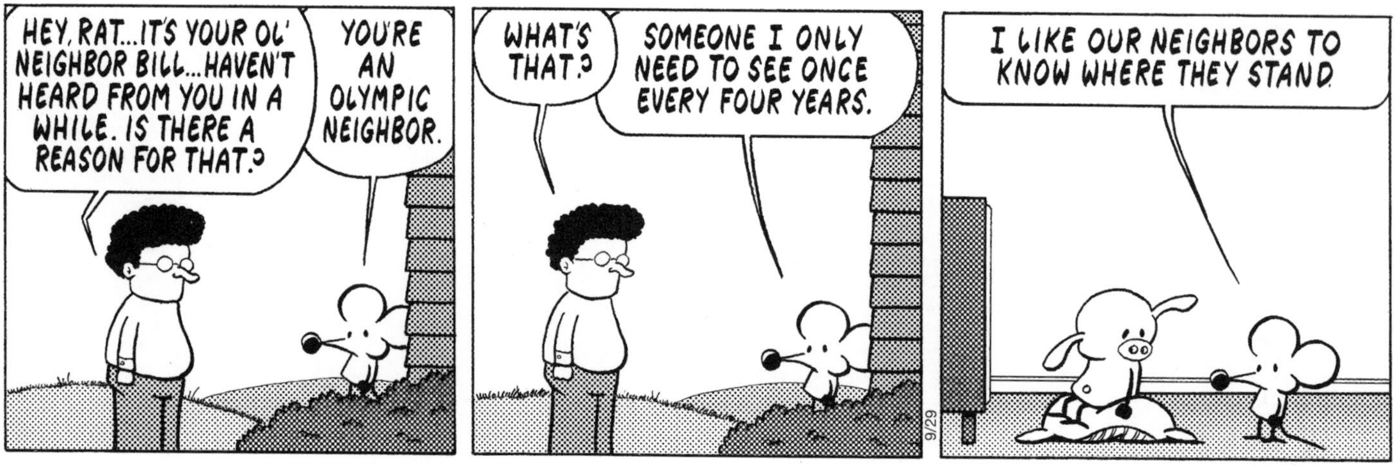
HEY, RAT...IT'S YOUR OL' NEIGHBOR BILL...HAVEN'T HEARD FROM YOU IN A WHILE. IS THERE A REASON FOR THAT?
YOU'RE AN OLYMPIC NEIGHBOR.
WHAT'S THAT?
SOMEONE I ONLY NEED TO SEE ONCE EVERY FOUR YEARS.
9/29
I LIKE OUR NEIGHBORS TO KNOW WHERE THEY STAND.

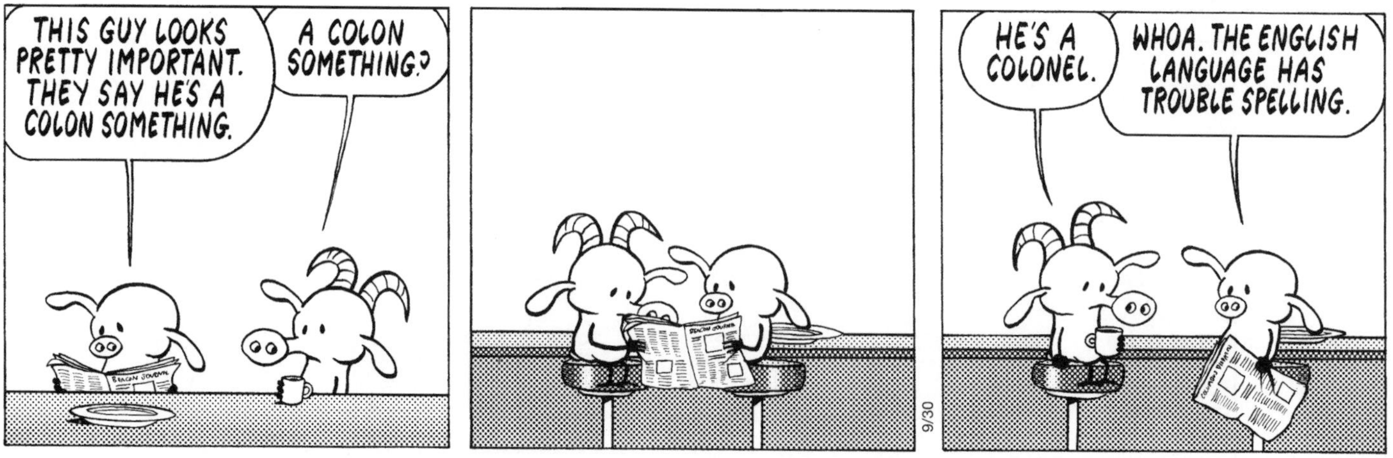
THIS GUY LOOKS PRETTY IMPORTANT. THEY SAY HE'S A COLON SOMETHING.
A COLON SOMETHING?
9/30
HE'S A COLONEL.
WHOA. THE ENGLISH LANGUAGE HAS TROUBLE SPELLING.

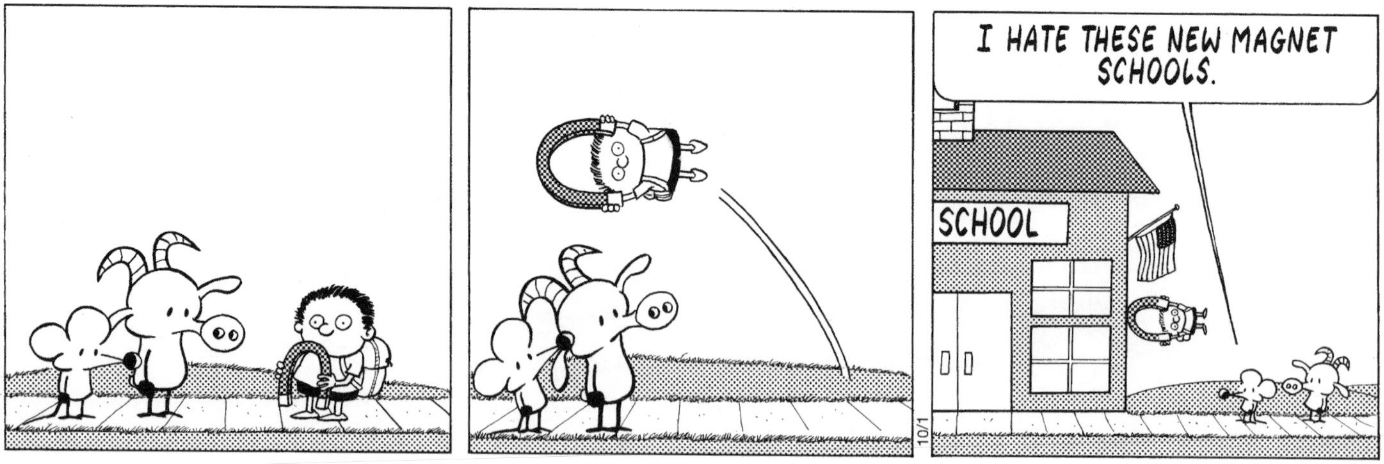
10/1
I HATE THESE NEW MAGNET SCHOOLS.
SCHOOL

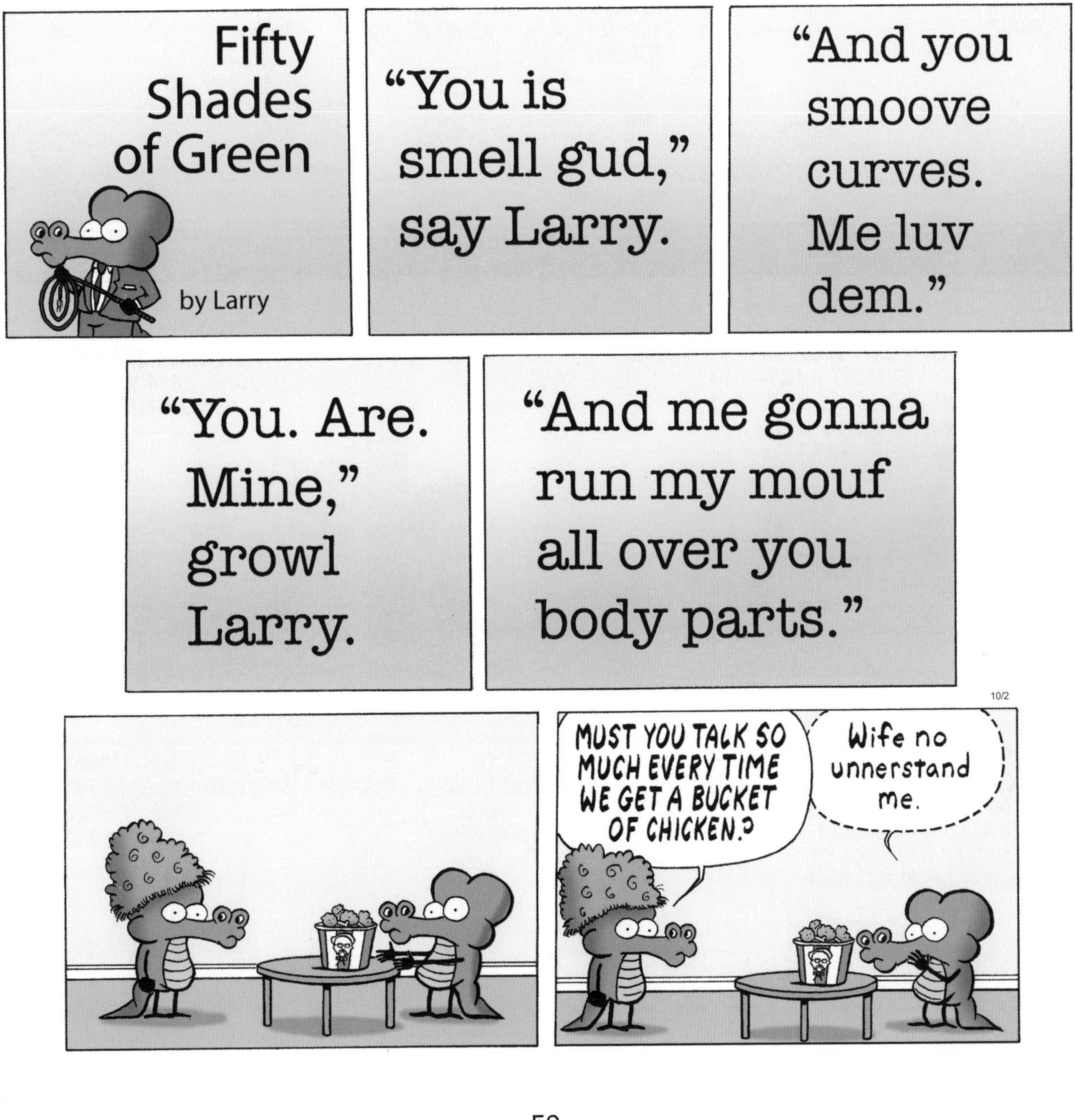
Fifty Shades of Green
by Larry
"You is smell gud," say Larry.
"And you smoove curves. Me luv dem."
"You. Are. Mine," growl Larry.
"And me gonna run my mouf all over you body parts."
10/2
MUST YOU TALK SO MUCH EVERY TIME WE GET A BUCKET OF CHICKEN?
Wife no unnerstand me.

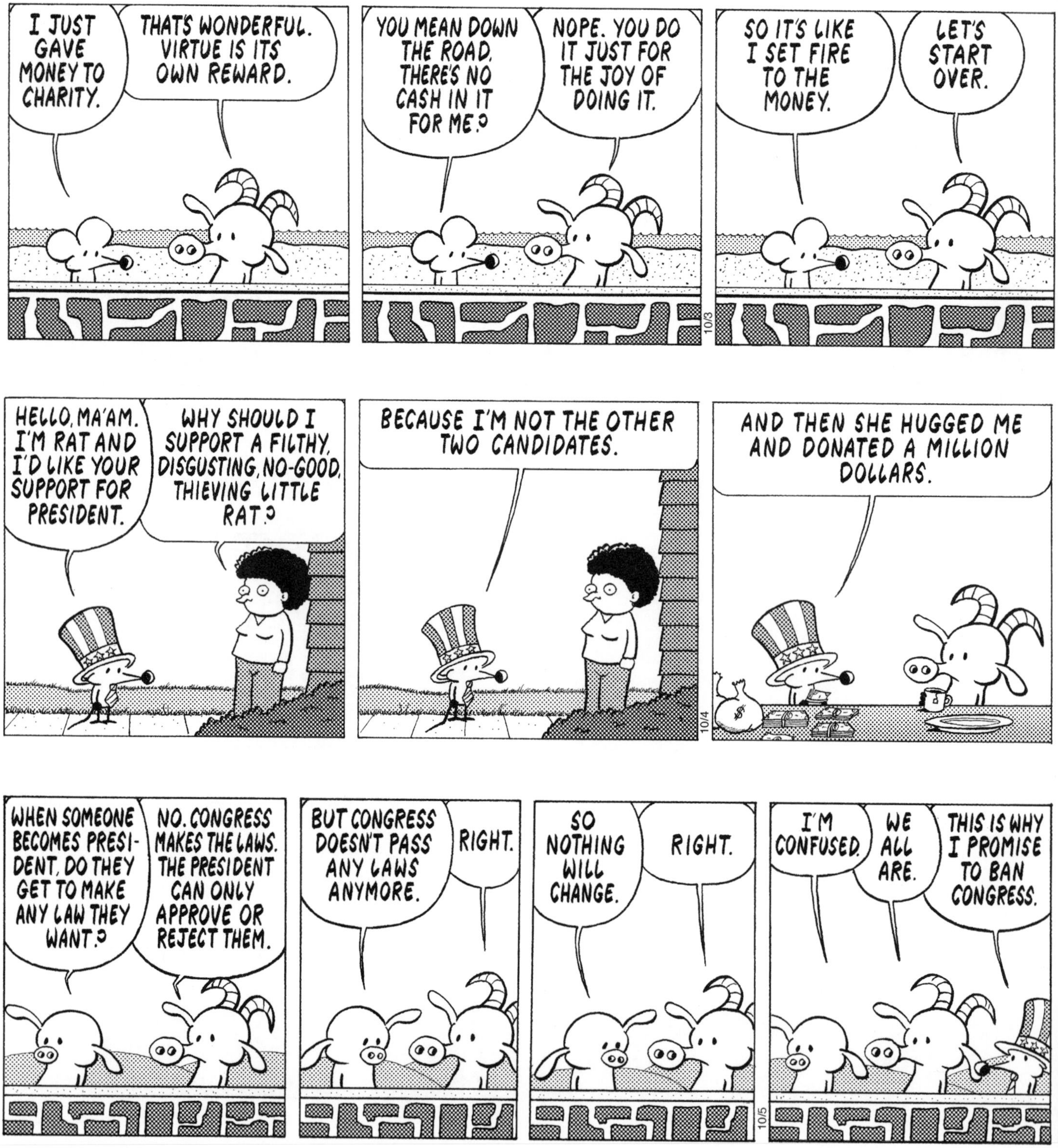
I JUST GAVE MONEY TO CHARITY.
THAT'S WONDERFUL. VIRTUE IS ITS OWN REWARD.
YOU MEAN DOWN THE ROAD, THERE'S NO CASH IN IT FOR ME?
NOPE. YOU DO IT JUST FOR THE JOY OF DOING IT.
SO IT'S LIKE I SET FIRE TO THE MONEY.
LET'S START OVER.
10/3
HELLO, MA'AM. I'M RAT AND I'D LIKE YOUR SUPPORT FOR PRESIDENT.
WHY SHOULD I SUPPORT A FILTHY, DISGUSTING, NO-GOOD, THIEVING LITTLE RAT?
BECAUSE I'M NOT THE OTHER TWO CANDIDATES.
AND THEN SHE HUGGED ME AND DONATED A MILLION DOLLARS.
10/4
WHEN SOMEONE BECOMES PRESIDENT, DO THEY GET TO MAKE ANY LAW THEY WANT?
NO. CONGRESS MAKES THE LAWS. THE PRESIDENT CAN ONLY APPROVE OR REJECT THEM.
BUT CONGRESS DOESN'T PASS ANY LAWS ANYMORE.
RIGHT.
SO NOTHING WILL CHANGE.
RIGHT.
I'M CONFUSED.
WE ALL ARE.
THIS IS WHY I PROMISE TO BAN CONGRESS.
10/5

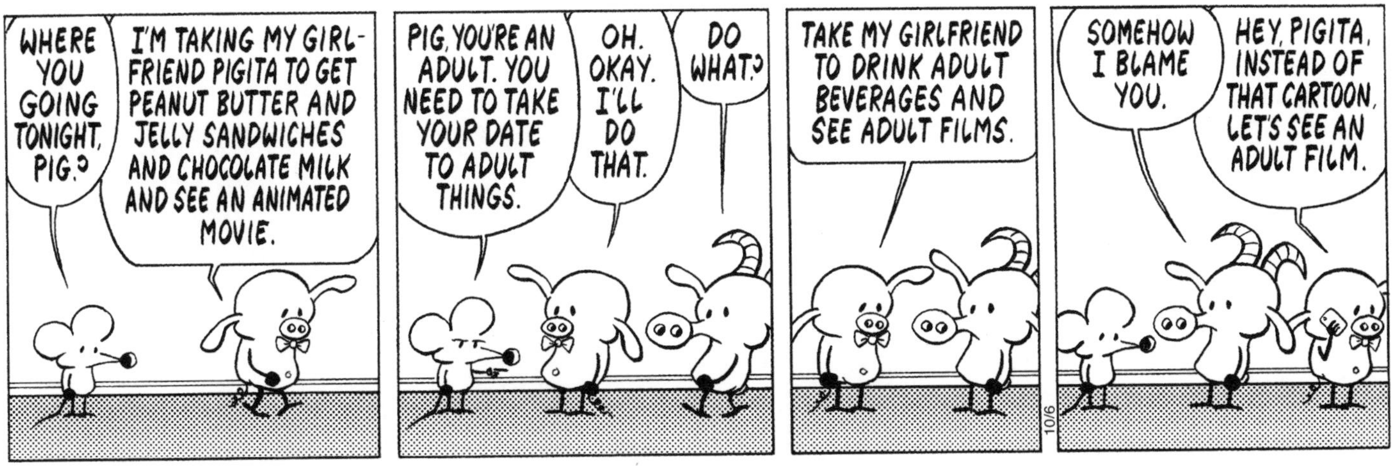
WHERE YOU GOING TONIGHT, PIG?
I'M TAKING MY GIRLFRIEND PIGITA TO GET PEANUT BUTTER AND JELLY SANDWICHES AND CHOCOLATE MILK AND SEE AN ANIMATED MOVIE.
PIG, YOU'RE AN ADULT. YOU NEED TO TAKE YOUR DATE TO ADULT THINGS.
OH. OKAY. I'LL DO THAT.
DO WHAT?
TAKE MY GIRLFRIEND TO DRINK ADULT BEVERAGES AND SEE ADULT FILMS.
10/6
SOMEHOW I BLAME YOU.
HEY, PIGITA, INSTEAD OF THAT CARTOON, LET'S SEE AN ADULT FILM.

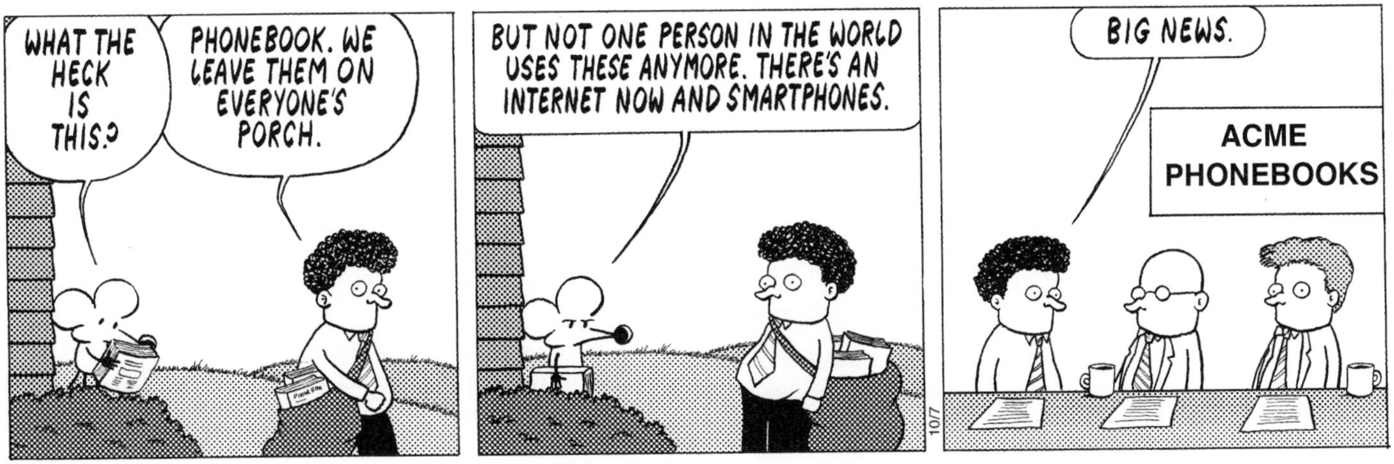
WHAT THE HECK IS THIS?
PHONEBOOK. WE LEAVE THEM ON EVERYONE'S PORCH.
BUT NOT ONE PERSON IN THE WORLD USES THESE ANYMORE. THERE'S AN INTERNET NOW AND SMARTPHONES.
10/7
BIG NEWS.
ACME PHONEBOOKS

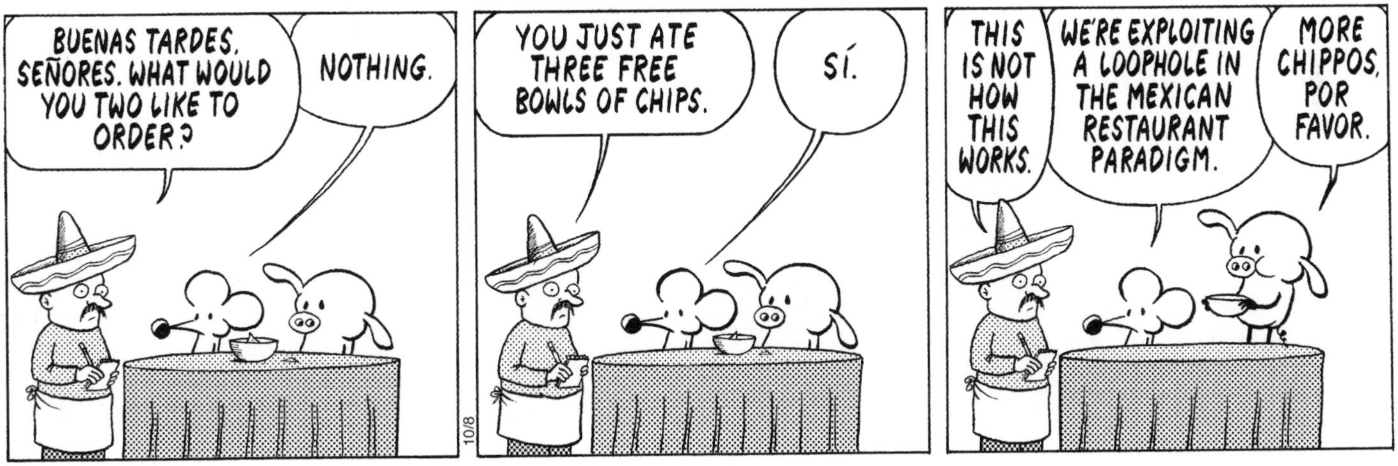
BUENAS TARDES, SEÑORES. WHAT WOULD YOU TWO LIKE TO ORDER?
NOTHING.
10/8
YOU JUST ATE THREE FREE BOWLS OF CHIPS.
SÍ.
THIS IS NOT HOW THIS WORKS.
WE'RE EXPLOITING A LOOPHOLE IN THE MEXICAN RESTAURANT PARADIGM.
MORE CHIPPOS, POR FAVOR.

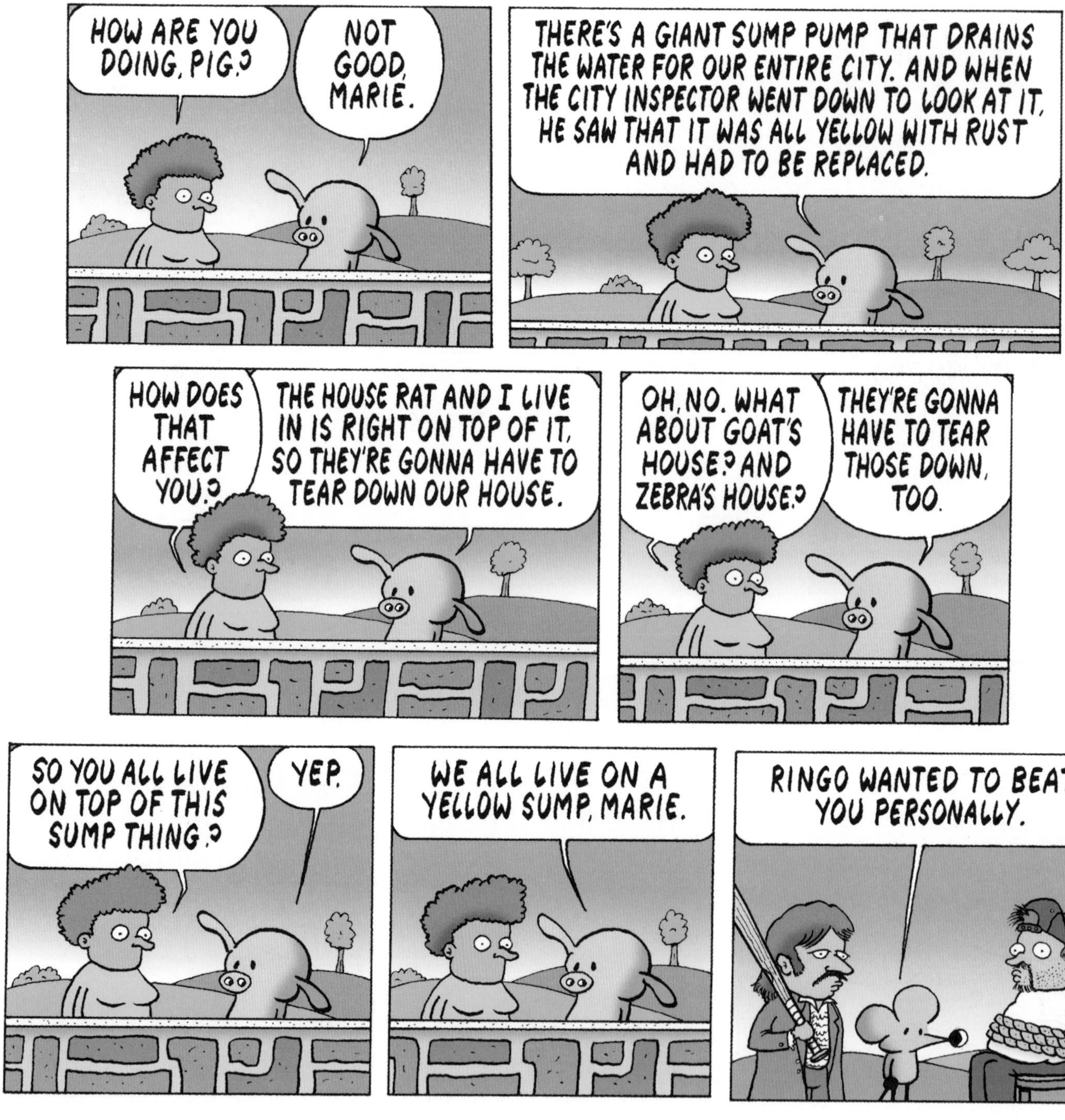
HOW ARE YOU DOING, PIG?
NOT GOOD, MARIE.
THERE'S A GIANT SUMP PUMP THAT DRAINS THE WATER FOR OUR ENTIRE CITY. AND WHEN THE CITY INSPECTOR WENT DOWN TO LOOK AT IT, HE SAW THAT IT WAS ALL YELLOW WITH RUST AND HAD TO BE REPLACED.
HOW DOES THAT AFFECT YOU?
THE HOUSE RAT AND I LIVE IN IS RIGHT ON TOP OF IT, SO THEY'RE GONNA HAVE TO TEAR DOWN OUR HOUSE.
OH, NO. WHAT ABOUT GOAT'S HOUSE? AND ZEBRA'S HOUSE?
THEY'RE GONNA HAVE TO TEAR THOSE DOWN, TOO.
10/9
SO YOU ALL LIVE ON TOP OF THIS SUMP THING?
YEP.
WE ALL LIVE ON A YELLOW SUMP, MARIE.
RINGO WANTED TO BEAT YOU PERSONALLY.

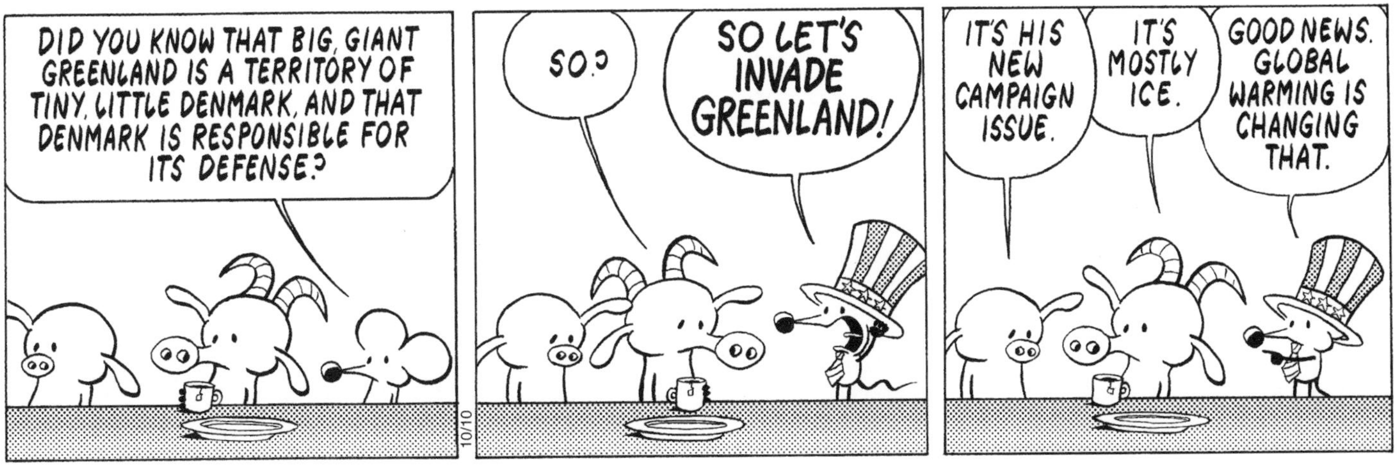
DID YOU KNOW THAT BIG, GIANT GREENLAND IS A TERRITORY OF TINY, LITTLE DENMARK, AND THAT DENMARK IS RESPONSIBLE FOR ITS DEFENSE?
10/10
SO?
SO LET'S INVADE GREENLAND!
IT'S HIS NEW CAMPAIGN ISSUE.
IT'S MOSTLY ICE.
GOOD NEWS. GLOBAL WARMING IS CHANGING THAT.

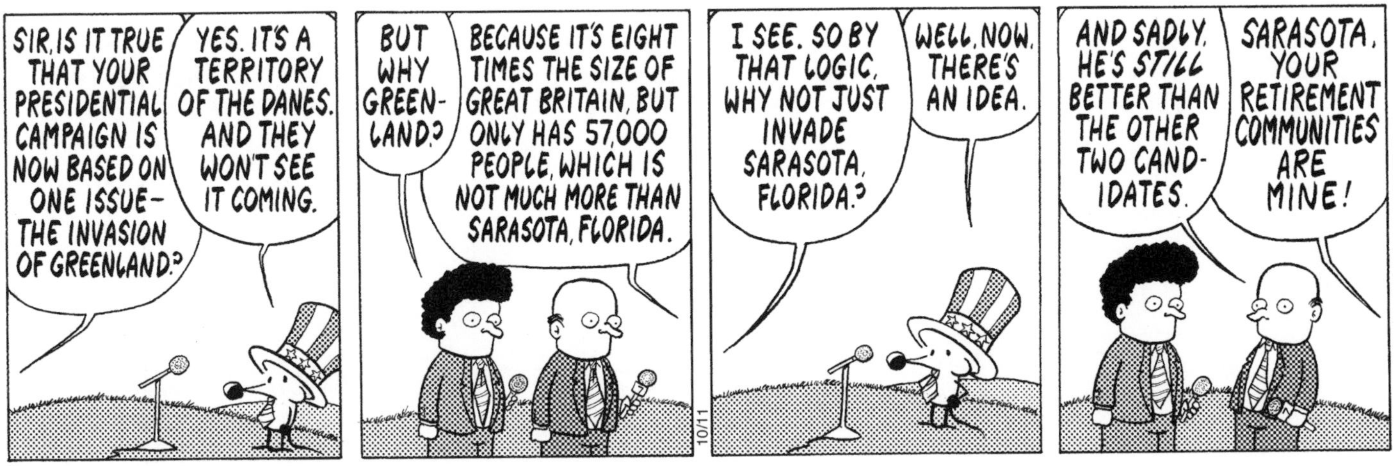
SIR, IS IT TRUE THAT YOUR PRESIDENTIAL CAMPAIGN IS NOW BASED ON ONE ISSUE– THE INVASION OF GREENLAND?
YES. IT'S A TERRITORY OF THE DANES. AND THEY WON'T SEE IT COMING.
10/11
BUT WHY GREEN-LAND?
BECAUSE IT'S EIGHT TIMES THE SIZE OF GREAT BRITAIN, BUT ONLY HAS 57,000 PEOPLE, WHICH IS NOT MUCH MORE THAN SARASOTA, FLORIDA.
I SEE. SO BY THAT LOGIC, WHY NOT JUST INVADE SARASOTA, FLORIDA?
WELL, NOW, THERE'S AN IDEA.
AND SADLY, HE'S STILL BETTER THAN THE OTHER TWO CAND-IDATES.
SARASOTA, YOUR RETIREMENT COMMUNITIES ARE MINE!

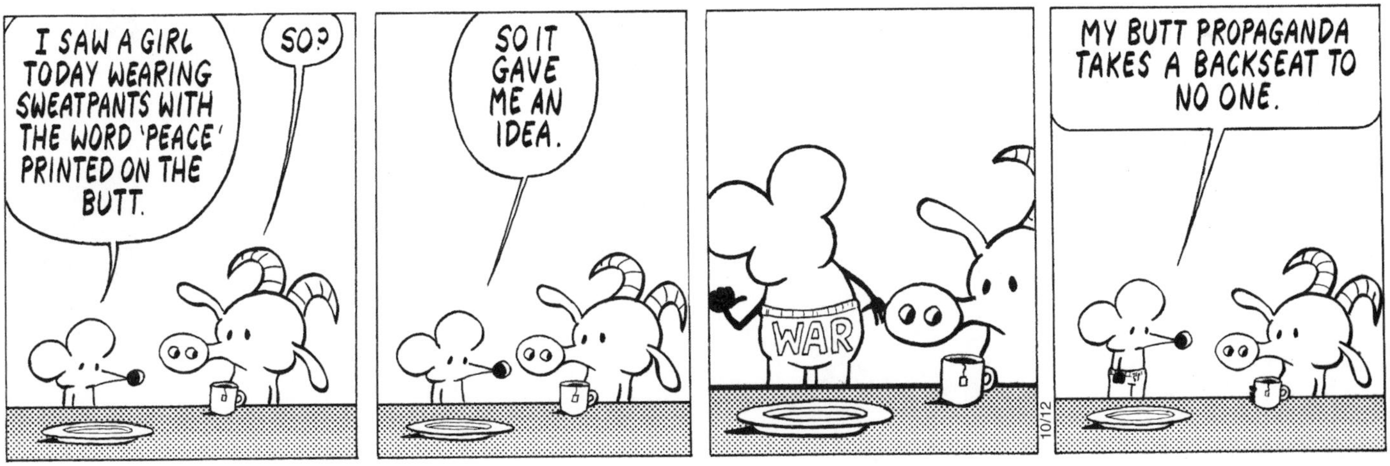
I SAW A GIRL TODAY WEARING SWEATPANTS WITH THE WORD 'PEACE' PRINTED ON THE BUTT.
SO?
SO IT GAVE ME AN IDEA.
WAR
10/12
MY BUTT PROPAGANDA TAKES A BACKSEAT TO NO ONE.

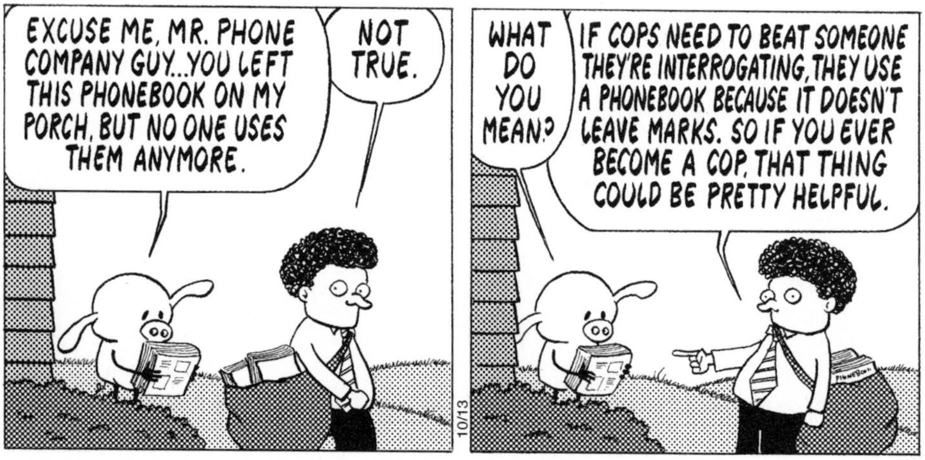
EXCUSE ME, MR. PHONE COMPANY GUY...YOU LEFT THIS PHONEBOOK ON MY PORCH, BUT NO ONE USES THEM ANYMORE.
NOT TRUE.
10/13
WHAT DO YOU MEAN?
IF COPS NEED TO BEAT SOMEONE THEY'RE INTERROGATING, THEY USE A PHONEBOOK BECAUSE IT DOESN'T LEAVE MARKS. SO IF YOU EVER BECOME A COP, THAT THING COULD BE PRETTY HELPFUL.
IT'S NICE TO SEE THE PHONE COMPANY ADAPTING.

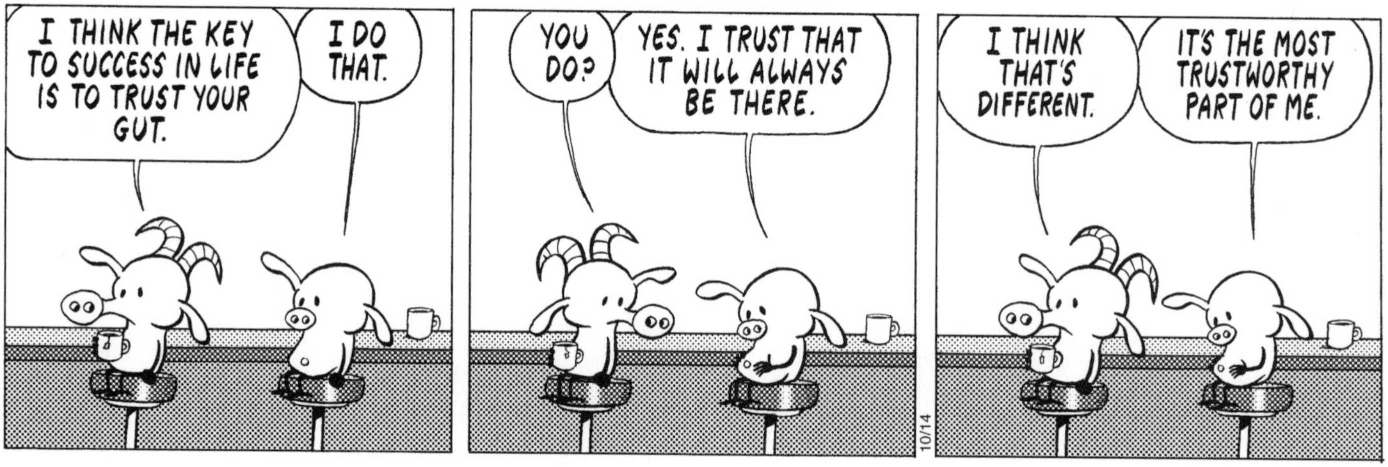
I THINK THE KEY TO SUCCESS IN LIFE IS TO TRUST YOUR GUT.
I DO THAT.
YOU DO?
YES. I TRUST THAT IT WILL ALWAYS BE THERE.
10/14
I THINK THAT'S DIFFERENT.
IT'S THE MOST TRUSTWORTHY PART OF ME.

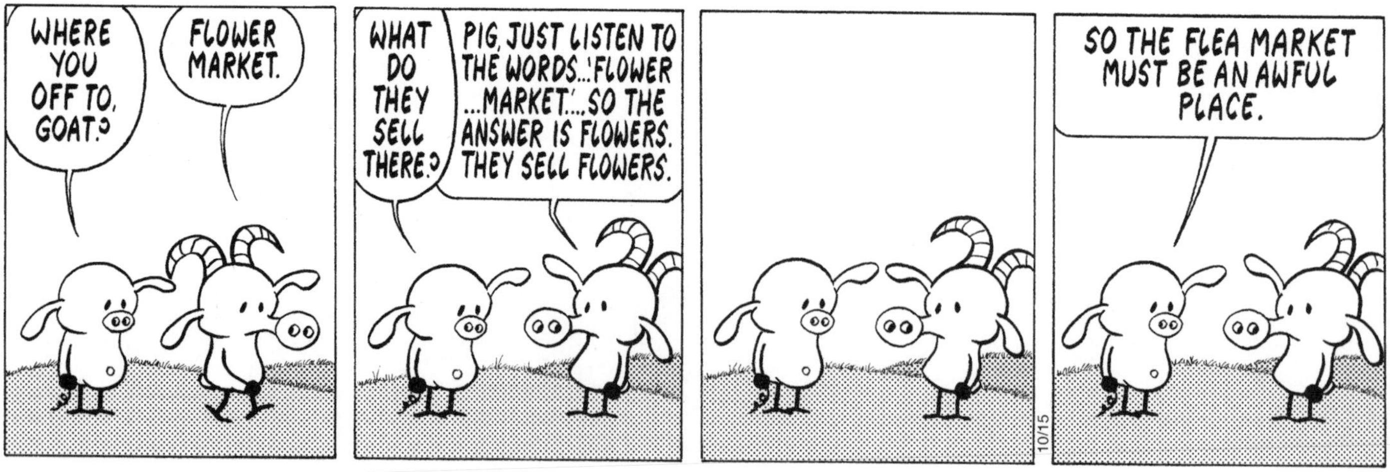
WHERE YOU OFF TO, GOAT?
FLOWER MARKET.
WHAT DO THEY SELL THERE?
PIG, JUST LISTEN TO THE WORDS...'FLOWER ...MARKET'...SO THE ANSWER IS FLOWERS. THEY SELL FLOWERS.
10/15
SO THE FLEA MARKET MUST BE AN AWFUL PLACE.

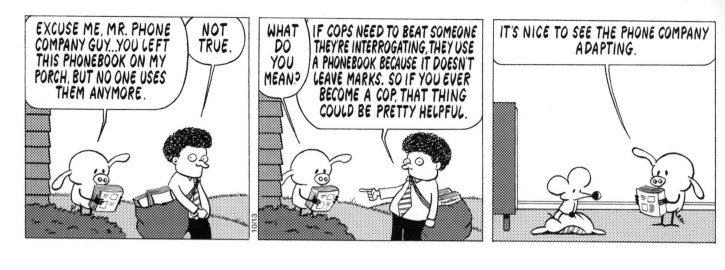

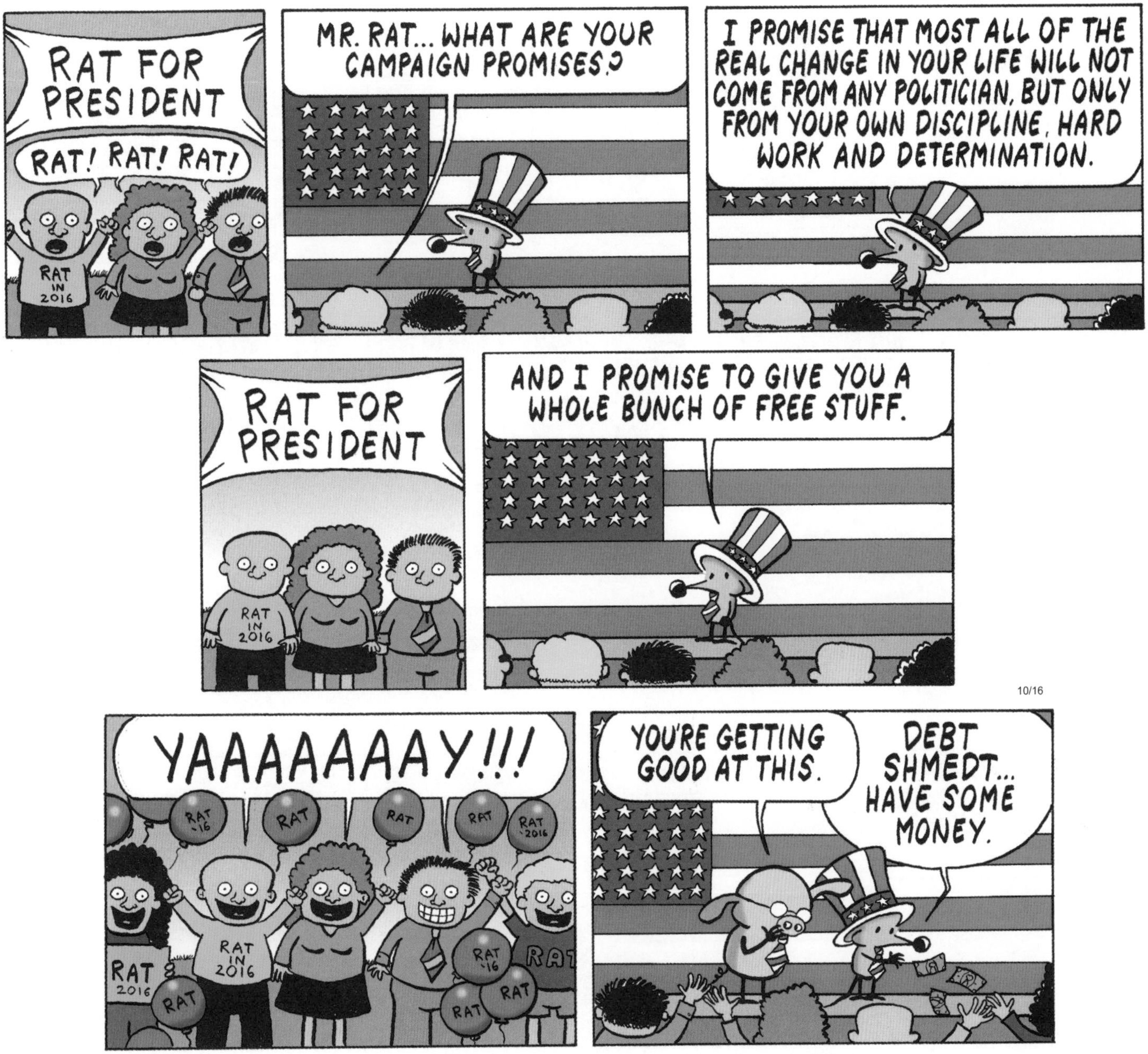
RAT FOR PRESIDENT
RAT! RAT! RAT!
RAT IN 2016
MR. RAT... WHAT ARE YOUR CAMPAIGN PROMISES?
I PROMISE THAT MOST ALL OF THE REAL CHANGE IN YOUR LIFE WILL NOT COME FROM ANY POLITICIAN, BUT ONLY FROM YOUR OWN DISCIPLINE, HARD WORK AND DETERMINATION.
RAT FOR PRESIDENT
RAT IN 2016
AND I PROMISE TO GIVE YOU A WHOLE BUNCH OF FREE STUFF.
10/16
YAAAAAAAY!!!
RAT
RAT IN 2016
YOU'RE GETTING GOOD AT THIS.
DEBT SHMEDT... HAVE SOME MONEY.

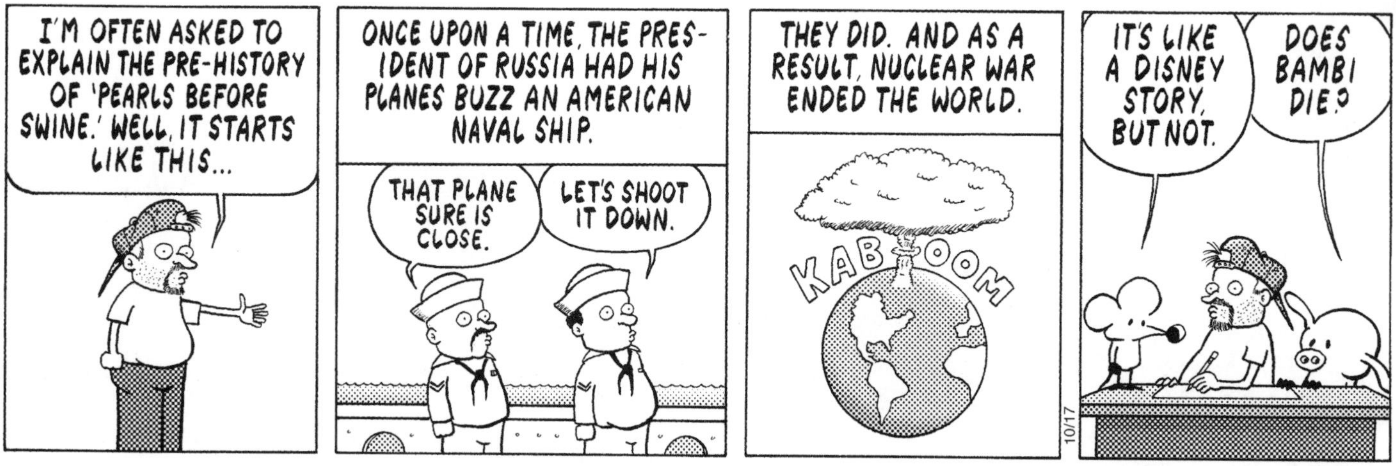
I'M OFTEN ASKED TO EXPLAIN THE PRE-HISTORY OF 'PEARLS BEFORE SWINE.' WELL, IT STARTS LIKE THIS...
ONCE UPON A TIME, THE PRES-IDENT OF RUSSIA HAD HIS PLANES BUZZ AN AMERICAN NAVAL SHIP.
THAT PLANE SURE IS CLOSE.
LET'S SHOOT IT DOWN.
THEY DID. AND AS A RESULT, NUCLEAR WAR ENDED THE WORLD.
KABOOOM
10/17
IT'S LIKE A DISNEY STORY, BUT NOT.
DOES BAMBI DIE?

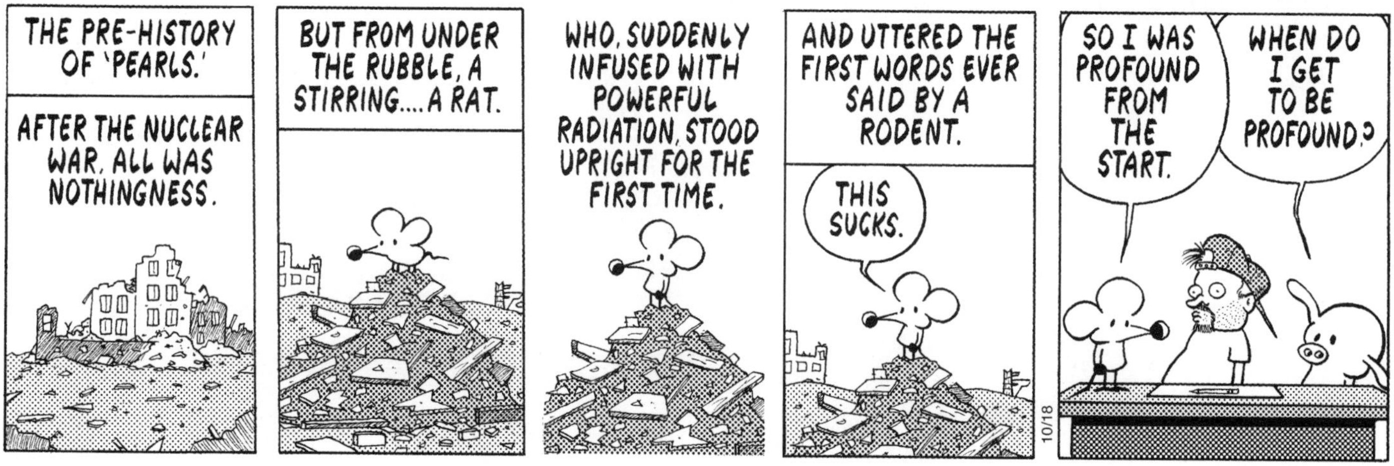
THE PRE-HISTORY OF 'PEARLS.'
AFTER THE NUCLEAR WAR, ALL WAS NOTHINGNESS.
BUT FROM UNDER THE RUBBLE, A STIRRING.... A RAT.
WHO, SUDDENLY INFUSED WITH POWERFUL RADIATION, STOOD UPRIGHT FOR THE FIRST TIME.
AND UTTERED THE FIRST WORDS EVER SAID BY A RODENT.
THIS SUCKS.
10/18
SO I WAS PROFOUND FROM THE START.
WHEN DO I GET TO BE PROFOUND?

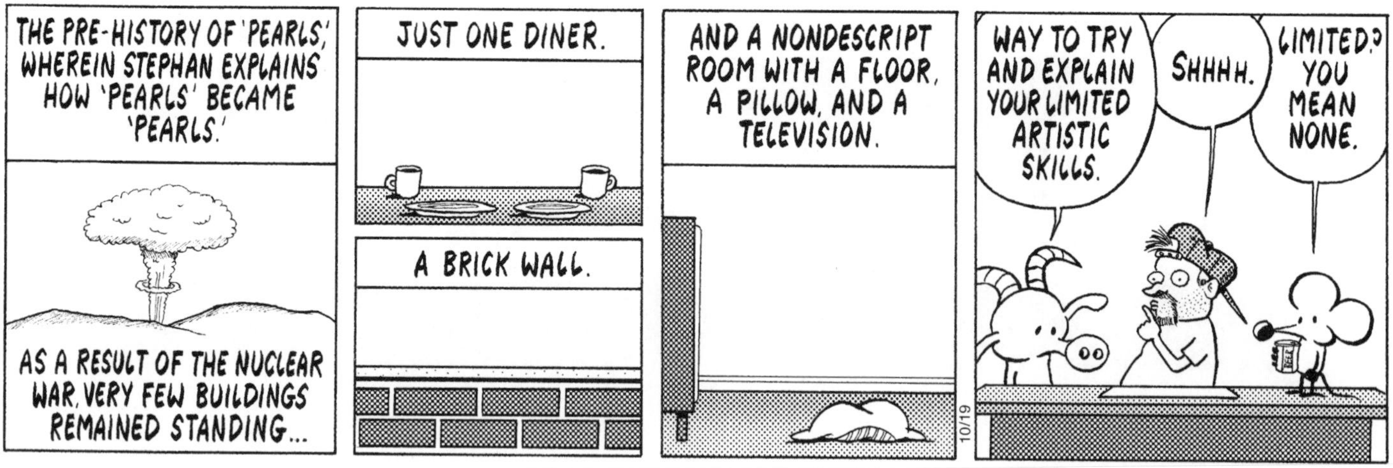
THE PRE-HISTORY OF 'PEARLS,' WHEREIN STEPHAN EXPLAINS HOW 'PEARLS' BECAME 'PEARLS.'
AS A RESULT OF THE NUCLEAR WAR, VERY FEW BUILDINGS REMAINED STANDING...
JUST ONE DINER.
A BRICK WALL.
AND A NONDESCRIPT ROOM WITH A FLOOR, A PILLOW, AND A TELEVISION.
10/19
WAY TO TRY AND EXPLAIN YOUR LIMITED ARTISTIC SKILLS.
SHHHH.
LIMITED? YOU MEAN NONE.

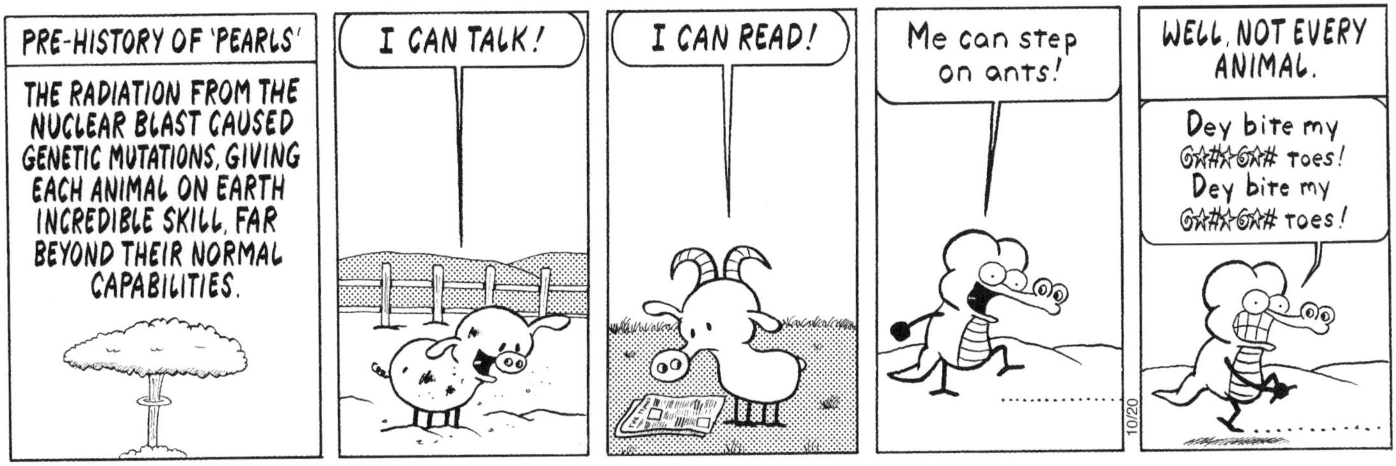
PRE-HISTORY OF 'PEARLS'
THE RADIATION FROM THE NUCLEAR BLAST CAUSED GENETIC MUTATIONS, GIVING EACH ANIMAL ON EARTH INCREDIBLE SKILL, FAR BEYOND THEIR NORMAL CAPABILITIES.
I CAN TALK!
I CAN READ!
Me can step on ants!
10/20
WELL, NOT EVERY ANIMAL.
Dey bite my G☆#☆G☆# toes! Dey bite my G☆#☆G☆# toes!

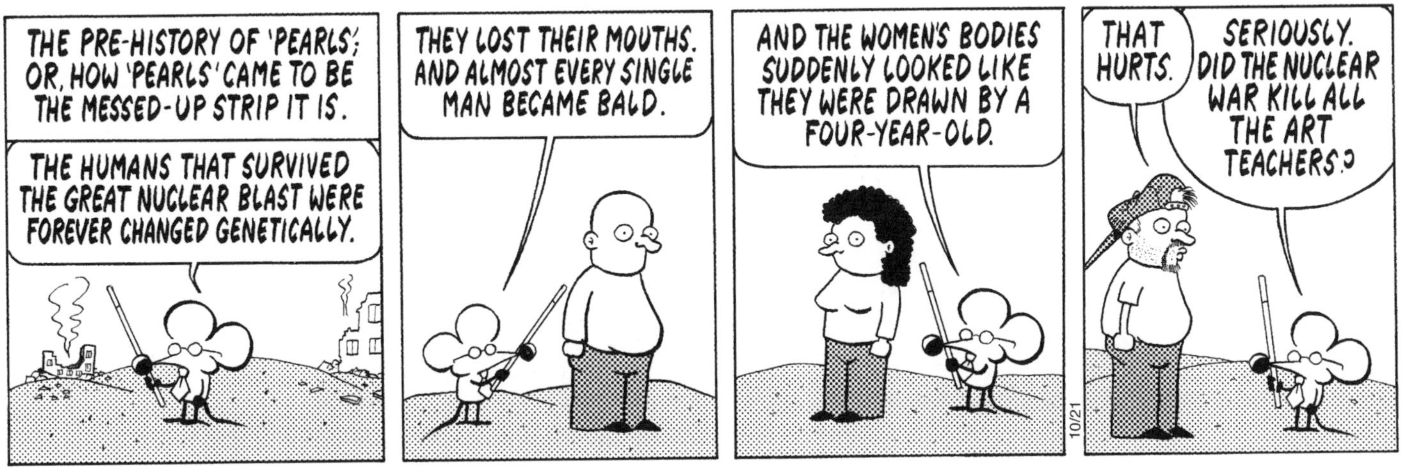
THE PRE-HISTORY OF 'PEARLS'; OR, HOW 'PEARLS' CAME TO BE THE MESSED-UP STRIP IT IS.
THE HUMANS THAT SURVIVED THE GREAT NUCLEAR BLAST WERE FOREVER CHANGED GENETICALLY.
THEY LOST THEIR MOUTHS. AND ALMOST EVERY SINGLE MAN BECAME BALD.
AND THE WOMEN'S BODIES SUDDENLY LOOKED LIKE THEY WERE DRAWN BY A FOUR-YEAR-OLD.
10/21
THAT HURTS.
SERIOUSLY. DID THE NUCLEAR WAR KILL ALL THE ART TEACHERS?

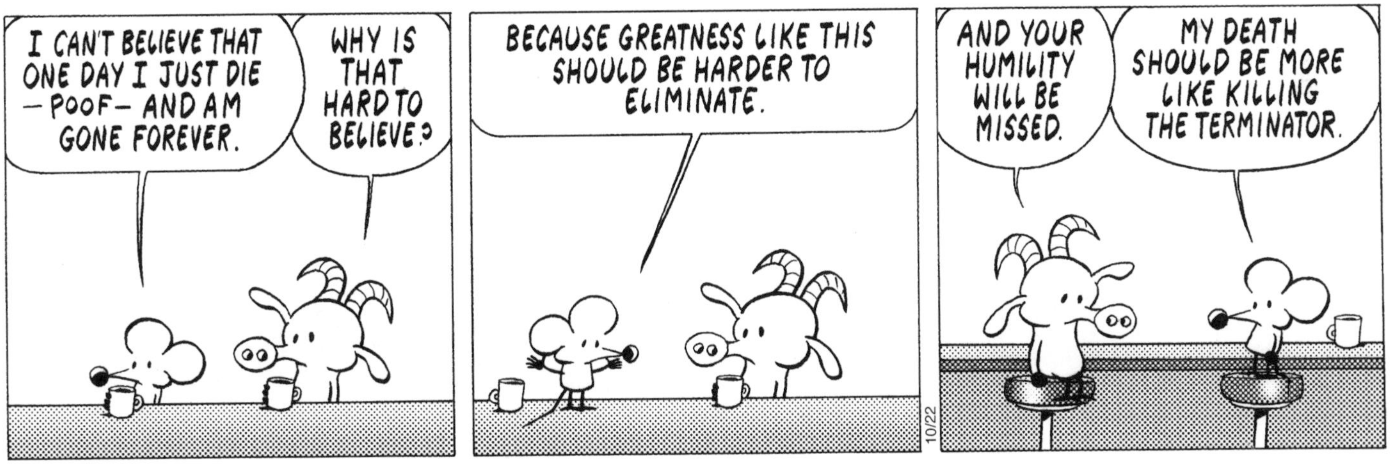
I CAN'T BELIEVE THAT ONE DAY I JUST DIE — POOF— AND AM GONE FOREVER.
WHY IS THAT HARD TO BELIEVE?
BECAUSE GREATNESS LIKE THIS SHOULD BE HARDER TO ELIMINATE.
10/22
AND YOUR HUMILITY WILL BE MISSED.
MY DEATH SHOULD BE MORE LIKE KILLING THE TERMINATOR.

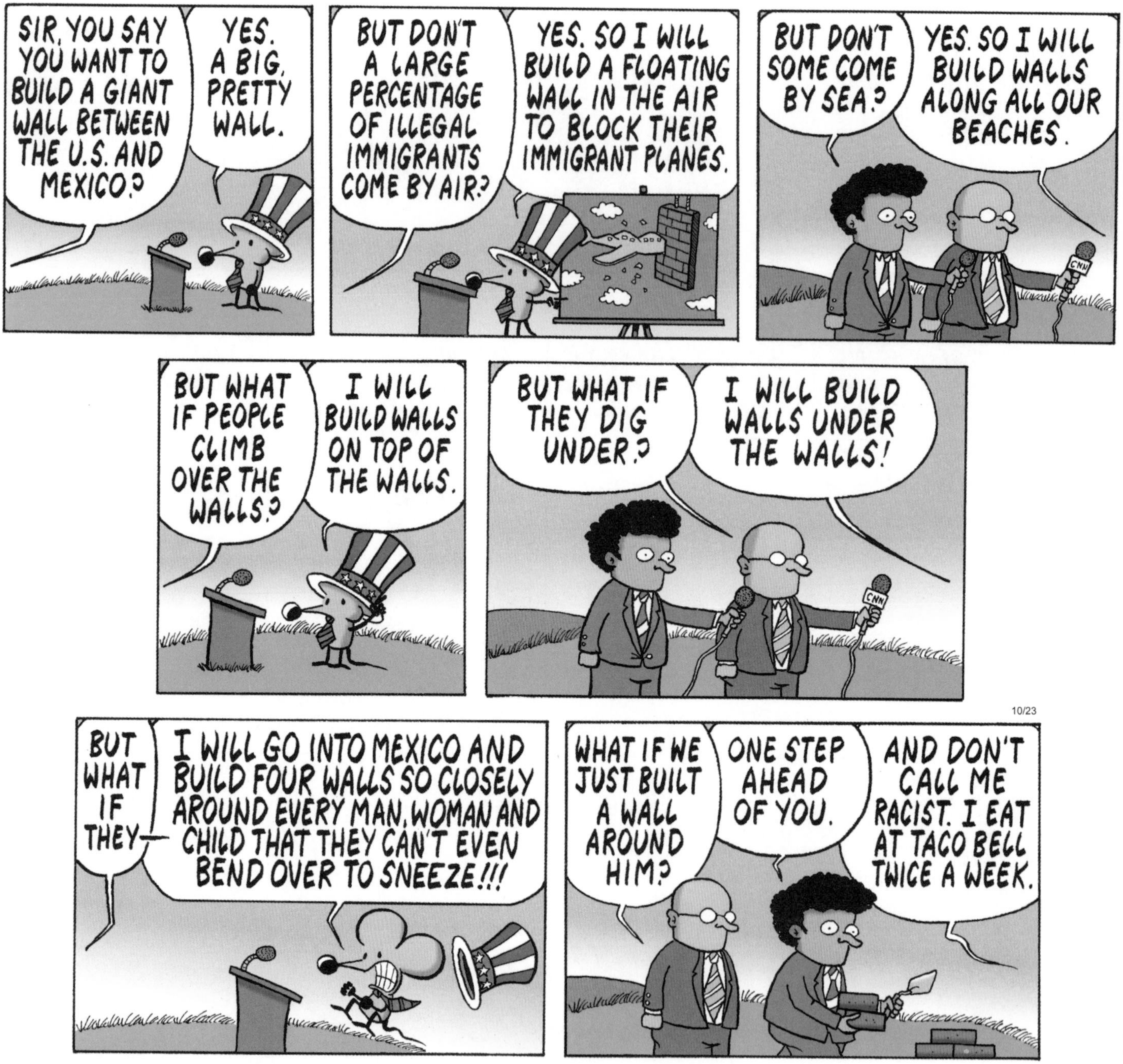
SIR, YOU SAY YOU WANT TO BUILD A GIANT WALL BETWEEN THE U.S. AND MEXICO?
YES. A BIG, PRETTY WALL.
BUT DON'T A LARGE PERCENTAGE OF ILLEGAL IMMIGRANTS COME BY AIR?
YES. SO I WILL BUILD A FLOATING WALL IN THE AIR TO BLOCK THEIR IMMIGRANT PLANES.
BUT DON'T SOME COME BY SEA?
YES. SO I WILL BUILD WALLS ALONG ALL OUR BEACHES.
CNN
BUT WHAT IF PEOPLE CLIMB OVER THE WALLS?
I WILL BUILD WALLS ON TOP OF THE WALLS.
BUT WHAT IF THEY DIG UNDER?
I WILL BUILD WALLS UNDER THE WALLS!
CNN
10/23
BUT WHAT IF THEY—
I WILL GO INTO MEXICO AND BUILD FOUR WALLS SO CLOSELY AROUND EVERY MAN, WOMAN AND CHILD THAT THEY CAN'T EVEN BEND OVER TO SNEEZE!!!
WHAT IF WE JUST BUILT A WALL AROUND HIM?
ONE STEP AHEAD OF YOU.
AND DON'T CALL ME RACIST. I EAT AT TACO BELL TWICE A WEEK.

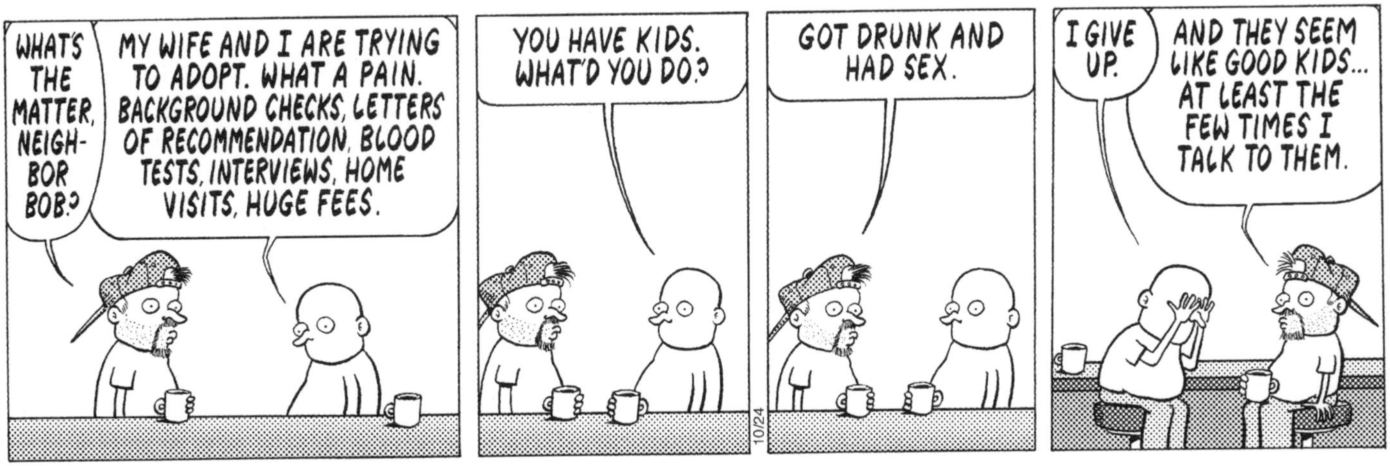
WHAT'S THE MATTER, NEIGHBOR BOB?
MY WIFE AND I ARE TRYING TO ADOPT. WHAT A PAIN. BACKGROUND CHECKS, LETTERS OF RECOMMENDATION, BLOOD TESTS, INTERVIEWS, HOME VISITS, HUGE FEES.
YOU HAVE KIDS. WHAT'D YOU DO?
GOT DRUNK AND HAD SEX.
10/24
I GIVE UP.
AND THEY SEEM LIKE GOOD KIDS... AT LEAST THE FEW TIMES I TALK TO THEM.

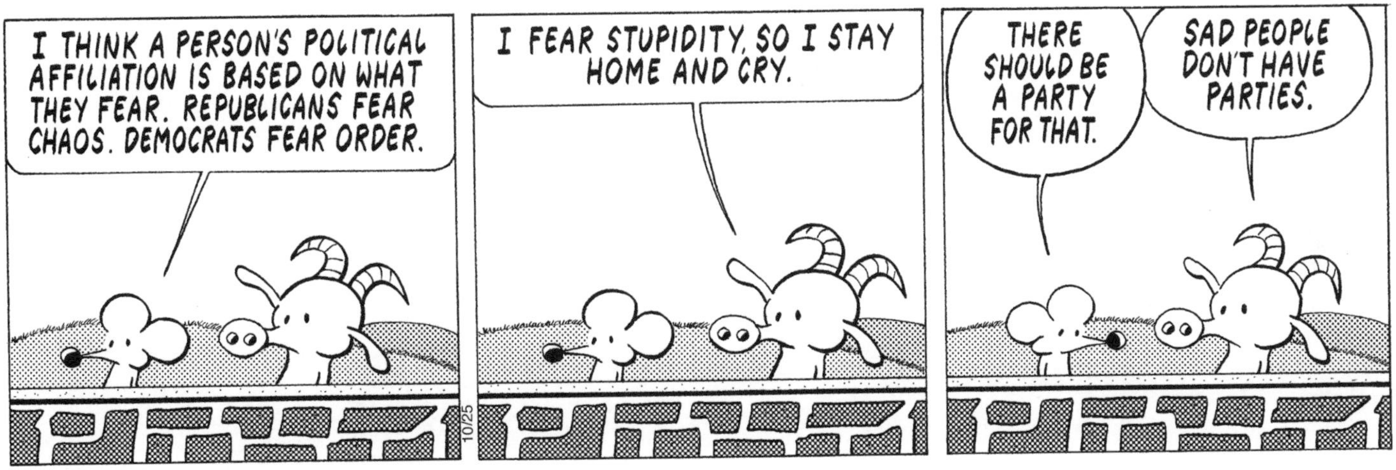
I THINK A PERSON'S POLITICAL AFFILIATION IS BASED ON WHAT THEY FEAR. REPUBLICANS FEAR CHAOS. DEMOCRATS FEAR ORDER.
10/25
I FEAR STUPIDITY, SO I STAY HOME AND CRY.
THERE SHOULD BE A PARTY FOR THAT.
SAD PEOPLE DON'T HAVE PARTIES.

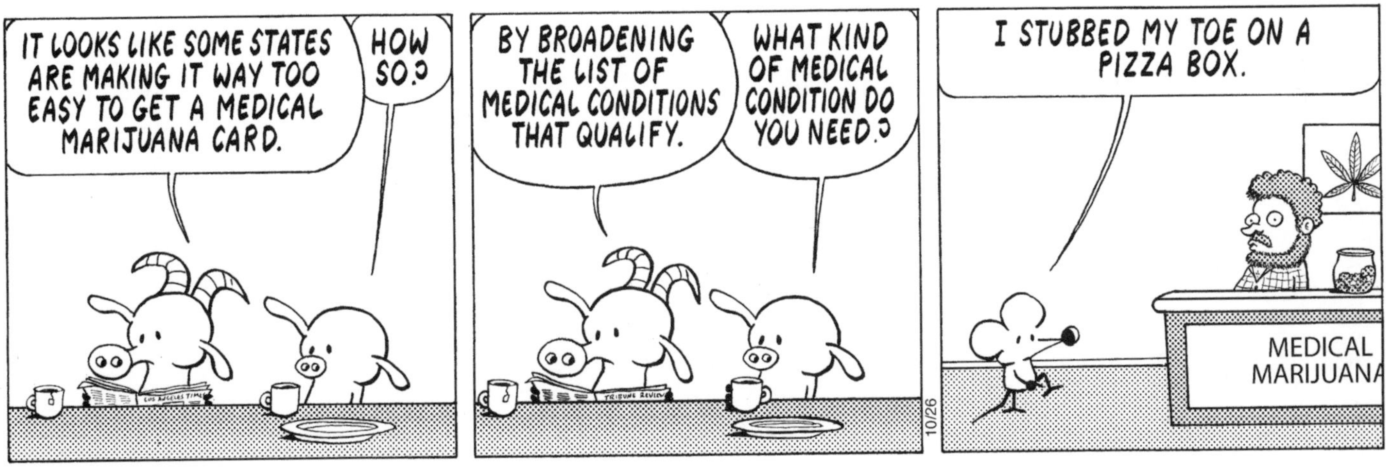
IT LOOKS LIKE SOME STATES ARE MAKING IT WAY TOO EASY TO GET A MEDICAL MARIJUANA CARD.
HOW SO?
BY BROADENING THE LIST OF MEDICAL CONDITIONS THAT QUALIFY.
WHAT KIND OF MEDICAL CONDITION DO YOU NEED?
10/26
I STUBBED MY TOE ON A PIZZA BOX.
MEDICAL MARIJUANA

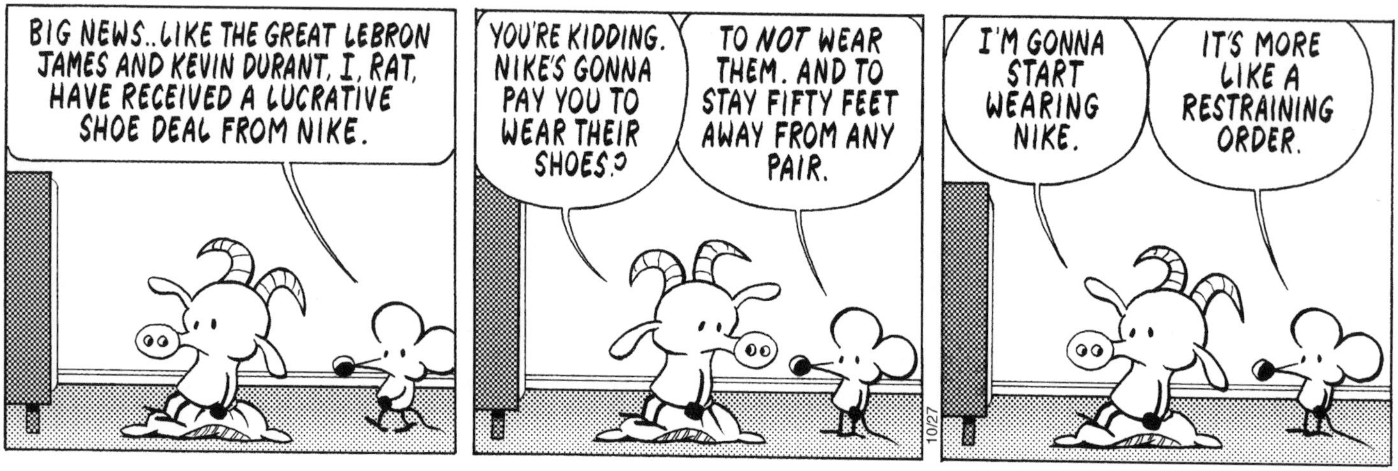
BIG NEWS..LIKE THE GREAT LEBRON JAMES AND KEVIN DURANT, I, RAT, HAVE RECEIVED A LUCRATIVE SHOE DEAL FROM NIKE.
YOU'RE KIDDING. NIKE'S GONNA PAY YOU TO WEAR THEIR SHOES?
TO *NOT* WEAR THEM. AND TO STAY FIFTY FEET AWAY FROM ANY PAIR.
10/27
I'M GONNA START WEARING NIKE.
IT'S MORE LIKE A RESTRAINING ORDER.

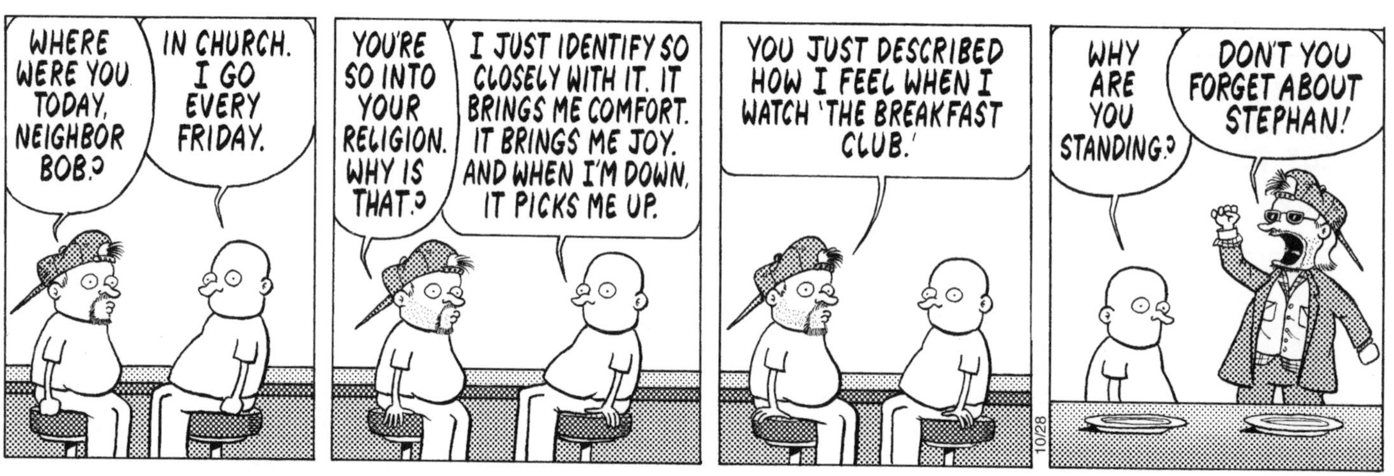
WHERE WERE YOU TODAY, NEIGHBOR BOB?
IN CHURCH. I GO EVERY FRIDAY.
YOU'RE SO INTO YOUR RELIGION. WHY IS THAT?
I JUST IDENTIFY SO CLOSELY WITH IT. IT BRINGS ME COMFORT. IT BRINGS ME JOY. AND WHEN I'M DOWN, IT PICKS ME UP.
YOU JUST DESCRIBED HOW I FEEL WHEN I WATCH 'THE BREAKFAST CLUB.'
10/28
WHY ARE YOU STANDING?
DON'T YOU FORGET ABOUT STEPHAN!

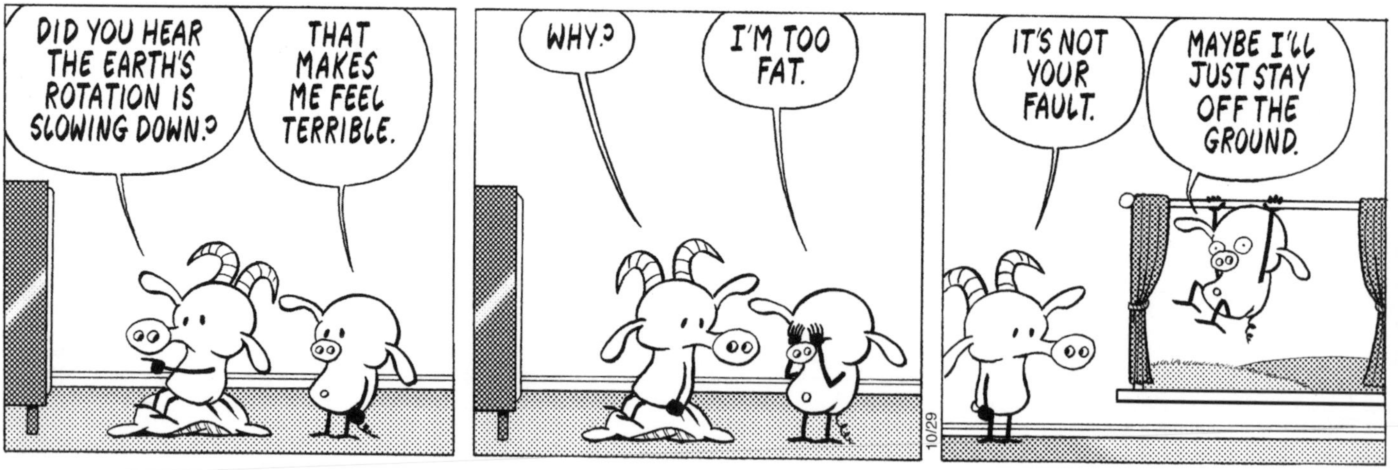
DID YOU HEAR THE EARTH'S ROTATION IS SLOWING DOWN?
THAT MAKES ME FEEL TERRIBLE.
WHY?
I'M TOO FAT.
10/29
IT'S NOT YOUR FAULT.
MAYBE I'LL JUST STAY OFF THE GROUND.

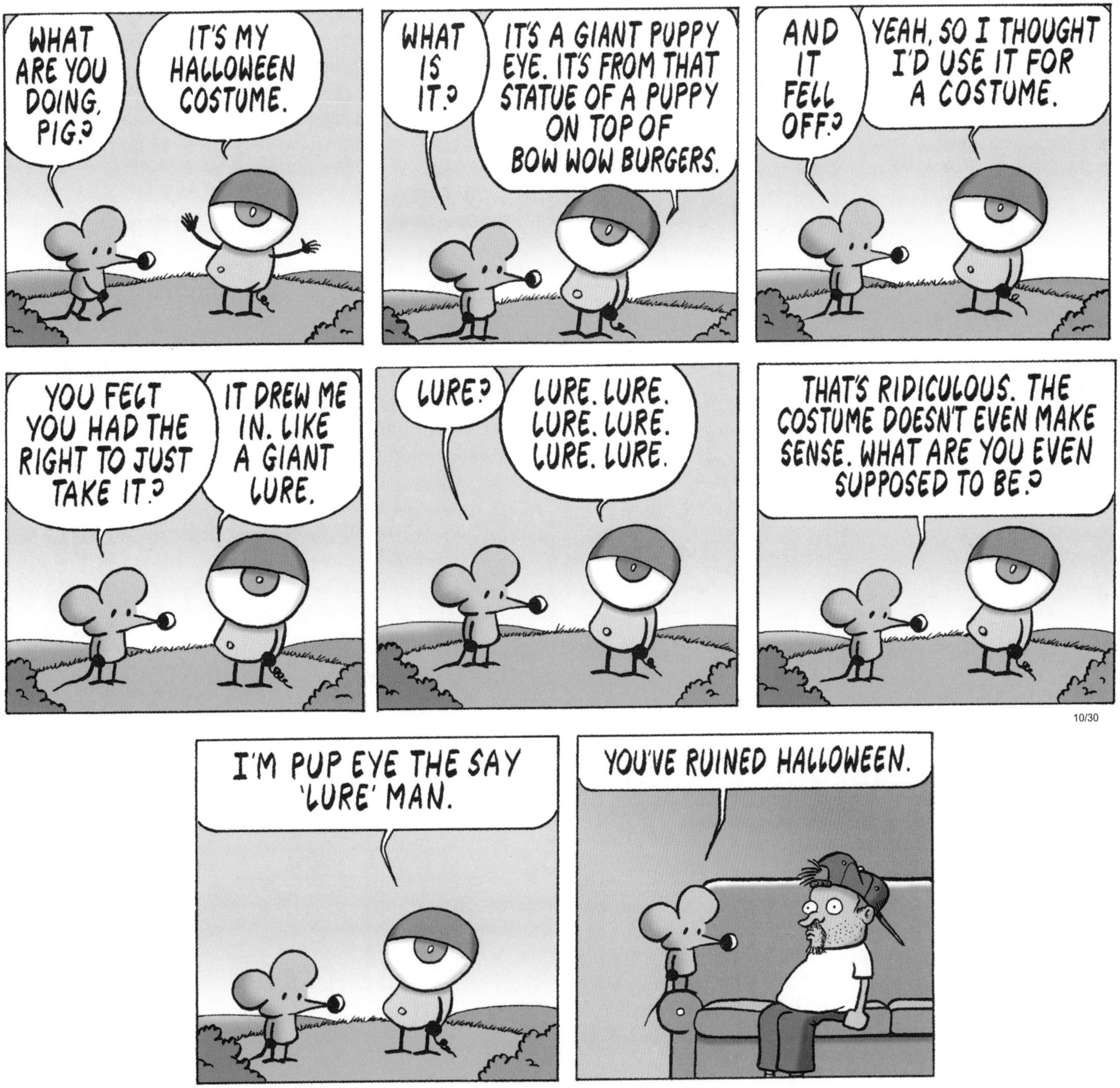
WHAT ARE YOU DOING, PIG?
IT'S MY HALLOWEEN COSTUME.
WHAT IS IT?
IT'S A GIANT PUPPY EYE. IT'S FROM THAT STATUE OF A PUPPY ON TOP OF BOW WOW BURGERS.
AND IT FELL OFF?
YEAH, SO I THOUGHT I'D USE IT FOR A COSTUME.
YOU FELT YOU HAD THE RIGHT TO JUST TAKE IT?
IT DREW ME IN. LIKE A GIANT LURE.
LURE?
LURE. LURE. LURE. LURE. LURE. LURE.
THAT'S RIDICULOUS. THE COSTUME DOESN'T EVEN MAKE SENSE. WHAT ARE YOU EVEN SUPPOSED TO BE?
10/30
I'M PUP EYE THE SAY 'LURE' MAN.
YOU'VE RUINED HALLOWEEN.

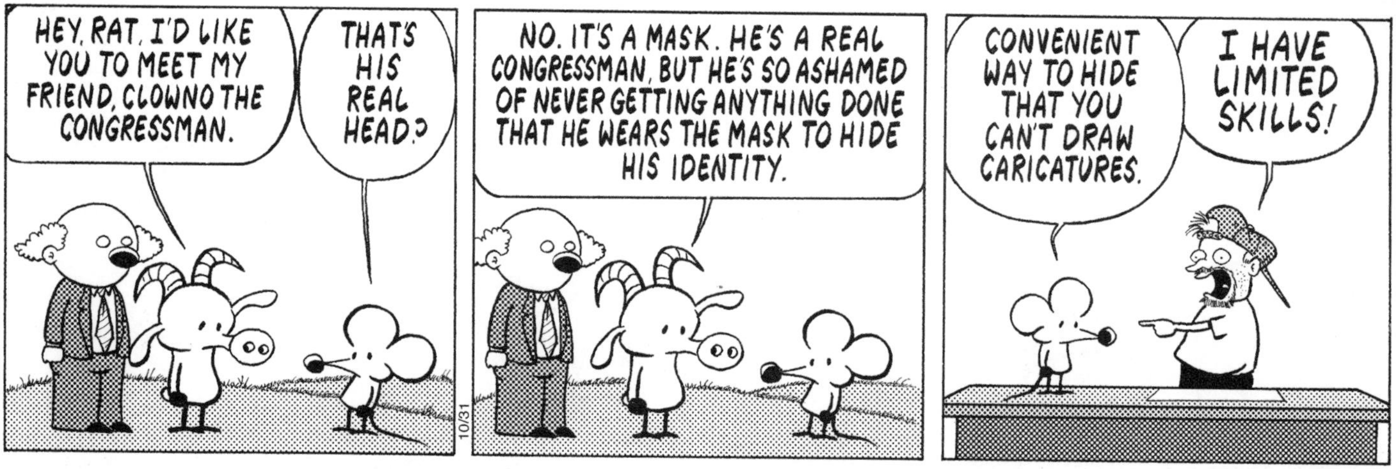
HEY, RAT. I'D LIKE YOU TO MEET MY FRIEND, CLOWNO THE CONGRESSMAN.
THAT'S HIS REAL HEAD?
NO. IT'S A MASK. HE'S A REAL CONGRESSMAN, BUT HE'S SO ASHAMED OF NEVER GETTING ANYTHING DONE THAT HE WEARS THE MASK TO HIDE HIS IDENTITY.
CONVENIENT WAY TO HIDE THAT YOU CAN'T DRAW CARICATURES.
I HAVE LIMITED SKILLS!
10/31

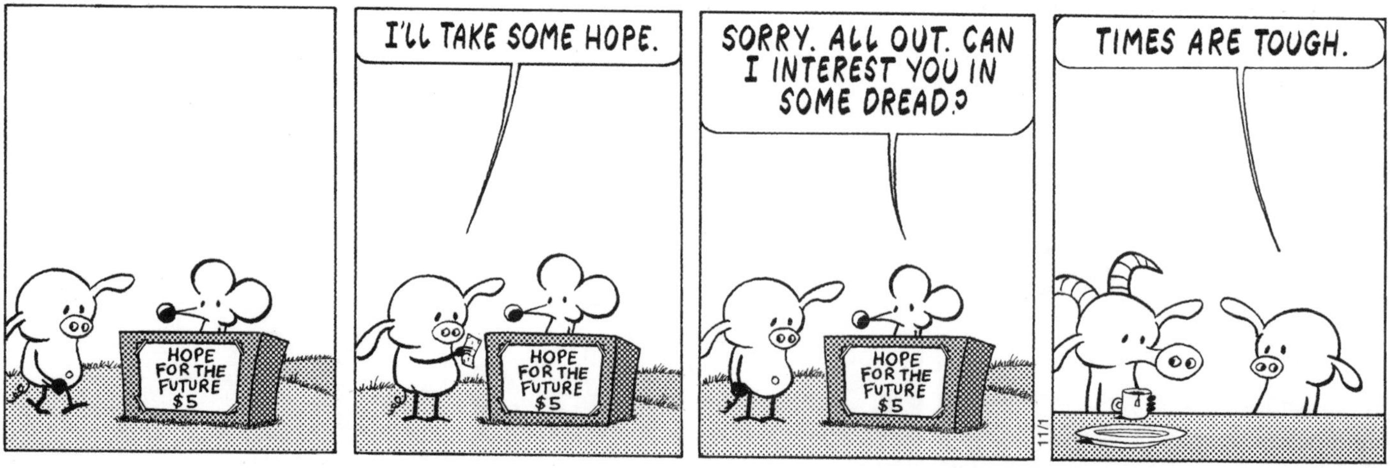
HOPE FOR THE FUTURE $5
I'LL TAKE SOME HOPE.
SORRY. ALL OUT. CAN I INTEREST YOU IN SOME DREAD?
TIMES ARE TOUGH.
11/1

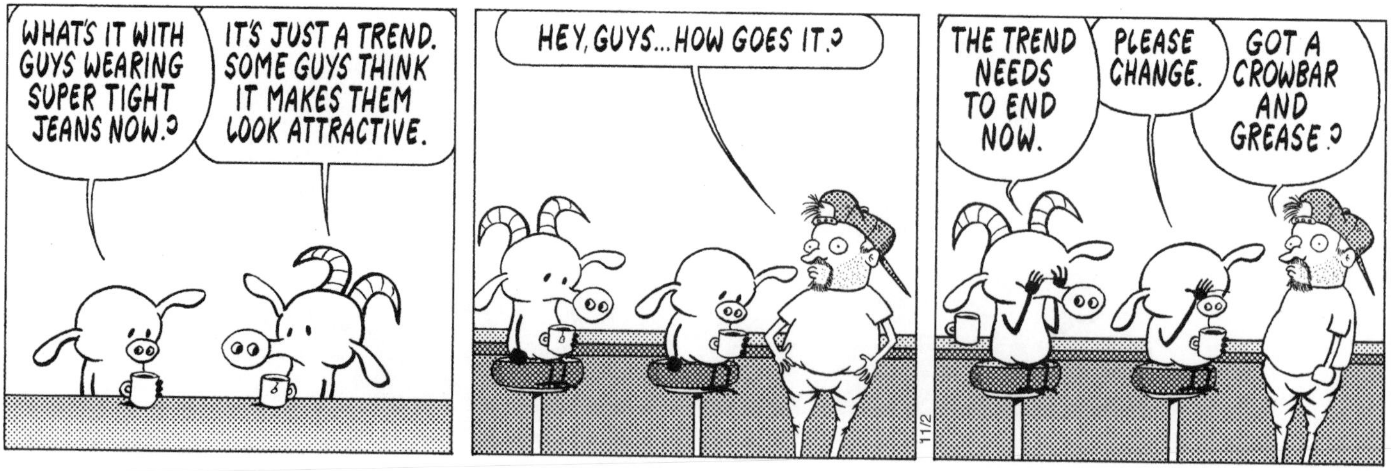
WHAT'S IT WITH GUYS WEARING SUPER TIGHT JEANS NOW?
IT'S JUST A TREND. SOME GUYS THINK IT MAKES THEM LOOK ATTRACTIVE.
HEY, GUYS... HOW GOES IT?
THE TREND NEEDS TO END NOW.
PLEASE CHANGE.
GOT A CROWBAR AND GREASE?
11/2

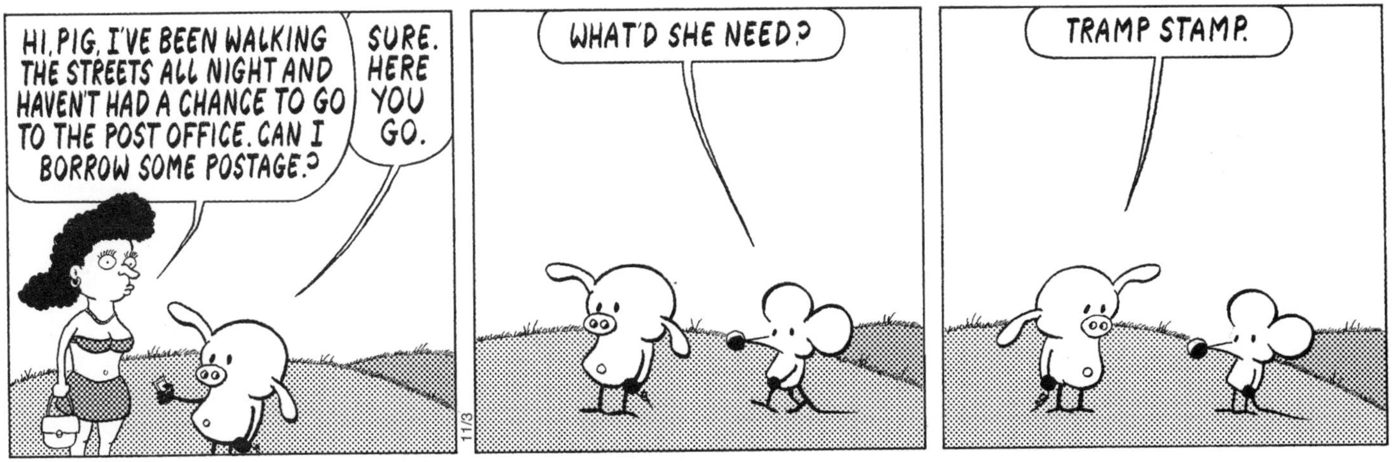
HI, PIG. I'VE BEEN WALKING THE STREETS ALL NIGHT AND HAVEN'T HAD A CHANCE TO GO TO THE POST OFFICE. CAN I BORROW SOME POSTAGE?
SURE. HERE YOU GO.
11/3
WHAT'D SHE NEED?
TRAMP STAMP.

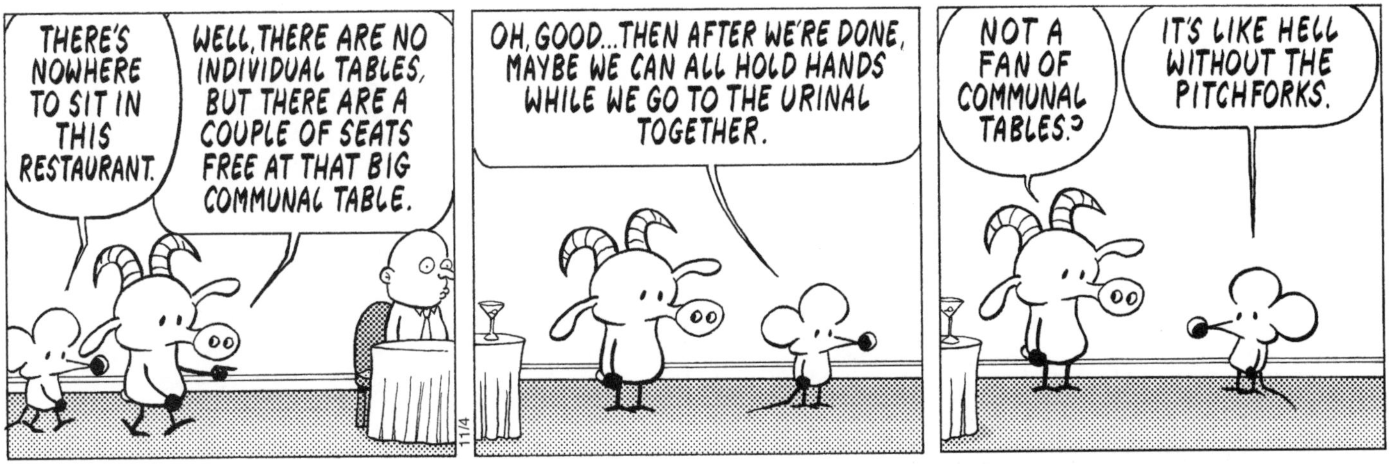
THERE'S NOWHERE TO SIT IN THIS RESTAURANT.
WELL, THERE ARE NO INDIVIDUAL TABLES, BUT THERE ARE A COUPLE OF SEATS FREE AT THAT BIG COMMUNAL TABLE.
11/4
OH, GOOD...THEN AFTER WE'RE DONE, MAYBE WE CAN ALL HOLD HANDS WHILE WE GO TO THE URINAL TOGETHER.
NOT A FAN OF COMMUNAL TABLES?
IT'S LIKE HELL WITHOUT THE PITCHFORKS.

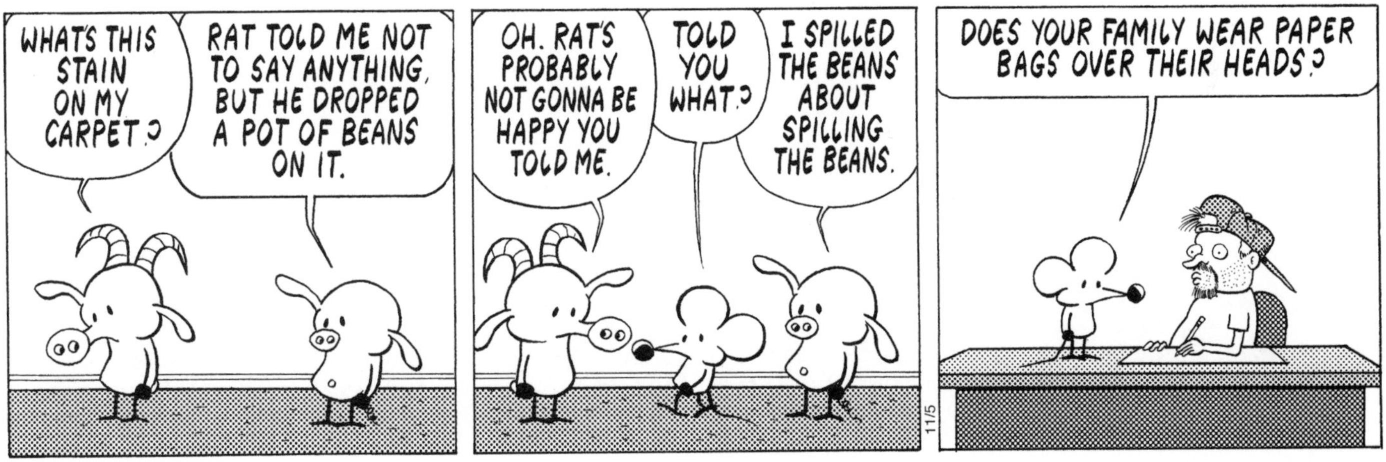
WHAT'S THIS STAIN ON MY CARPET?
RAT TOLD ME NOT TO SAY ANYTHING, BUT HE DROPPED A POT OF BEANS ON IT.
OH. RAT'S PROBABLY NOT GONNA BE HAPPY YOU TOLD ME.
TOLD YOU WHAT?
I SPILLED THE BEANS ABOUT SPILLING THE BEANS.
11/5
DOES YOUR FAMILY WEAR PAPER BAGS OVER THEIR HEADS?

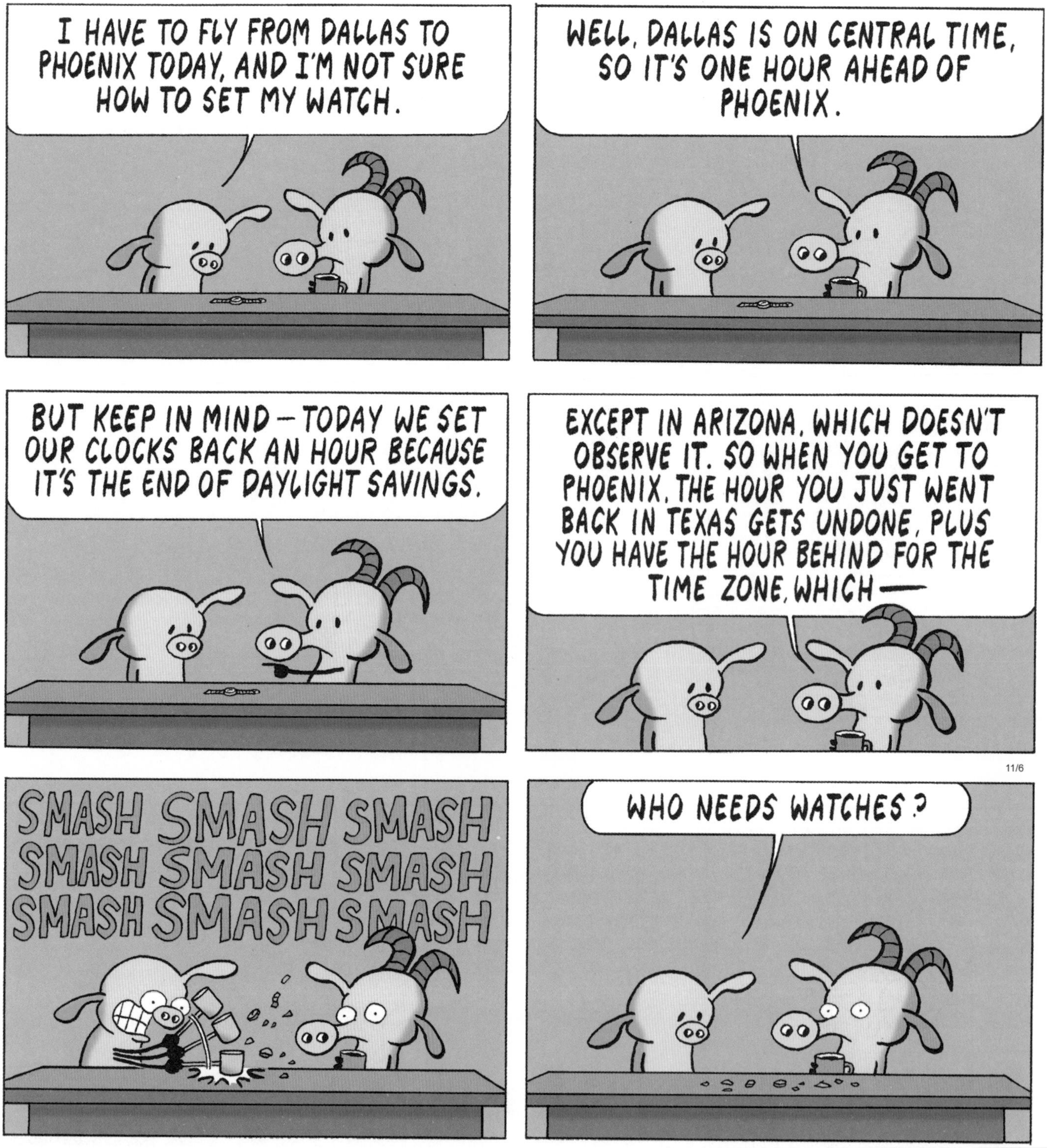
I HAVE TO FLY FROM DALLAS TO PHOENIX TODAY, AND I'M NOT SURE HOW TO SET MY WATCH.
WELL, DALLAS IS ON CENTRAL TIME, SO IT'S ONE HOUR AHEAD OF PHOENIX.
BUT KEEP IN MIND — TODAY WE SET OUR CLOCKS BACK AN HOUR BECAUSE IT'S THE END OF DAYLIGHT SAVINGS.
EXCEPT IN ARIZONA, WHICH DOESN'T OBSERVE IT. SO WHEN YOU GET TO PHOENIX, THE HOUR YOU JUST WENT BACK IN TEXAS GETS UNDONE, PLUS YOU HAVE THE HOUR BEHIND FOR THE TIME ZONE, WHICH —
11/6
SMASH SMASH SMASH SMASH SMASH SMASH SMASH SMASH SMASH
WHO NEEDS WATCHES?

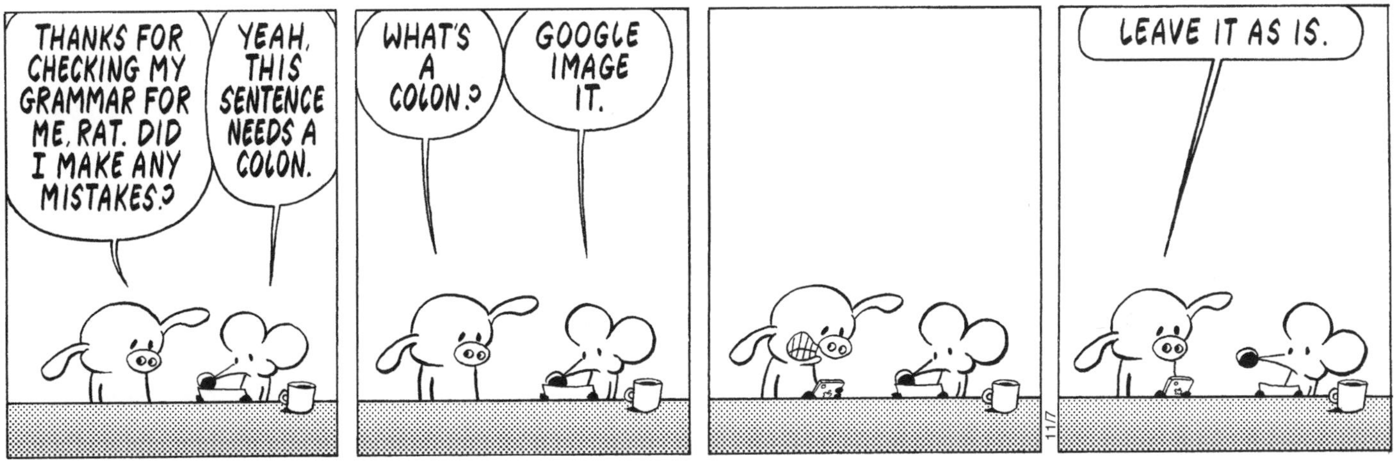
THANKS FOR CHECKING MY GRAMMAR FOR ME, RAT. DID I MAKE ANY MISTAKES?
YEAH, THIS SENTENCE NEEDS A COLON.
WHAT'S A COLON?
GOOGLE IMAGE IT.
LEAVE IT AS IS.
11/7

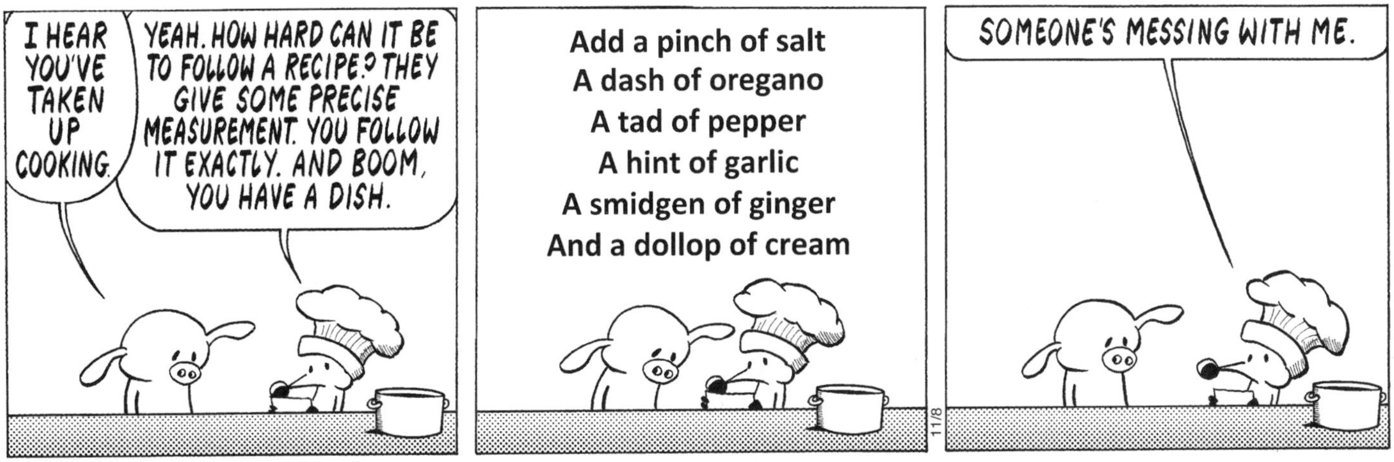
I HEAR YOU'VE TAKEN UP COOKING.
YEAH. HOW HARD CAN IT BE TO FOLLOW A RECIPE? THEY GIVE SOME PRECISE MEASUREMENT. YOU FOLLOW IT EXACTLY. AND BOOM, YOU HAVE A DISH.
Add a pinch of salt
A dash of oregano
A tad of pepper
A hint of garlic
A smidgen of ginger
And a dollop of cream
SOMEONE'S MESSING WITH ME.
11/8

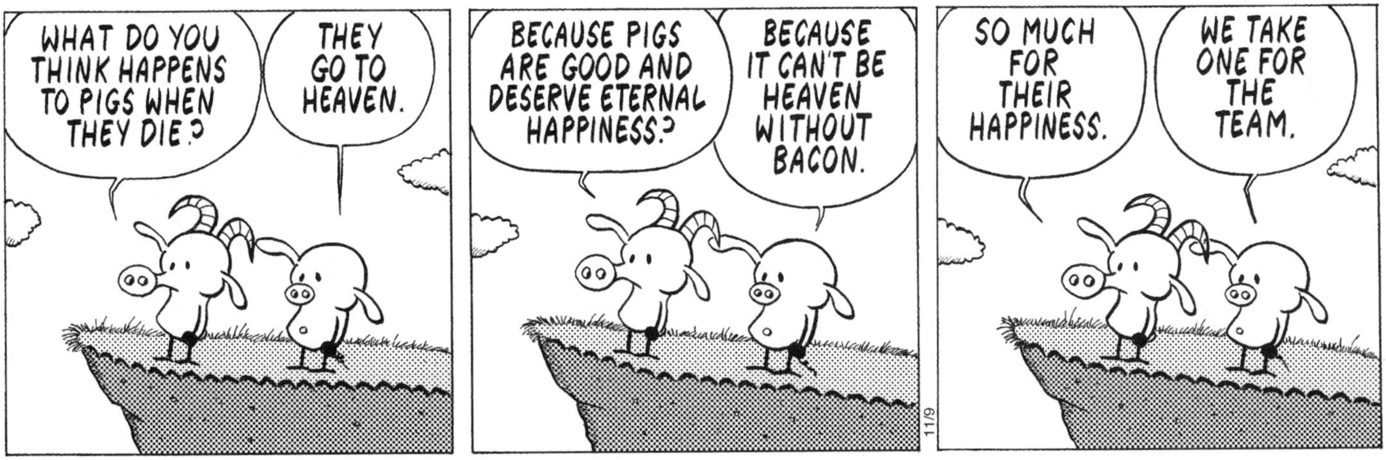
WHAT DO YOU THINK HAPPENS TO PIGS WHEN THEY DIE?
THEY GO TO HEAVEN.
BECAUSE PIGS ARE GOOD AND DESERVE ETERNAL HAPPINESS?
BECAUSE IT CAN'T BE HEAVEN WITHOUT BACON.
SO MUCH FOR THEIR HAPPINESS.
WE TAKE ONE FOR THE TEAM.
11/9

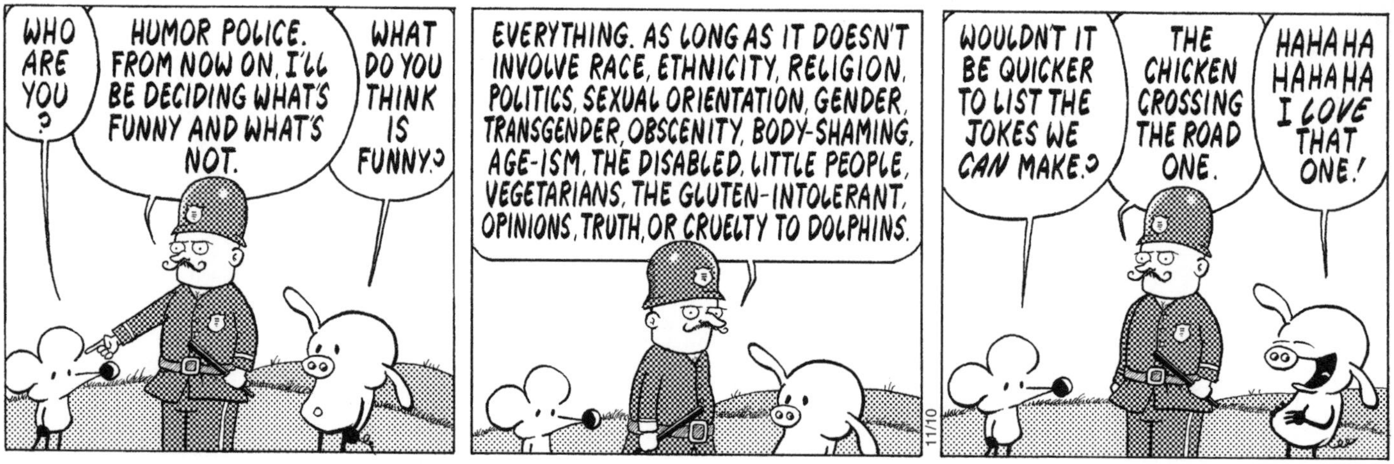
WHO ARE YOU?
HUMOR POLICE. FROM NOW ON, I'LL BE DECIDING WHAT'S FUNNY AND WHAT'S NOT.
WHAT DO YOU THINK IS FUNNY?
EVERYTHING. AS LONG AS IT DOESN'T INVOLVE RACE, ETHNICITY, RELIGION, POLITICS, SEXUAL ORIENTATION, GENDER, TRANSGENDER, OBSCENITY, BODY-SHAMING, AGE-ISM, THE DISABLED, LITTLE PEOPLE, VEGETARIANS, THE GLUTEN-INTOLERANT, OPINIONS, TRUTH, OR CRUELTY TO DOLPHINS.
WOULDN'T IT BE QUICKER TO LIST THE JOKES WE *CAN* MAKE?
THE CHICKEN CROSSING THE ROAD ONE.
HAHAHA HAHAHA I *LOVE* THAT ONE!
11/10

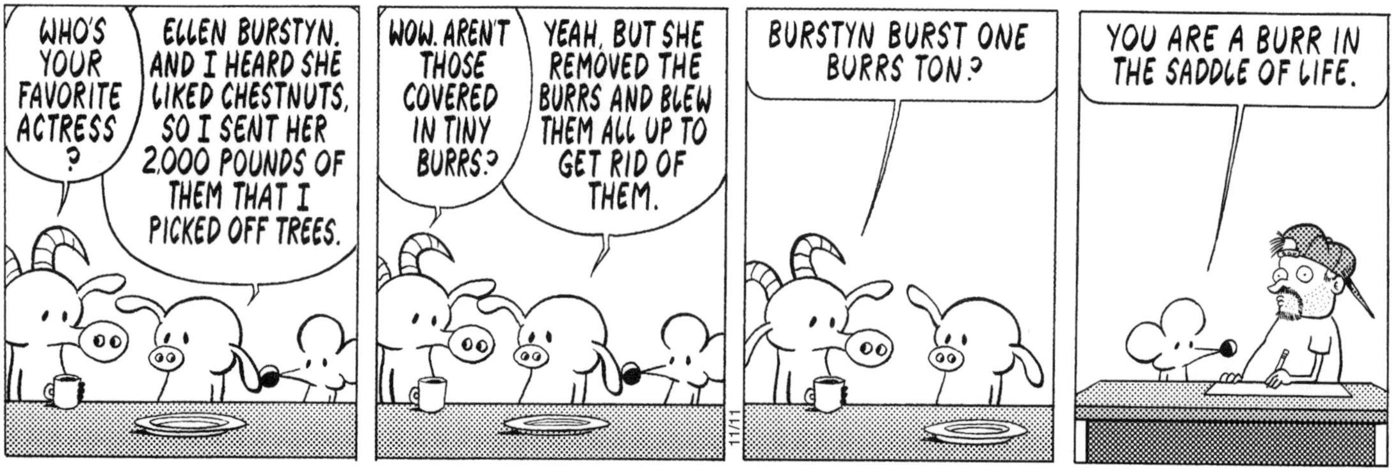
WHO'S YOUR FAVORITE ACTRESS?
ELLEN BURSTYN. AND I HEARD SHE LIKED CHESTNUTS, SO I SENT HER 2,000 POUNDS OF THEM THAT I PICKED OFF TREES.
WOW. AREN'T THOSE COVERED IN TINY BURRS?
YEAH, BUT SHE REMOVED THE BURRS AND BLEW THEM ALL UP TO GET RID OF THEM.
BURSTYN BURST ONE BURRS TON?
11/11
YOU ARE A BURR IN THE SADDLE OF LIFE.

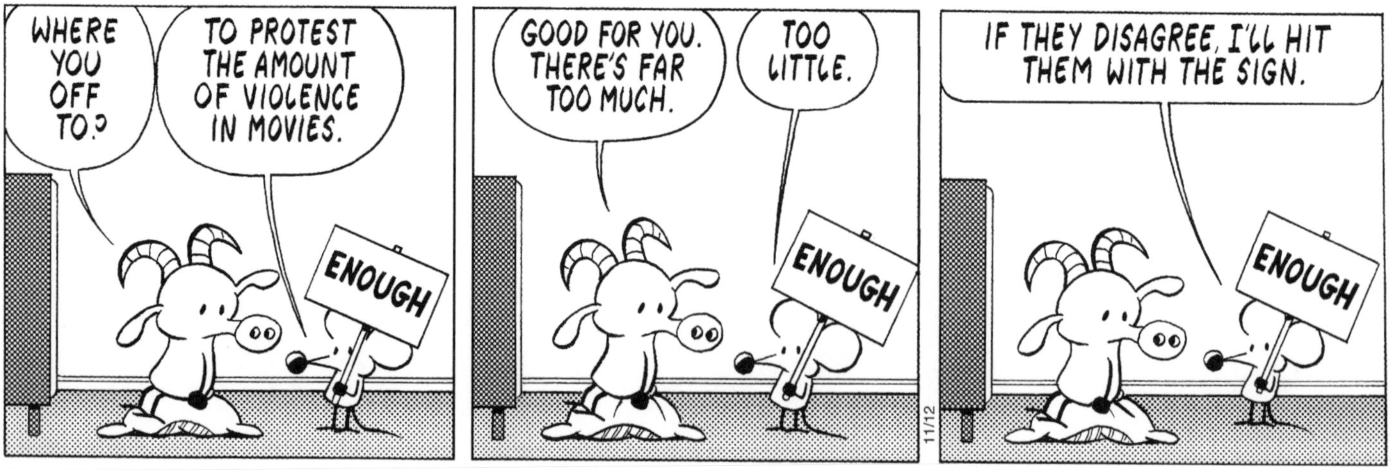
WHERE YOU OFF TO?
TO PROTEST THE AMOUNT OF VIOLENCE IN MOVIES.
ENOUGH
GOOD FOR YOU. THERE'S FAR TOO MUCH.
TOO LITTLE.
ENOUGH
11/12
IF THEY DISAGREE, I'LL HIT THEM WITH THE SIGN.
ENOUGH

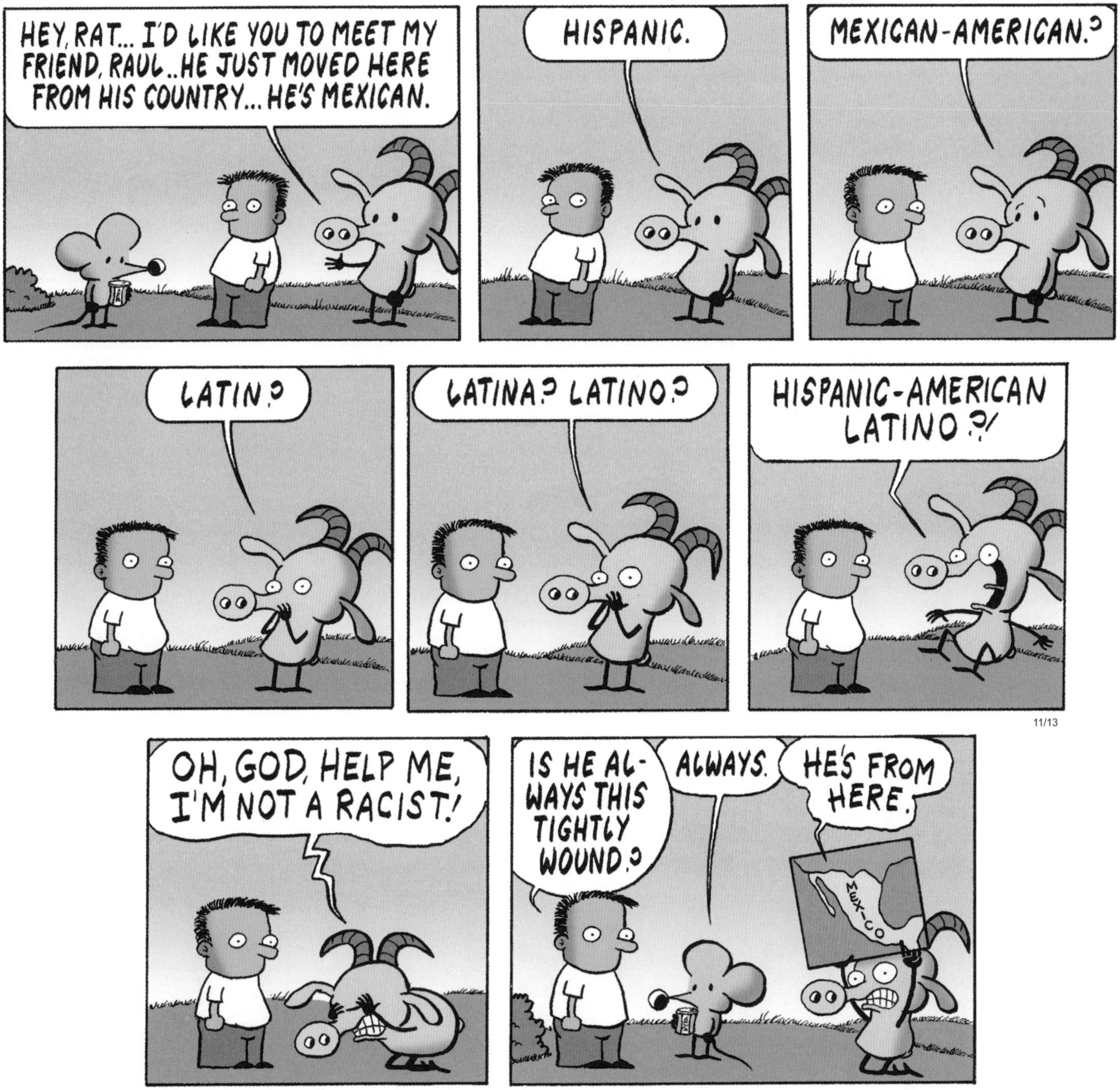
HEY, RAT... I'D LIKE YOU TO MEET MY FRIEND, RAUL.. HE JUST MOVED HERE FROM HIS COUNTRY... HE'S MEXICAN.
HISPANIC.
MEXICAN-AMERICAN.?
LATIN.?
LATINA.? LATINO.?
HISPANIC-AMERICAN LATINO.?!
11/13
OH, GOD, HELP ME, I'M NOT A RACIST!
IS HE ALWAYS THIS TIGHTLY WOUND.?
ALWAYS.
HE'S FROM HERE.
MEXICO

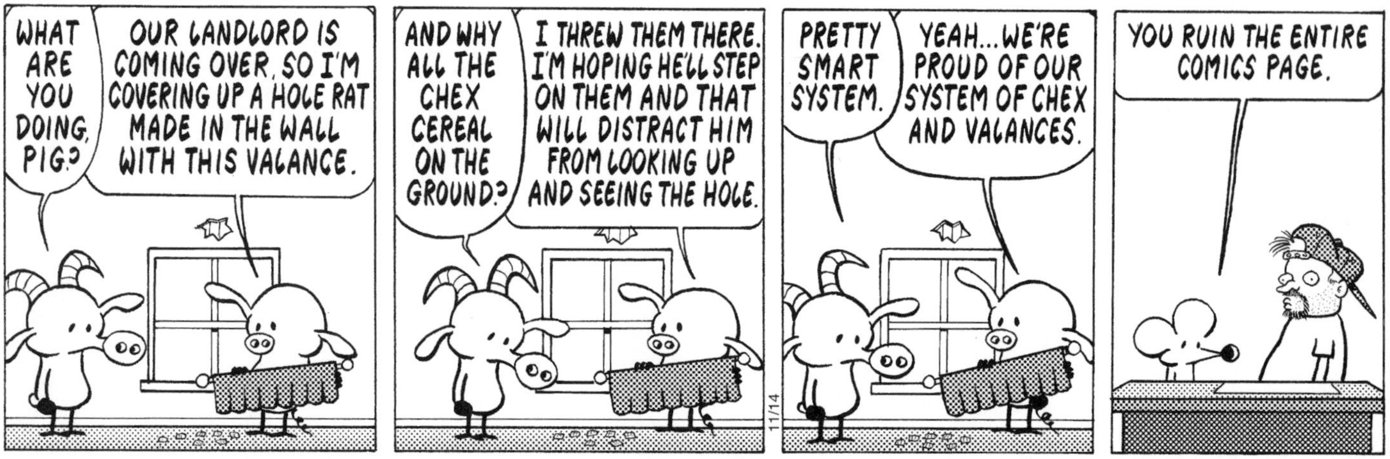
WHAT ARE YOU DOING, PIG?
OUR LANDLORD IS COMING OVER, SO I'M COVERING UP A HOLE RAT MADE IN THE WALL WITH THIS VALANCE.
AND WHY ALL THE CHEX CEREAL ON THE GROUND?
I THREW THEM THERE. I'M HOPING HE'LL STEP ON THEM AND THAT WILL DISTRACT HIM FROM LOOKING UP AND SEEING THE HOLE.
11/14
PRETTY SMART SYSTEM.
YEAH... WE'RE PROUD OF OUR SYSTEM OF CHEX AND VALANCES.
YOU RUIN THE ENTIRE COMICS PAGE.

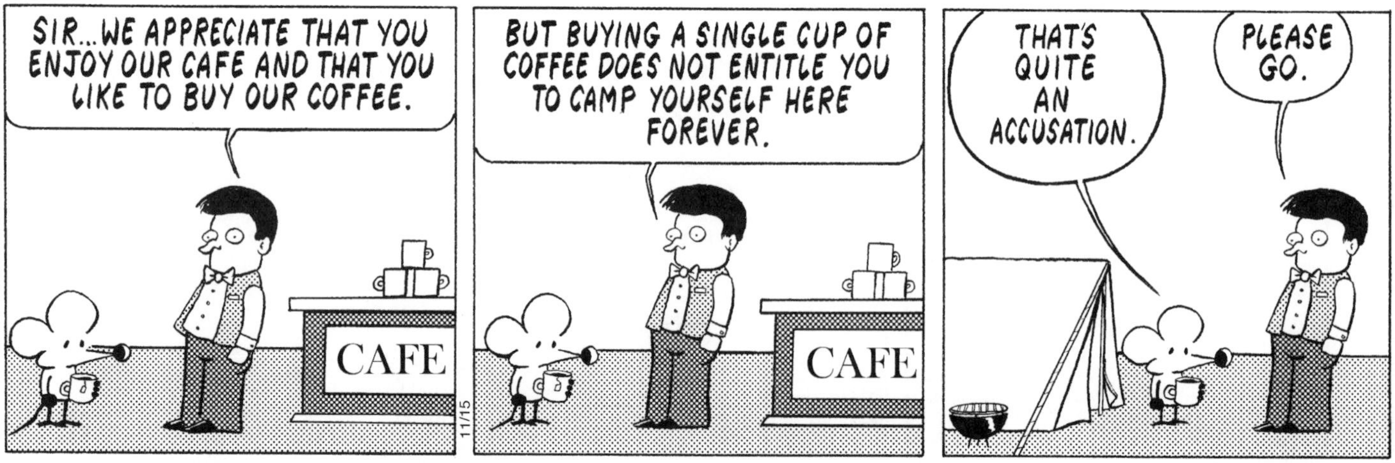
SIR... WE APPRECIATE THAT YOU ENJOY OUR CAFE AND THAT YOU LIKE TO BUY OUR COFFEE.
CAFE
11/15
BUT BUYING A SINGLE CUP OF COFFEE DOES NOT ENTITLE YOU TO CAMP YOURSELF HERE FOREVER.
CAFE
THAT'S QUITE AN ACCUSATION.
PLEASE GO.

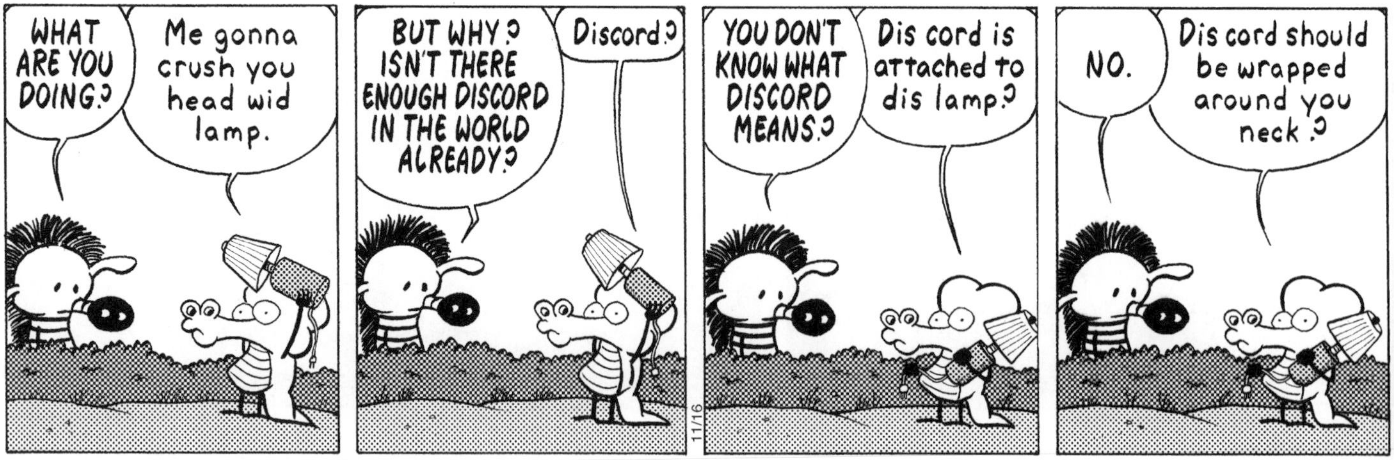
WHAT ARE YOU DOING?
Me gonna crush you head wid lamp.
BUT WHY? ISN'T THERE ENOUGH DISCORD IN THE WORLD ALREADY?
Discord?
11/16
YOU DON'T KNOW WHAT DISCORD MEANS?
Dis cord is attached to dis lamp?
NO.
Dis cord should be wrapped around you neck?

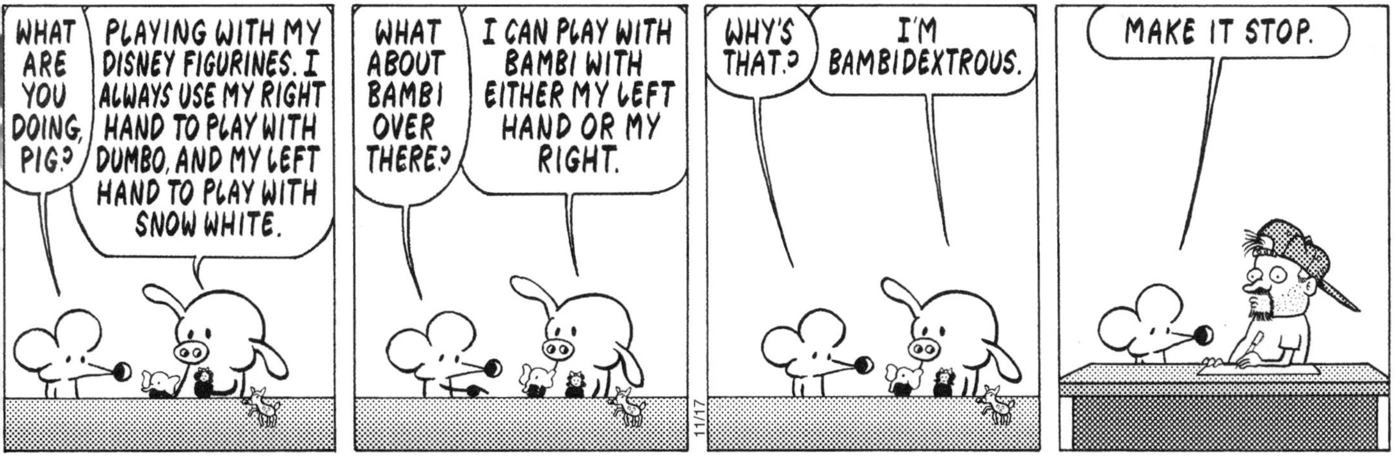
WHAT ARE YOU DOING, PIG?
PLAYING WITH MY DISNEY FIGURINES. I ALWAYS USE MY RIGHT HAND TO PLAY WITH DUMBO, AND MY LEFT HAND TO PLAY WITH SNOW WHITE.
WHAT ABOUT BAMBI OVER THERE?
I CAN PLAY WITH BAMBI WITH EITHER MY LEFT HAND OR MY RIGHT.
WHY'S THAT?
I'M BAMBIDEXTROUS.
MAKE IT STOP.
11/17

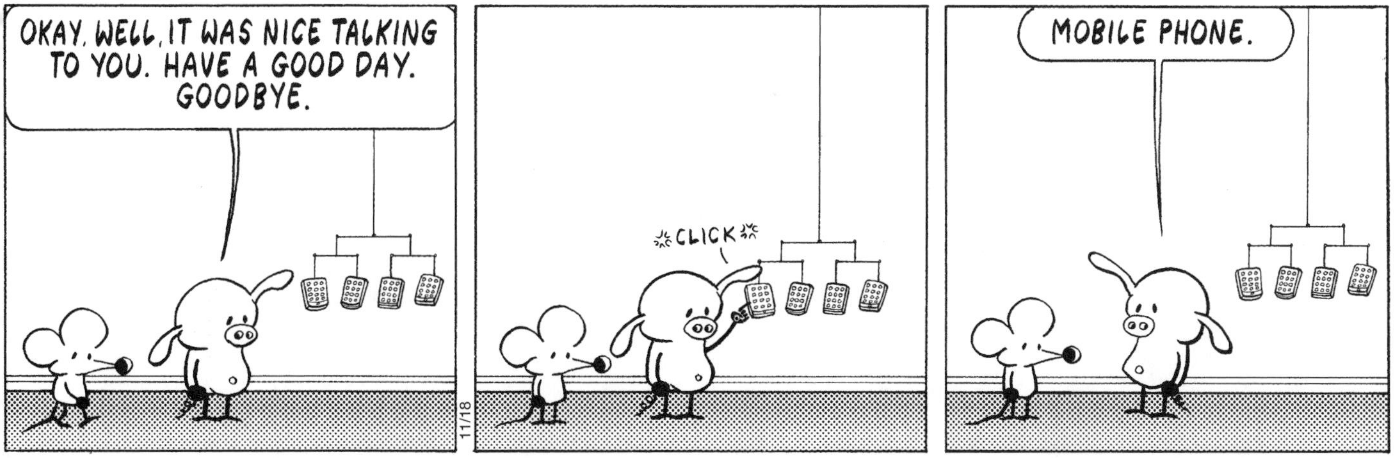
OKAY, WELL, IT WAS NICE TALKING TO YOU. HAVE A GOOD DAY. GOODBYE.
CLICK
MOBILE PHONE.
11/18

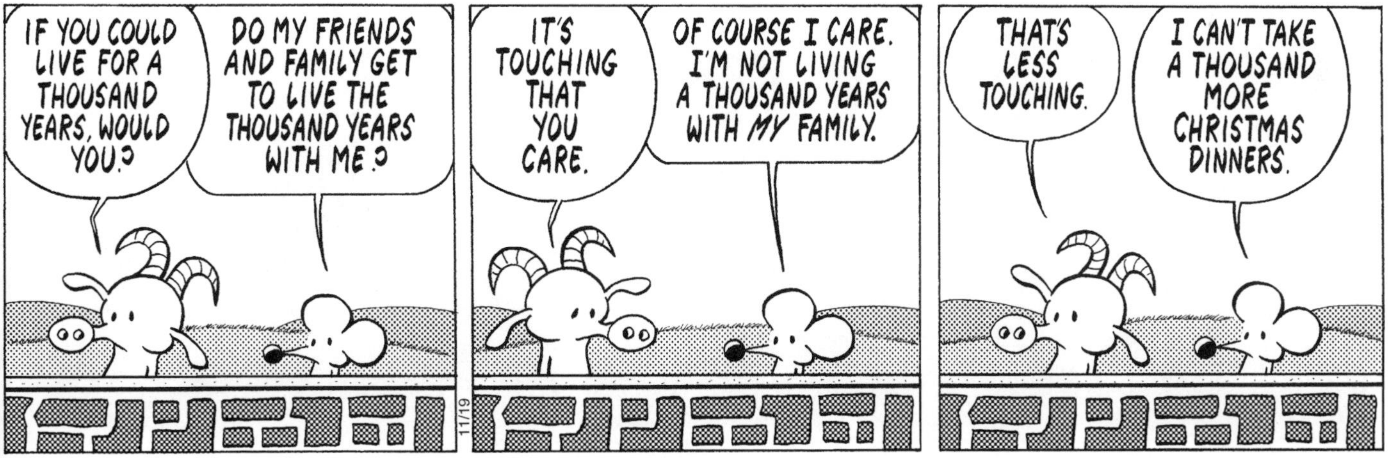
IF YOU COULD LIVE FOR A THOUSAND YEARS, WOULD YOU?
DO MY FRIENDS AND FAMILY GET TO LIVE THE THOUSAND YEARS WITH ME?
IT'S TOUCHING THAT YOU CARE.
OF COURSE I CARE. I'M NOT LIVING A THOUSAND YEARS WITH MY FAMILY.
THAT'S LESS TOUCHING.
I CAN'T TAKE A THOUSAND MORE CHRISTMAS DINNERS.
11/19

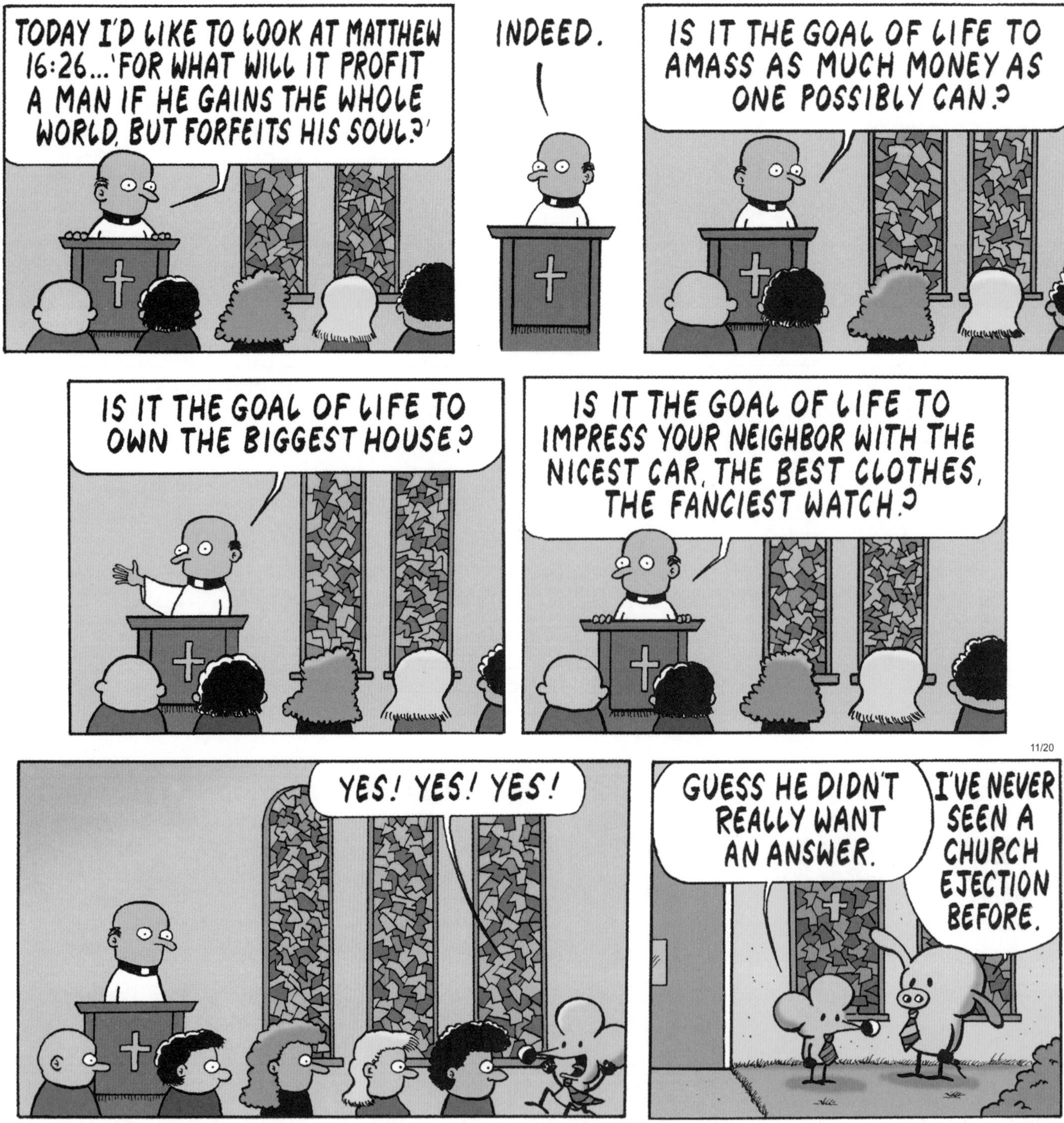
TODAY I'D LIKE TO LOOK AT MATTHEW 16:26...'FOR WHAT WILL IT PROFIT A MAN IF HE GAINS THE WHOLE WORLD, BUT FORFEITS HIS SOUL?'
INDEED.
IS IT THE GOAL OF LIFE TO AMASS AS MUCH MONEY AS ONE POSSIBLY CAN?
IS IT THE GOAL OF LIFE TO OWN THE BIGGEST HOUSE?
IS IT THE GOAL OF LIFE TO IMPRESS YOUR NEIGHBOR WITH THE NICEST CAR, THE BEST CLOTHES, THE FANCIEST WATCH?
11/20
YES! YES! YES!
GUESS HE DIDN'T REALLY WANT AN ANSWER.
I'VE NEVER SEEN A CHURCH EJECTION BEFORE.

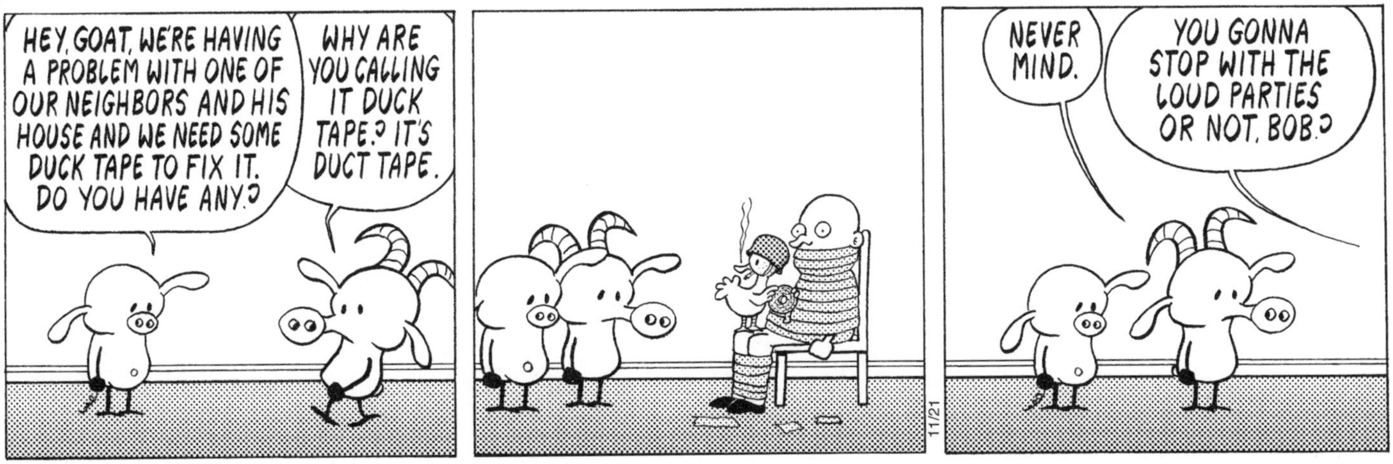
HEY, GOAT, WE'RE HAVING A PROBLEM WITH ONE OF OUR NEIGHBORS AND HIS HOUSE AND WE NEED SOME DUCK TAPE TO FIX IT. DO YOU HAVE ANY?
WHY ARE YOU CALLING IT DUCK TAPE? IT'S DUCT TAPE.
11/21
NEVER MIND.
YOU GONNA STOP WITH THE LOUD PARTIES OR NOT, BOB?

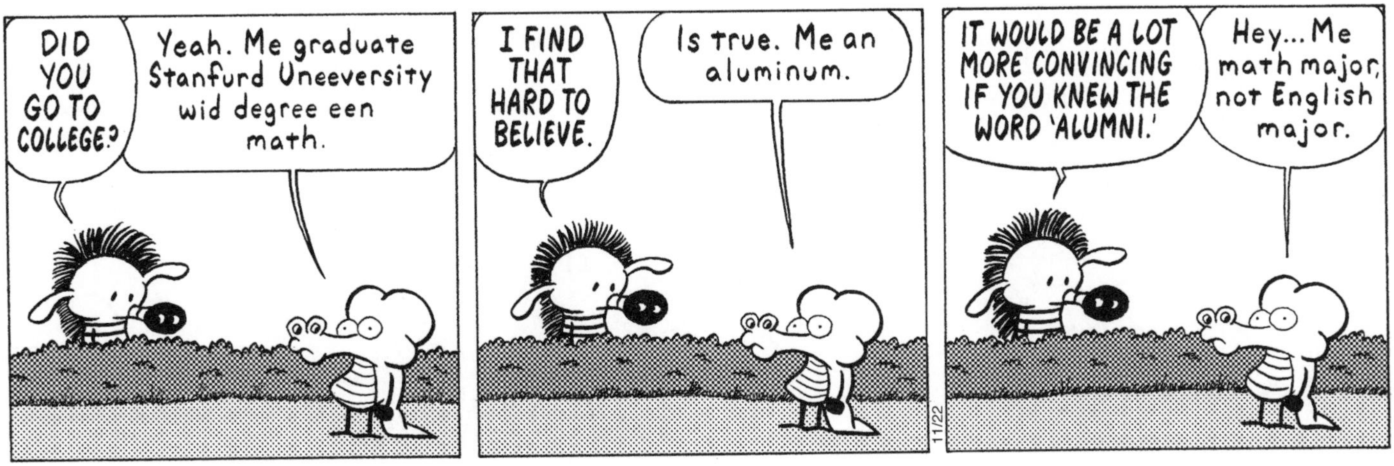
DID YOU GO TO COLLEGE?
Yeah. Me graduate Stanfurd Uneeversity wid degree een math.
I FIND THAT HARD TO BELIEVE.
Is true. Me an aluminum.
11/22
IT WOULD BE A LOT MORE CONVINCING IF YOU KNEW THE WORD 'ALUMNI.'
Hey... Me math major, not English major.

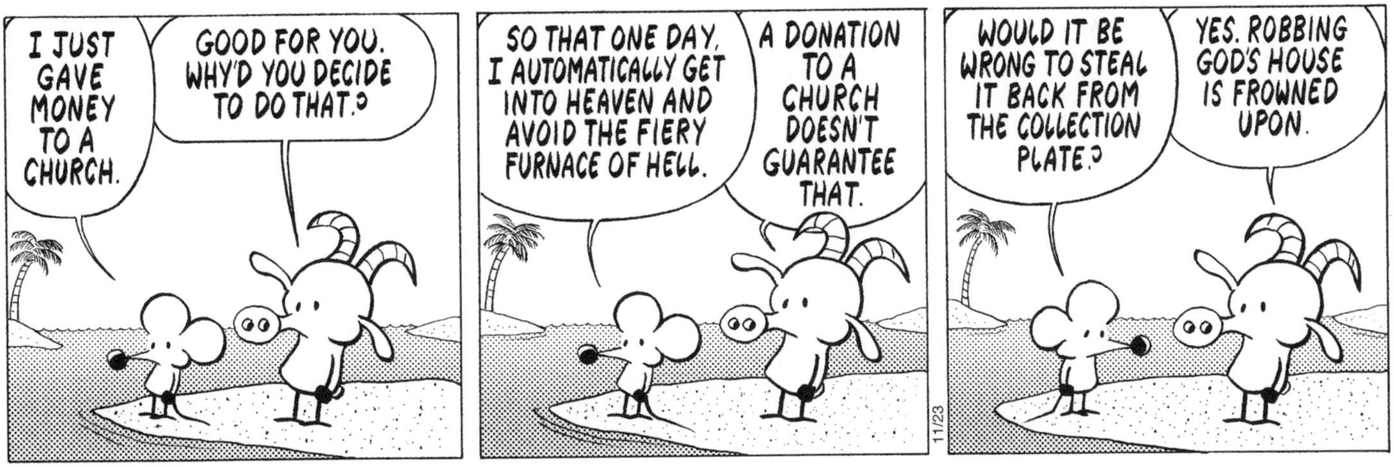
I JUST GAVE MONEY TO A CHURCH.
GOOD FOR YOU. WHY'D YOU DECIDE TO DO THAT?
SO THAT ONE DAY, I AUTOMATICALLY GET INTO HEAVEN AND AVOID THE FIERY FURNACE OF HELL.
A DONATION TO A CHURCH DOESN'T GUARANTEE THAT.
11/23
WOULD IT BE WRONG TO STEAL IT BACK FROM THE COLLECTION PLATE?
YES. ROBBING GOD'S HOUSE IS FROWNED UPON.

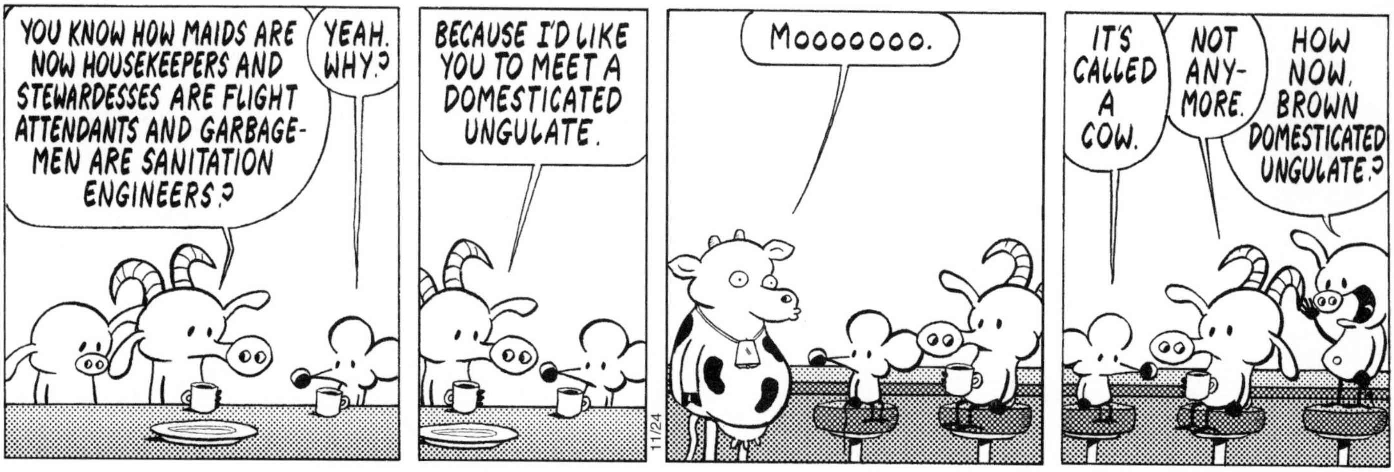
YOU KNOW HOW MAIDS ARE NOW HOUSEKEEPERS AND STEWARDESSES ARE FLIGHT ATTENDANTS AND GARBAGEMEN ARE SANITATION ENGINEERS?
YEAH. WHY?
BECAUSE I'D LIKE YOU TO MEET A DOMESTICATED UNGULATE.
11/24
Mooooooo.
IT'S CALLED A COW.
NOT ANYMORE.
HOW NOW, BROWN DOMESTICATED UNGULATE?

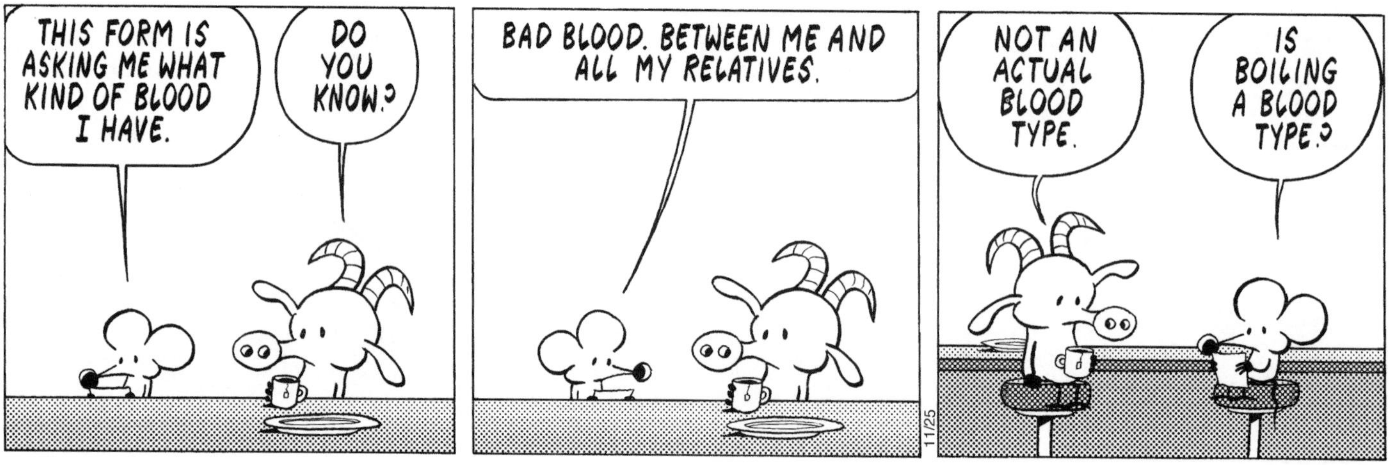
THIS FORM IS ASKING ME WHAT KIND OF BLOOD I HAVE.
DO YOU KNOW?
BAD BLOOD. BETWEEN ME AND ALL MY RELATIVES.
11/25
NOT AN ACTUAL BLOOD TYPE.
IS BOILING A BLOOD TYPE?

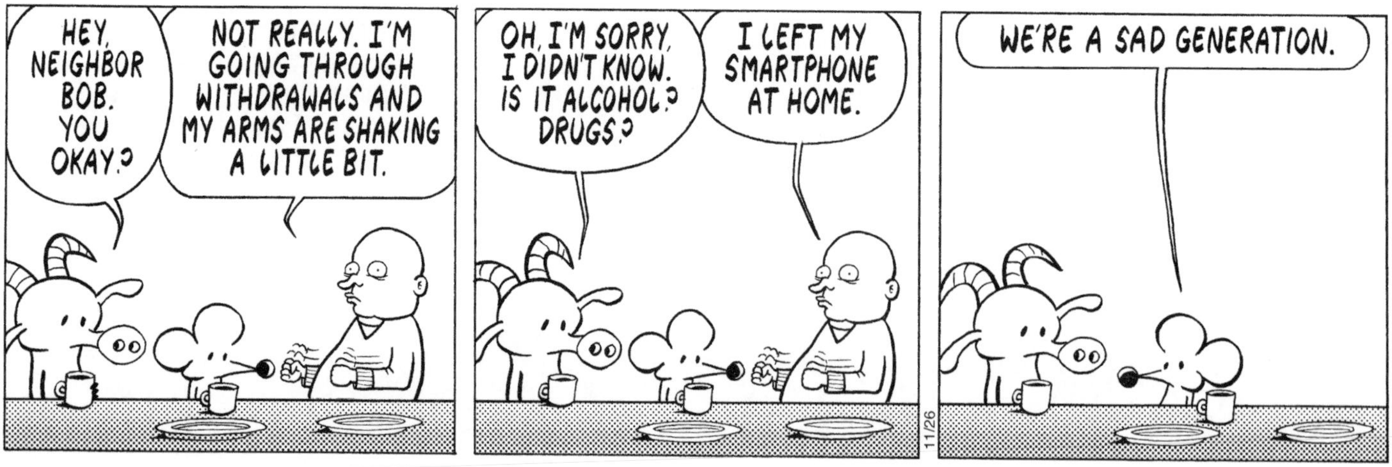
HEY, NEIGHBOR BOB. YOU OKAY?
NOT REALLY. I'M GOING THROUGH WITHDRAWALS AND MY ARMS ARE SHAKING A LITTLE BIT.
OH, I'M SORRY, I DIDN'T KNOW. IS IT ALCOHOL? DRUGS?
I LEFT MY SMARTPHONE AT HOME.
11/26
WE'RE A SAD GENERATION.

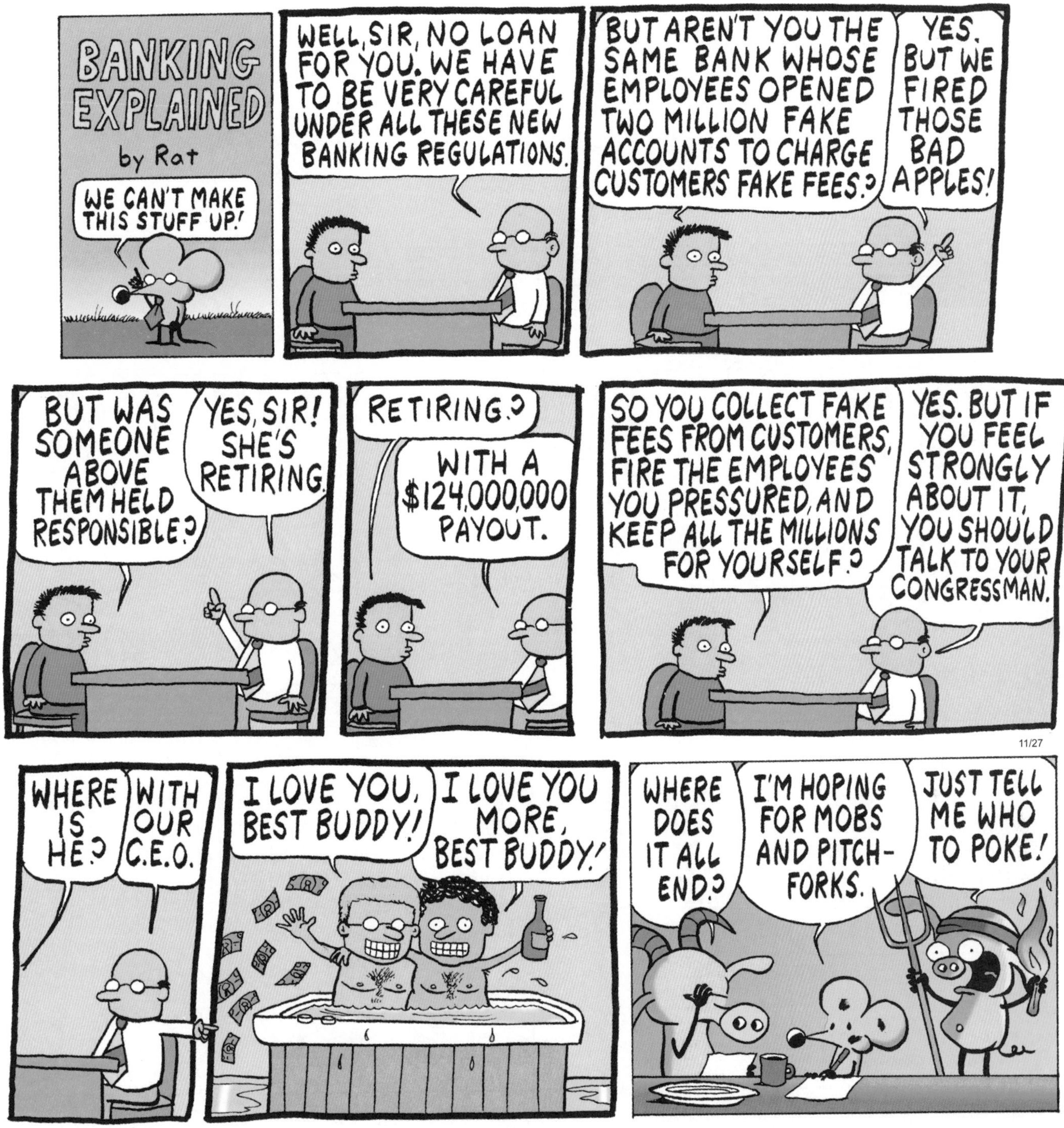
BANKING EXPLAINED
by Rat
WE CAN'T MAKE THIS STUFF UP!
WELL, SIR, NO LOAN FOR YOU. WE HAVE TO BE VERY CAREFUL UNDER ALL THESE NEW BANKING REGULATIONS.
BUT AREN'T YOU THE SAME BANK WHOSE EMPLOYEES OPENED TWO MILLION FAKE ACCOUNTS TO CHARGE CUSTOMERS FAKE FEES?
YES. BUT WE FIRED THOSE BAD APPLES!
BUT WAS SOMEONE ABOVE THEM HELD RESPONSIBLE?
YES, SIR! SHE'S RETIRING.
RETIRING?
WITH A $124,000,000 PAYOUT.
SO YOU COLLECT FAKE FEES FROM CUSTOMERS, FIRE THE EMPLOYEES YOU PRESSURED, AND KEEP ALL THE MILLIONS FOR YOURSELF?
YES. BUT IF YOU FEEL STRONGLY ABOUT IT, YOU SHOULD TALK TO YOUR CONGRESSMAN.
11/27
WHERE IS HE?
WITH OUR C.E.O.
I LOVE YOU, BEST BUDDY!
I LOVE YOU MORE, BEST BUDDY!
WHERE DOES IT ALL END?
I'M HOPING FOR MOBS AND PITCH-FORKS.
JUST TELL ME WHO TO POKE!

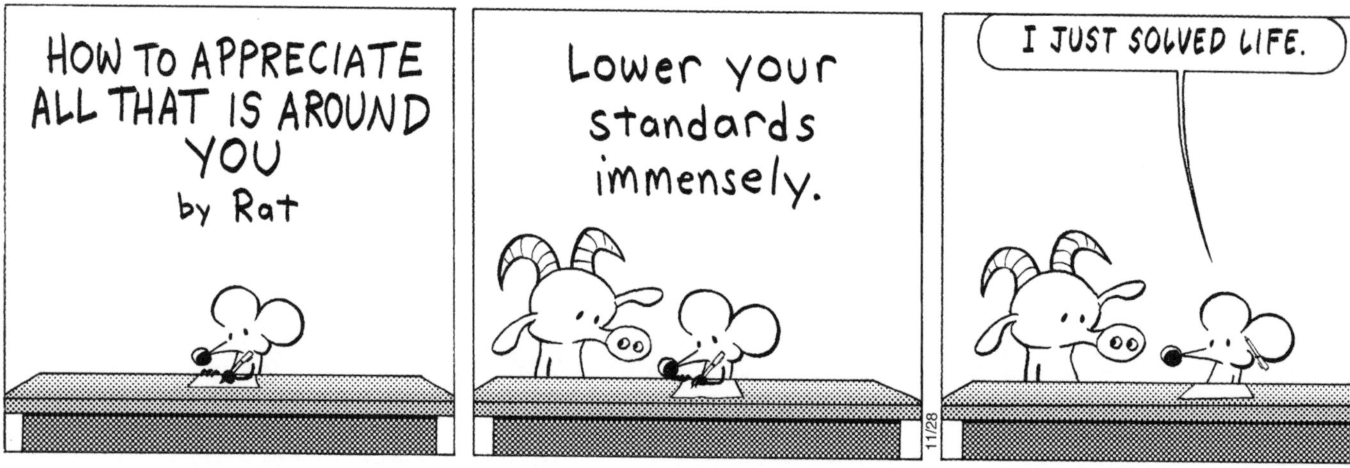
HOW TO APPRECIATE ALL THAT IS AROUND YOU by Rat
Lower your standards immensely.
11/28
I JUST SOLVED LIFE.

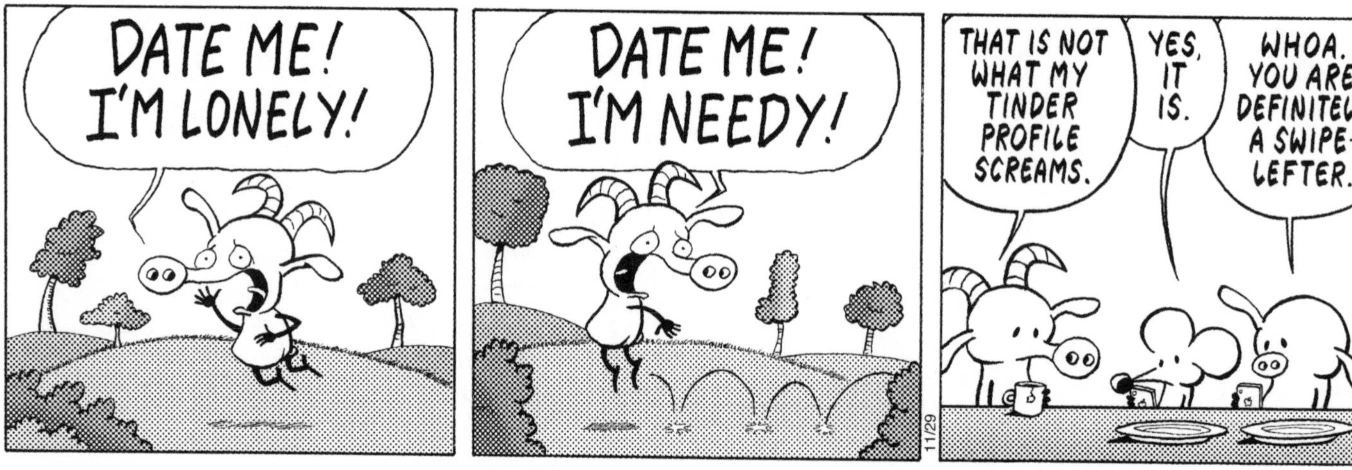
DATE ME! I'M LONELY!
DATE ME! I'M NEEDY!
11/29
THAT IS NOT WHAT MY TINDER PROFILE SCREAMS.
YES, IT IS.
WHOA. YOU ARE DEFINITELY A SWIPE-LEFTER.

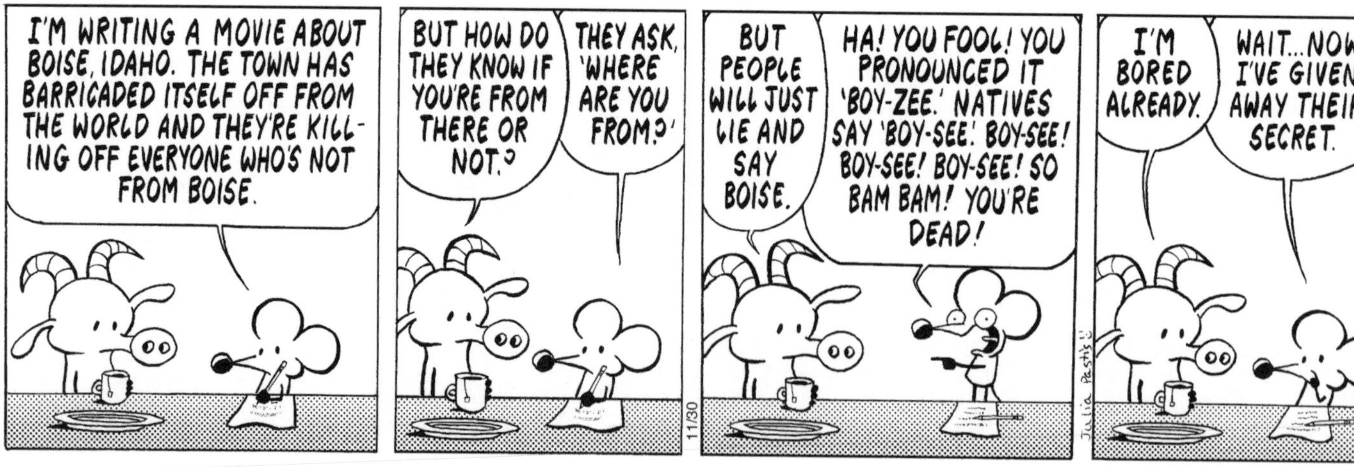
I'M WRITING A MOVIE ABOUT BOISE, IDAHO. THE TOWN HAS BARRICADED ITSELF OFF FROM THE WORLD AND THEY'RE KILLING OFF EVERYONE WHO'S NOT FROM BOISE.
BUT HOW DO THEY KNOW IF YOU'RE FROM THERE OR NOT?
THEY ASK, 'WHERE ARE YOU FROM?'
11/30
BUT PEOPLE WILL JUST LIE AND SAY BOISE.
HA! YOU FOOL! YOU PRONOUNCED IT 'BOY-ZEE.' NATIVES SAY 'BOY-SEE.' BOY-SEE! BOY-SEE! BOY-SEE! SO BAM BAM! YOU'RE DEAD!
I'M BORED ALREADY.
WAIT...NOW I'VE GIVEN AWAY THEIR SECRET.

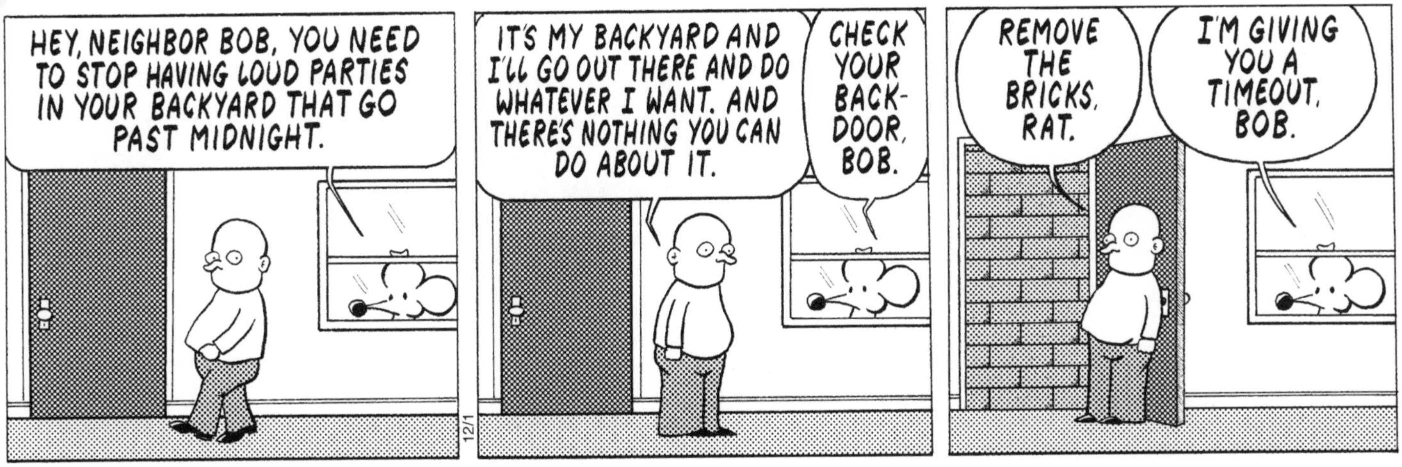
HEY, NEIGHBOR BOB, YOU NEED TO STOP HAVING LOUD PARTIES IN YOUR BACKYARD THAT GO PAST MIDNIGHT.
12/1
IT'S MY BACKYARD AND I'LL GO OUT THERE AND DO WHATEVER I WANT. AND THERE'S NOTHING YOU CAN DO ABOUT IT.
CHECK YOUR BACK-DOOR, BOB.
REMOVE THE BRICKS, RAT.
I'M GIVING YOU A TIMEOUT, BOB.

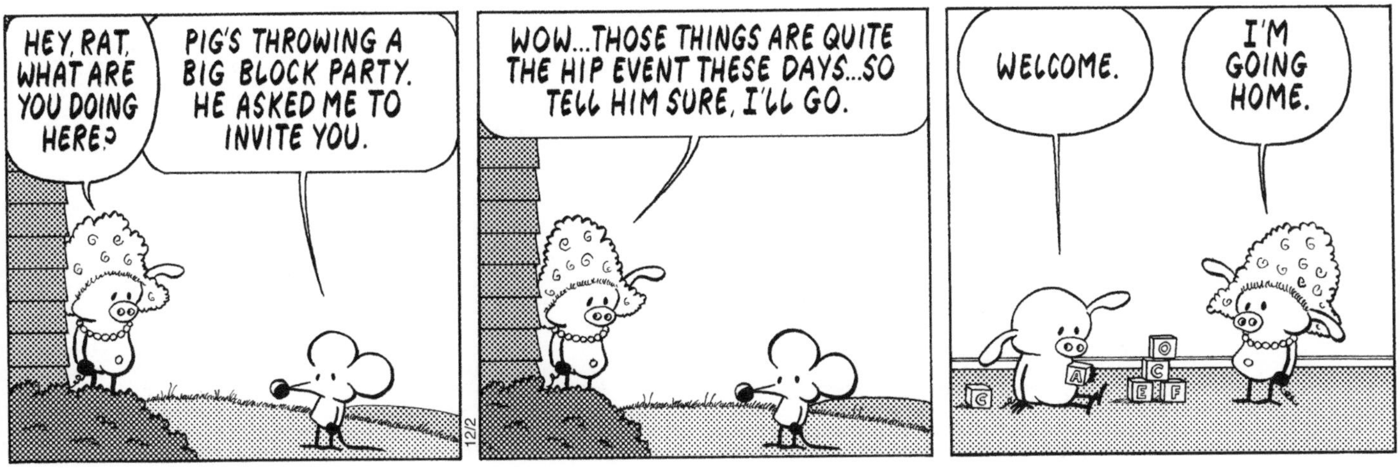
HEY, RAT, WHAT ARE YOU DOING HERE?
PIG'S THROWING A BIG BLOCK PARTY. HE ASKED ME TO INVITE YOU.
12/2
WOW...THOSE THINGS ARE QUITE THE HIP EVENT THESE DAYS...SO TELL HIM SURE, I'LL GO.
WELCOME.
I'M GOING HOME.

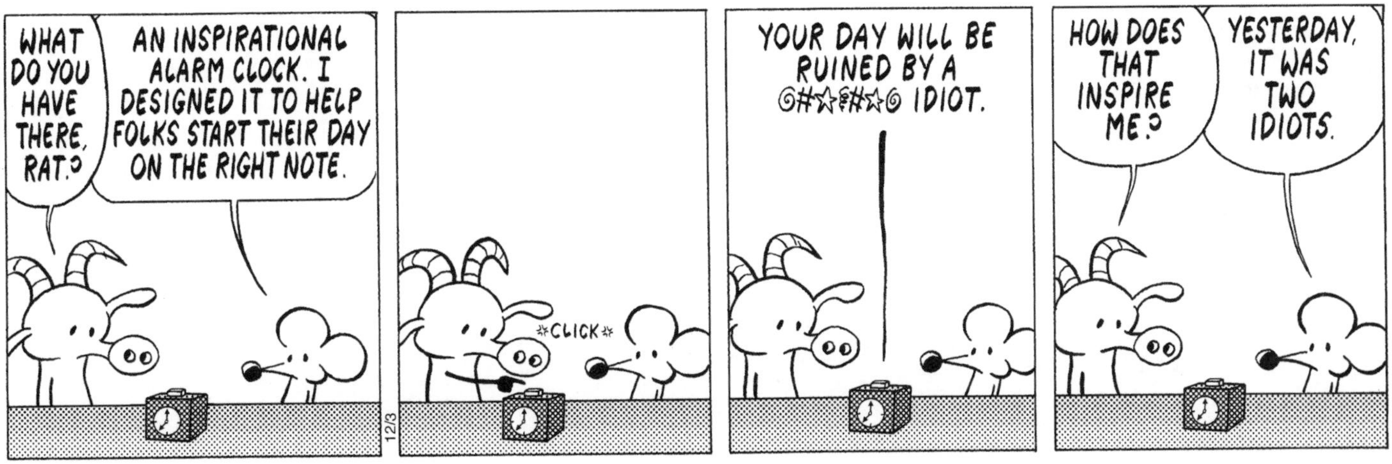
WHAT DO YOU HAVE THERE, RAT?
AN INSPIRATIONAL ALARM CLOCK. I DESIGNED IT TO HELP FOLKS START THEIR DAY ON THE RIGHT NOTE.
12/3
CLICK
YOUR DAY WILL BE RUINED BY A @#☆$#☆@ IDIOT.
HOW DOES THAT INSPIRE ME?
YESTERDAY, IT WAS TWO IDIOTS.

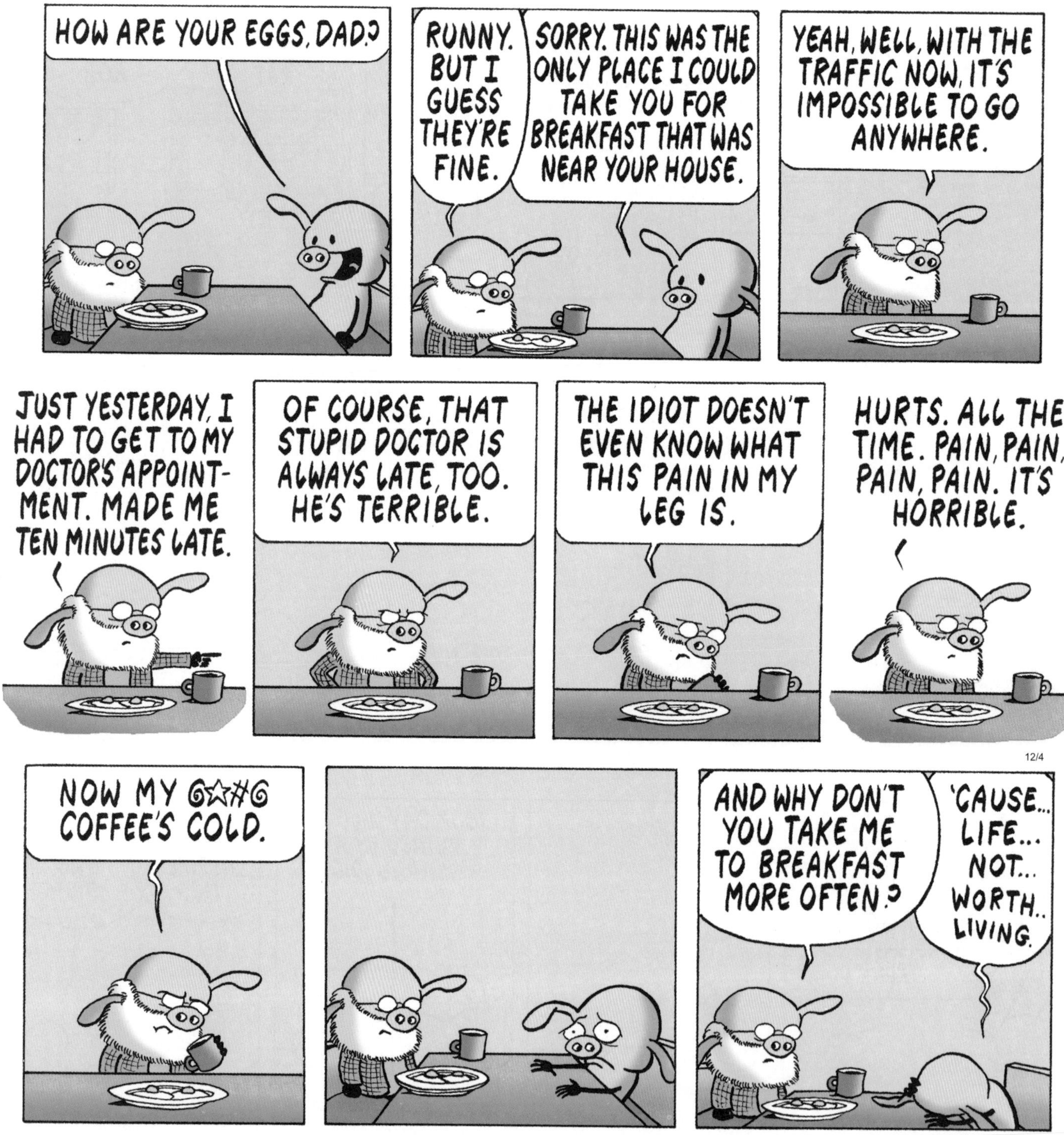
HOW ARE YOUR EGGS, DAD?
RUNNY. BUT I GUESS THEY'RE FINE.
SORRY. THIS WAS THE ONLY PLACE I COULD TAKE YOU FOR BREAKFAST THAT WAS NEAR YOUR HOUSE.
YEAH, WELL, WITH THE TRAFFIC NOW, IT'S IMPOSSIBLE TO GO ANYWHERE.
JUST YESTERDAY, I HAD TO GET TO MY DOCTOR'S APPOINTMENT. MADE ME TEN MINUTES LATE.
OF COURSE, THAT STUPID DOCTOR IS ALWAYS LATE, TOO. HE'S TERRIBLE.
THE IDIOT DOESN'T EVEN KNOW WHAT THIS PAIN IN MY LEG IS.
HURTS. ALL THE TIME. PAIN, PAIN, PAIN, PAIN. IT'S HORRIBLE.
12/4
NOW MY @☆#@ COFFEE'S COLD.
AND WHY DON'T YOU TAKE ME TO BREAKFAST MORE OFTEN?
'CAUSE... LIFE... NOT... WORTH.. LIVING.

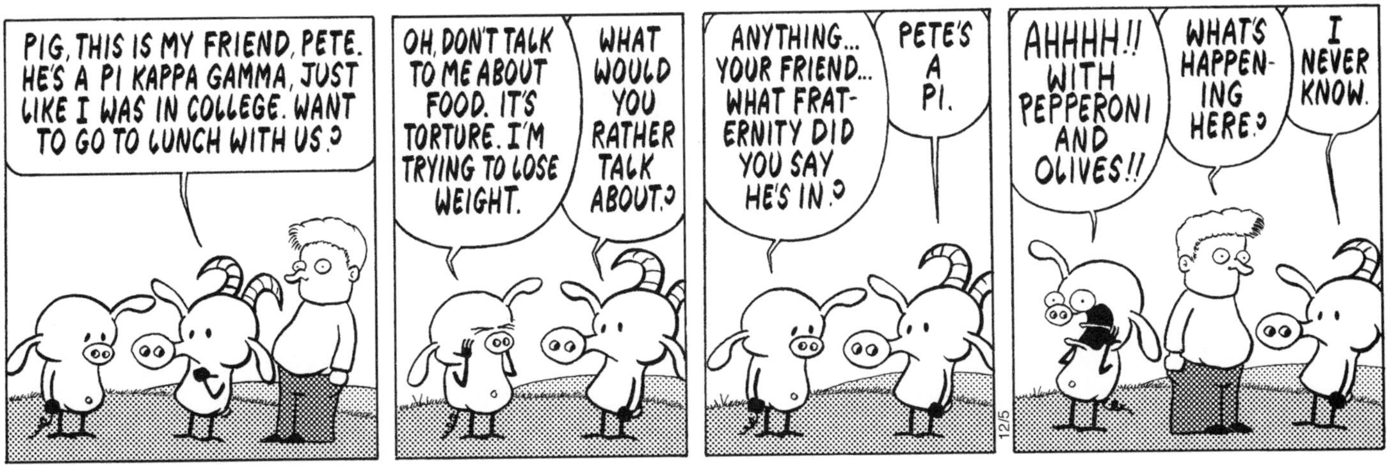
PIG, THIS IS MY FRIEND, PETE. HE'S A PI KAPPA GAMMA, JUST LIKE I WAS IN COLLEGE. WANT TO GO TO LUNCH WITH US?
OH, DON'T TALK TO ME ABOUT FOOD. IT'S TORTURE. I'M TRYING TO LOSE WEIGHT.
WHAT WOULD YOU RATHER TALK ABOUT?
ANYTHING... YOUR FRIEND... WHAT FRATERNITY DID YOU SAY HE'S IN?
PETE'S A PI.
12/5
AHHHH!! WITH PEPPERONI AND OLIVES!!
WHAT'S HAPPENING HERE?
I NEVER KNOW.

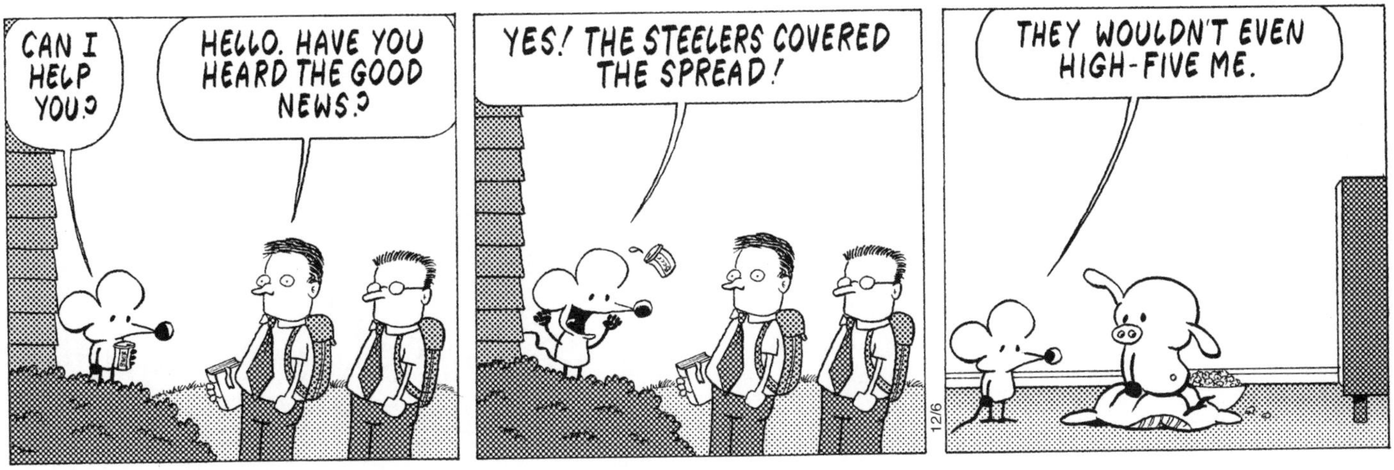
CAN I HELP YOU?
HELLO. HAVE YOU HEARD THE GOOD NEWS?
YES! THE STEELERS COVERED THE SPREAD!
12/6
THEY WOULDN'T EVEN HIGH-FIVE ME.

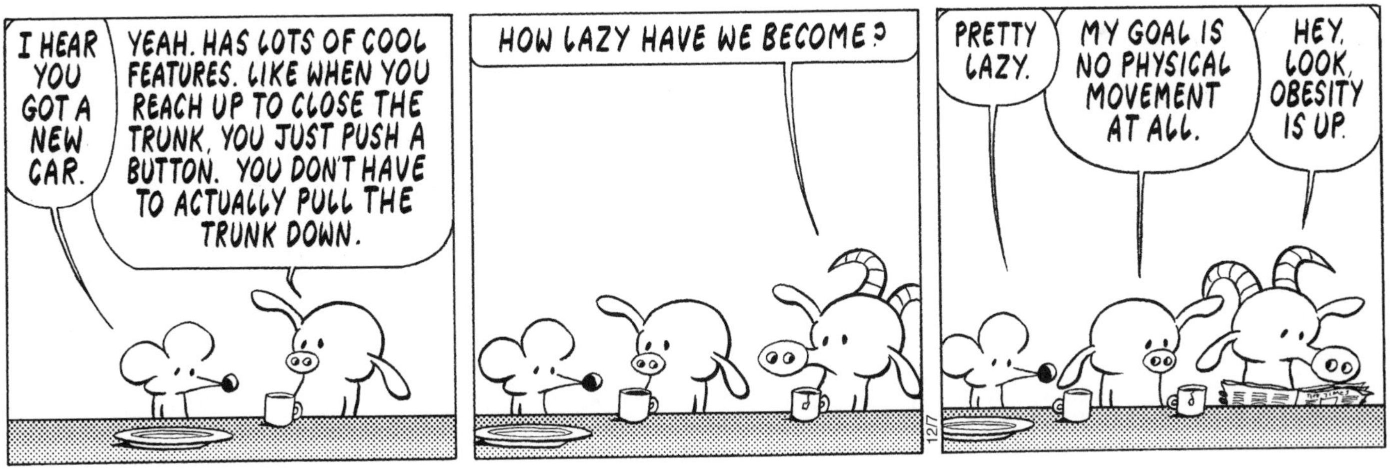
I HEAR YOU GOT A NEW CAR.
YEAH. HAS LOTS OF COOL FEATURES. LIKE WHEN YOU REACH UP TO CLOSE THE TRUNK, YOU JUST PUSH A BUTTON. YOU DON'T HAVE TO ACTUALLY PULL THE TRUNK DOWN.
HOW LAZY HAVE WE BECOME?
12/7
PRETTY LAZY.
MY GOAL IS NO PHYSICAL MOVEMENT AT ALL.
HEY, LOOK, OBESITY IS UP.

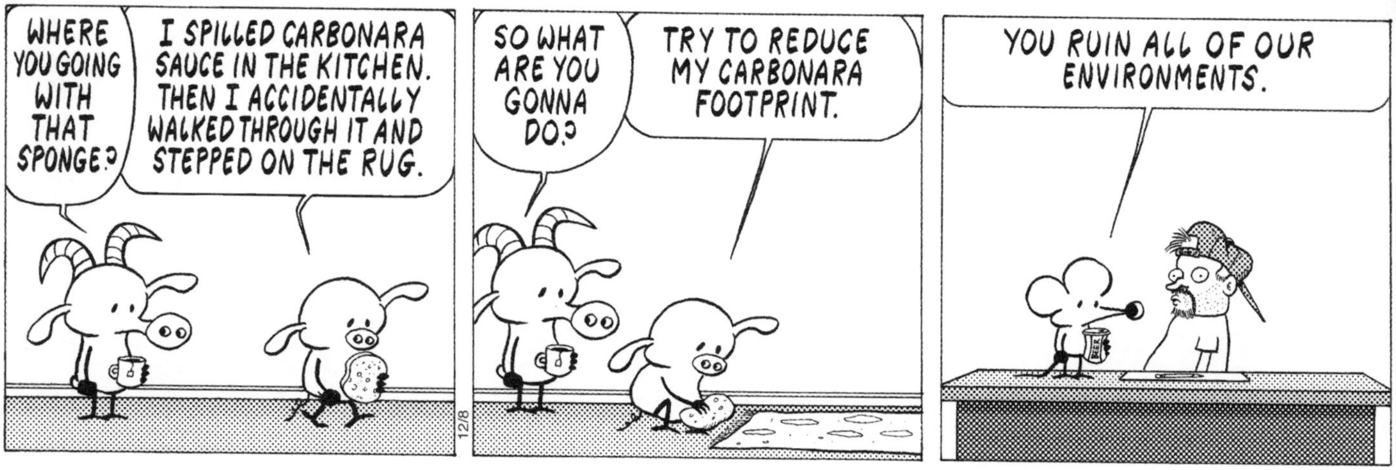
WHERE YOU GOING WITH THAT SPONGE?
I SPILLED CARBONARA SAUCE IN THE KITCHEN. THEN I ACCIDENTALLY WALKED THROUGH IT AND STEPPED ON THE RUG.
12/8
SO WHAT ARE YOU GONNA DO?
TRY TO REDUCE MY CARBONARA FOOTPRINT.
YOU RUIN ALL OF OUR ENVIRONMENTS.
BEER

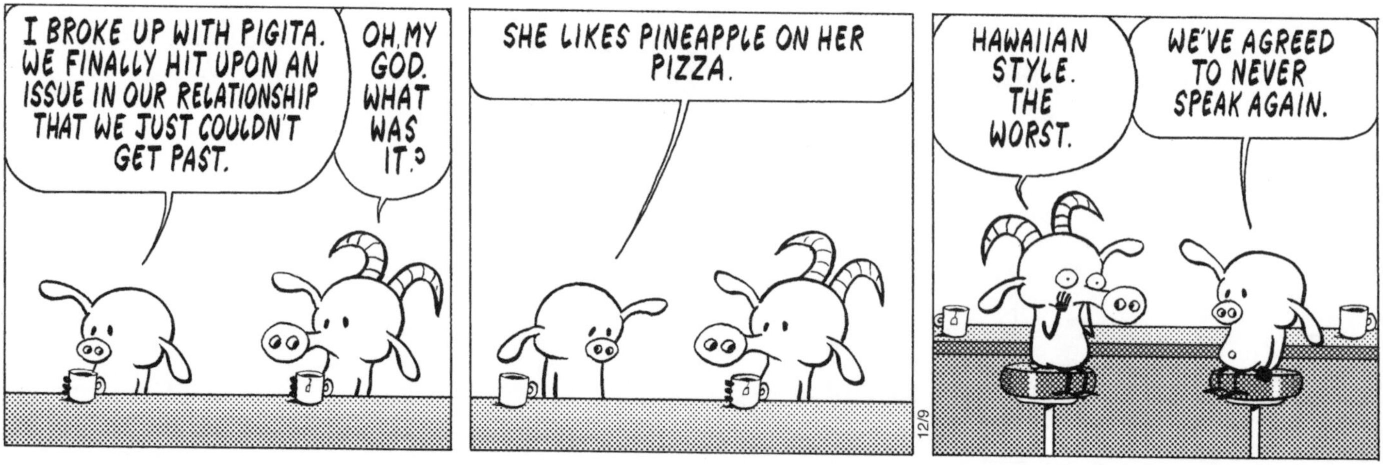
I BROKE UP WITH PIGITA. WE FINALLY HIT UPON AN ISSUE IN OUR RELATIONSHIP THAT WE JUST COULDN'T GET PAST.
OH, MY GOD. WHAT WAS IT?
SHE LIKES PINEAPPLE ON HER PIZZA.
12/9
HAWAIIAN STYLE. THE WORST.
WE'VE AGREED TO NEVER SPEAK AGAIN.

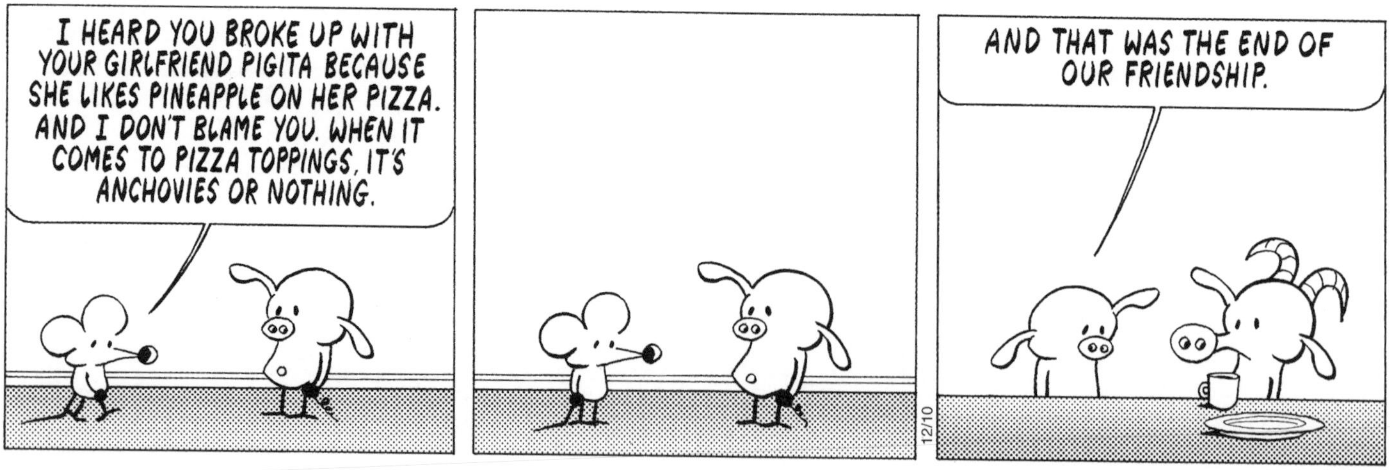
I HEARD YOU BROKE UP WITH YOUR GIRLFRIEND PIGITA BECAUSE SHE LIKES PINEAPPLE ON HER PIZZA. AND I DON'T BLAME YOU. WHEN IT COMES TO PIZZA TOPPINGS, IT'S ANCHOVIES OR NOTHING.
12/10
AND THAT WAS THE END OF OUR FRIENDSHIP.

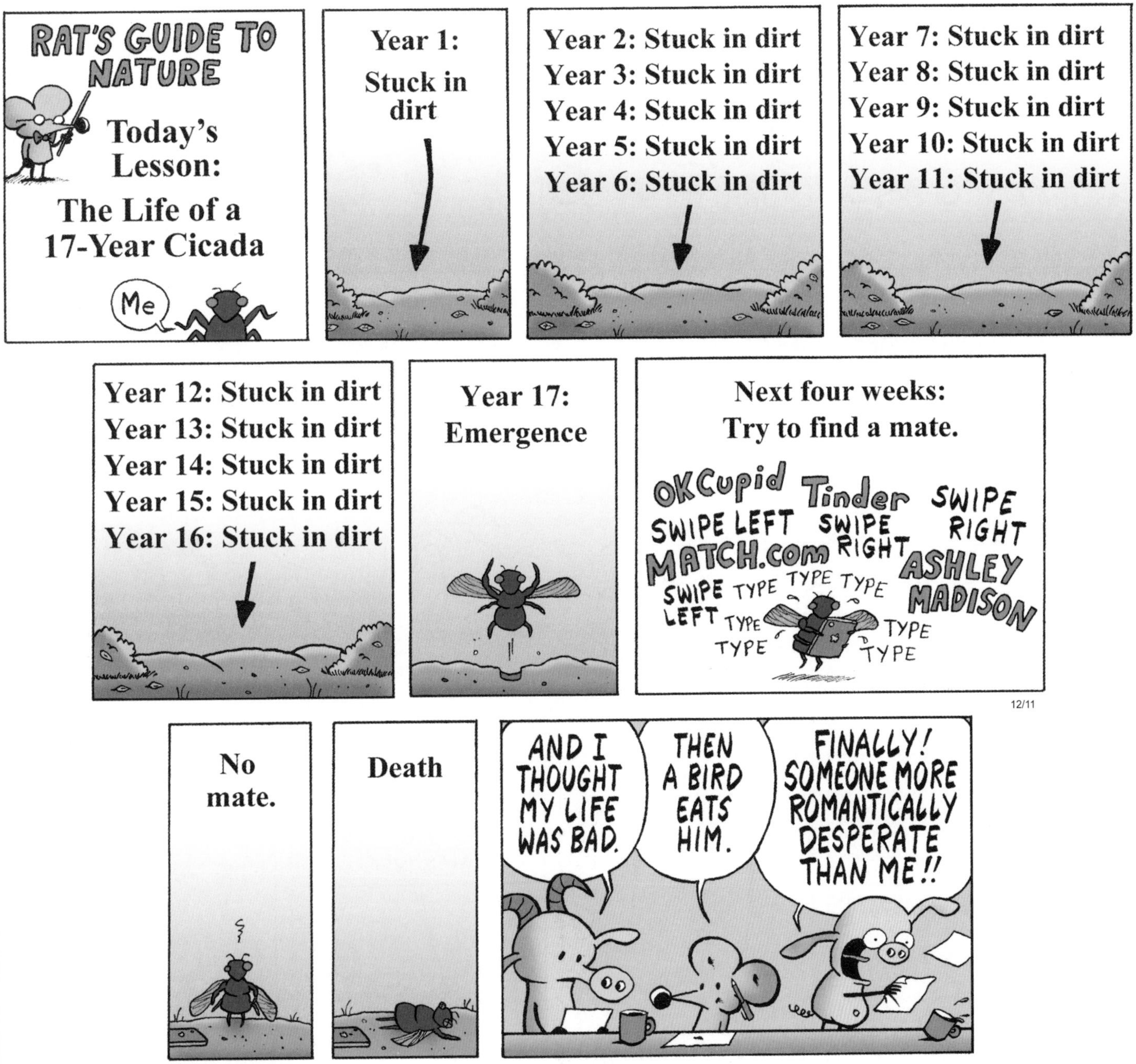
RAT'S GUIDE TO NATURE
Today's Lesson:
The Life of a 17-Year Cicada
Me
Year 1:
Stuck in dirt
Year 2: Stuck in dirt
Year 3: Stuck in dirt
Year 4: Stuck in dirt
Year 5: Stuck in dirt
Year 6: Stuck in dirt
Year 7: Stuck in dirt
Year 8: Stuck in dirt
Year 9: Stuck in dirt
Year 10: Stuck in dirt
Year 11: Stuck in dirt
Year 12: Stuck in dirt
Year 13: Stuck in dirt
Year 14: Stuck in dirt
Year 15: Stuck in dirt
Year 16: Stuck in dirt
Year 17:
Emergence
Next four weeks:
Try to find a mate.
OKCupid
Tinder
SWIPE RIGHT
SWIPE LEFT
SWIPE RIGHT
MATCH.com
ASHLEY MADISON
SWIPE LEFT
TYPE TYPE TYPE
TYPE
TYPE
TYPE
TYPE
12/11
No mate.
Death
AND I THOUGHT MY LIFE WAS BAD.
THEN A BIRD EATS HIM.
FINALLY! SOMEONE MORE ROMANTICALLY DESPERATE THAN ME!!

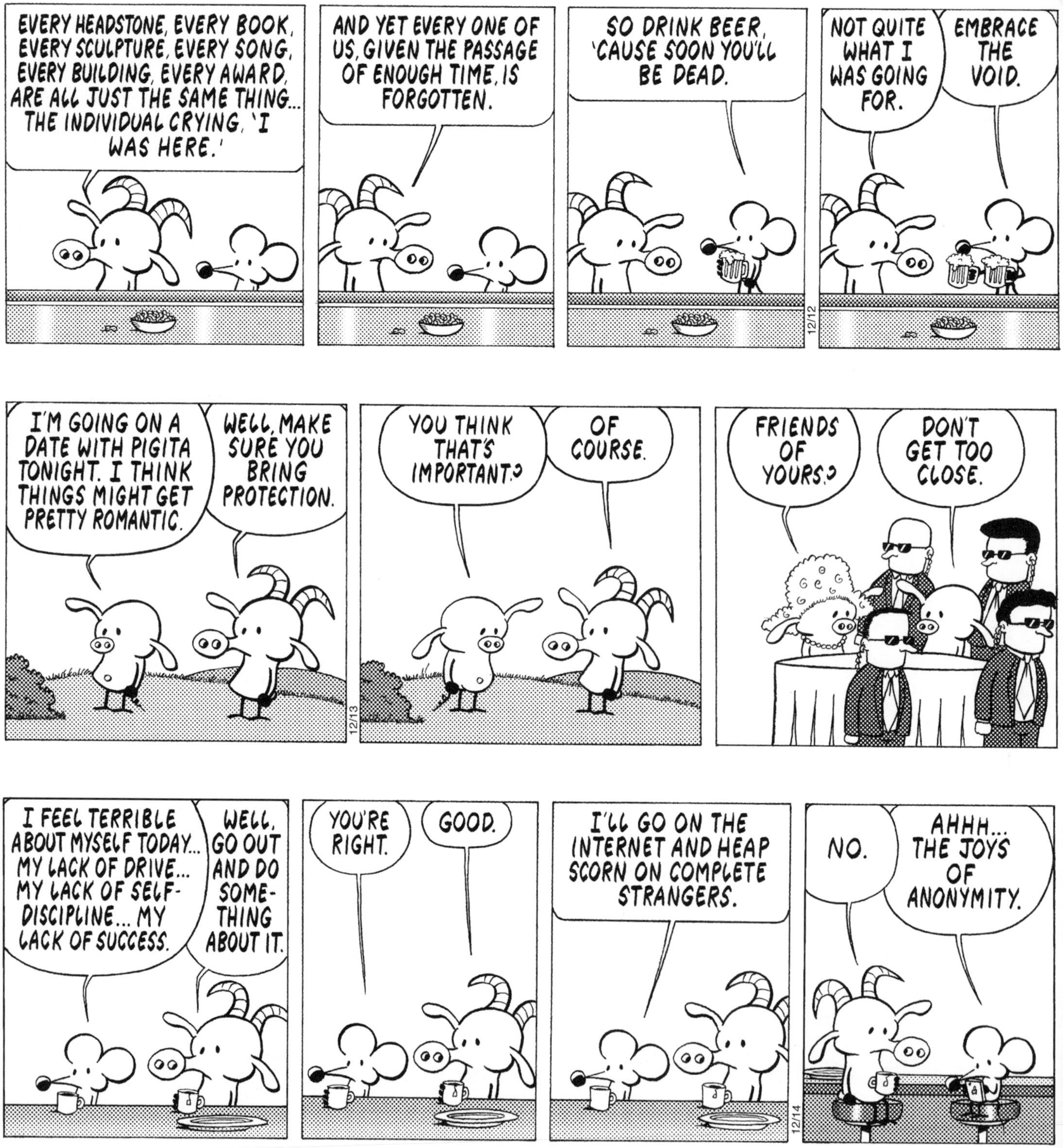
EVERY HEADSTONE, EVERY BOOK, EVERY SCULPTURE, EVERY SONG, EVERY BUILDING, EVERY AWARD, ARE ALL JUST THE SAME THING... THE INDIVIDUAL CRYING, 'I WAS HERE.'
AND YET EVERY ONE OF US, GIVEN THE PASSAGE OF ENOUGH TIME, IS FORGOTTEN.
SO DRINK BEER, 'CAUSE SOON YOU'LL BE DEAD.
12/12
NOT QUITE WHAT I WAS GOING FOR.
EMBRACE THE VOID.
I'M GOING ON A DATE WITH PIGITA TONIGHT. I THINK THINGS MIGHT GET PRETTY ROMANTIC.
WELL, MAKE SURE YOU BRING PROTECTION.
12/13
YOU THINK THAT'S IMPORTANT?
OF COURSE.
FRIENDS OF YOURS?
DON'T GET TOO CLOSE.
I FEEL TERRIBLE ABOUT MYSELF TODAY... MY LACK OF DRIVE... MY LACK OF SELF-DISCIPLINE... MY LACK OF SUCCESS.
WELL, GO OUT AND DO SOMETHING ABOUT IT.
YOU'RE RIGHT.
GOOD.
I'LL GO ON THE INTERNET AND HEAP SCORN ON COMPLETE STRANGERS.
12/14
NO.
AHHH... THE JOYS OF ANONYMITY.

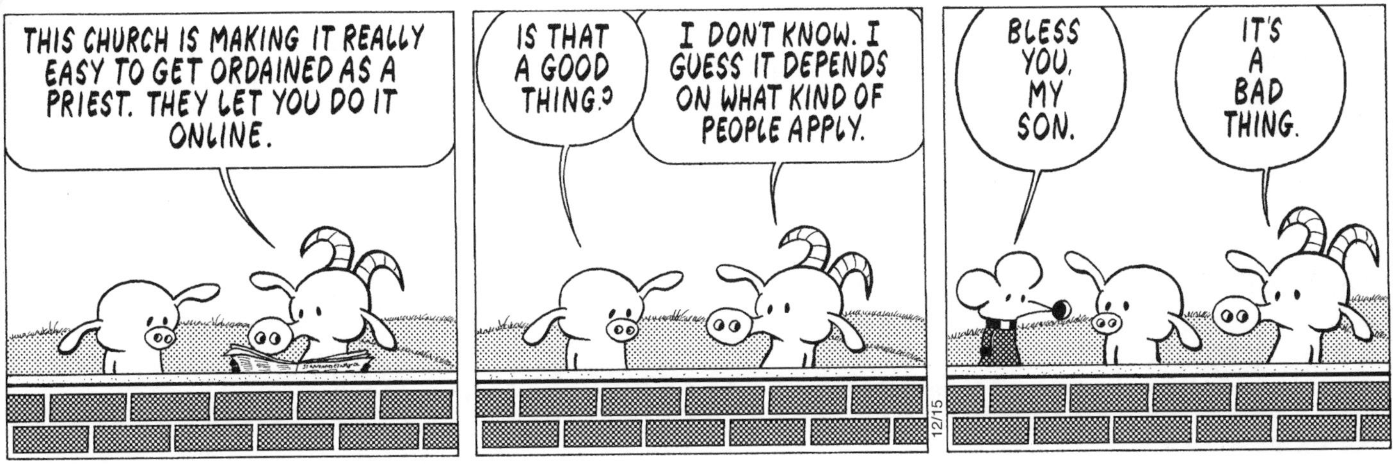
THIS CHURCH IS MAKING IT REALLY EASY TO GET ORDAINED AS A PRIEST. THEY LET YOU DO IT ONLINE.
IS THAT A GOOD THING?
I DON'T KNOW. I GUESS IT DEPENDS ON WHAT KIND OF PEOPLE APPLY.
12/15
BLESS YOU, MY SON.
IT'S A BAD THING.

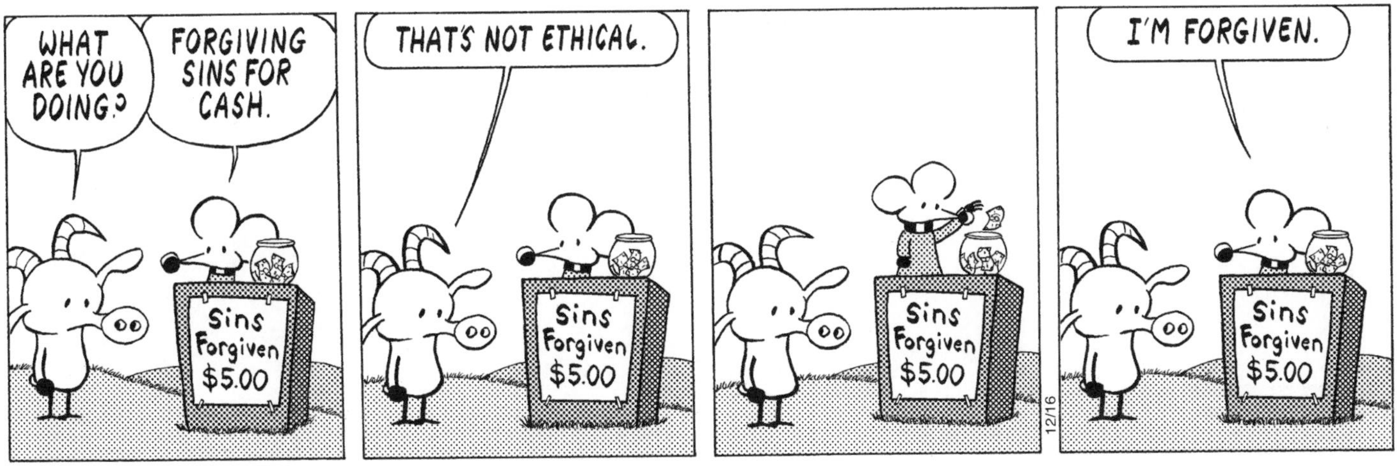
WHAT ARE YOU DOING?
FORGIVING SINS FOR CASH.
Sins Forgiven $5.00
THAT'S NOT ETHICAL.
Sins Forgiven $5.00
Sins Forgiven $5.00
12/16
I'M FORGIVEN.
Sins Forgiven $5.00

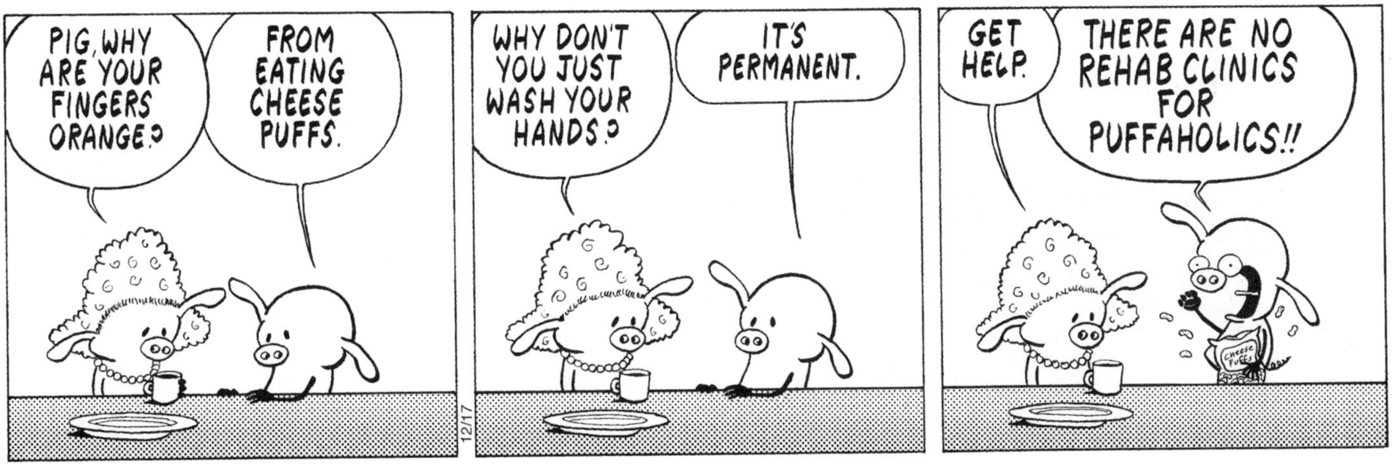
PIG, WHY ARE YOUR FINGERS ORANGE?
FROM EATING CHEESE PUFFS.
12/17
WHY DON'T YOU JUST WASH YOUR HANDS?
IT'S PERMANENT.
GET HELP.
THERE ARE NO REHAB CLINICS FOR PUFFAHOLICS!!
Cheese Puffs

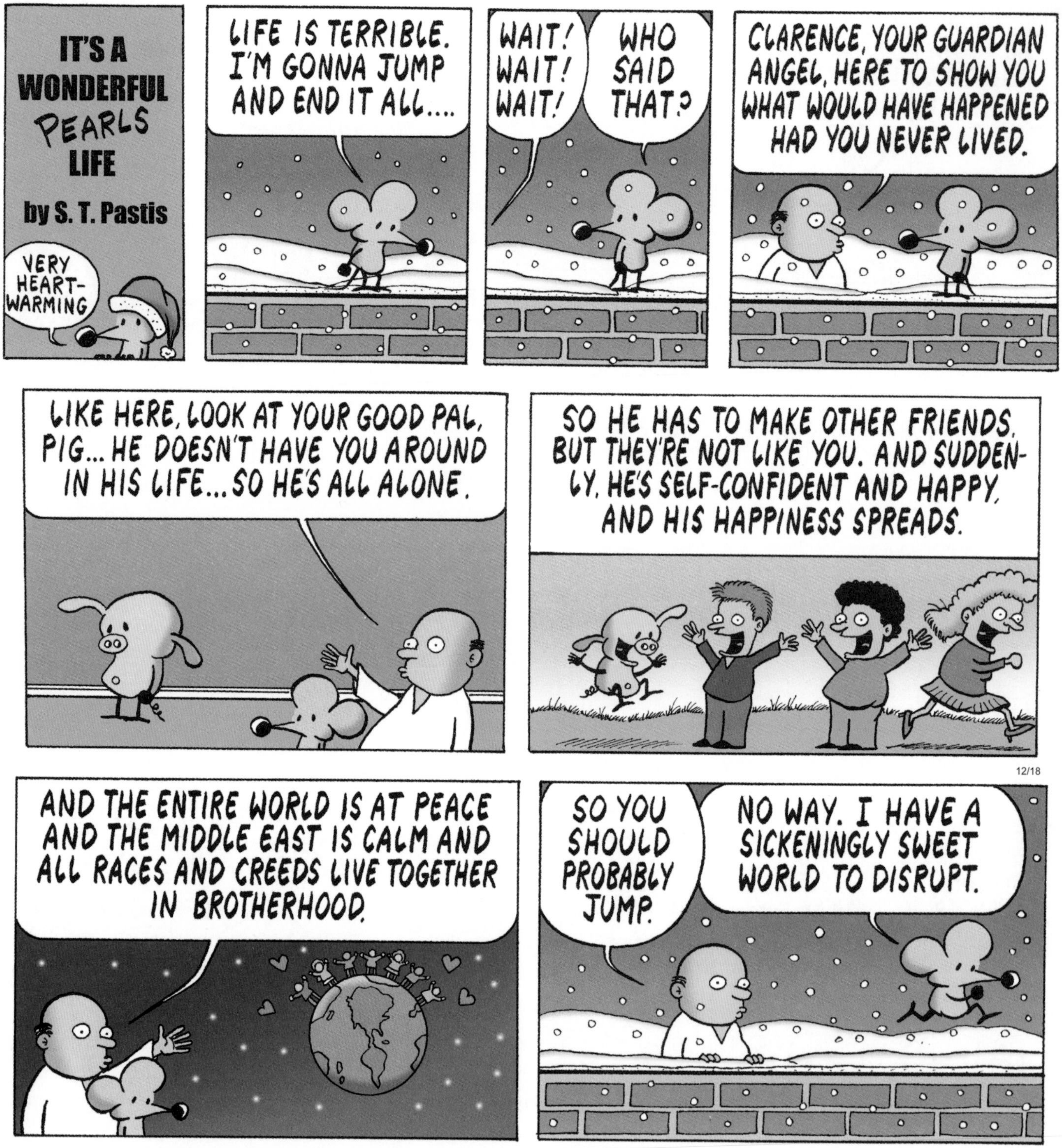
IT'S A WONDERFUL PEARLS LIFE
by S. T. Pastis
VERY HEART-WARMING
LIFE IS TERRIBLE. I'M GONNA JUMP AND END IT ALL....
WAIT! WAIT! WAIT!
WHO SAID THAT?
CLARENCE, YOUR GUARDIAN ANGEL, HERE TO SHOW YOU WHAT WOULD HAVE HAPPENED HAD YOU NEVER LIVED.
LIKE HERE, LOOK AT YOUR GOOD PAL, PIG... HE DOESN'T HAVE YOU AROUND IN HIS LIFE... SO HE'S ALL ALONE.
SO HE HAS TO MAKE OTHER FRIENDS, BUT THEY'RE NOT LIKE YOU. AND SUDDENLY, HE'S SELF-CONFIDENT AND HAPPY, AND HIS HAPPINESS SPREADS.
12/18
AND THE ENTIRE WORLD IS AT PEACE AND THE MIDDLE EAST IS CALM AND ALL RACES AND CREEDS LIVE TOGETHER IN BROTHERHOOD.
SO YOU SHOULD PROBABLY JUMP.
NO WAY. I HAVE A SICKENINGLY SWEET WORLD TO DISRUPT.

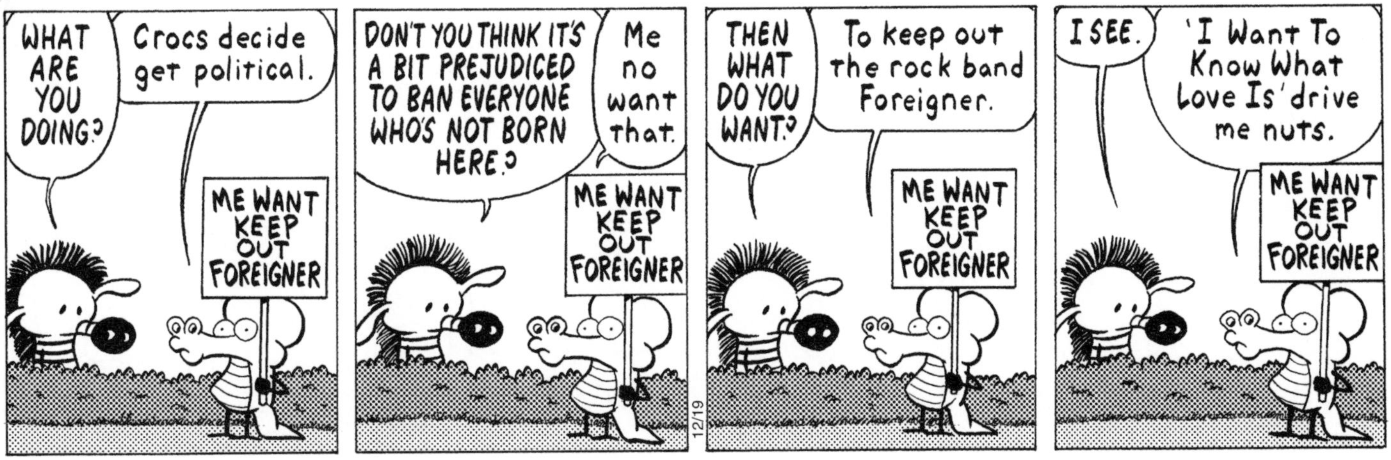
WHAT ARE YOU DOING?
Crocs decide get political.
ME WANT KEEP OUT FOREIGNER
DON'T YOU THINK IT'S A BIT PREJUDICED TO BAN EVERYONE WHO'S NOT BORN HERE?
Me no want that.
ME WANT KEEP OUT FOREIGNER
THEN WHAT DO YOU WANT?
To keep out the rock band Foreigner.
ME WANT KEEP OUT FOREIGNER
I SEE.
'I Want To Know What Love Is' drive me nuts.
ME WANT KEEP OUT FOREIGNER
12/19

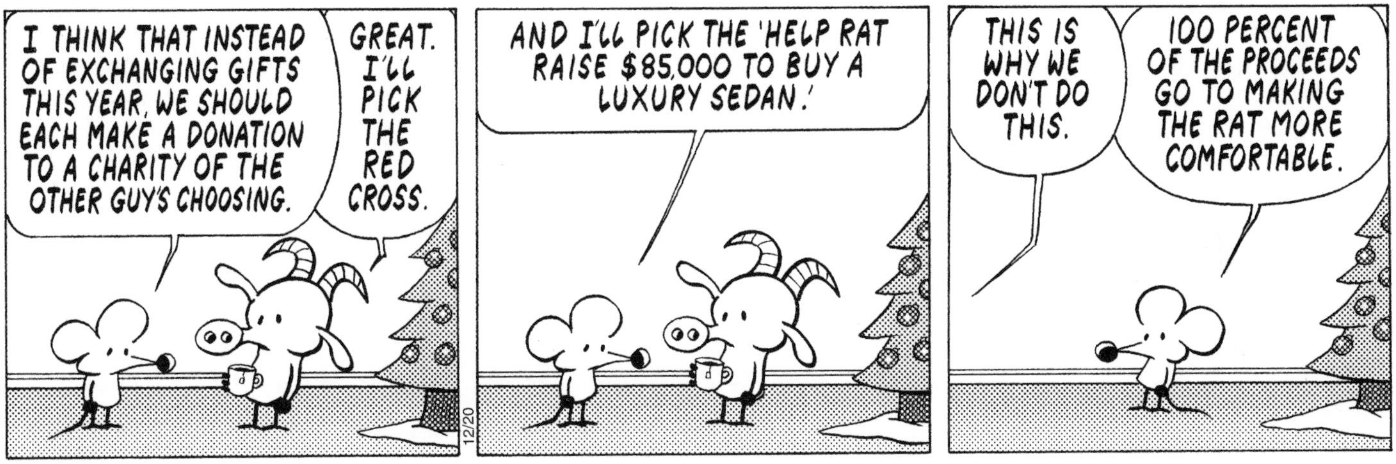
I THINK THAT INSTEAD OF EXCHANGING GIFTS THIS YEAR, WE SHOULD EACH MAKE A DONATION TO A CHARITY OF THE OTHER GUY'S CHOOSING.
GREAT. I'LL PICK THE RED CROSS.
AND I'LL PICK THE 'HELP RAT RAISE $85,000 TO BUY A LUXURY SEDAN.'
THIS IS WHY WE DON'T DO THIS.
100 PERCENT OF THE PROCEEDS GO TO MAKING THE RAT MORE COMFORTABLE.
12/20

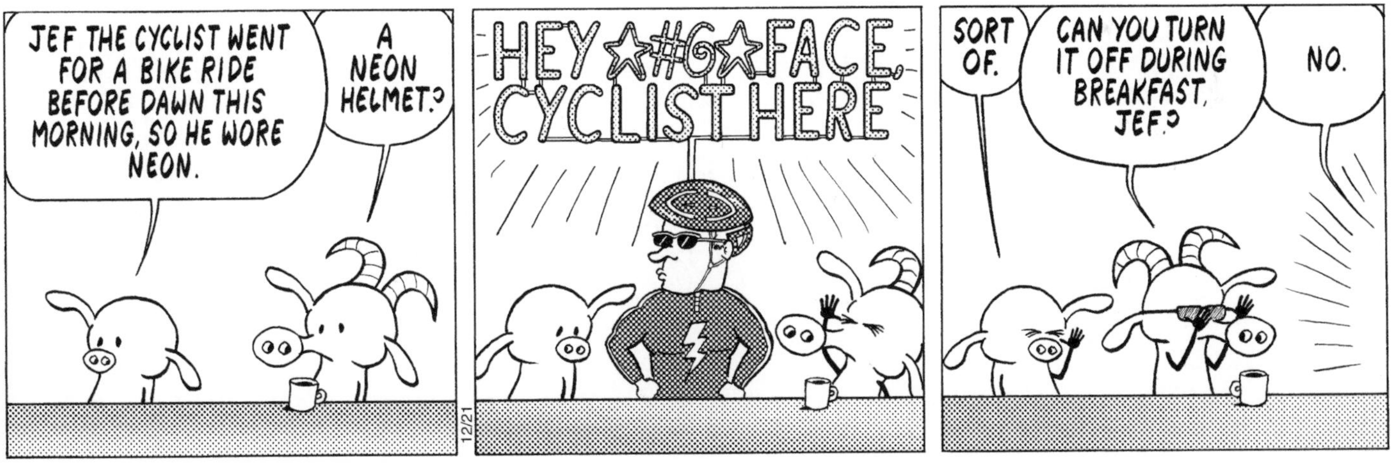
JEF THE CYCLIST WENT FOR A BIKE RIDE BEFORE DAWN THIS MORNING, SO HE WORE NEON.
A NEON HELMET?
HEY ☆#G☆FACE, CYCLIST HERE
SORT OF.
CAN YOU TURN IT OFF DURING BREAKFAST, JEF?
NO.
12/21

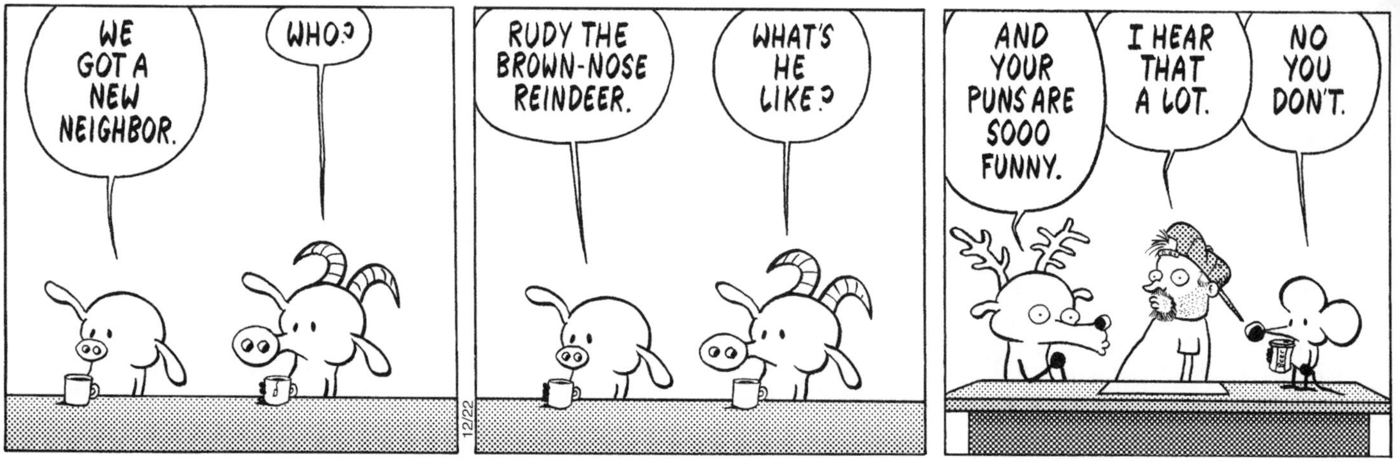
WE GOT A NEW NEIGHBOR.
WHO?
RUDY THE BROWN-NOSE REINDEER.
WHAT'S HE LIKE?
AND YOUR PUNS ARE SOOO FUNNY.
I HEAR THAT A LOT.
NO YOU DON'T.
12/22

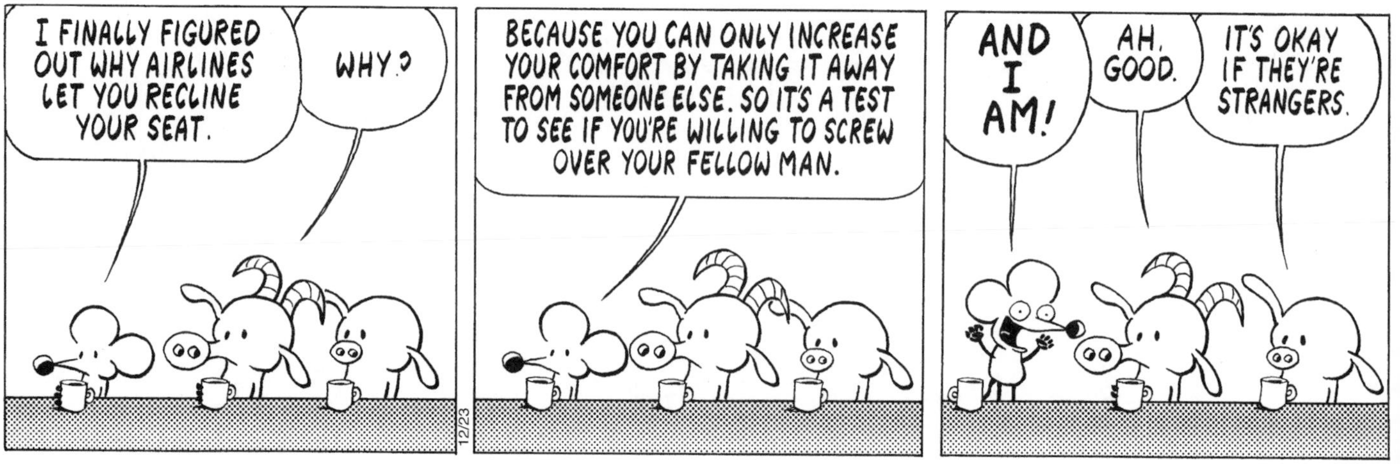
I FINALLY FIGURED OUT WHY AIRLINES LET YOU RECLINE YOUR SEAT.
WHY?
BECAUSE YOU CAN ONLY INCREASE YOUR COMFORT BY TAKING IT AWAY FROM SOMEONE ELSE. SO IT'S A TEST TO SEE IF YOU'RE WILLING TO SCREW OVER YOUR FELLOW MAN.
AND I AM!
AH, GOOD.
IT'S OKAY IF THEY'RE STRANGERS.
12/23

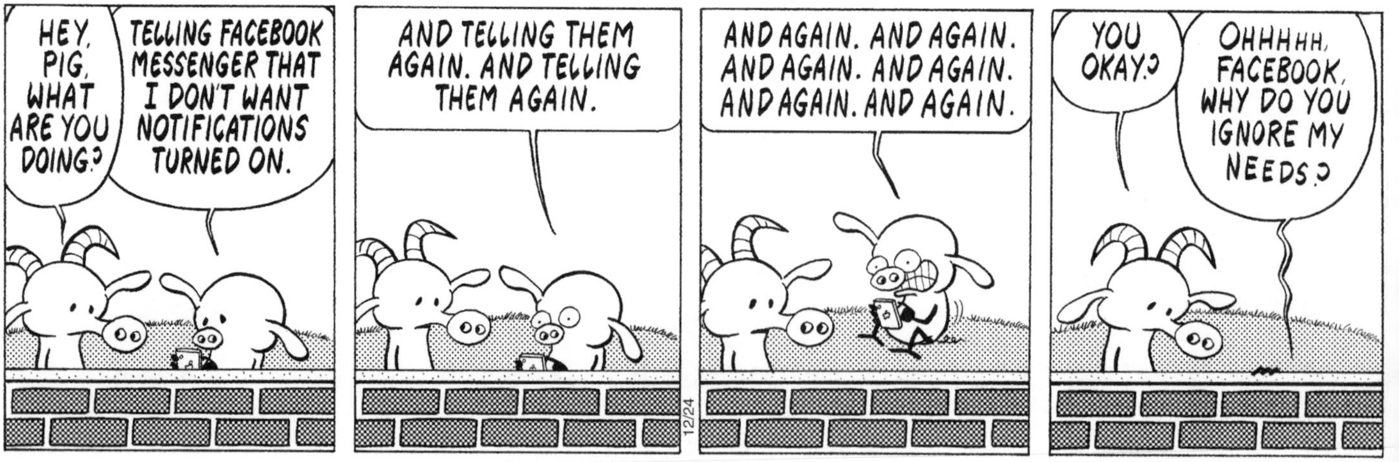
HEY, PIG, WHAT ARE YOU DOING?
TELLING FACEBOOK MESSENGER THAT I DON'T WANT NOTIFICATIONS TURNED ON.
AND TELLING THEM AGAIN. AND TELLING THEM AGAIN.
AND AGAIN. AND AGAIN. AND AGAIN. AND AGAIN. AND AGAIN. AND AGAIN.
YOU OKAY?
OHHHHH, FACEBOOK, WHY DO YOU IGNORE MY NEEDS?
12/24

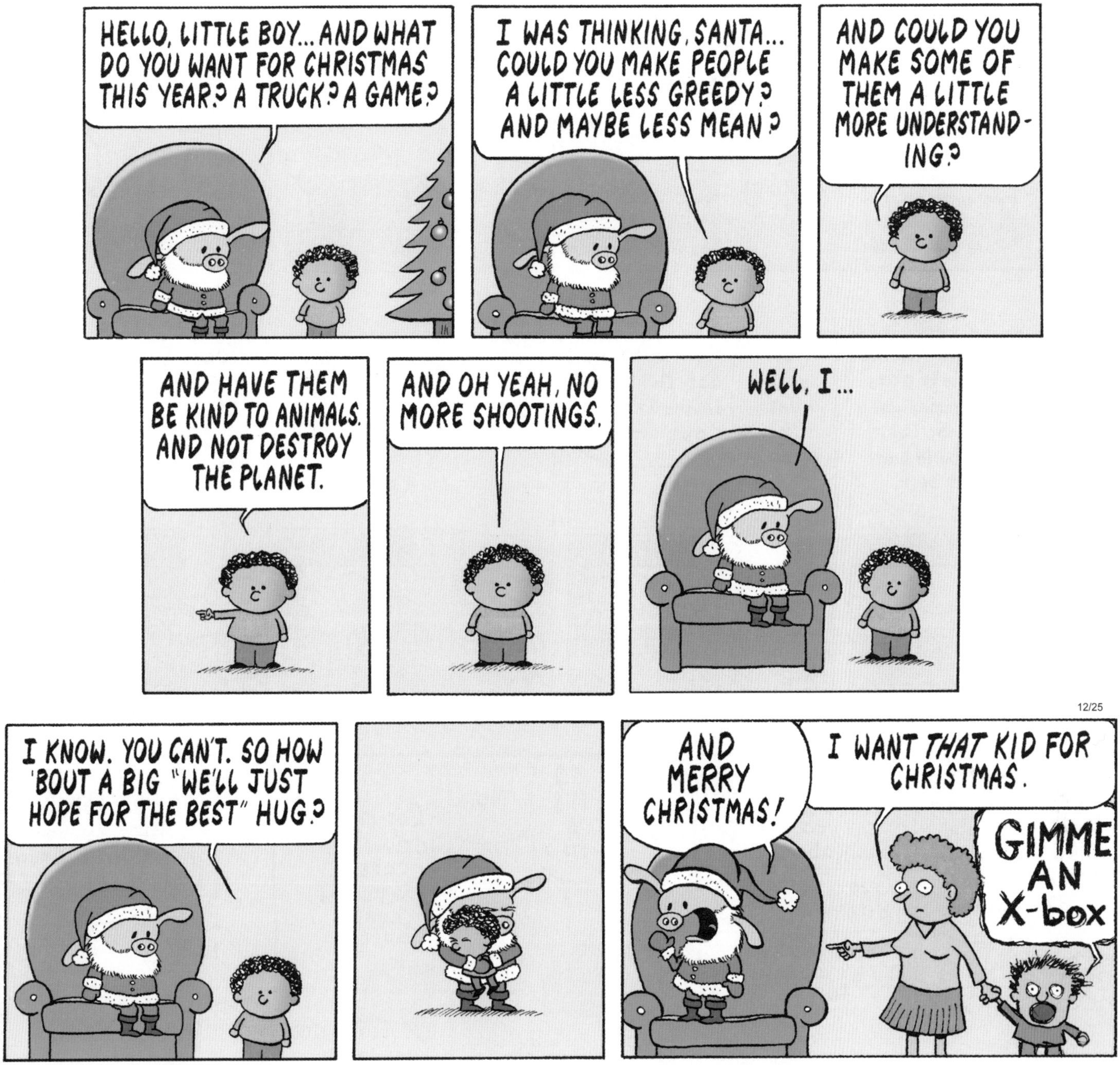
HELLO, LITTLE BOY... AND WHAT DO YOU WANT FOR CHRISTMAS THIS YEAR? A TRUCK? A GAME?
I WAS THINKING, SANTA... COULD YOU MAKE PEOPLE A LITTLE LESS GREEDY? AND MAYBE LESS MEAN?
AND COULD YOU MAKE SOME OF THEM A LITTLE MORE UNDERSTAND-ING?
AND HAVE THEM BE KIND TO ANIMALS. AND NOT DESTROY THE PLANET.
AND OH YEAH, NO MORE SHOOTINGS.
WELL, I...
I KNOW. YOU CAN'T. SO HOW 'BOUT A BIG "WE'LL JUST HOPE FOR THE BEST" HUG?
AND MERRY CHRISTMAS!
I WANT *THAT* KID FOR CHRISTMAS.
GIMME AN X-box
12/25

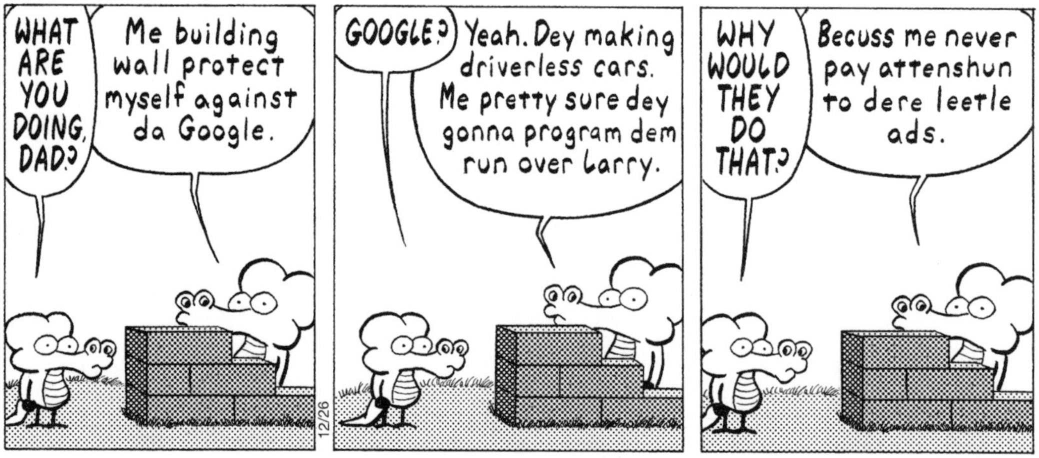
WHAT ARE YOU DOING, DAD?
Me building wall protect myself against da Google.
12/26
GOOGLE?
Yeah. Dey making driverless cars. Me pretty sure dey gonna program dem run over Larry.
WHY WOULD THEY DO THAT?
Becuss me never pay attenshun to dere leetle ads.
THEY PROBABLY WON'T KILL YOU FOR THAT.
Never trust da Google, son.

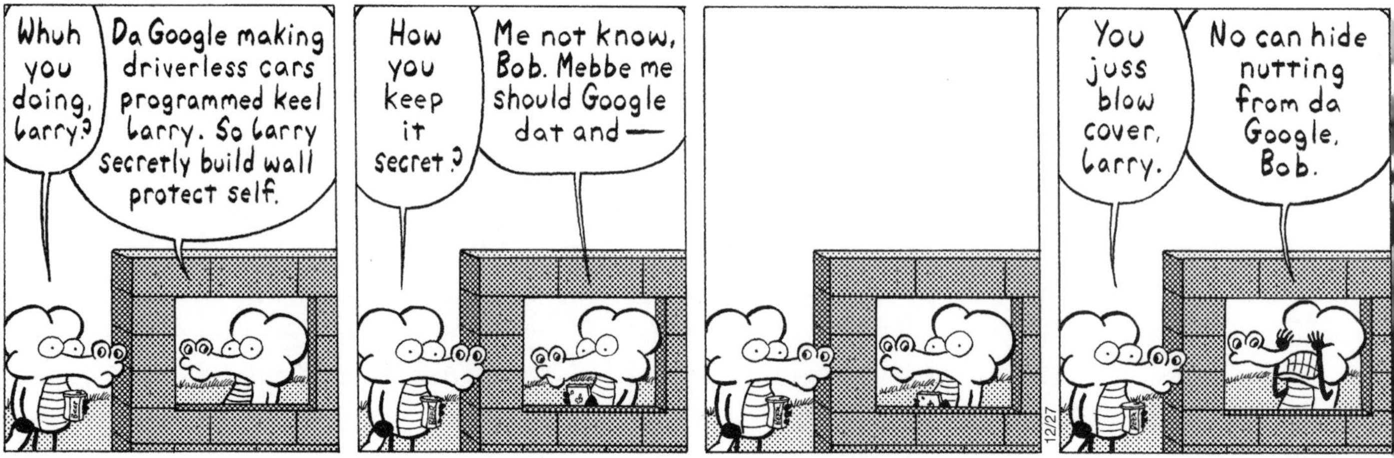
Whuh you doing, Larry?
Da Google making driverless cars programmed keel Larry. So Larry secretly build wall protect self.
How you keep it secret?
Me not know, Bob. Mebbe me should Google dat and—
12/27
You juss blow cover, Larry.
No can hide nutting from da Google, Bob.

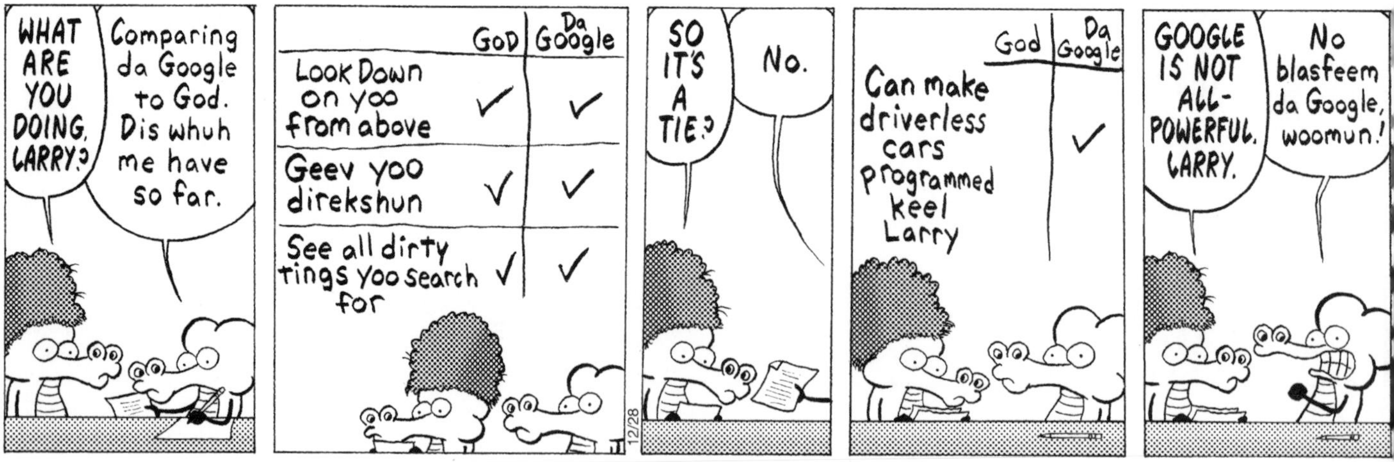
WHAT ARE YOU DOING, LARRY?
Comparing da Google to God. Dis whuh me have so far.
GOD
Da Google
Look Down on yoo from above ✓ ✓
Geev yoo direkshun ✓ ✓
See all dirty tings yoo search for ✓ ✓
12/28
SO IT'S A TIE?
No.
God
Da Google
Can make driverless cars programmed keel Larry ✓
GOOGLE IS NOT ALL-POWERFUL, LARRY.
No blasfeem da Google, woomun!

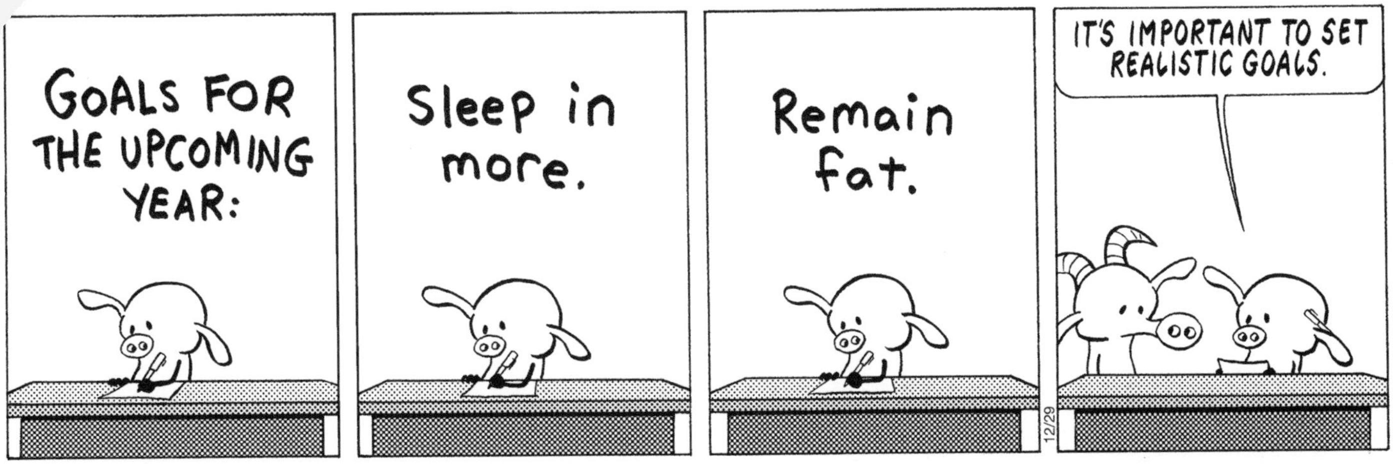
GOALS FOR THE UPCOMING YEAR:
Sleep in more.
Remain fat.
IT'S IMPORTANT TO SET REALISTIC GOALS.
12/29

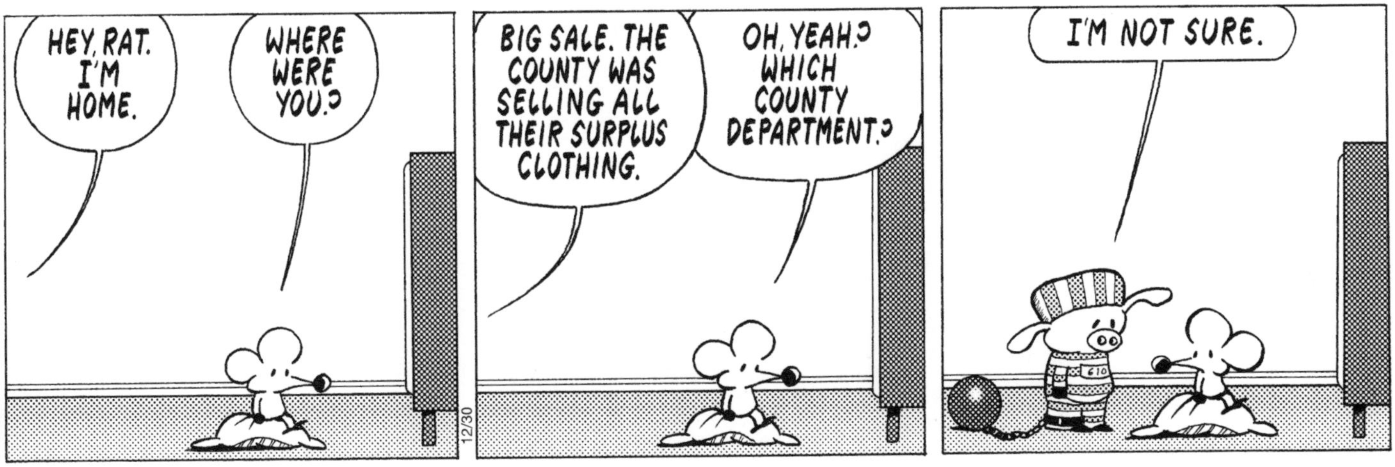
HEY, RAT. I'M HOME.
WHERE WERE YOU?
12/30
BIG SALE. THE COUNTY WAS SELLING ALL THEIR SURPLUS CLOTHING.
OH, YEAH? WHICH COUNTY DEPARTMENT?
I'M NOT SURE.
610

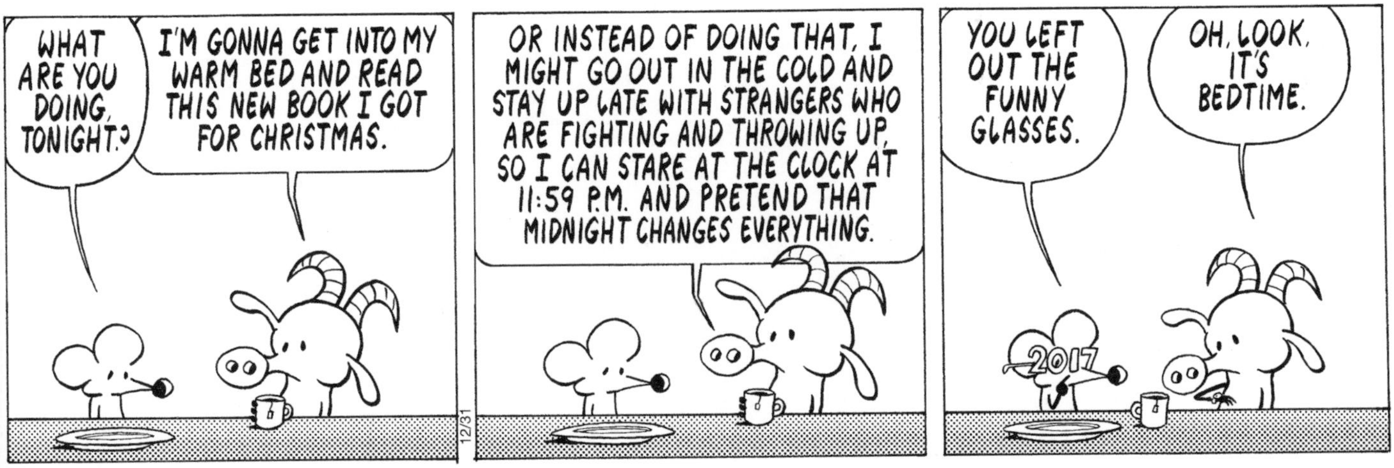
WHAT ARE YOU DOING, TONIGHT?
I'M GONNA GET INTO MY WARM BED AND READ THIS NEW BOOK I GOT FOR CHRISTMAS.
12/31
OR INSTEAD OF DOING THAT, I MIGHT GO OUT IN THE COLD AND STAY UP LATE WITH STRANGERS WHO ARE FIGHTING AND THROWING UP, SO I CAN STARE AT THE CLOCK AT 11:59 P.M. AND PRETEND THAT MIDNIGHT CHANGES EVERYTHING.
YOU LEFT OUT THE FUNNY GLASSES.
2017
OH, LOOK. IT'S BEDTIME.

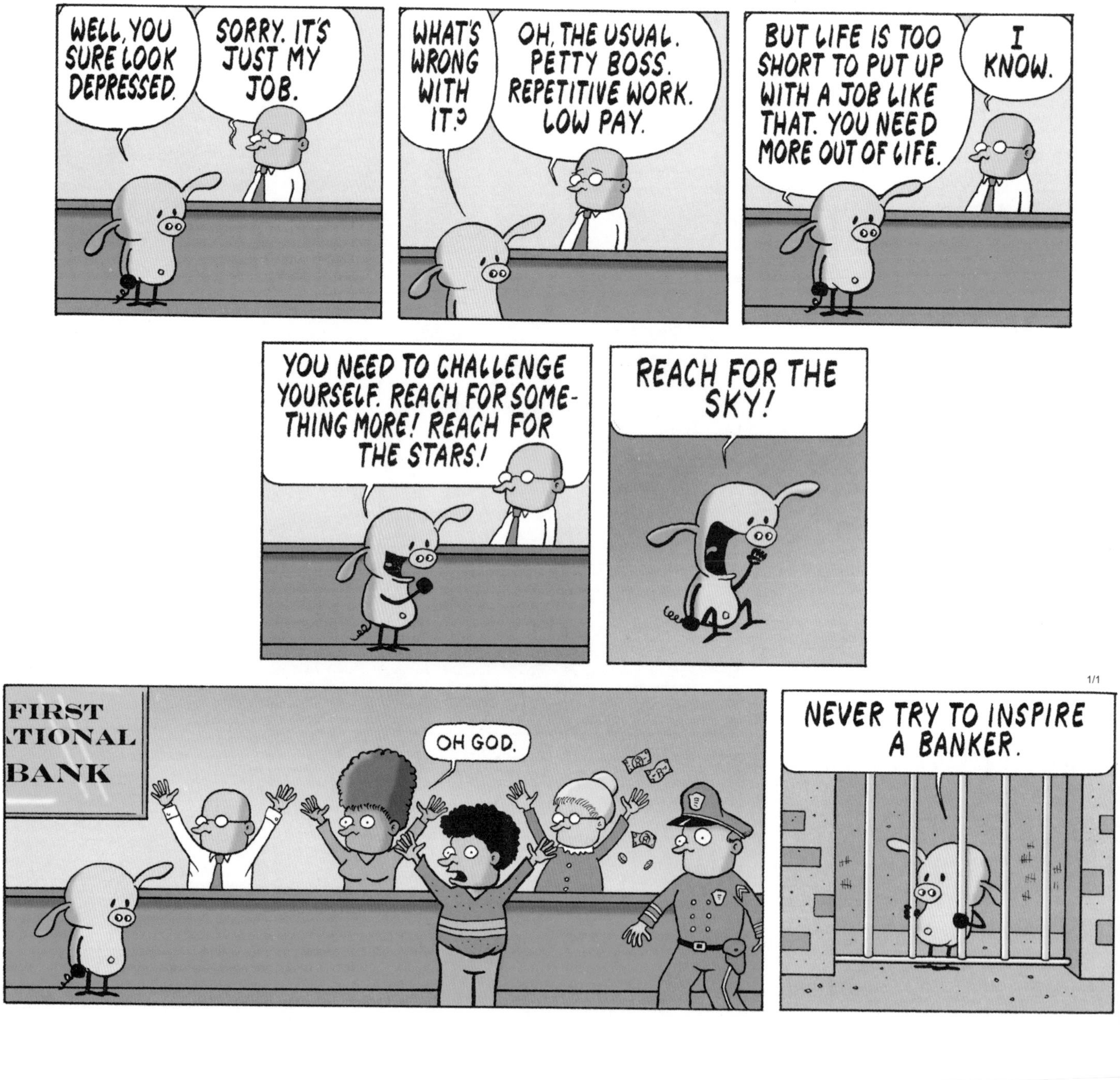
WELL, YOU SURE LOOK DEPRESSED.
SORRY. IT'S JUST MY JOB.
WHAT'S WRONG WITH IT?
OH, THE USUAL. PETTY BOSS. REPETITIVE WORK. LOW PAY.
BUT LIFE IS TOO SHORT TO PUT UP WITH A JOB LIKE THAT. YOU NEED MORE OUT OF LIFE.
I KNOW.
YOU NEED TO CHALLENGE YOURSELF. REACH FOR SOME-THING MORE! REACH FOR THE STARS!
REACH FOR THE SKY!
FIRST
TIONAL
BANK
OH GOD.
NEVER TRY TO INSPIRE A BANKER.
1/1

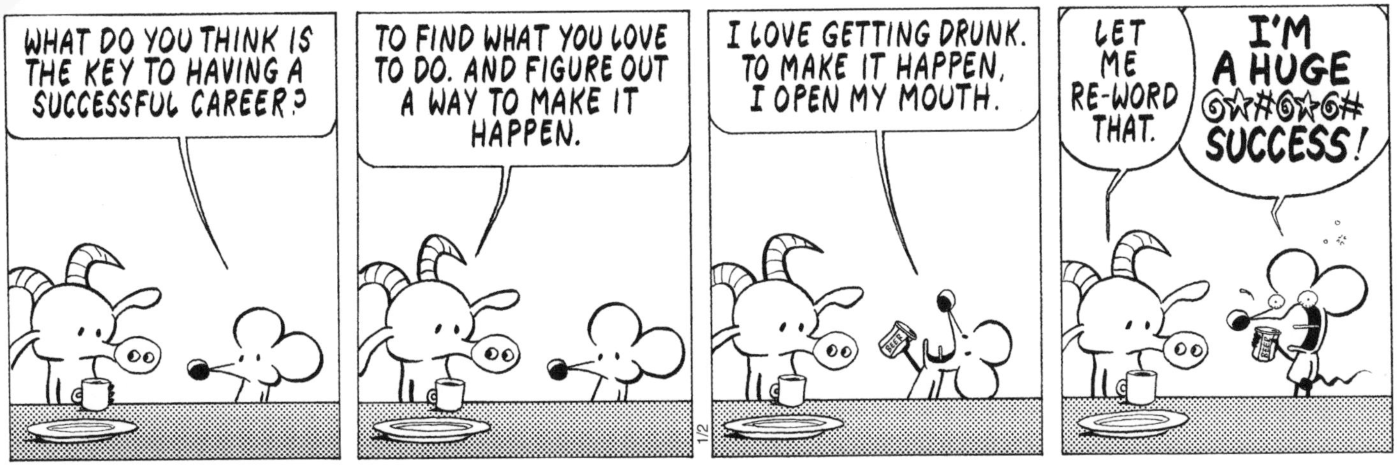
WHAT DO YOU THINK IS THE KEY TO HAVING A SUCCESSFUL CAREER?
TO FIND WHAT YOU LOVE TO DO. AND FIGURE OUT A WAY TO MAKE IT HAPPEN.
I LOVE GETTING DRUNK. TO MAKE IT HAPPEN, I OPEN MY MOUTH.
BEER
LET ME RE-WORD THAT.
I'M A HUGE @☆#@☆@# SUCCESS!
1/2

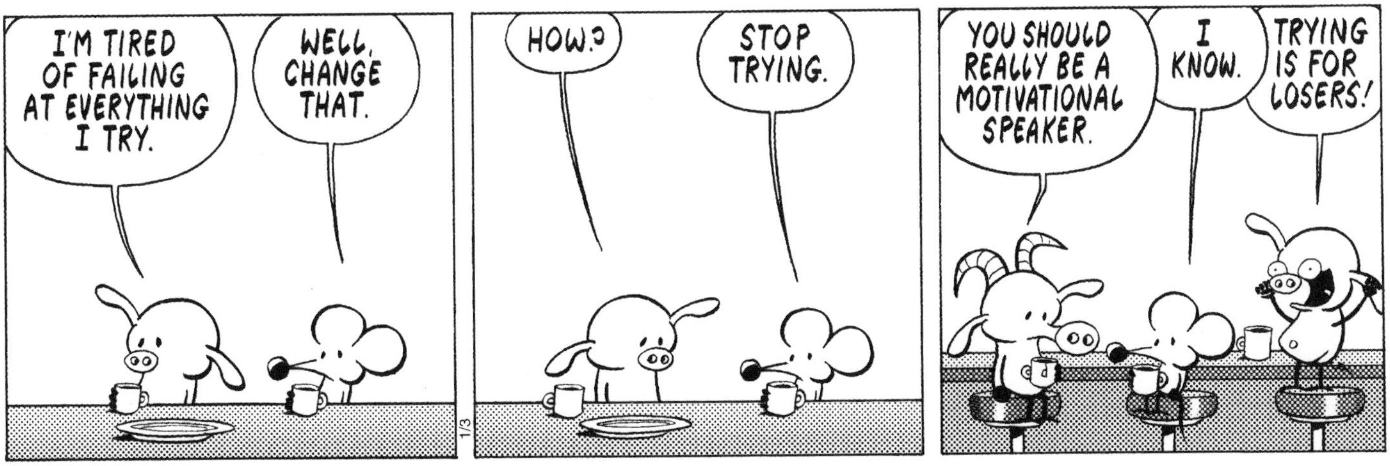
I'M TIRED OF FAILING AT EVERYTHING I TRY.
WELL, CHANGE THAT.
HOW?
STOP TRYING.
YOU SHOULD REALLY BE A MOTIVATIONAL SPEAKER.
I KNOW.
TRYING IS FOR LOSERS!
1/3

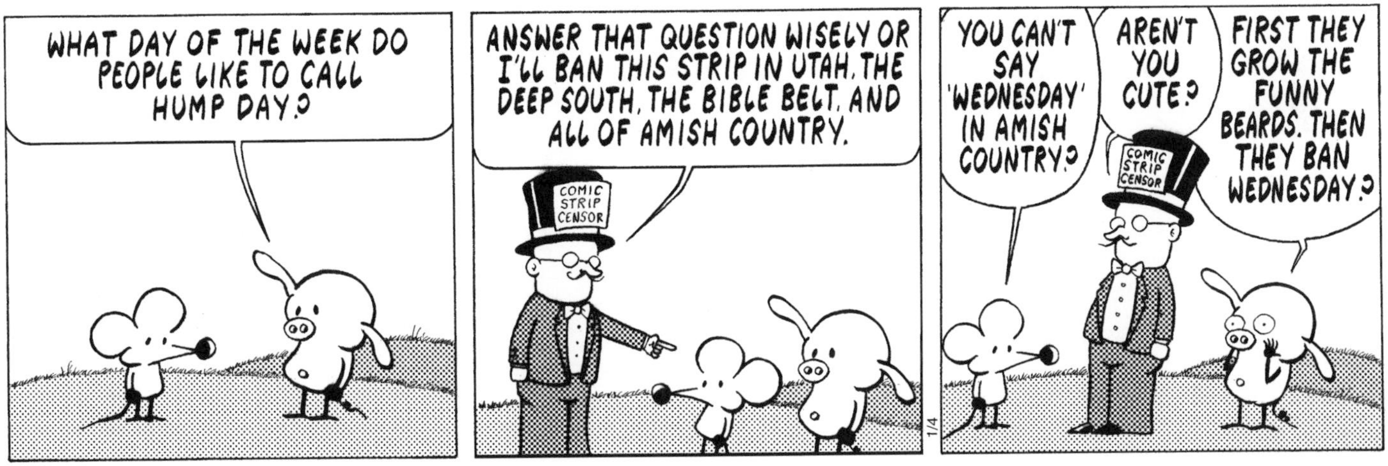
WHAT DAY OF THE WEEK DO PEOPLE LIKE TO CALL HUMP DAY?
ANSWER THAT QUESTION WISELY OR I'LL BAN THIS STRIP IN UTAH, THE DEEP SOUTH, THE BIBLE BELT, AND ALL OF AMISH COUNTRY.
COMIC STRIP CENSOR
YOU CAN'T SAY 'WEDNESDAY' IN AMISH COUNTRY?
AREN'T YOU CUTE?
FIRST THEY GROW THE FUNNY BEARDS. THEN THEY BAN WEDNESDAY?
COMIC STRIP CENSOR
1/4

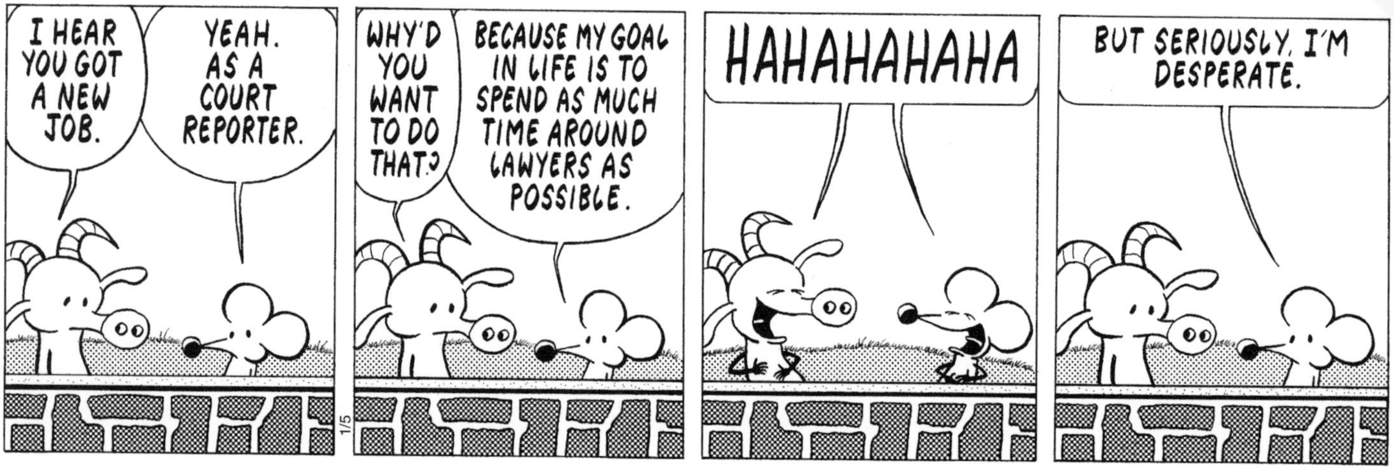
I HEAR YOU GOT A NEW JOB.
YEAH. AS A COURT REPORTER.
WHY'D YOU WANT TO DO THAT?
BECAUSE MY GOAL IN LIFE IS TO SPEND AS MUCH TIME AROUND LAWYERS AS POSSIBLE.
HAHAHAHAHA
BUT SERIOUSLY, I'M DESPERATE.
1/5

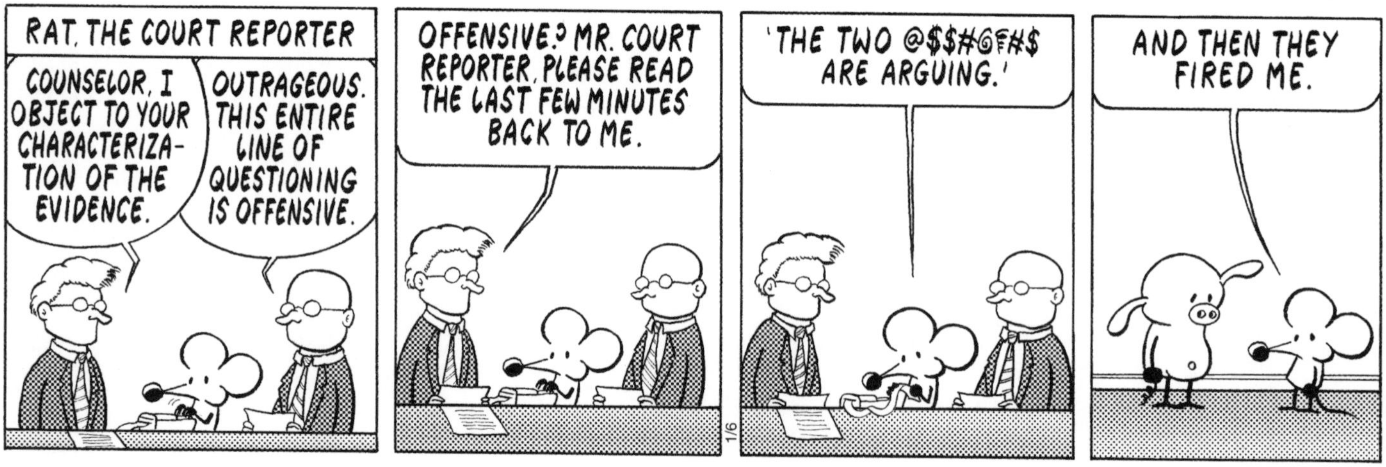
RAT, THE COURT REPORTER
COUNSELOR, I OBJECT TO YOUR CHARACTERIZATION OF THE EVIDENCE.
OUTRAGEOUS. THIS ENTIRE LINE OF QUESTIONING IS OFFENSIVE.
OFFENSIVE? MR. COURT REPORTER, PLEASE READ THE LAST FEW MINUTES BACK TO ME.
'THE TWO @$$#@F#$ ARE ARGUING.'
AND THEN THEY FIRED ME.
1/6

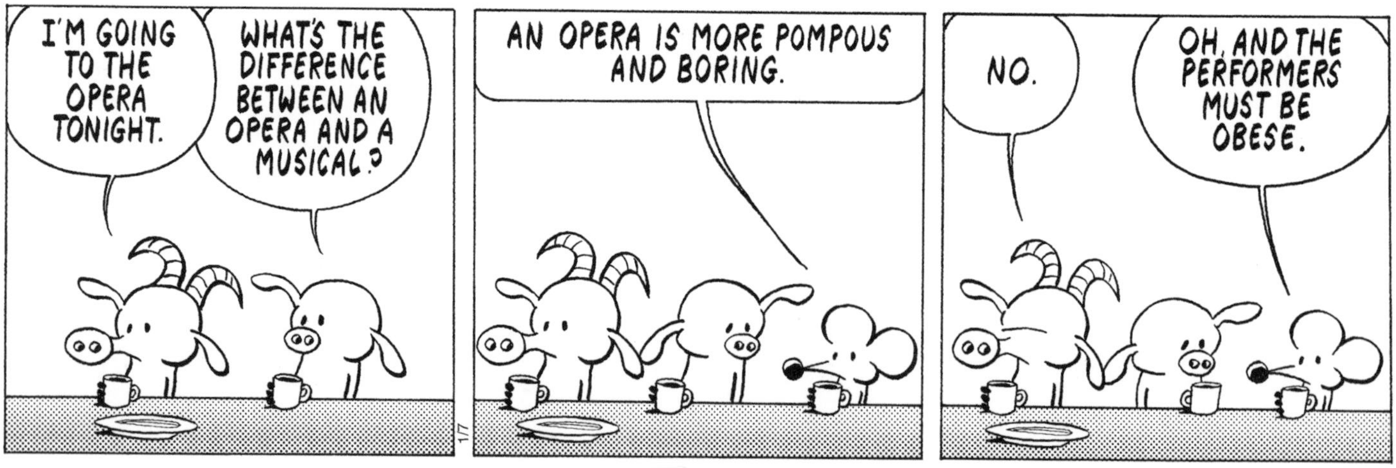
I'M GOING TO THE OPERA TONIGHT.
WHAT'S THE DIFFERENCE BETWEEN AN OPERA AND A MUSICAL?
AN OPERA IS MORE POMPOUS AND BORING.
NO.
OH, AND THE PERFORMERS MUST BE OBESE.
1/7

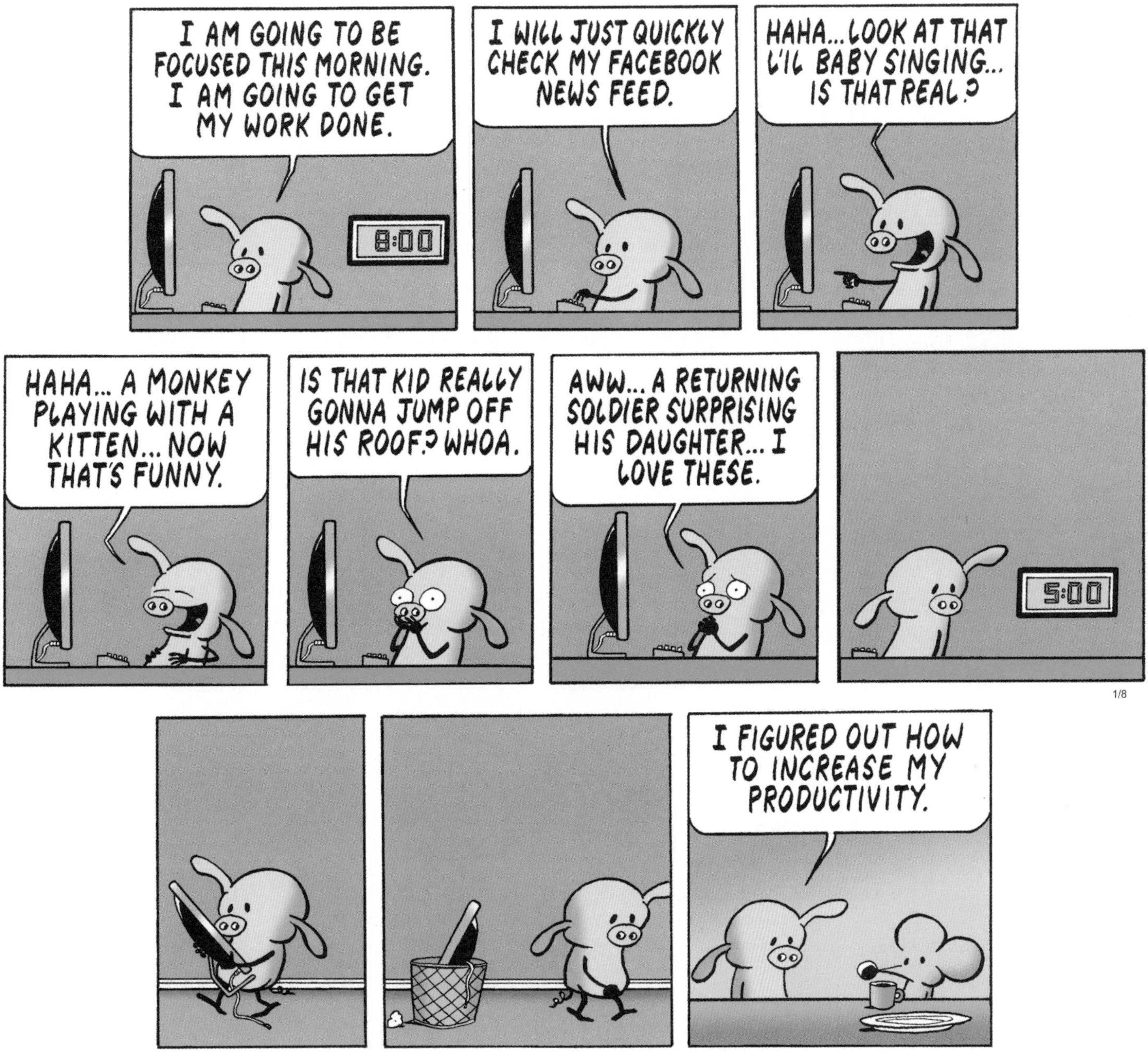
I AM GOING TO BE FOCUSED THIS MORNING. I AM GOING TO GET MY WORK DONE.
8:00
I WILL JUST QUICKLY CHECK MY FACEBOOK NEWS FEED.
HAHA...LOOK AT THAT LI'L BABY SINGING... IS THAT REAL?
HAHA... A MONKEY PLAYING WITH A KITTEN... NOW THAT'S FUNNY.
IS THAT KID REALLY GONNA JUMP OFF HIS ROOF? WHOA.
AWW... A RETURNING SOLDIER SURPRISING HIS DAUGHTER... I LOVE THESE.
5:00
1/8
I FIGURED OUT HOW TO INCREASE MY PRODUCTIVITY.

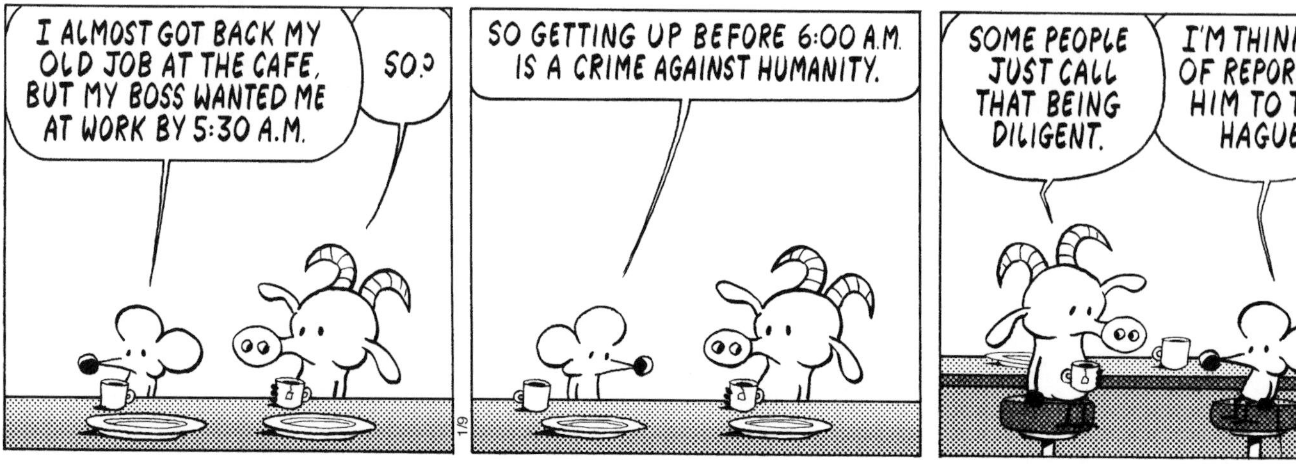
I ALMOST GOT BACK MY OLD JOB AT THE CAFE, BUT MY BOSS WANTED ME AT WORK BY 5:30 A.M.
SO?
1/9
SO GETTING UP BEFORE 6:00 A.M. IS A CRIME AGAINST HUMANITY.
SOME PEOPLE JUST CALL THAT BEING DILIGENT.
I'M THINKING OF REPORTING HIM TO THE HAGUE.

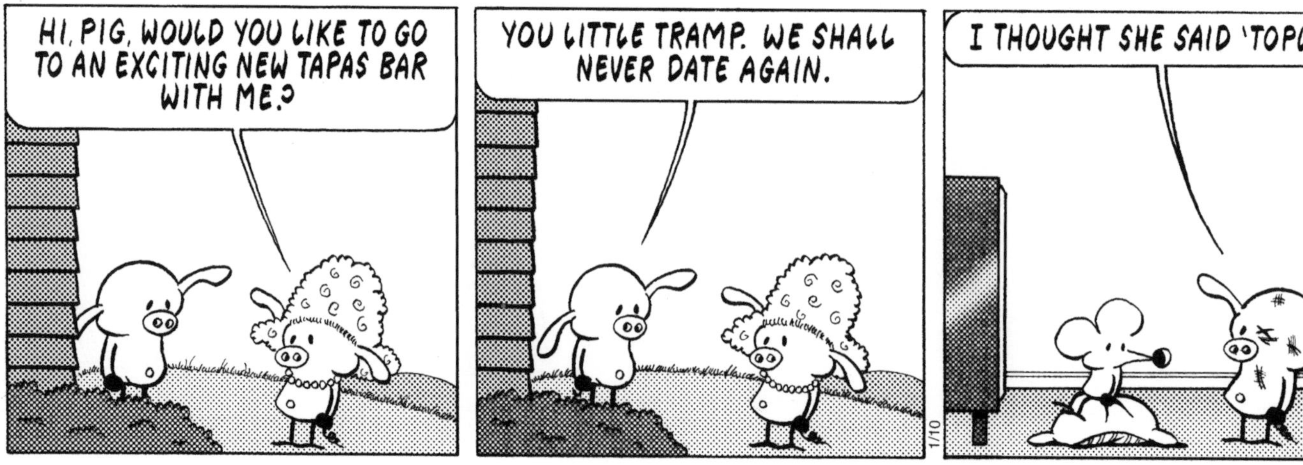
HI, PIG, WOULD YOU LIKE TO GO TO AN EXCITING NEW TAPAS BAR WITH ME?
YOU LITTLE TRAMP. WE SHALL NEVER DATE AGAIN.
1/10
I THOUGHT SHE SAID 'TOPLESS.'

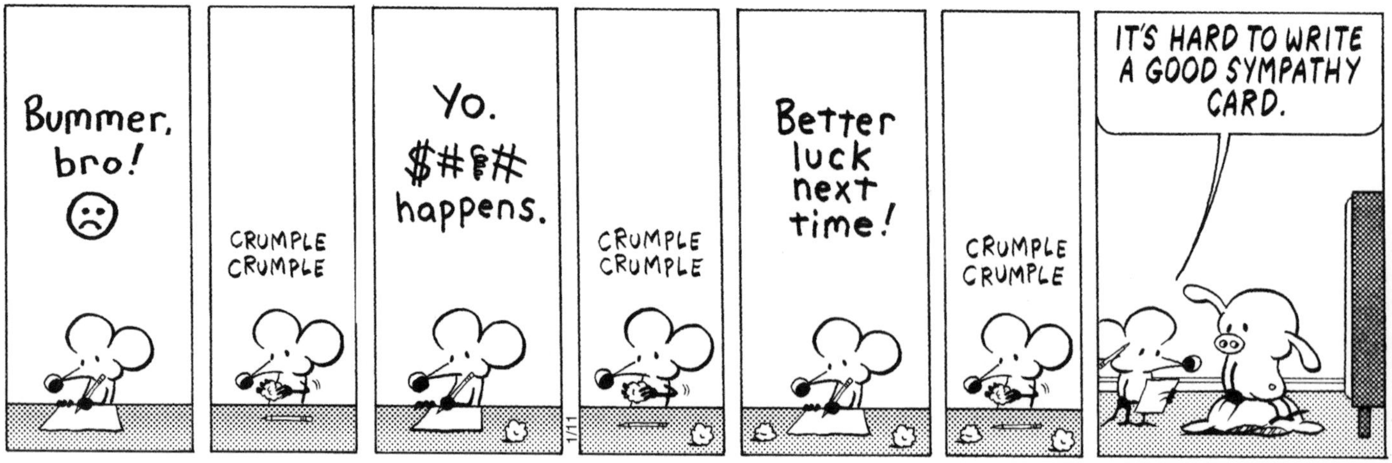
Bummer, bro! ☹
CRUMPLE CRUMPLE
Yo. $#$# happens.
1/11
CRUMPLE CRUMPLE
Better luck next time!
CRUMPLE CRUMPLE
IT'S HARD TO WRITE A GOOD SYMPATHY CARD.

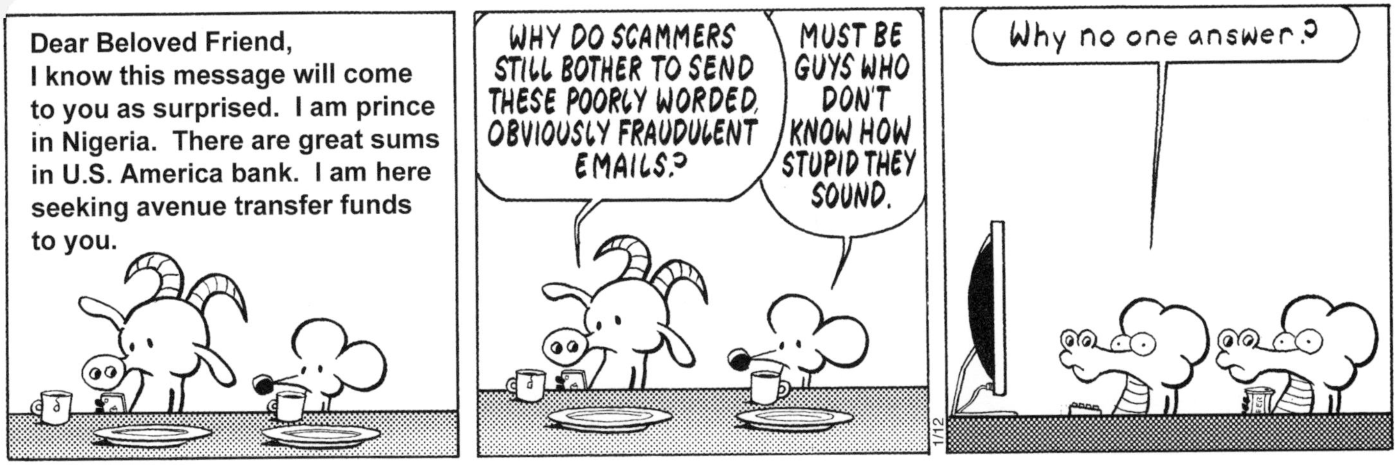
Dear Beloved Friend,
I know this message will come to you as surprised. I am prince in Nigeria. There are great sums in U.S. America bank. I am here seeking avenue transfer funds to you.
WHY DO SCAMMERS STILL BOTHER TO SEND THESE POORLY WORDED, OBVIOUSLY FRAUDULENT EMAILS?
MUST BE GUYS WHO DON'T KNOW HOW STUPID THEY SOUND.
1/12
Why no one answer?

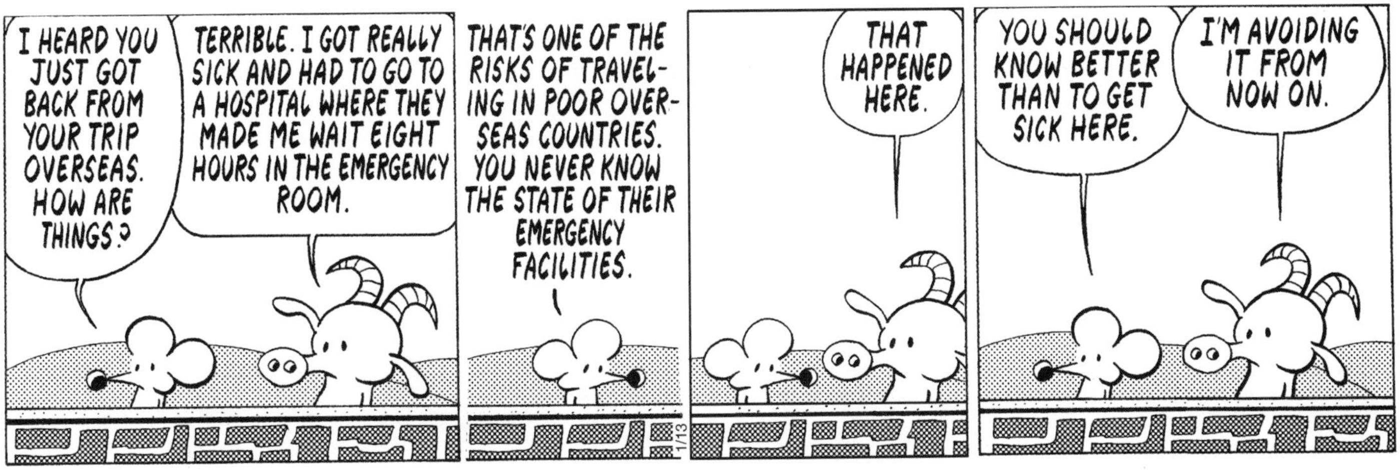
I HEARD YOU JUST GOT BACK FROM YOUR TRIP OVERSEAS. HOW ARE THINGS?
TERRIBLE. I GOT REALLY SICK AND HAD TO GO TO A HOSPITAL WHERE THEY MADE ME WAIT EIGHT HOURS IN THE EMERGENCY ROOM.
THAT'S ONE OF THE RISKS OF TRAVELING IN POOR OVERSEAS COUNTRIES. YOU NEVER KNOW THE STATE OF THEIR EMERGENCY FACILITIES.
1/13
THAT HAPPENED HERE.
YOU SHOULD KNOW BETTER THAN TO GET SICK HERE.
I'M AVOIDING IT FROM NOW ON.

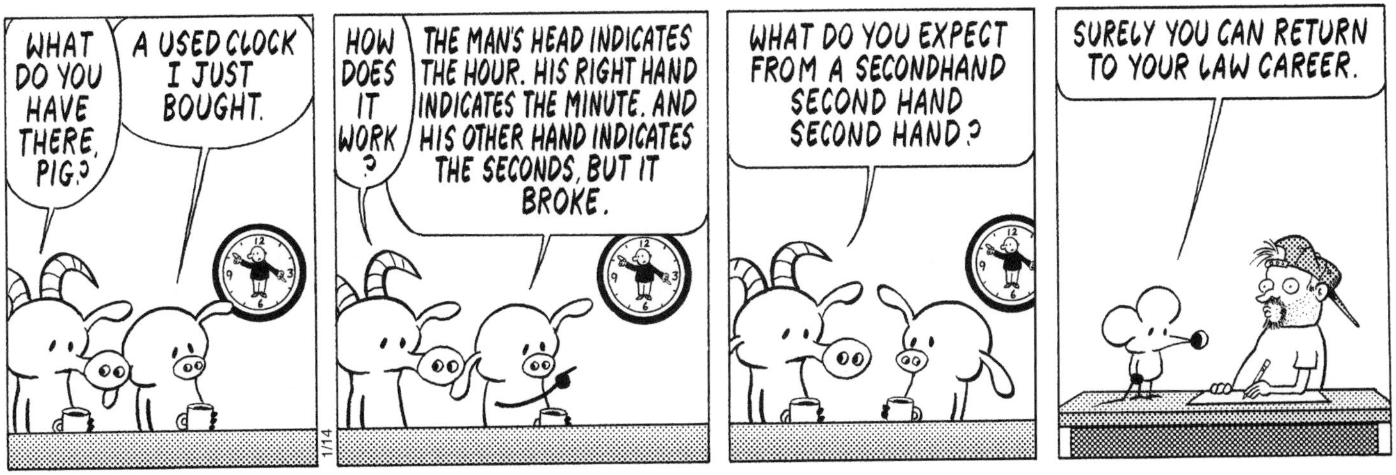
WHAT DO YOU HAVE THERE, PIG?
A USED CLOCK I JUST BOUGHT.
1/14
HOW DOES IT WORK?
THE MAN'S HEAD INDICATES THE HOUR. HIS RIGHT HAND INDICATES THE MINUTE. AND HIS OTHER HAND INDICATES THE SECONDS, BUT IT BROKE.
WHAT DO YOU EXPECT FROM A SECONDHAND SECOND HAND SECOND HAND?
SURELY YOU CAN RETURN TO YOUR LAW CAREER.

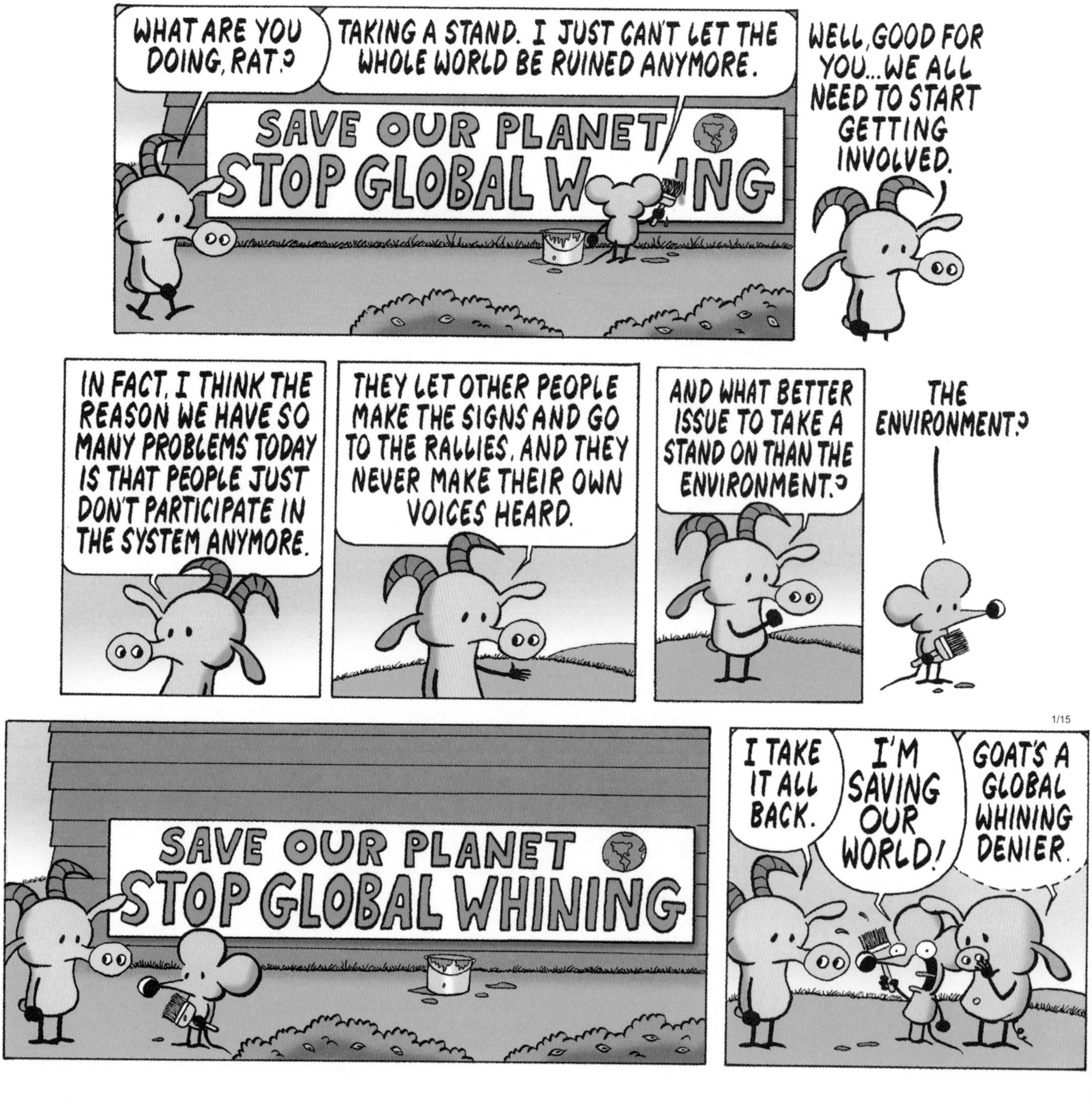
WHAT ARE YOU DOING, RAT?
TAKING A STAND. I JUST CAN'T LET THE WHOLE WORLD BE RUINED ANYMORE.
SAVE OUR PLANET
STOP GLOBAL W
NG
WELL, GOOD FOR YOU...WE ALL NEED TO START GETTING INVOLVED.
IN FACT, I THINK THE REASON WE HAVE SO MANY PROBLEMS TODAY IS THAT PEOPLE JUST DON'T PARTICIPATE IN THE SYSTEM ANYMORE.
THEY LET OTHER PEOPLE MAKE THE SIGNS AND GO TO THE RALLIES, AND THEY NEVER MAKE THEIR OWN VOICES HEARD.
AND WHAT BETTER ISSUE TO TAKE A STAND ON THAN THE ENVIRONMENT?
THE ENVIRONMENT?
SAVE OUR PLANET
STOP GLOBAL WHINING
1/15
I TAKE IT ALL BACK.
I'M SAVING OUR WORLD!
GOAT'S A GLOBAL WHINING DENIER.

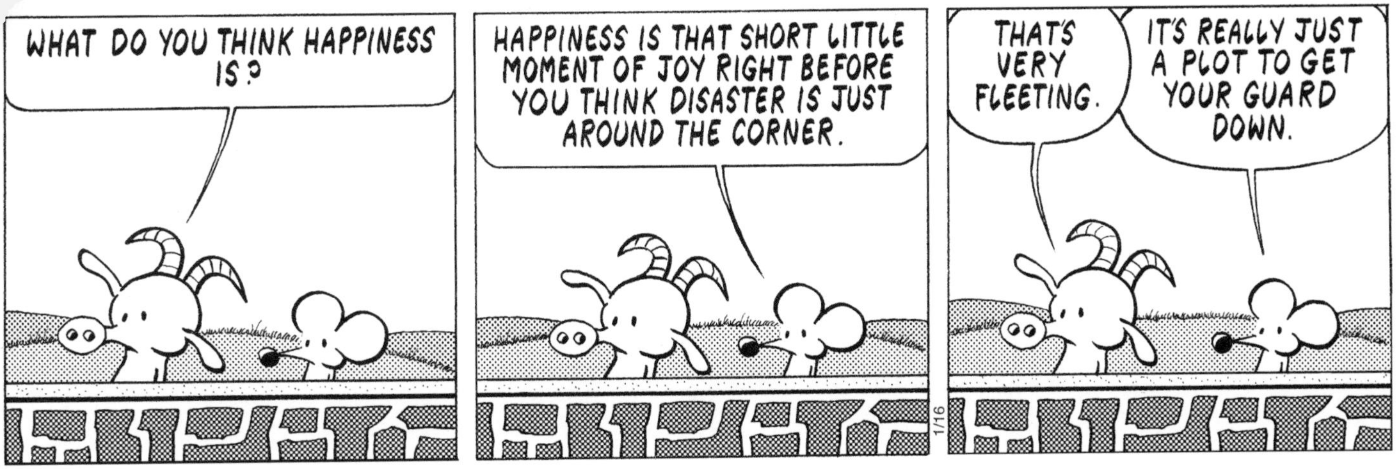
WHAT DO YOU THINK HAPPINESS IS?
HAPPINESS IS THAT SHORT LITTLE MOMENT OF JOY RIGHT BEFORE YOU THINK DISASTER IS JUST AROUND THE CORNER.
THAT'S VERY FLEETING.
IT'S REALLY JUST A PLOT TO GET YOUR GUARD DOWN.
1/16

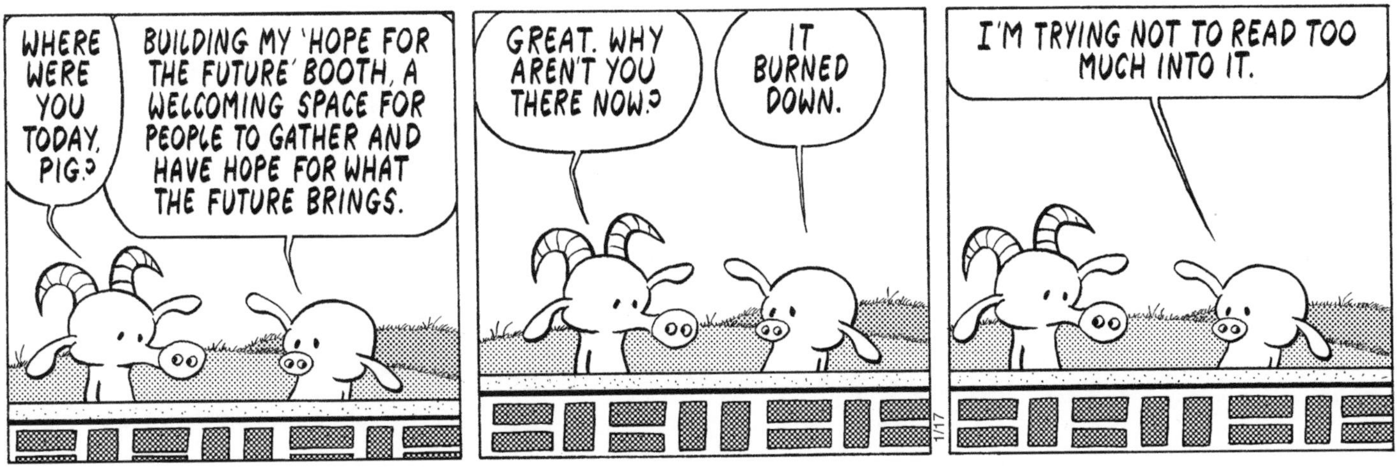
WHERE WERE YOU TODAY, PIG?
BUILDING MY 'HOPE FOR THE FUTURE' BOOTH, A WELCOMING SPACE FOR PEOPLE TO GATHER AND HAVE HOPE FOR WHAT THE FUTURE BRINGS.
GREAT. WHY AREN'T YOU THERE NOW?
IT BURNED DOWN.
I'M TRYING NOT TO READ TOO MUCH INTO IT.
1/17

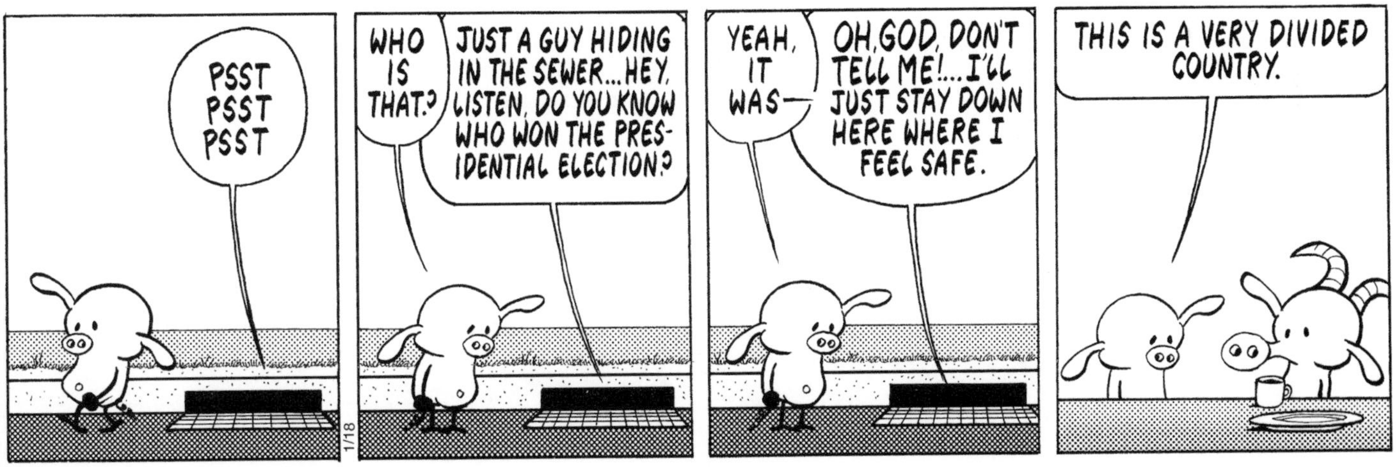
PSST PSST PSST
WHO IS THAT?
JUST A GUY HIDING IN THE SEWER... HEY, LISTEN, DO YOU KNOW WHO WON THE PRESIDENTIAL ELECTION?
YEAH, IT WAS—
OH, GOD, DON'T TELL ME!... I'LL JUST STAY DOWN HERE WHERE I FEEL SAFE.
THIS IS A VERY DIVIDED COUNTRY.
1/18

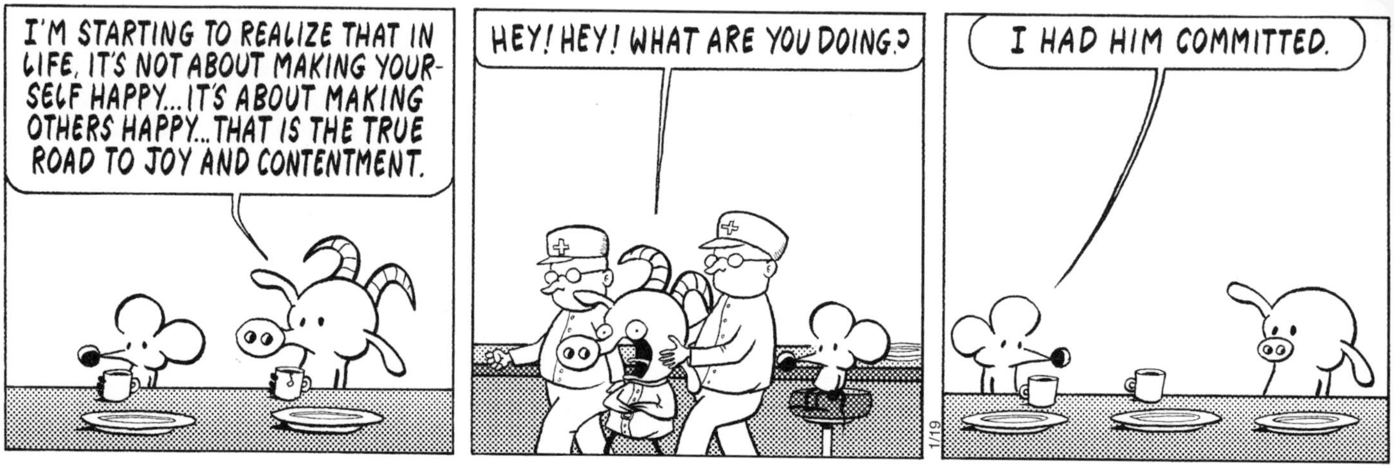
I'M STARTING TO REALIZE THAT IN LIFE, IT'S NOT ABOUT MAKING YOURSELF HAPPY... IT'S ABOUT MAKING OTHERS HAPPY... THAT IS THE TRUE ROAD TO JOY AND CONTENTMENT.
HEY! HEY! WHAT ARE YOU DOING?
I HAD HIM COMMITTED.
1/19

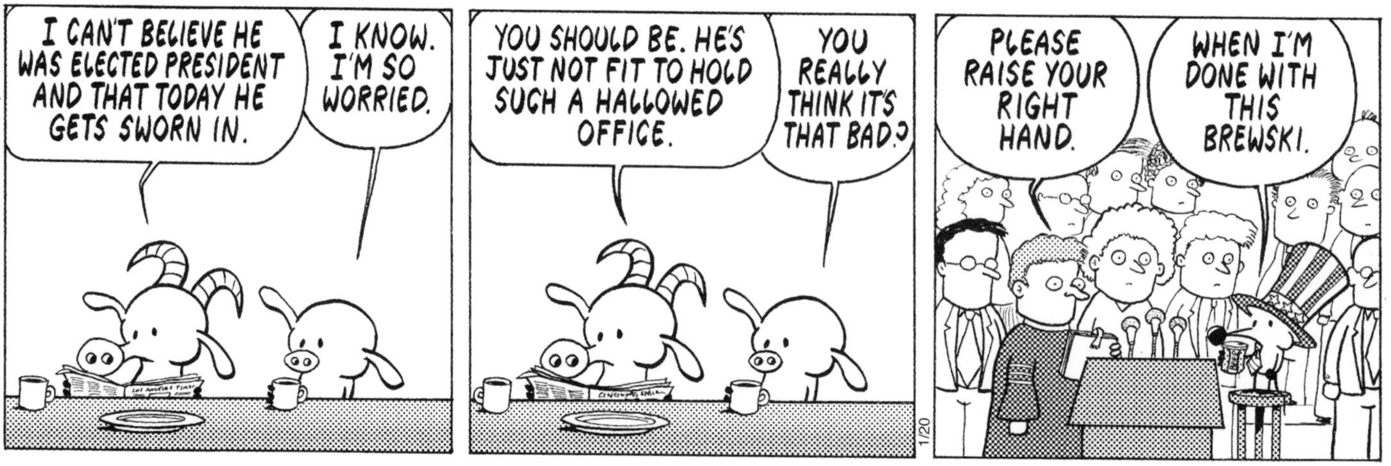
I CAN'T BELIEVE HE WAS ELECTED PRESIDENT AND THAT TODAY HE GETS SWORN IN.
I KNOW. I'M SO WORRIED.
YOU SHOULD BE. HE'S JUST NOT FIT TO HOLD SUCH A HALLOWED OFFICE.
YOU REALLY THINK IT'S THAT BAD?
PLEASE RAISE YOUR RIGHT HAND.
WHEN I'M DONE WITH THIS BREWSKI.
1/20

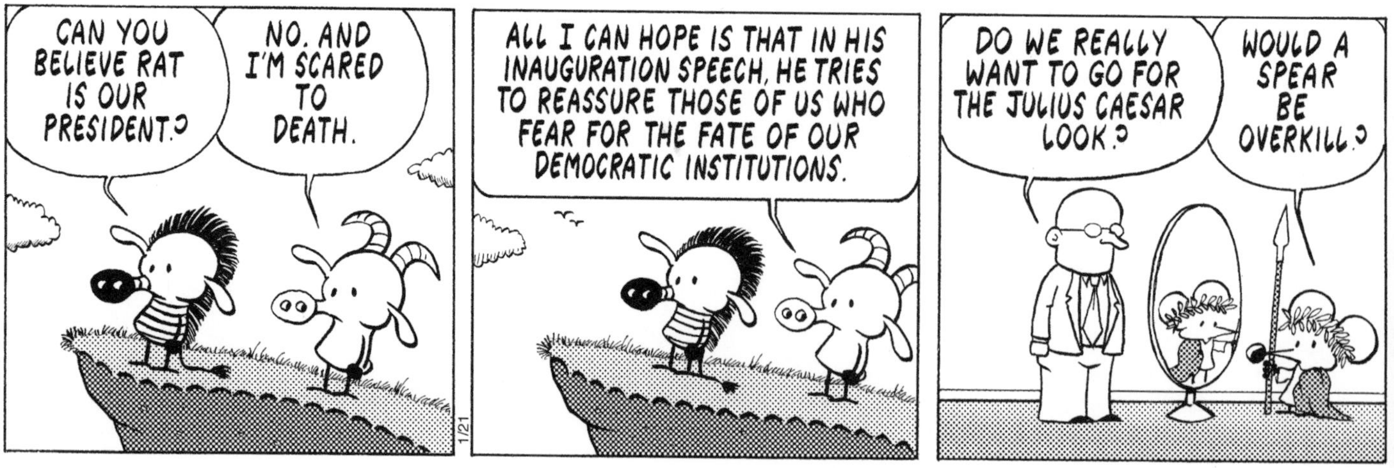
CAN YOU BELIEVE RAT IS OUR PRESIDENT?
NO. AND I'M SCARED TO DEATH.
ALL I CAN HOPE IS THAT IN HIS INAUGURATION SPEECH, HE TRIES TO REASSURE THOSE OF US WHO FEAR FOR THE FATE OF OUR DEMOCRATIC INSTITUTIONS.
DO WE REALLY WANT TO GO FOR THE JULIUS CAESAR LOOK?
WOULD A SPEAR BE OVERKILL?
1/21

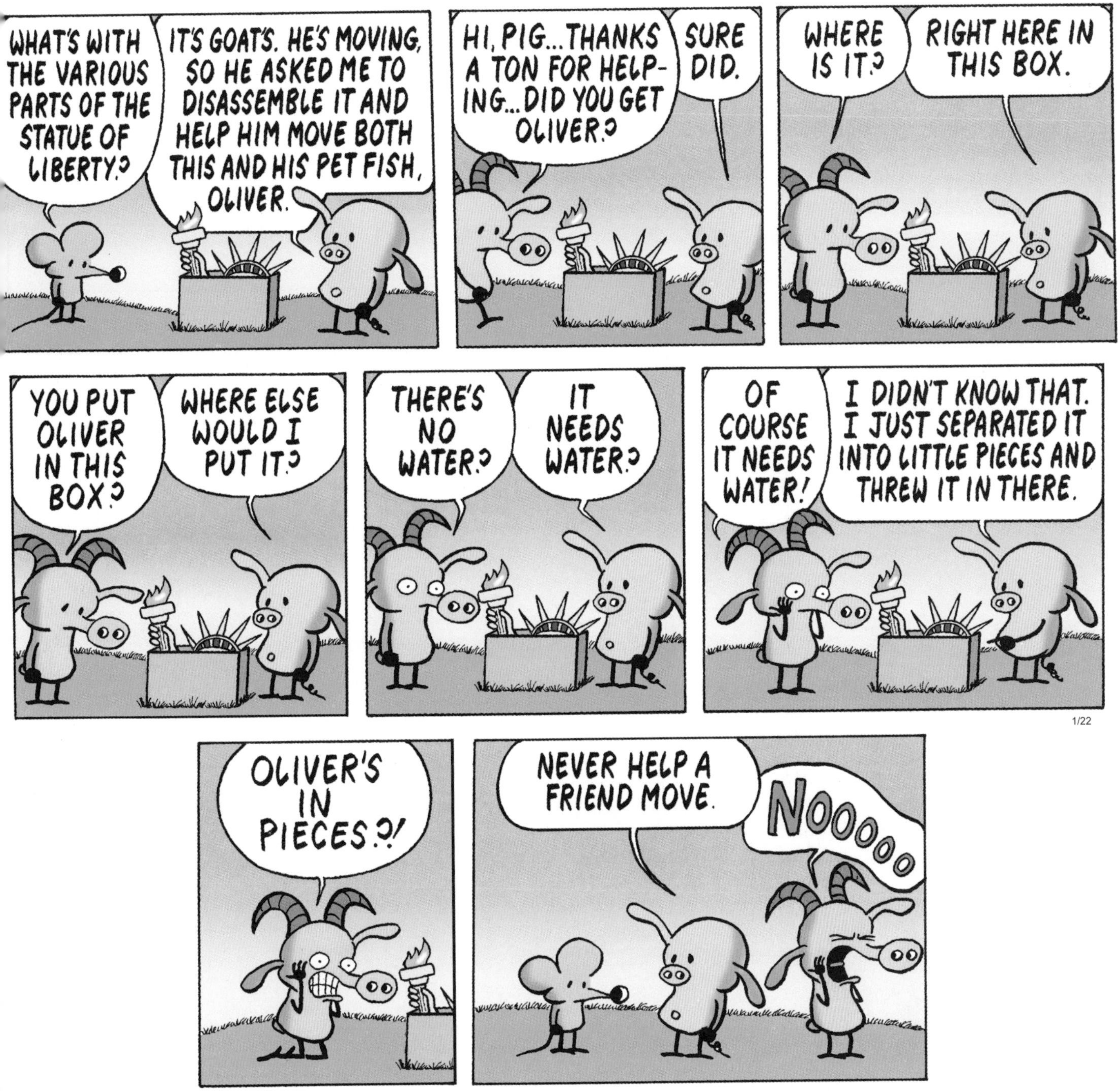
WHAT'S WITH THE VARIOUS PARTS OF THE STATUE OF LIBERTY?
IT'S GOAT'S. HE'S MOVING, SO HE ASKED ME TO DISASSEMBLE IT AND HELP HIM MOVE BOTH THIS AND HIS PET FISH, OLIVER.
HI, PIG...THANKS A TON FOR HELPING...DID YOU GET OLIVER?
SURE DID.
WHERE IS IT?
RIGHT HERE IN THIS BOX.
YOU PUT OLIVER IN THIS BOX?
WHERE ELSE WOULD I PUT IT?
THERE'S NO WATER?
IT NEEDS WATER?
OF COURSE IT NEEDS WATER!
I DIDN'T KNOW THAT. I JUST SEPARATED IT INTO LITTLE PIECES AND THREW IT IN THERE.
1/22
OLIVER'S IN PIECES?!
NEVER HELP A FRIEND MOVE.
NOOOOOO

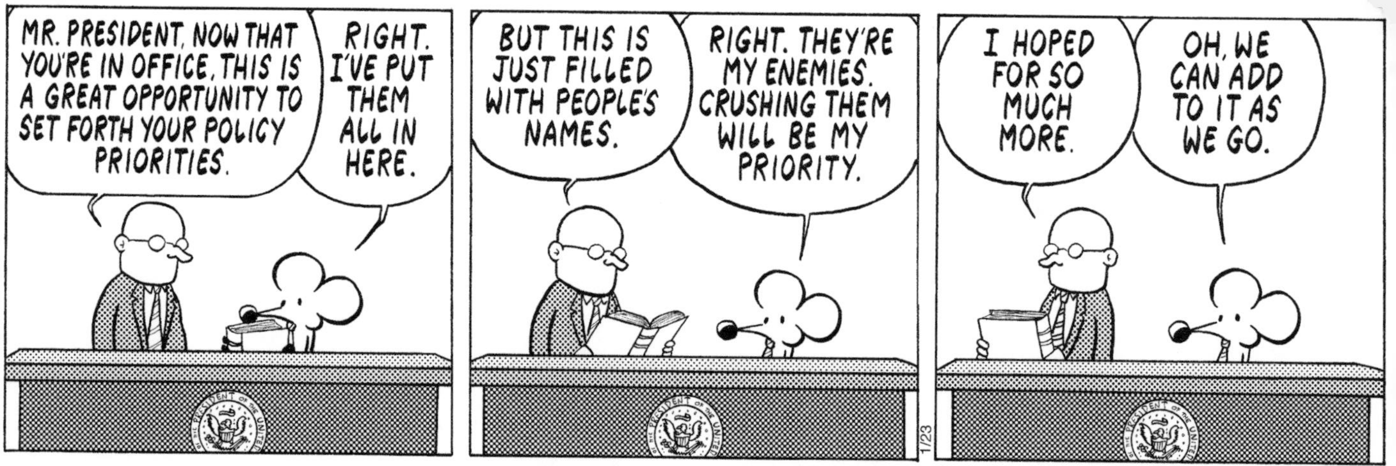
MR. PRESIDENT, NOW THAT YOU'RE IN OFFICE, THIS IS A GREAT OPPORTUNITY TO SET FORTH YOUR POLICY PRIORITIES.
RIGHT. I'VE PUT THEM ALL IN HERE.
BUT THIS IS JUST FILLED WITH PEOPLE'S NAMES.
RIGHT. THEY'RE MY ENEMIES. CRUSHING THEM WILL BE MY PRIORITY.
1/23
I HOPED FOR SO MUCH MORE.
OH, WE CAN ADD TO IT AS WE GO.

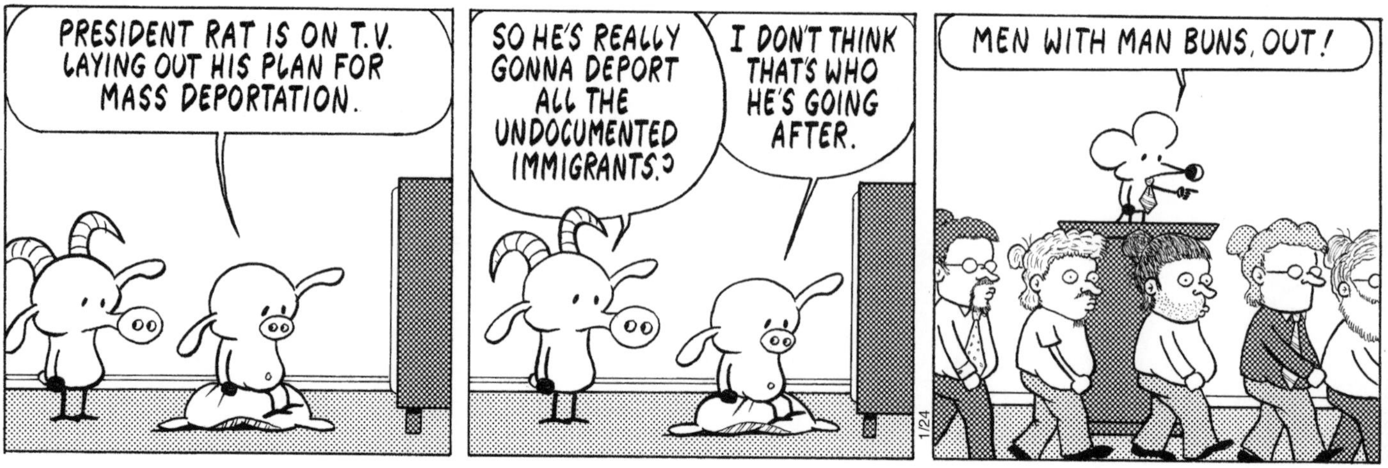
PRESIDENT RAT IS ON T.V. LAYING OUT HIS PLAN FOR MASS DEPORTATION.
SO HE'S REALLY GONNA DEPORT ALL THE UNDOCUMENTED IMMIGRANTS?
I DON'T THINK THAT'S WHO HE'S GOING AFTER.
1/24
MEN WITH MAN BUNS, OUT!

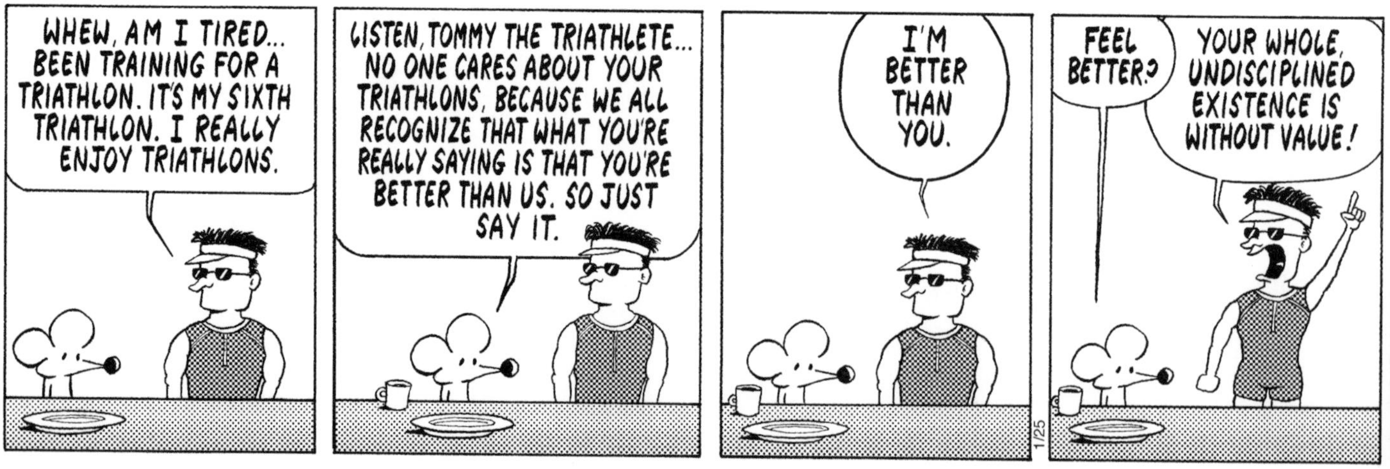
WHEW, AM I TIRED... BEEN TRAINING FOR A TRIATHLON. IT'S MY SIXTH TRIATHLON. I REALLY ENJOY TRIATHLONS.
LISTEN, TOMMY THE TRIATHLETE... NO ONE CARES ABOUT YOUR TRIATHLONS, BECAUSE WE ALL RECOGNIZE THAT WHAT YOU'RE REALLY SAYING IS THAT YOU'RE BETTER THAN US. SO JUST SAY IT.
I'M BETTER THAN YOU.
1/25
FEEL BETTER?
YOUR WHOLE, UNDISCIPLINED EXISTENCE IS WITHOUT VALUE!

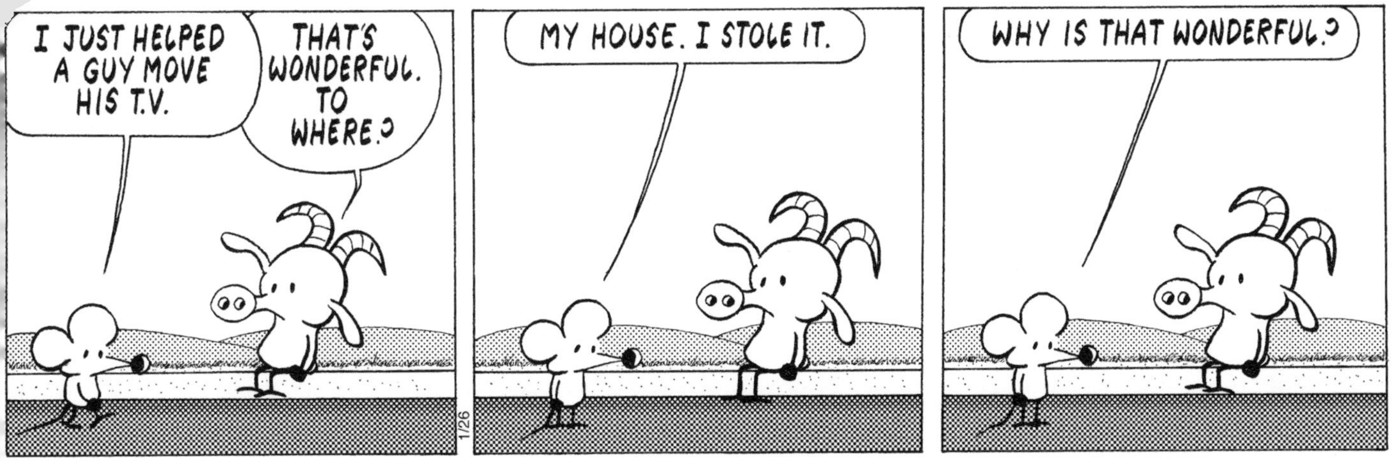
I JUST HELPED A GUY MOVE HIS T.V.
THAT'S WONDERFUL. TO WHERE?
MY HOUSE. I STOLE IT.
WHY IS THAT WONDERFUL?
1/26

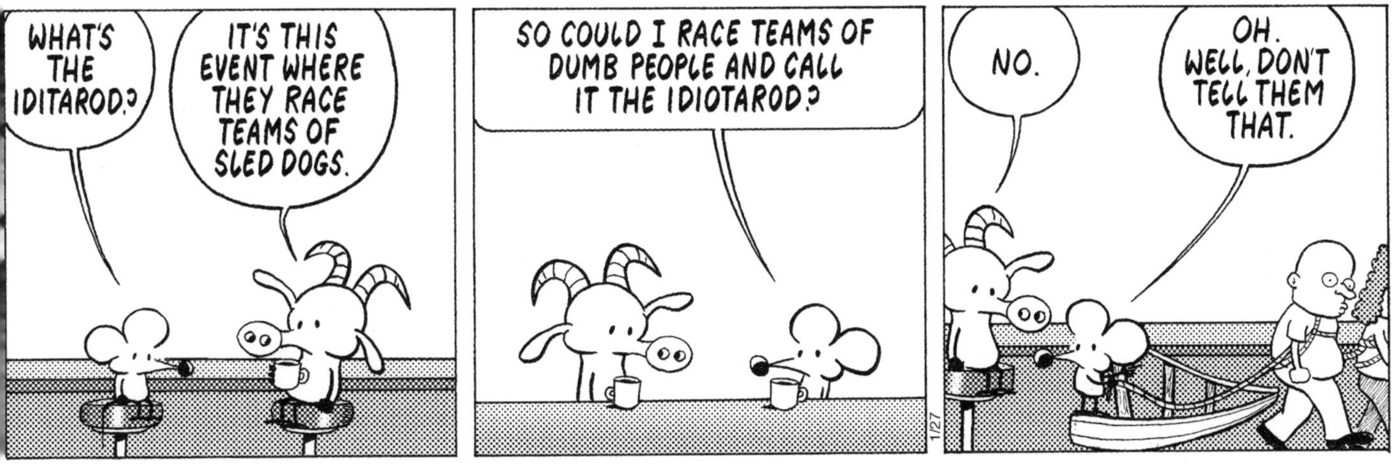
WHAT'S THE IDITAROD?
IT'S THIS EVENT WHERE THEY RACE TEAMS OF SLED DOGS.
SO COULD I RACE TEAMS OF DUMB PEOPLE AND CALL IT THE IDIOTAROD?
NO.
OH. WELL, DON'T TELL THEM THAT.
1/27

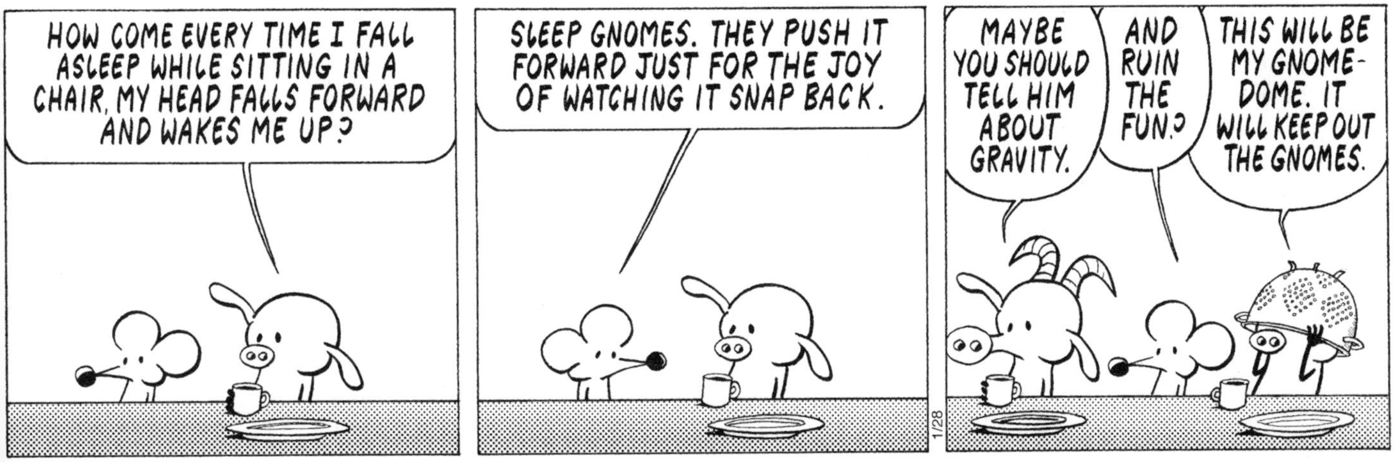
HOW COME EVERY TIME I FALL ASLEEP WHILE SITTING IN A CHAIR, MY HEAD FALLS FORWARD AND WAKES ME UP?
SLEEP GNOMES. THEY PUSH IT FORWARD JUST FOR THE JOY OF WATCHING IT SNAP BACK.
MAYBE YOU SHOULD TELL HIM ABOUT GRAVITY.
AND RUIN THE FUN?
THIS WILL BE MY GNOME-DOME. IT WILL KEEP OUT THE GNOMES.
1/28

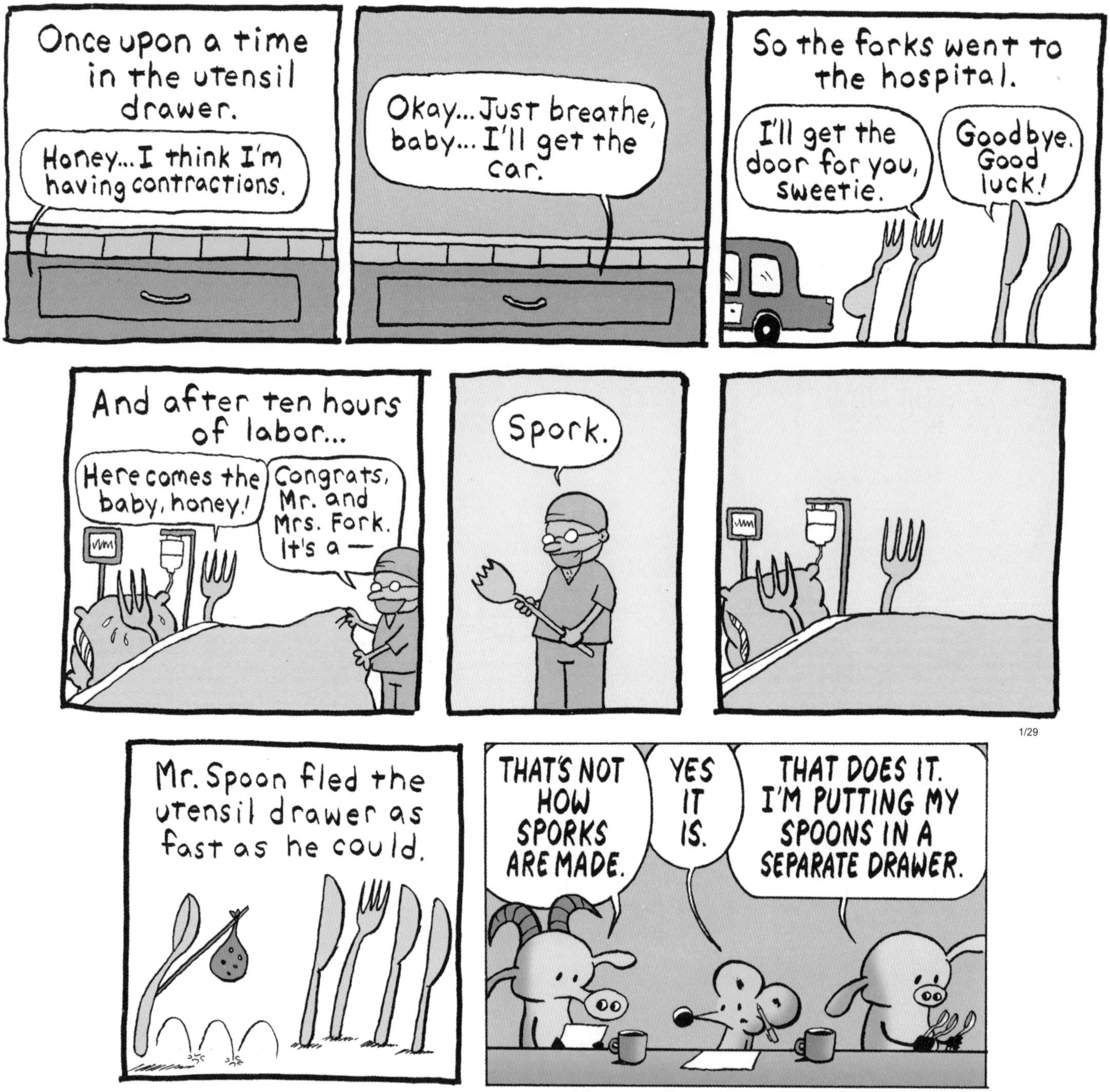
Once upon a time in the utensil drawer.
Honey... I think I'm having contractions.
Okay... Just breathe, baby... I'll get the car.
So the forks went to the hospital.
I'll get the door for you, sweetie.
Goodbye. Good luck!
And after ten hours of labor...
Here comes the baby, honey!
Congrats, Mr. and Mrs. Fork. It's a —
Spork.
1/29
Mr. Spoon fled the utensil drawer as fast as he could.
THAT'S NOT HOW SPORKS ARE MADE.
YES IT IS.
THAT DOES IT. I'M PUTTING MY SPOONS IN A SEPARATE DRAWER.

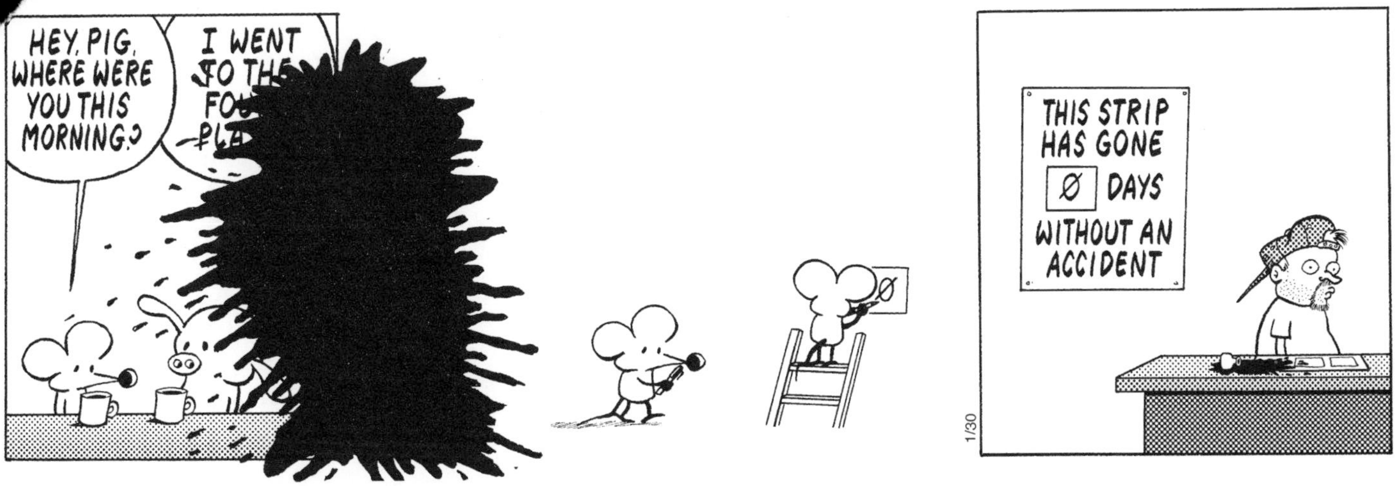

HEY, PIG, WHERE WERE YOU THIS MORNING?
I WENT
THIS STRIP HAS GONE Ø DAYS WITHOUT AN ACCIDENT
Ø
1/30

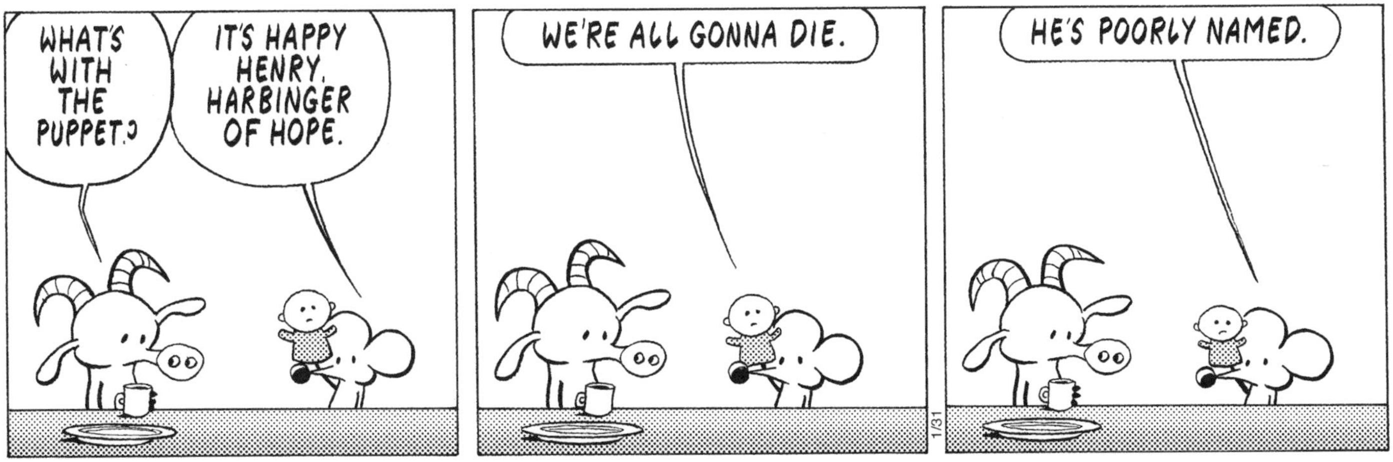

WHAT'S WITH THE PUPPET?
IT'S HAPPY HENRY, HARBINGER OF HOPE.
WE'RE ALL GONNA DIE.
HE'S POORLY NAMED.
1/31

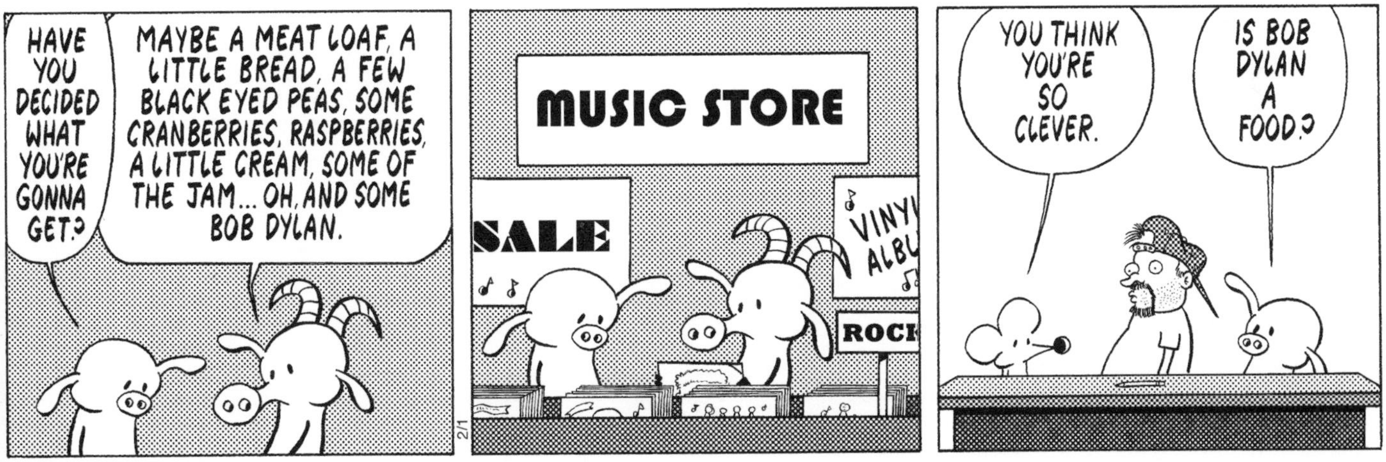

HAVE YOU DECIDED WHAT YOU'RE GONNA GET?
MAYBE A MEAT LOAF, A LITTLE BREAD, A FEW BLACK EYED PEAS, SOME CRANBERRIES, RASPBERRIES, A LITTLE CREAM, SOME OF THE JAM... OH, AND SOME BOB DYLAN.
2/1
MUSIC STORE
SALE
ROCK
YOU THINK YOU'RE SO CLEVER.
IS BOB DYLAN A FOOD?

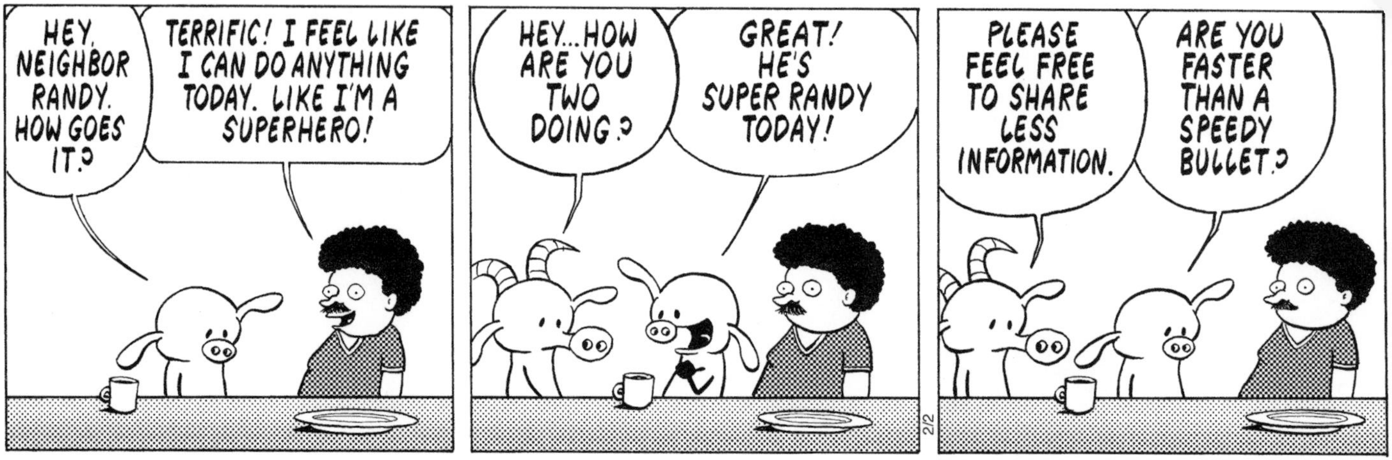
HEY, NEIGHBOR RANDY. HOW GOES IT?
TERRIFIC! I FEEL LIKE I CAN DO ANYTHING TODAY. LIKE I'M A SUPERHERO!
HEY...HOW ARE YOU TWO DOING?
GREAT! HE'S SUPER RANDY TODAY!
2/2
PLEASE FEEL FREE TO SHARE LESS INFORMATION.
ARE YOU FASTER THAN A SPEEDY BULLET?

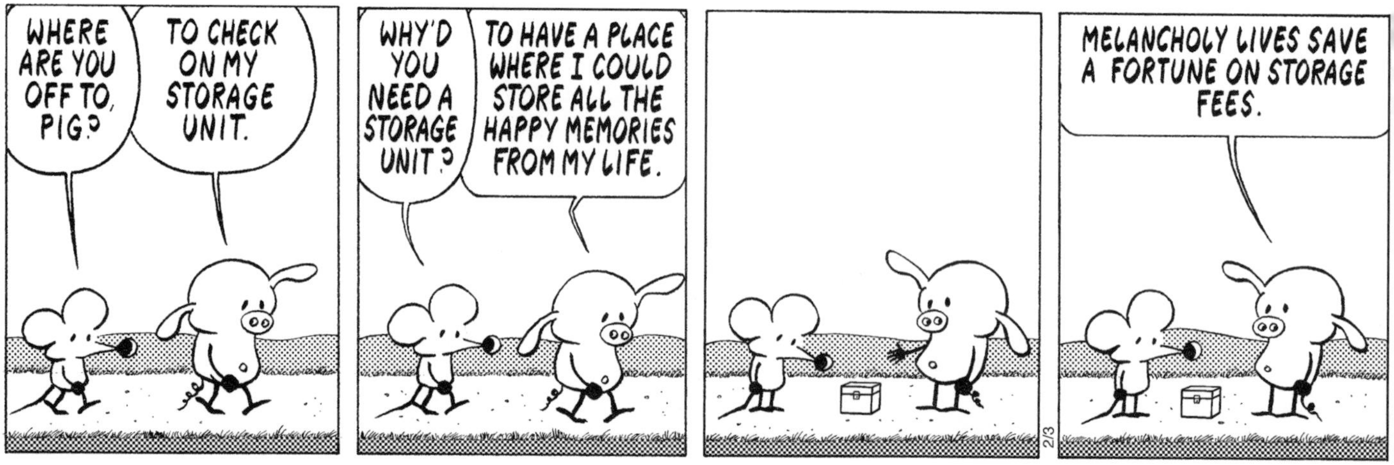
WHERE ARE YOU OFF TO, PIG?
TO CHECK ON MY STORAGE UNIT.
WHY'D YOU NEED A STORAGE UNIT?
TO HAVE A PLACE WHERE I COULD STORE ALL THE HAPPY MEMORIES FROM MY LIFE.
2/3
MELANCHOLY LIVES SAVE A FORTUNE ON STORAGE FEES.

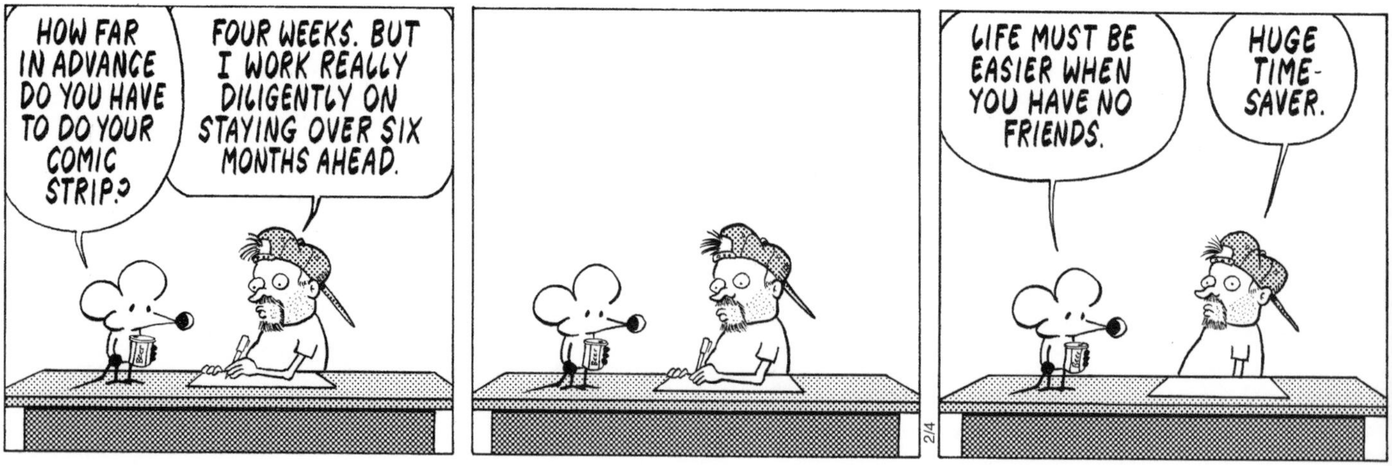
HOW FAR IN ADVANCE DO YOU HAVE TO DO YOUR COMIC STRIP?
FOUR WEEKS. BUT I WORK REALLY DILIGENTLY ON STAYING OVER SIX MONTHS AHEAD.
2/4
LIFE MUST BE EASIER WHEN YOU HAVE NO FRIENDS.
HUGE TIME-SAVER.

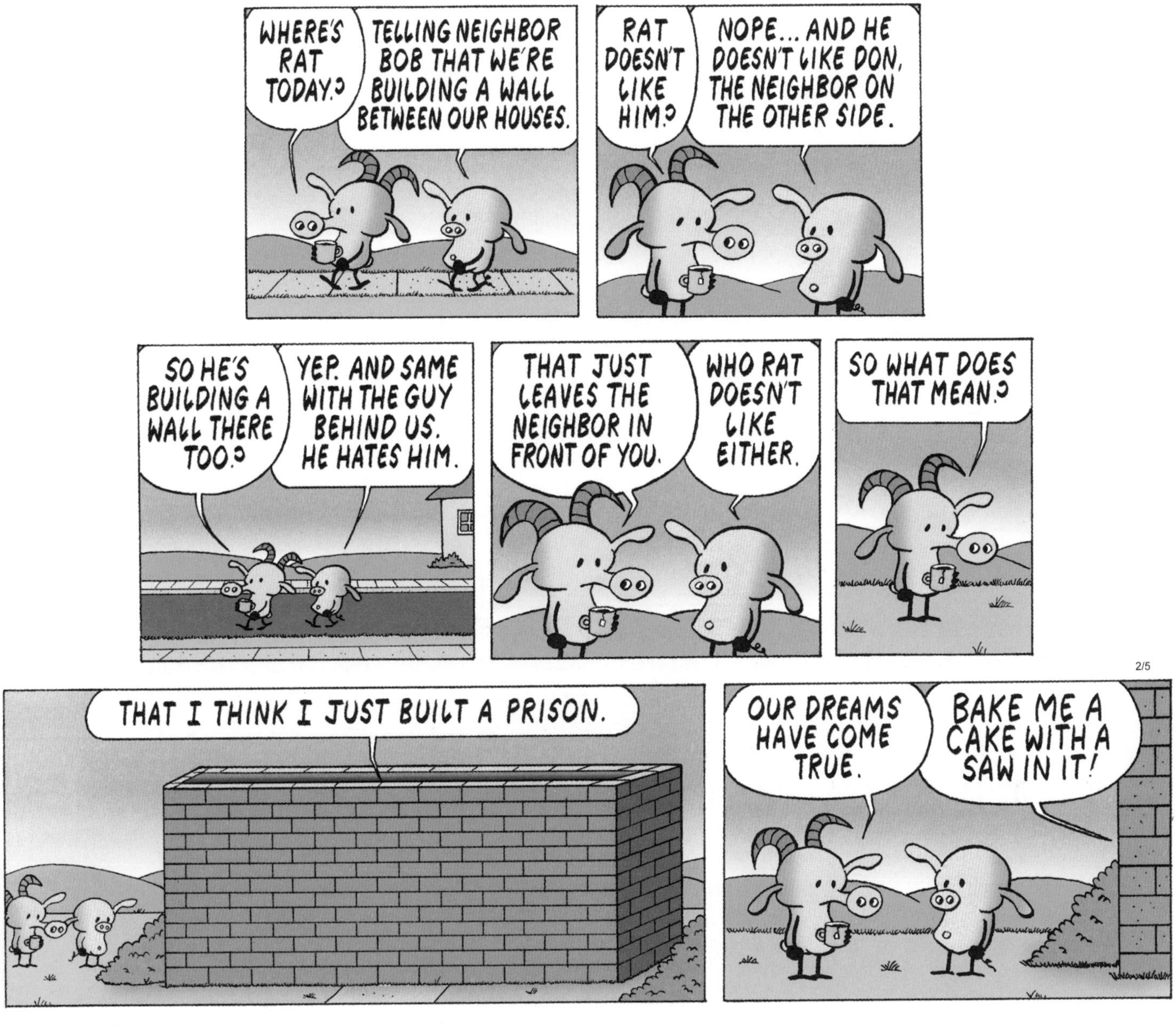
WHERE'S RAT TODAY?
TELLING NEIGHBOR BOB THAT WE'RE BUILDING A WALL BETWEEN OUR HOUSES.
RAT DOESN'T LIKE HIM?
NOPE... AND HE DOESN'T LIKE DON, THE NEIGHBOR ON THE OTHER SIDE.
SO HE'S BUILDING A WALL THERE TOO?
YEP. AND SAME WITH THE GUY BEHIND US. HE HATES HIM.
THAT JUST LEAVES THE NEIGHBOR IN FRONT OF YOU.
WHO RAT DOESN'T LIKE EITHER.
SO WHAT DOES THAT MEAN?
2/5
THAT I THINK I JUST BUILT A PRISON.
OUR DREAMS HAVE COME TRUE.
BAKE ME A CAKE WITH A SAW IN IT!

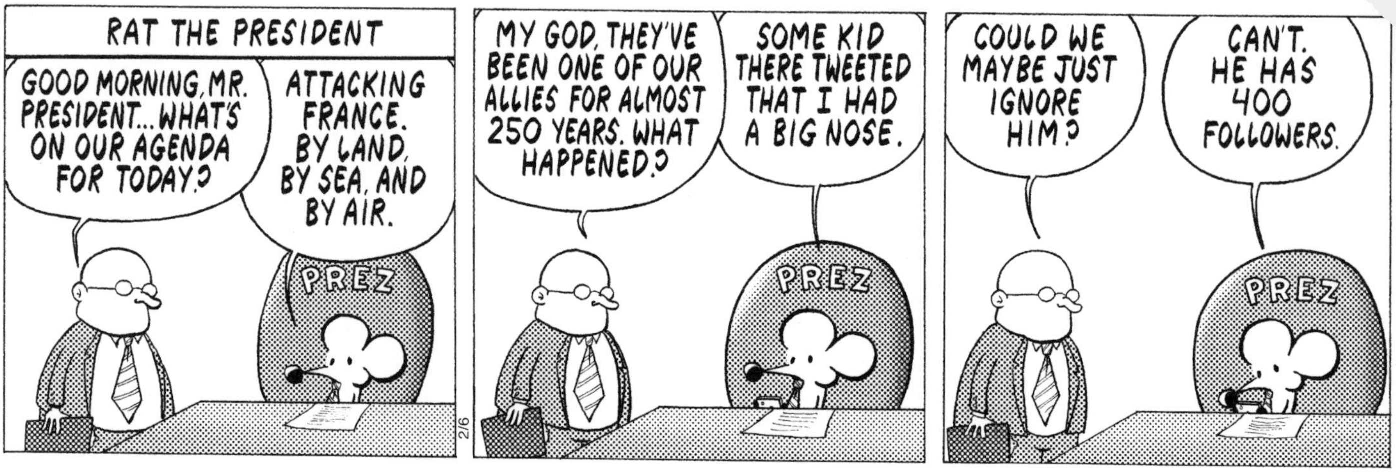
RAT THE PRESIDENT
GOOD MORNING, MR. PRESIDENT... WHAT'S ON OUR AGENDA FOR TODAY?
ATTACKING FRANCE. BY LAND, BY SEA, AND BY AIR.
PREZ
2/6
MY GOD, THEY'VE BEEN ONE OF OUR ALLIES FOR ALMOST 250 YEARS. WHAT HAPPENED?
SOME KID THERE TWEETED THAT I HAD A BIG NOSE.
PREZ
COULD WE MAYBE JUST IGNORE HIM?
CAN'T. HE HAS 400 FOLLOWERS.
PREZ

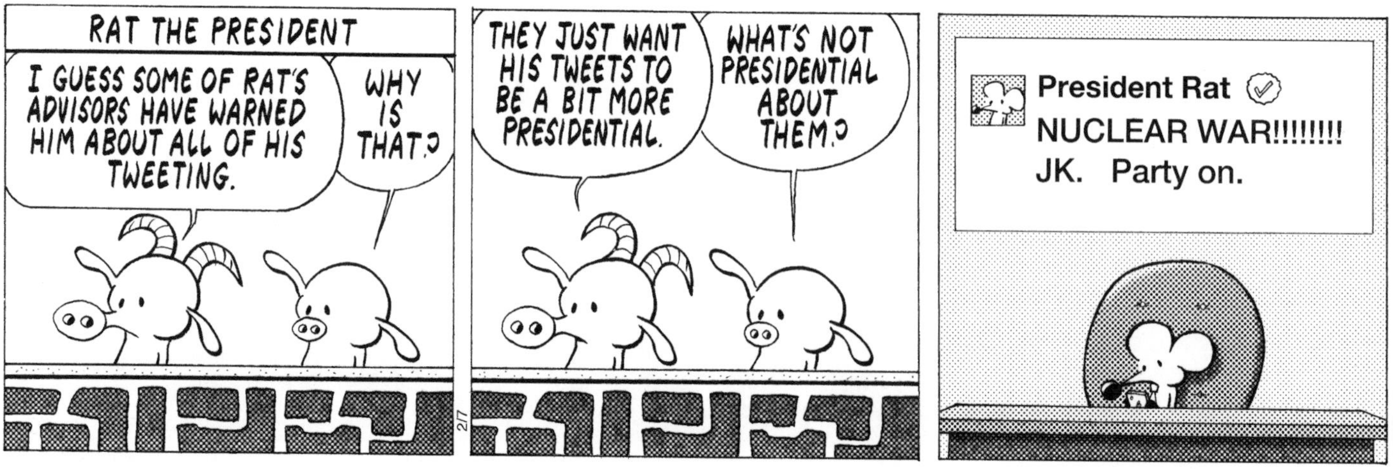
RAT THE PRESIDENT
I GUESS SOME OF RAT'S ADVISORS HAVE WARNED HIM ABOUT ALL OF HIS TWEETING.
WHY IS THAT?
2/7
THEY JUST WANT HIS TWEETS TO BE A BIT MORE PRESIDENTIAL.
WHAT'S NOT PRESIDENTIAL ABOUT THEM?
President Rat
NUCLEAR WAR!!!!!!!!
JK. Party on.

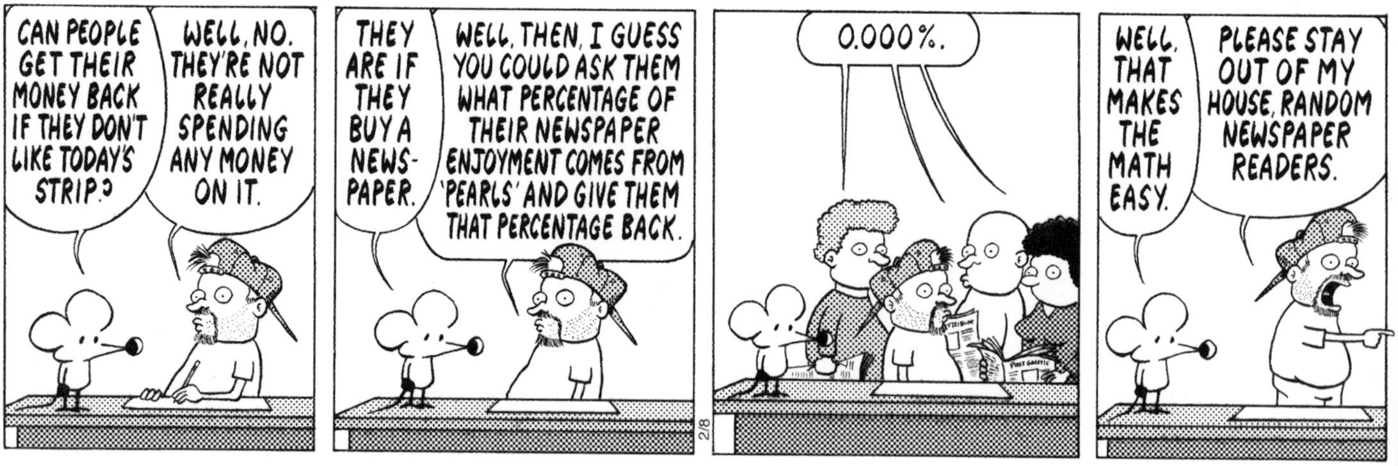
CAN PEOPLE GET THEIR MONEY BACK IF THEY DON'T LIKE TODAY'S STRIP?
WELL, NO. THEY'RE NOT REALLY SPENDING ANY MONEY ON IT.
THEY ARE IF THEY BUY A NEWS-PAPER.
WELL, THEN, I GUESS YOU COULD ASK THEM WHAT PERCENTAGE OF THEIR NEWSPAPER ENJOYMENT COMES FROM 'PEARLS' AND GIVE THEM THAT PERCENTAGE BACK.
2/8
0.000%.
WELL, THAT MAKES THE MATH EASY.
PLEASE STAY OUT OF MY HOUSE, RANDOM NEWSPAPER READERS.

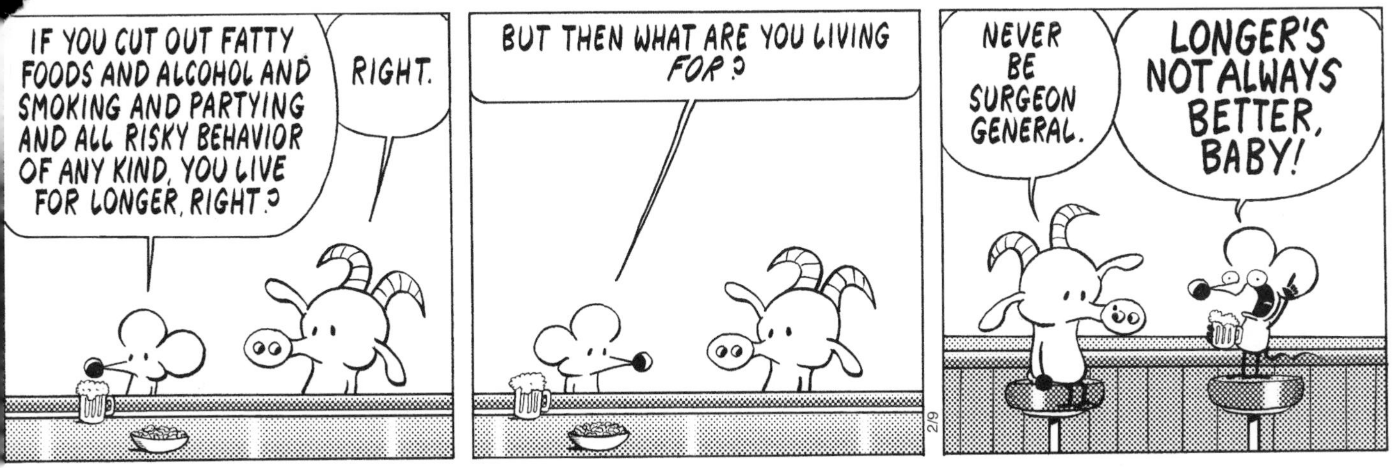
IF YOU CUT OUT FATTY FOODS AND ALCOHOL AND SMOKING AND PARTYING AND ALL RISKY BEHAVIOR OF ANY KIND, YOU LIVE FOR LONGER, RIGHT?
RIGHT.
BUT THEN WHAT ARE YOU LIVING *FOR*?
2/9
NEVER BE SURGEON GENERAL.
LONGER'S NOT ALWAYS BETTER, BABY!

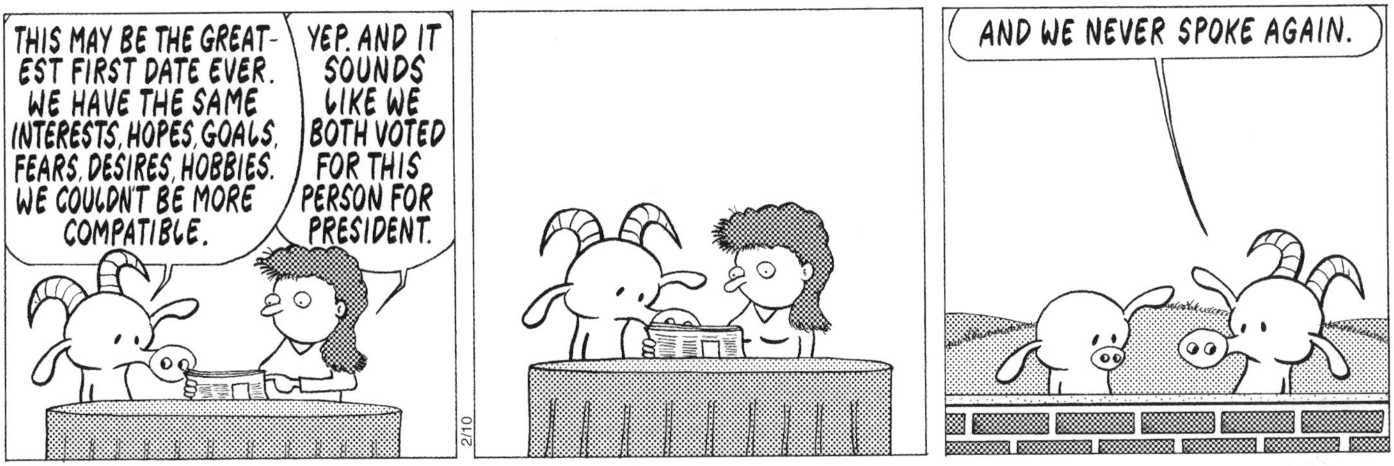
THIS MAY BE THE GREATEST FIRST DATE EVER. WE HAVE THE SAME INTERESTS, HOPES, GOALS, FEARS, DESIRES, HOBBIES. WE COULDN'T BE MORE COMPATIBLE.
YEP. AND IT SOUNDS LIKE WE BOTH VOTED FOR THIS PERSON FOR PRESIDENT.
2/10
AND WE NEVER SPOKE AGAIN.

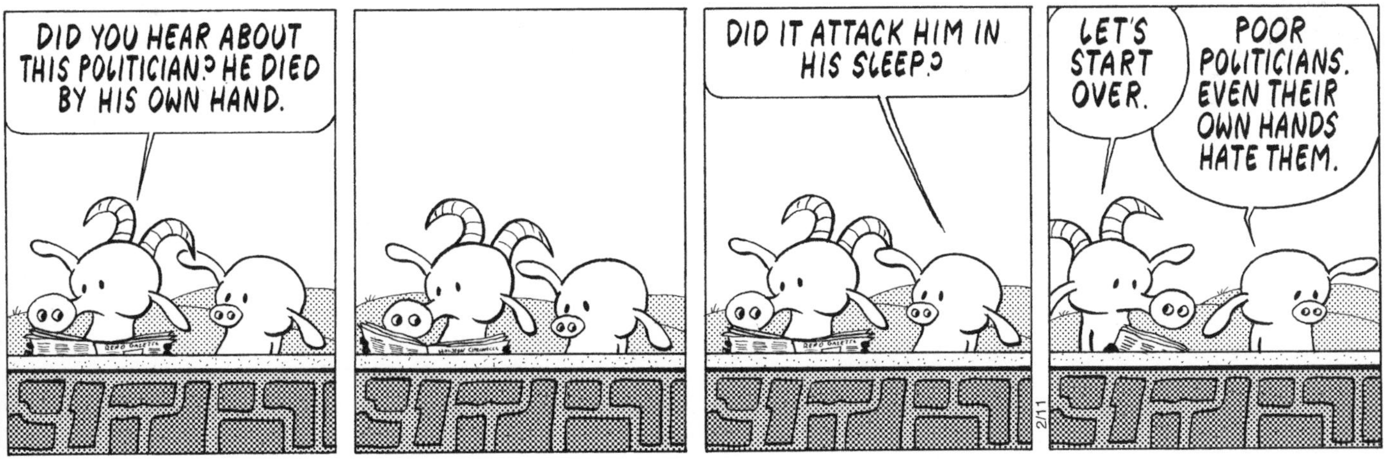
DID YOU HEAR ABOUT THIS POLITICIAN? HE DIED BY HIS OWN HAND.
DID IT ATTACK HIM IN HIS SLEEP?
2/11
LET'S START OVER.
POOR POLITICIANS. EVEN THEIR OWN HANDS HATE THEM.

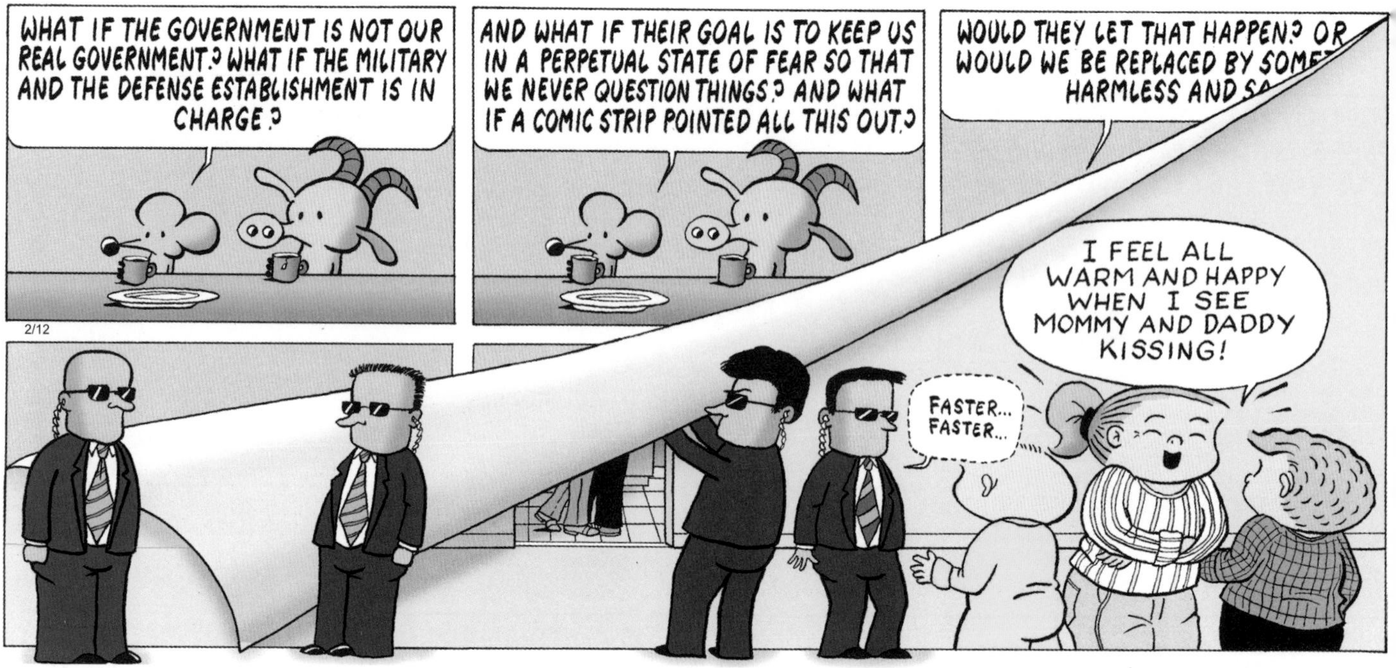
WHAT IF THE GOVERNMENT IS NOT OUR REAL GOVERNMENT? WHAT IF THE MILITARY AND THE DEFENSE ESTABLISHMENT IS IN CHARGE?
AND WHAT IF THEIR GOAL IS TO KEEP US IN A PERPETUAL STATE OF FEAR SO THAT WE NEVER QUESTION THINGS? AND WHAT IF A COMIC STRIP POINTED ALL THIS OUT?
WOULD THEY LET THAT HAPPEN? OR WOULD WE BE REPLACED BY SOME
HARMLESS AND
2/12
I FEEL ALL WARM AND HAPPY WHEN I SEE MOMMY AND DADDY KISSING!
FASTER... FASTER...

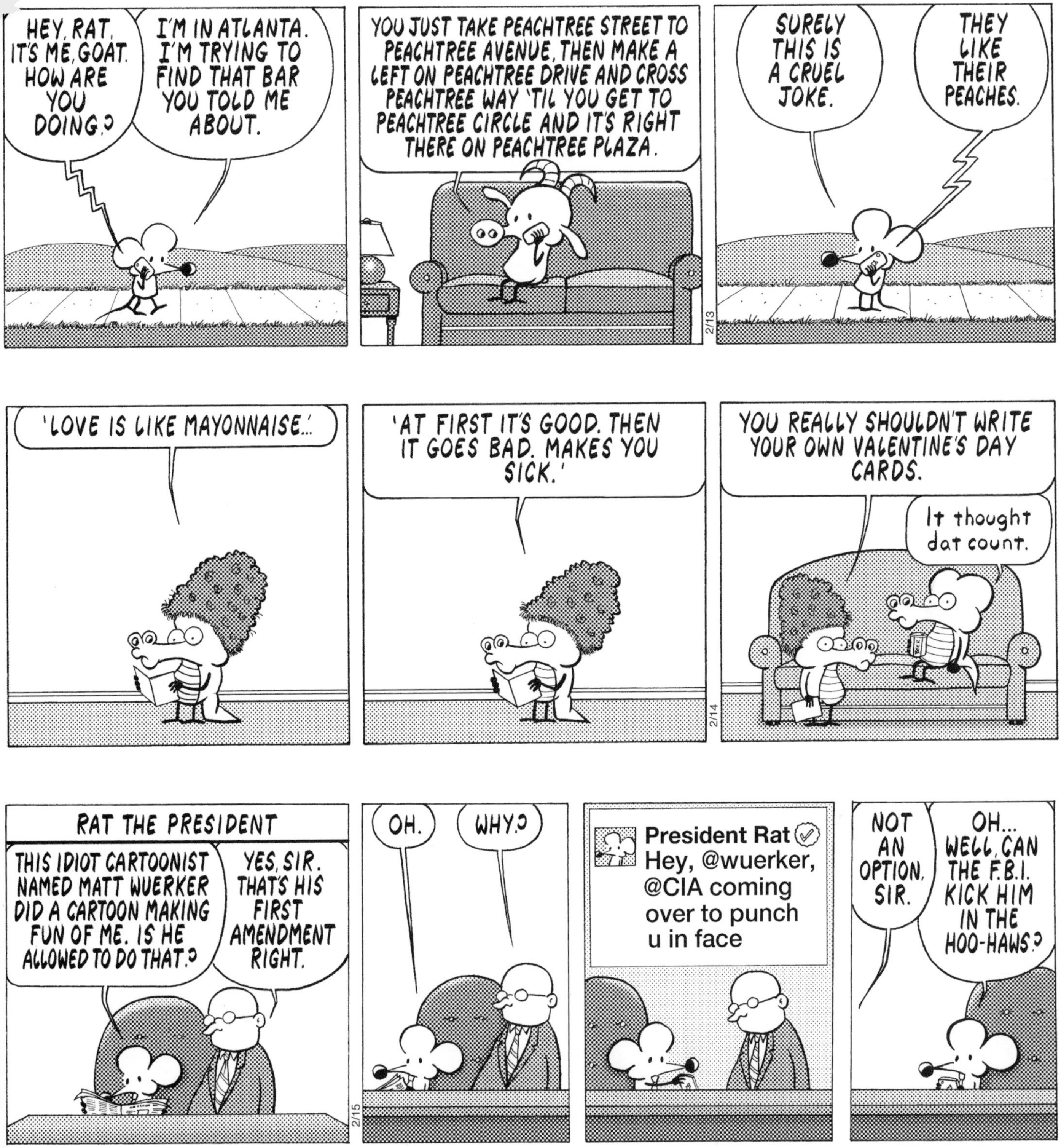
HEY, RAT. IT'S ME, GOAT. HOW ARE YOU DOING?
I'M IN ATLANTA. I'M TRYING TO FIND THAT BAR YOU TOLD ME ABOUT.
YOU JUST TAKE PEACHTREE STREET TO PEACHTREE AVENUE, THEN MAKE A LEFT ON PEACHTREE DRIVE AND CROSS PEACHTREE WAY 'TIL YOU GET TO PEACHTREE CIRCLE AND IT'S RIGHT THERE ON PEACHTREE PLAZA.
2/13
SURELY THIS IS A CRUEL JOKE.
THEY LIKE THEIR PEACHES.
'LOVE IS LIKE MAYONNAISE...'
'AT FIRST IT'S GOOD. THEN IT GOES BAD. MAKES YOU SICK.'
2/14
YOU REALLY SHOULDN'T WRITE YOUR OWN VALENTINE'S DAY CARDS.
It thought dat count.
RAT THE PRESIDENT
THIS IDIOT CARTOONIST NAMED MATT WUERKER DID A CARTOON MAKING FUN OF ME. IS HE ALLOWED TO DO THAT?
YES, SIR. THAT'S HIS FIRST AMENDMENT RIGHT.
2/15
OH.
WHY?
President Rat
Hey, @wuerker, @CIA coming over to punch u in face
NOT AN OPTION, SIR.
OH... WELL, CAN THE F.B.I. KICK HIM IN THE HOO-HAWS?

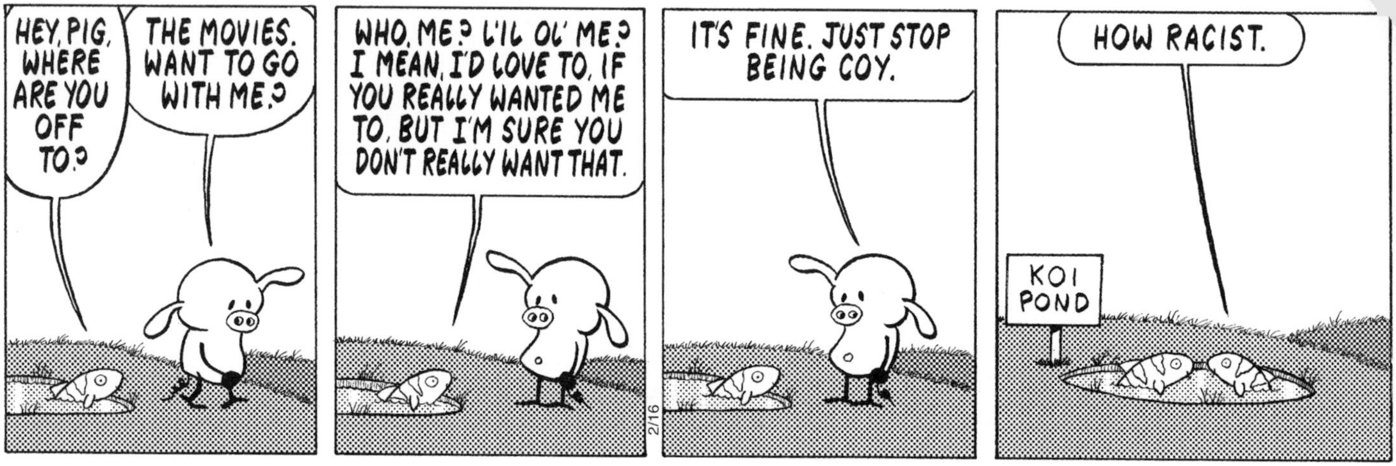
HEY, PIG, WHERE ARE YOU OFF TO?
THE MOVIES. WANT TO GO WITH ME?
WHO, ME? L'IL OL' ME? I MEAN, I'D LOVE TO, IF YOU REALLY WANTED ME TO, BUT I'M SURE YOU DON'T REALLY WANT THAT.
2/16
IT'S FINE. JUST STOP BEING COY.
KOI POND
HOW RACIST.

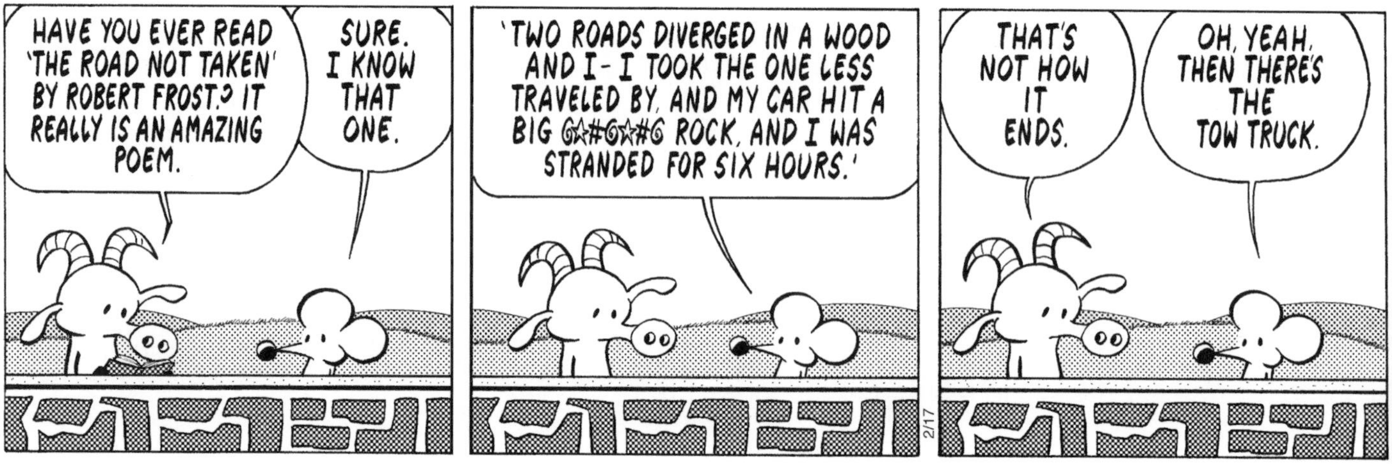
HAVE YOU EVER READ 'THE ROAD NOT TAKEN' BY ROBERT FROST? IT REALLY IS AN AMAZING POEM.
SURE. I KNOW THAT ONE.
'TWO ROADS DIVERGED IN A WOOD AND I - I TOOK THE ONE LESS TRAVELED BY, AND MY CAR HIT A BIG @☆#@☆#@ ROCK, AND I WAS STRANDED FOR SIX HOURS.'
2/17
THAT'S NOT HOW IT ENDS.
OH, YEAH. THEN THERE'S THE TOW TRUCK.

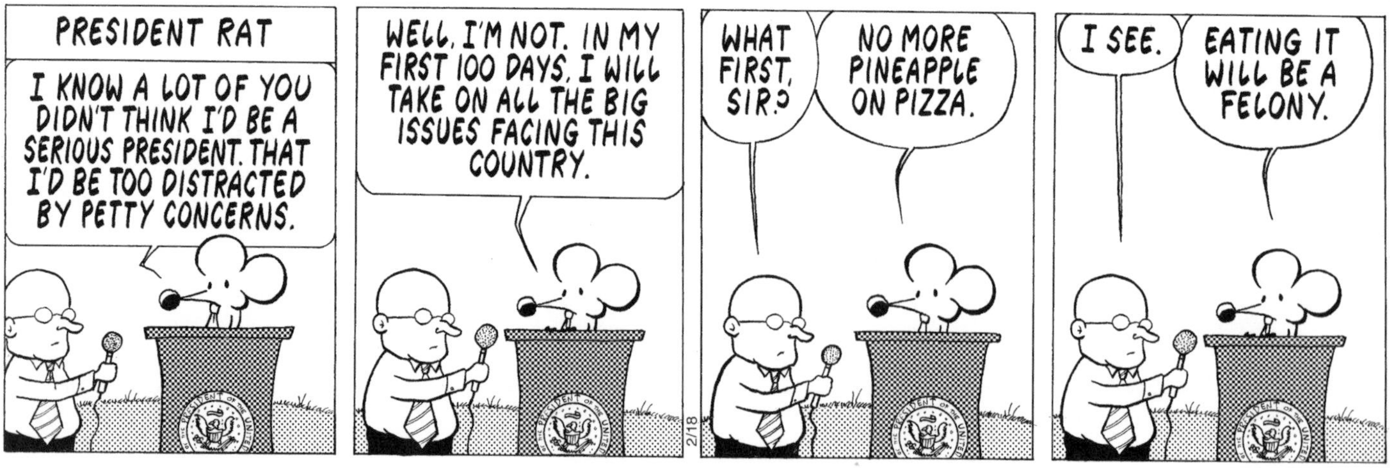
PRESIDENT RAT
I KNOW A LOT OF YOU DIDN'T THINK I'D BE A SERIOUS PRESIDENT. THAT I'D BE TOO DISTRACTED BY PETTY CONCERNS.
WELL, I'M NOT. IN MY FIRST 100 DAYS, I WILL TAKE ON ALL THE BIG ISSUES FACING THIS COUNTRY.
2/18
WHAT FIRST, SIR?
NO MORE PINEAPPLE ON PIZZA.
I SEE.
EATING IT WILL BE A FELONY.

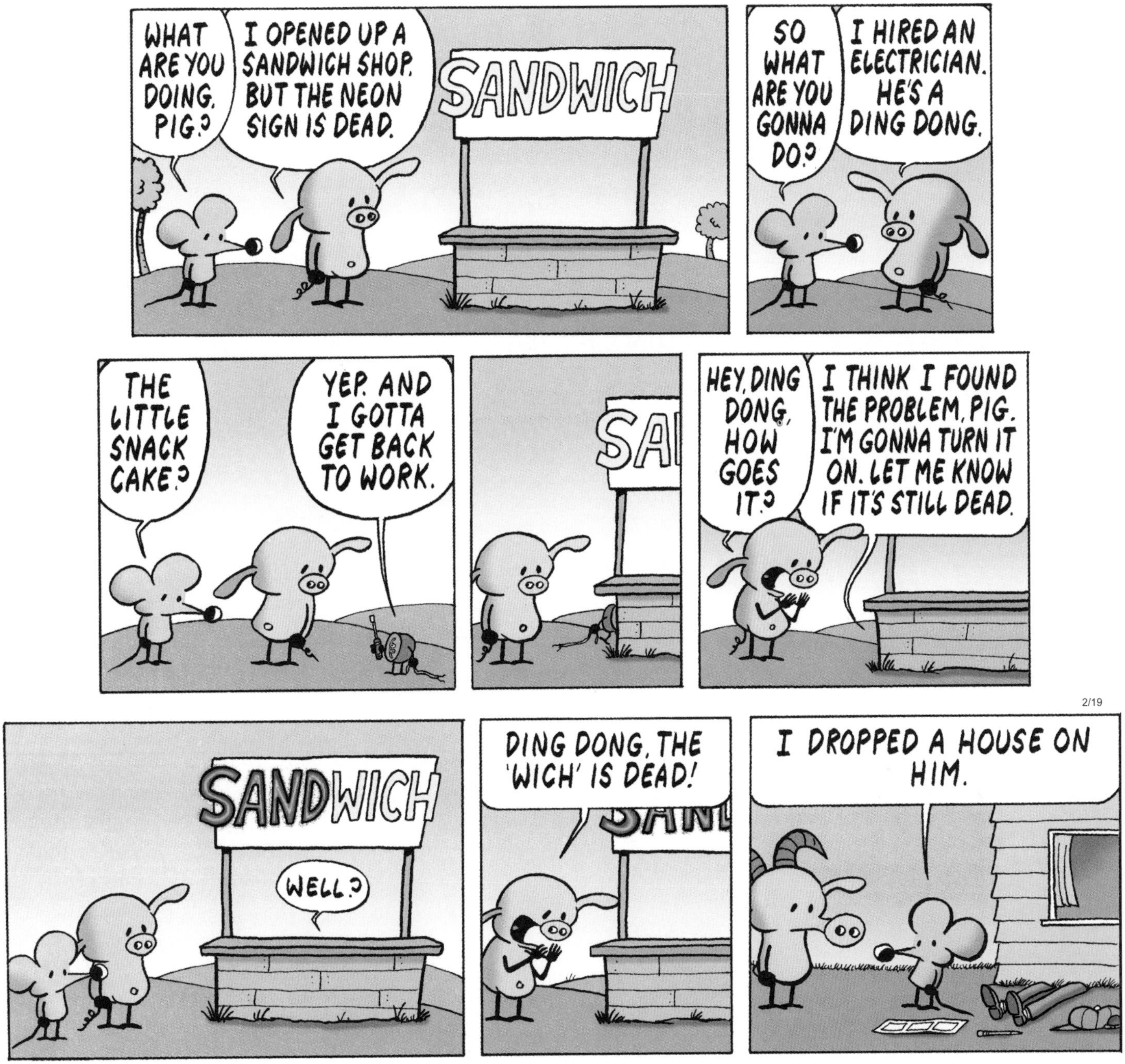
WHAT ARE YOU DOING, PIG?
I OPENED UP A SANDWICH SHOP, BUT THE NEON SIGN IS DEAD.
SANDWICH
SO WHAT ARE YOU GONNA DO?
I HIRED AN ELECTRICIAN. HE'S A DING DONG.
THE LITTLE SNACK CAKE?
YEP. AND I GOTTA GET BACK TO WORK.
HEY, DING DONG, HOW GOES IT?
I THINK I FOUND THE PROBLEM, PIG. I'M GONNA TURN IT ON. LET ME KNOW IF IT'S STILL DEAD.
2/19
SANDWICH
WELL?
DING DONG, THE 'WICH' IS DEAD!
I DROPPED A HOUSE ON HIM.

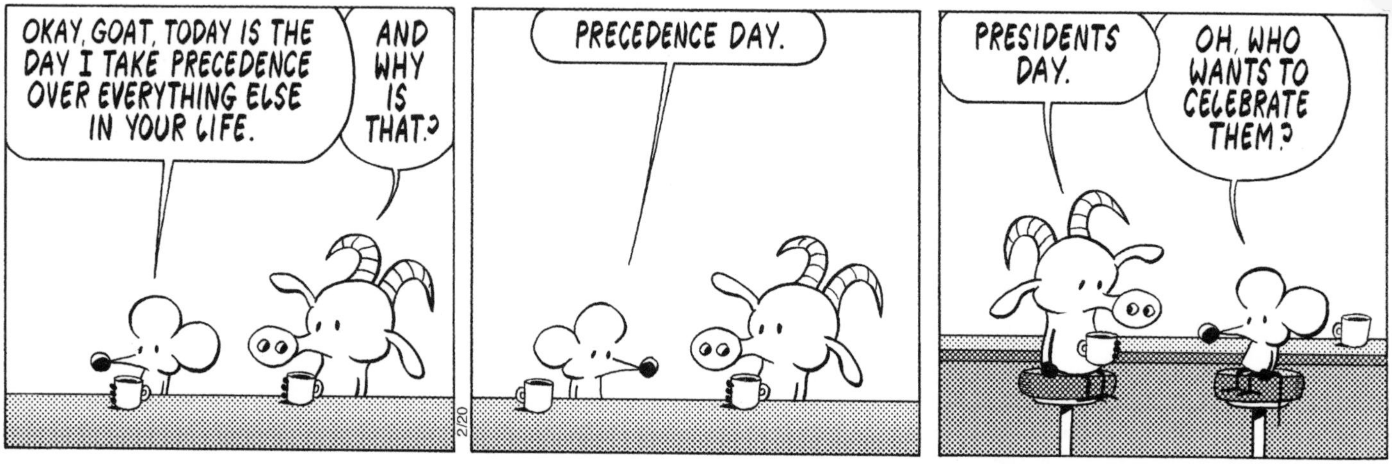
OKAY, GOAT, TODAY IS THE DAY I TAKE PRECEDENCE OVER EVERYTHING ELSE IN YOUR LIFE.
AND WHY IS THAT?
PRECEDENCE DAY.
PRESIDENTS DAY.
OH, WHO WANTS TO CELEBRATE THEM?
2/20

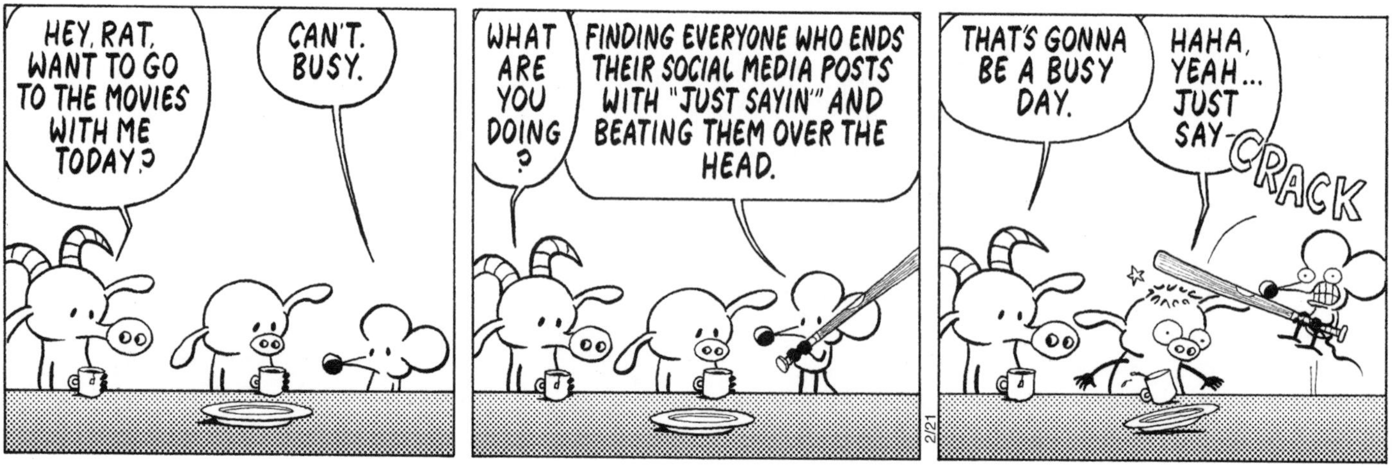
HEY, RAT, WANT TO GO TO THE MOVIES WITH ME TODAY?
CAN'T. BUSY.
WHAT ARE YOU DOING?
FINDING EVERYONE WHO ENDS THEIR SOCIAL MEDIA POSTS WITH "JUST SAYIN'" AND BEATING THEM OVER THE HEAD.
THAT'S GONNA BE A BUSY DAY.
HAHA, YEAH... JUST SAY-
CRACK
2/21

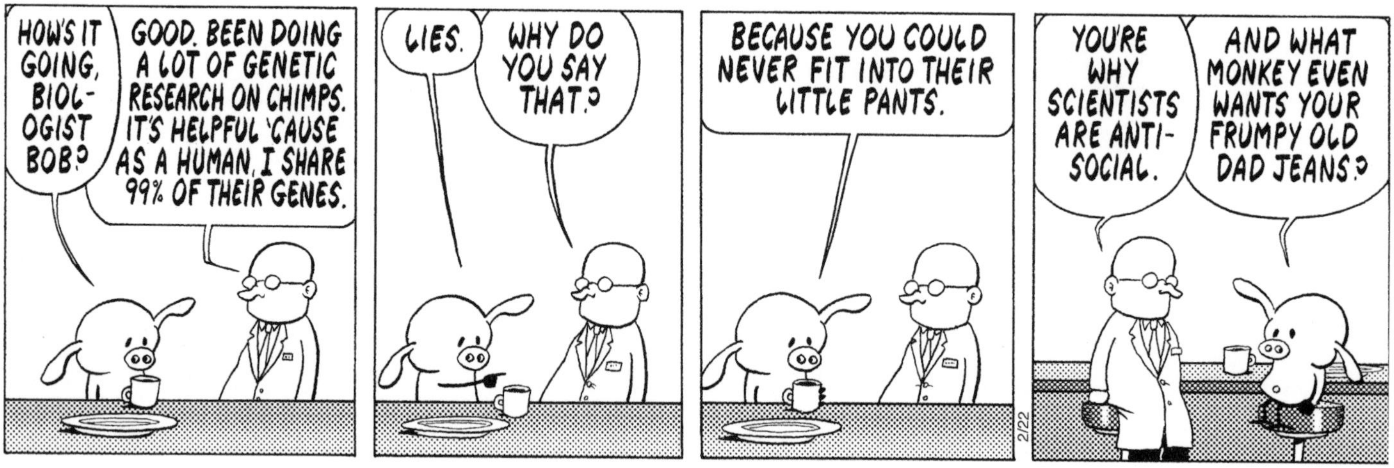
HOW'S IT GOING, BIOLOGIST BOB?
GOOD. BEEN DOING A LOT OF GENETIC RESEARCH ON CHIMPS. IT'S HELPFUL 'CAUSE AS A HUMAN, I SHARE 99% OF THEIR GENES.
LIES.
WHY DO YOU SAY THAT?
BECAUSE YOU COULD NEVER FIT INTO THEIR LITTLE PANTS.
YOU'RE WHY SCIENTISTS ARE ANTI-SOCIAL.
AND WHAT MONKEY EVEN WANTS YOUR FRUMPY OLD DAD JEANS?
2/22

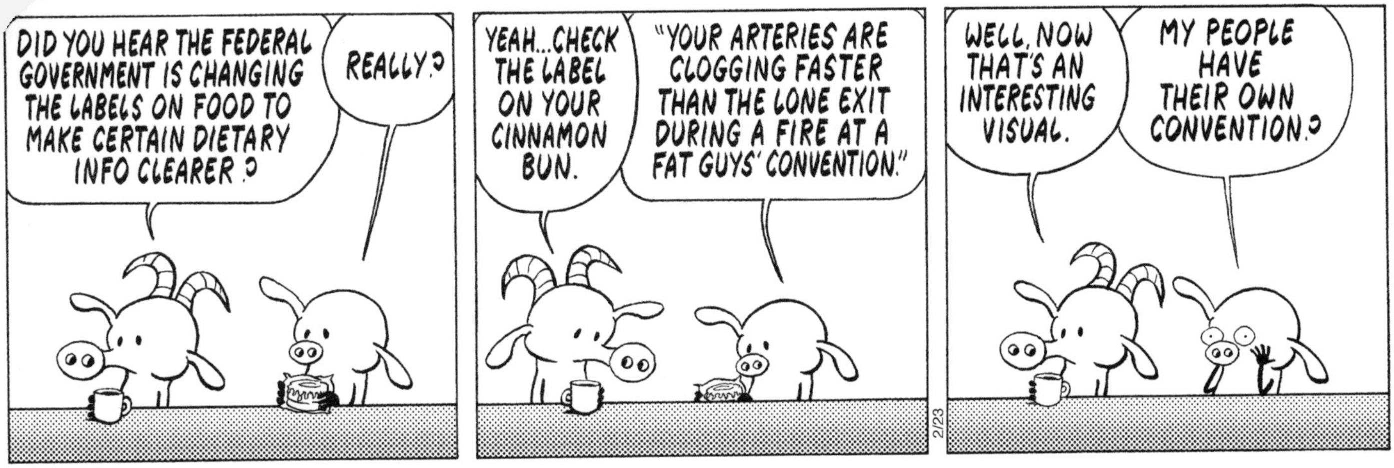
DID YOU HEAR THE FEDERAL GOVERNMENT IS CHANGING THE LABELS ON FOOD TO MAKE CERTAIN DIETARY INFO CLEARER?
REALLY?
YEAH...CHECK THE LABEL ON YOUR CINNAMON BUN.
"YOUR ARTERIES ARE CLOGGING FASTER THAN THE LONE EXIT DURING A FIRE AT A FAT GUYS' CONVENTION."
WELL, NOW THAT'S AN INTERESTING VISUAL.
MY PEOPLE HAVE THEIR OWN CONVENTION?
2/23

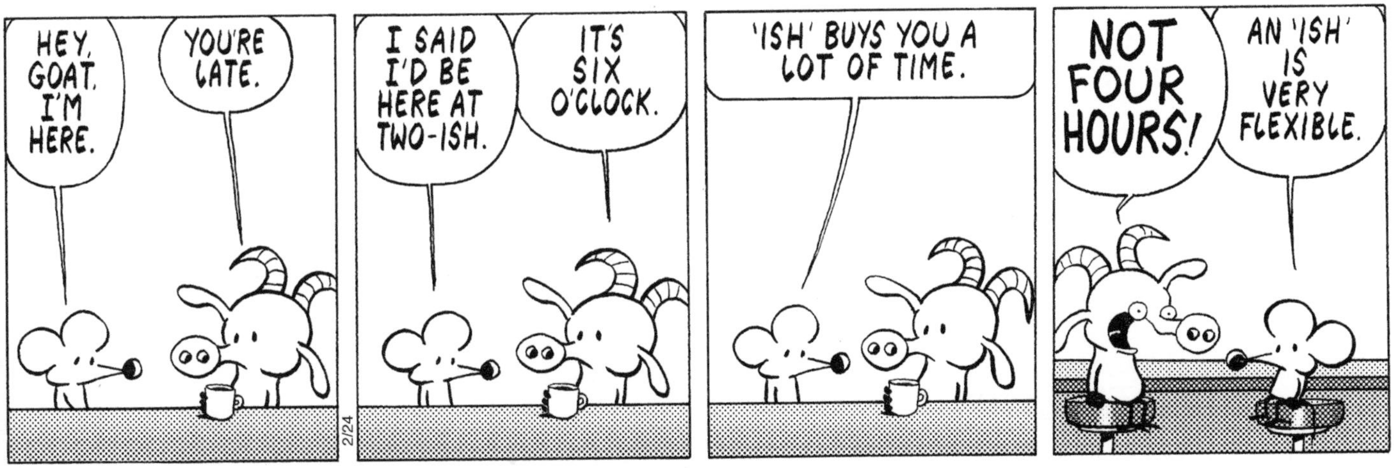
HEY, GOAT. I'M HERE.
YOU'RE LATE.
2/24
I SAID I'D BE HERE AT TWO-ISH.
IT'S SIX O'CLOCK.
'ISH' BUYS YOU A LOT OF TIME.
NOT FOUR HOURS!
AN 'ISH' IS VERY FLEXIBLE.

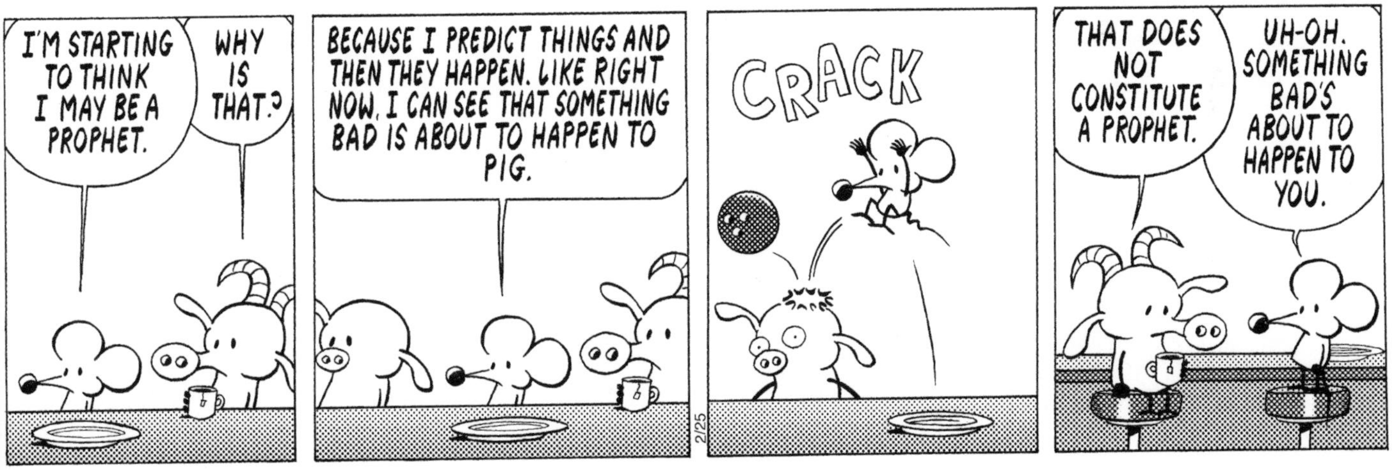
I'M STARTING TO THINK I MAY BE A PROPHET.
WHY IS THAT?
BECAUSE I PREDICT THINGS AND THEN THEY HAPPEN. LIKE RIGHT NOW, I CAN SEE THAT SOMETHING BAD IS ABOUT TO HAPPEN TO PIG.
2/25
CRACK
THAT DOES NOT CONSTITUTE A PROPHET.
UH-OH. SOMETHING BAD'S ABOUT TO HAPPEN TO YOU.

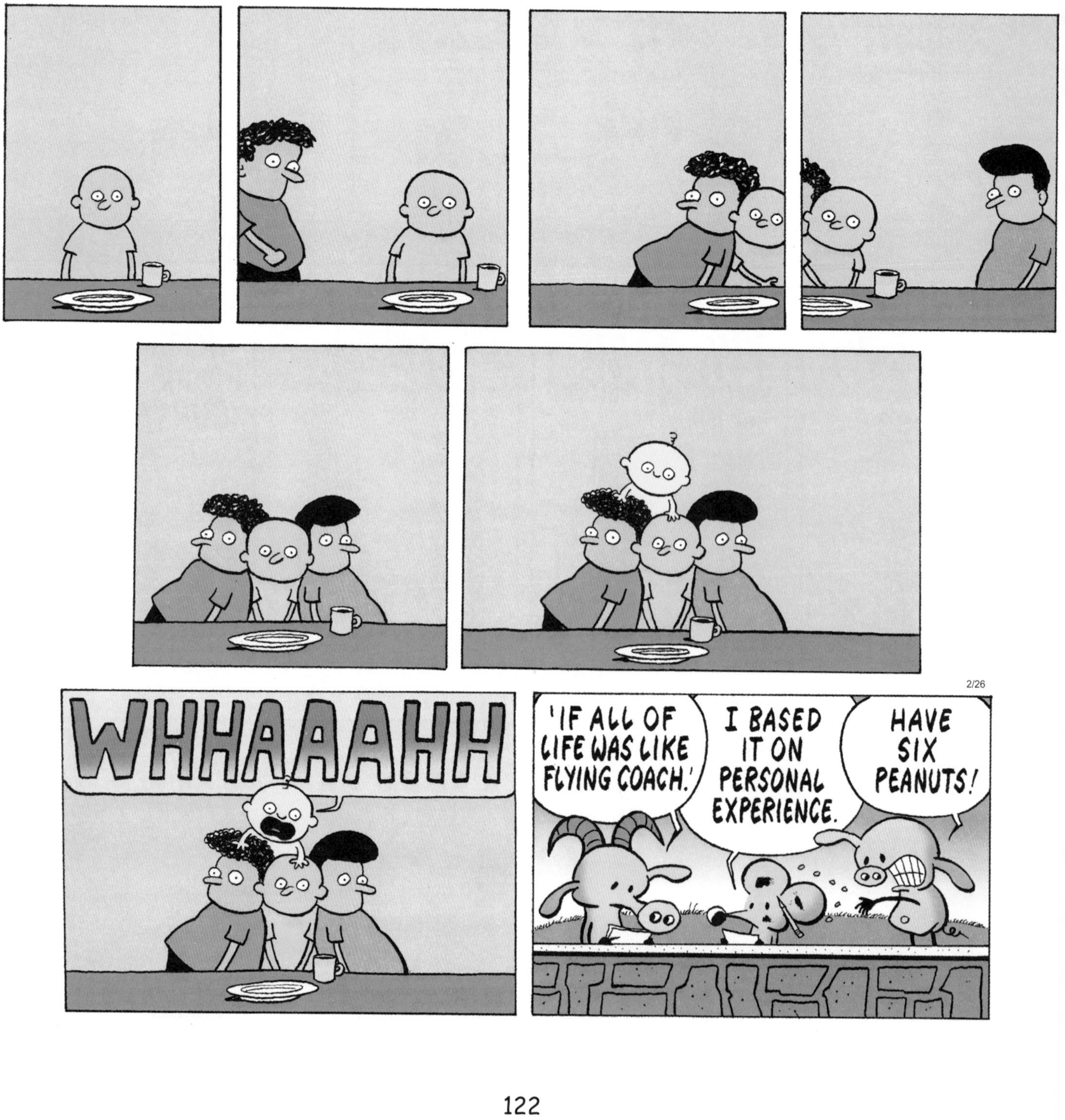
WHHAAAAHH
2/26
'IF ALL OF LIFE WAS LIKE FLYING COACH.'
I BASED IT ON PERSONAL EXPERIENCE.
HAVE SIX PEANUTS!

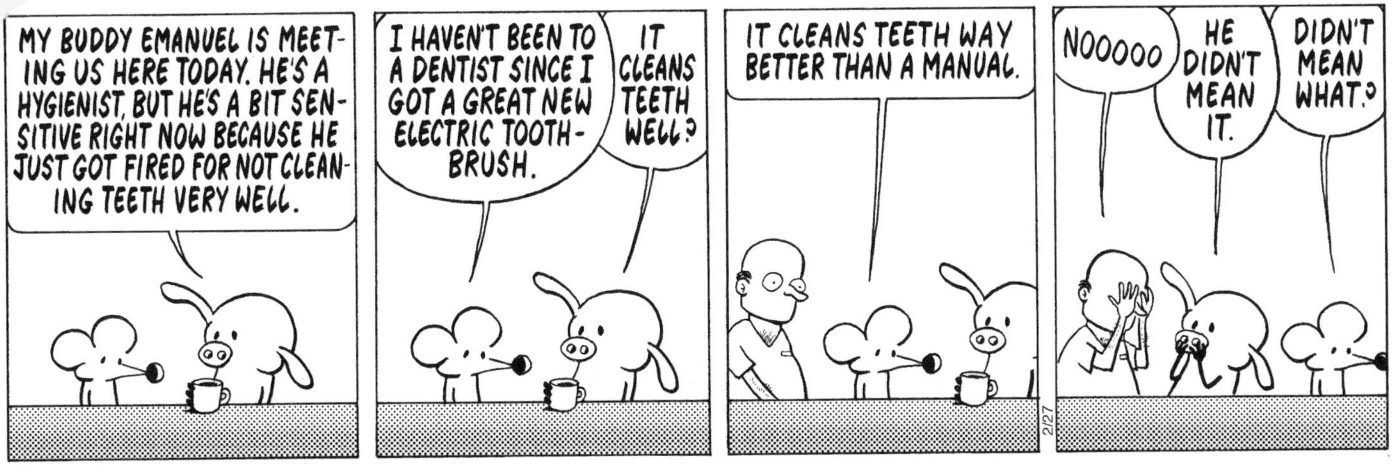
MY BUDDY EMANUEL IS MEETING US HERE TODAY. HE'S A HYGIENIST, BUT HE'S A BIT SENSITIVE RIGHT NOW BECAUSE HE JUST GOT FIRED FOR NOT CLEANING TEETH VERY WELL.
I HAVEN'T BEEN TO A DENTIST SINCE I GOT A GREAT NEW ELECTRIC TOOTHBRUSH.
IT CLEANS TEETH WELL?
IT CLEANS TEETH WAY BETTER THAN A MANUAL.
2/27
NOOOOO
HE DIDN'T MEAN IT.
DIDN'T MEAN WHAT?

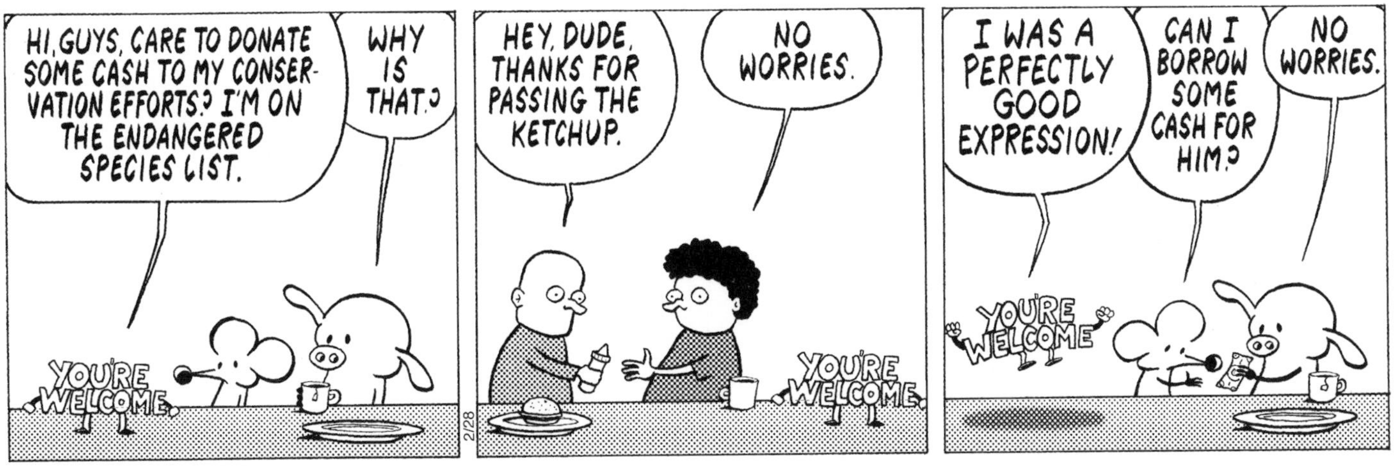
HI, GUYS, CARE TO DONATE SOME CASH TO MY CONSERVATION EFFORTS? I'M ON THE ENDANGERED SPECIES LIST.
WHY IS THAT?
YOU'RE WELCOME
2/28
HEY, DUDE, THANKS FOR PASSING THE KETCHUP.
NO WORRIES.
YOU'RE WELCOME
I WAS A PERFECTLY GOOD EXPRESSION!
CAN I BORROW SOME CASH FOR HIM?
NO WORRIES.
YOU'RE WELCOME

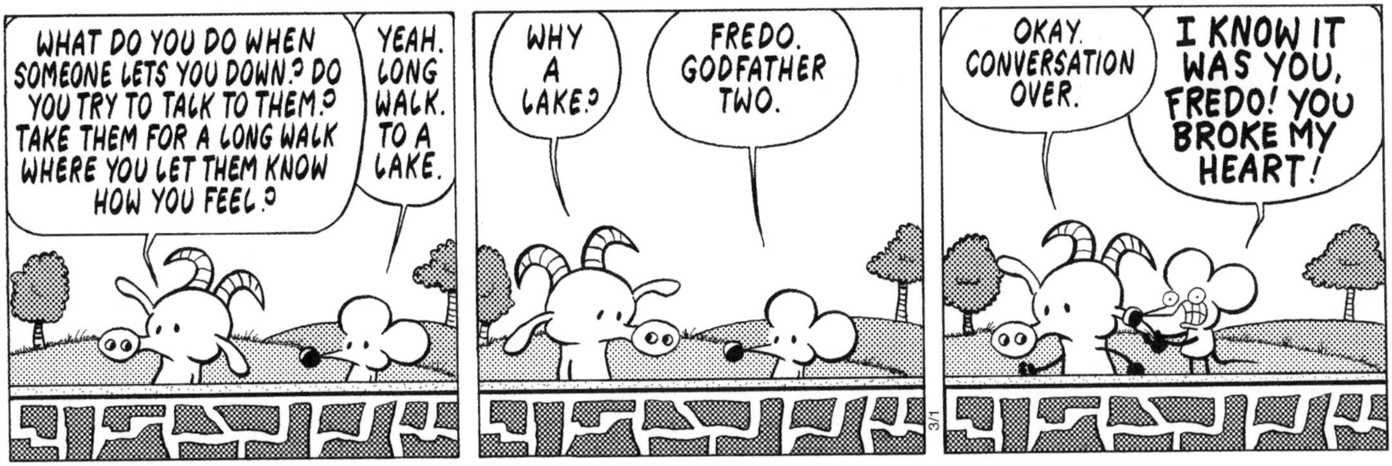
WHAT DO YOU DO WHEN SOMEONE LETS YOU DOWN? DO YOU TRY TO TALK TO THEM? TAKE THEM FOR A LONG WALK WHERE YOU LET THEM KNOW HOW YOU FEEL?
YEAH. LONG WALK. TO A LAKE.
WHY A LAKE?
FREDO. GODFATHER TWO.
3/1
OKAY. CONVERSATION OVER.
I KNOW IT WAS YOU, FREDO! YOU BROKE MY HEART!

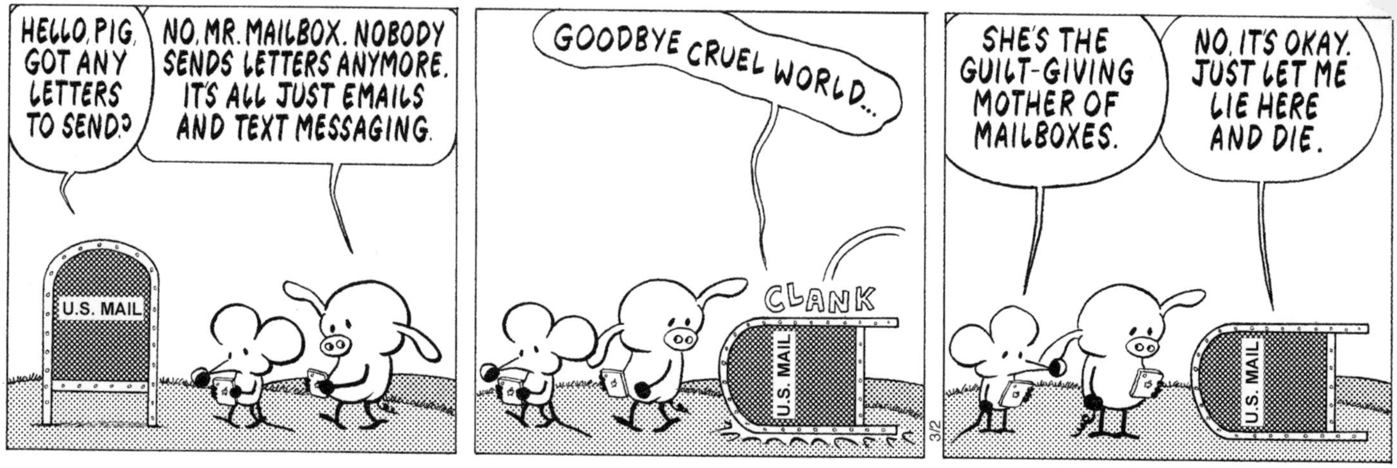
HELLO, PIG, GOT ANY LETTERS TO SEND?
NO, MR. MAILBOX. NOBODY SENDS LETTERS ANYMORE. IT'S ALL JUST EMAILS AND TEXT MESSAGING.
U.S. MAIL
GOODBYE CRUEL WORLD...
CLANK
U.S. MAIL
3/2
SHE'S THE GUILT-GIVING MOTHER OF MAILBOXES.
NO, IT'S OKAY. JUST LET ME LIE HERE AND DIE.
U.S. MAIL

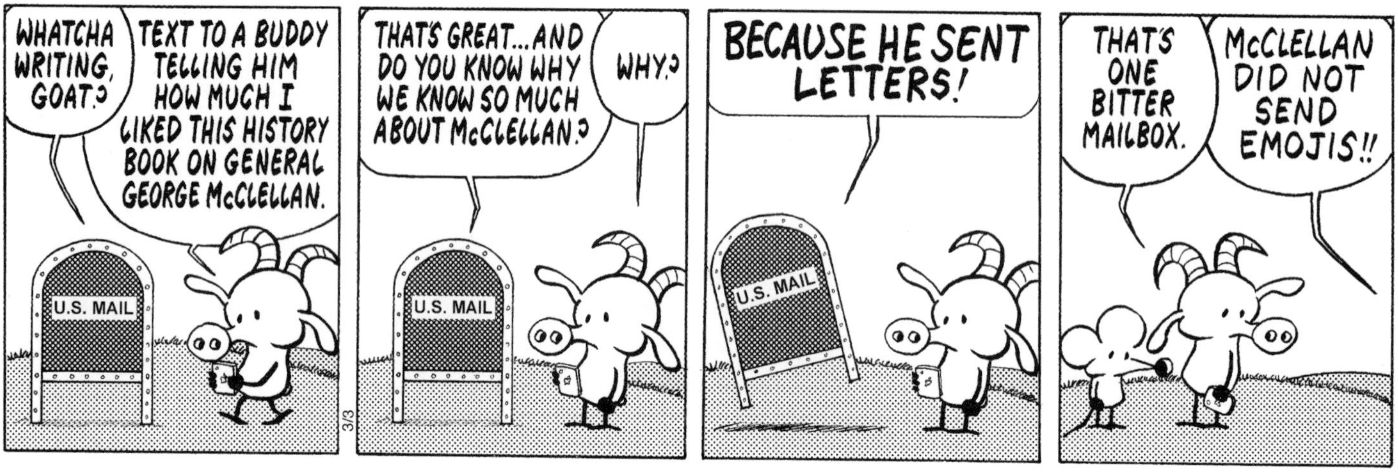
WHATCHA WRITING, GOAT?
TEXT TO A BUDDY TELLING HIM HOW MUCH I LIKED THIS HISTORY BOOK ON GENERAL GEORGE McCLELLAN.
U.S. MAIL
3/3
THAT'S GREAT...AND DO YOU KNOW WHY WE KNOW SO MUCH ABOUT McCLELLAN?
WHY?
U.S. MAIL
BECAUSE HE SENT LETTERS!
U.S. MAIL
THAT'S ONE BITTER MAILBOX.
McCLELLAN DID NOT SEND EMOJIS!!

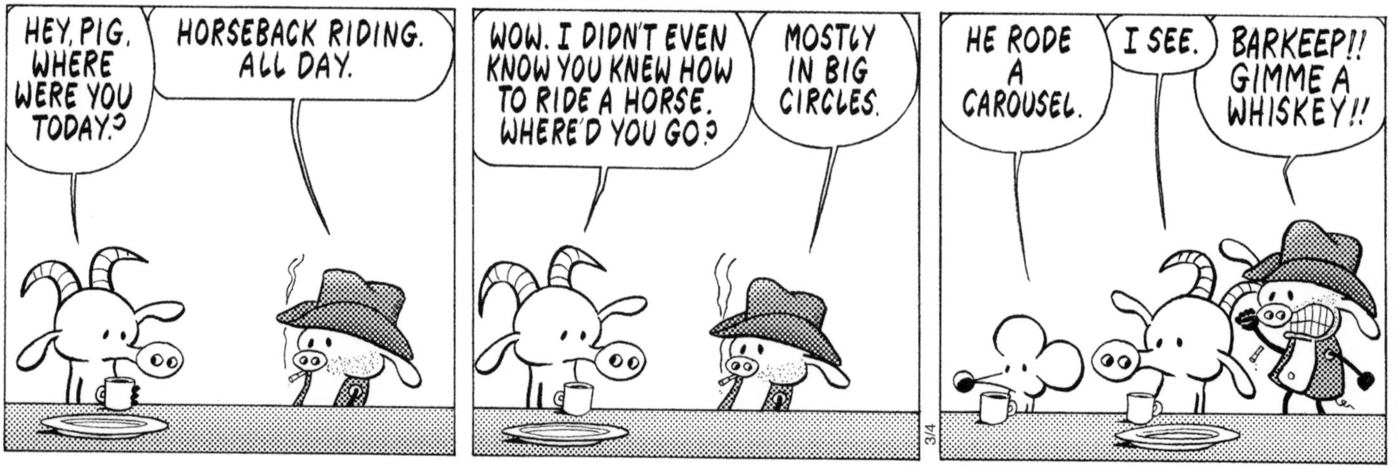
HEY, PIG. WHERE WERE YOU TODAY?
HORSEBACK RIDING. ALL DAY.
WOW. I DIDN'T EVEN KNOW YOU KNEW HOW TO RIDE A HORSE. WHERE'D YOU GO?
MOSTLY IN BIG CIRCLES.
3/4
HE RODE A CAROUSEL.
I SEE.
BARKEEP!! GIMME A WHISKEY!!

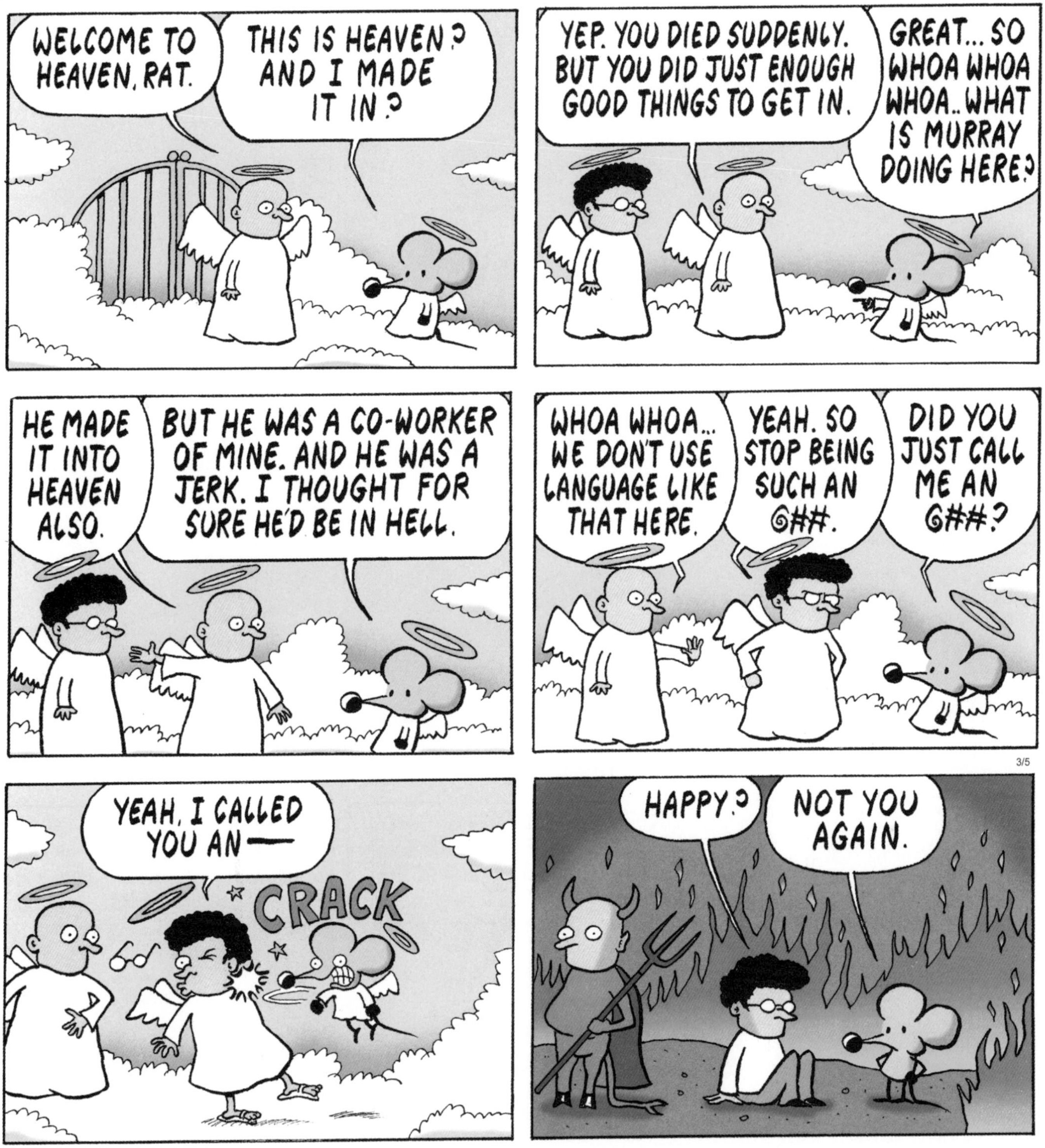
WELCOME TO HEAVEN, RAT.
THIS IS HEAVEN? AND I MADE IT IN?
YEP. YOU DIED SUDDENLY. BUT YOU DID JUST ENOUGH GOOD THINGS TO GET IN.
GREAT... SO WHOA WHOA WHOA.. WHAT IS MURRAY DOING HERE?
HE MADE IT INTO HEAVEN ALSO.
BUT HE WAS A CO-WORKER OF MINE. AND HE WAS A JERK. I THOUGHT FOR SURE HE'D BE IN HELL.
WHOA WHOA... WE DON'T USE LANGUAGE LIKE THAT HERE.
YEAH. SO STOP BEING SUCH AN @##.
DID YOU JUST CALL ME AN @##?
3/5
YEAH, I CALLED YOU AN—
CRACK
HAPPY?
NOT YOU AGAIN.

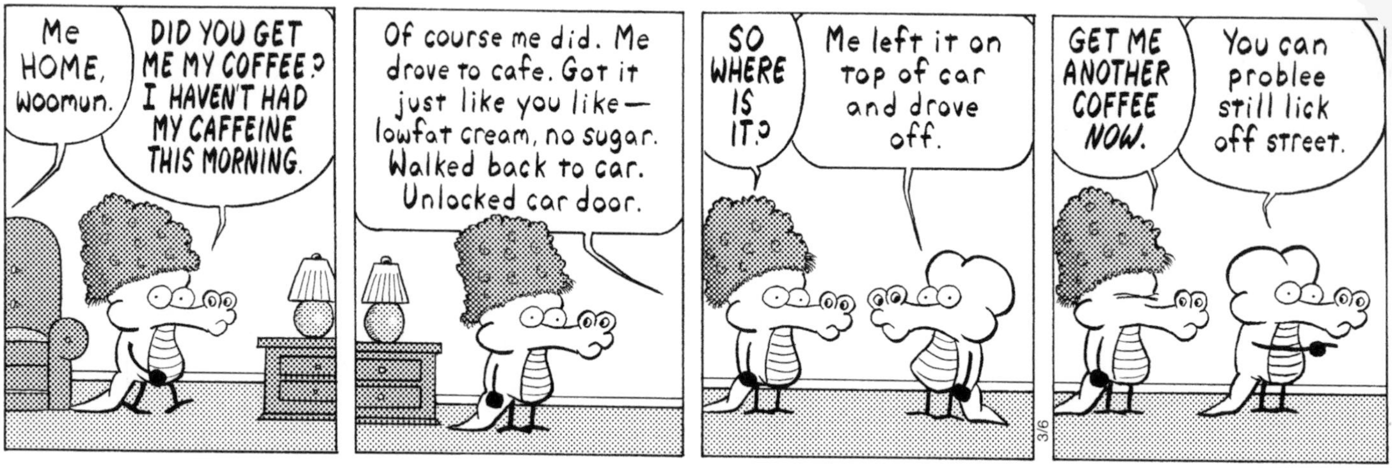
Me HOME, woomun.
DID YOU GET ME MY COFFEE? I HAVEN'T HAD MY CAFFEINE THIS MORNING.
Of course me did. Me drove to cafe. Got it just like you like— lowfat cream, no sugar. Walked back to car. Unlocked car door.
SO WHERE IS IT?
Me left it on top of car and drove off.
GET ME ANOTHER COFFEE NOW.
You can problee still lick off street.
3/6

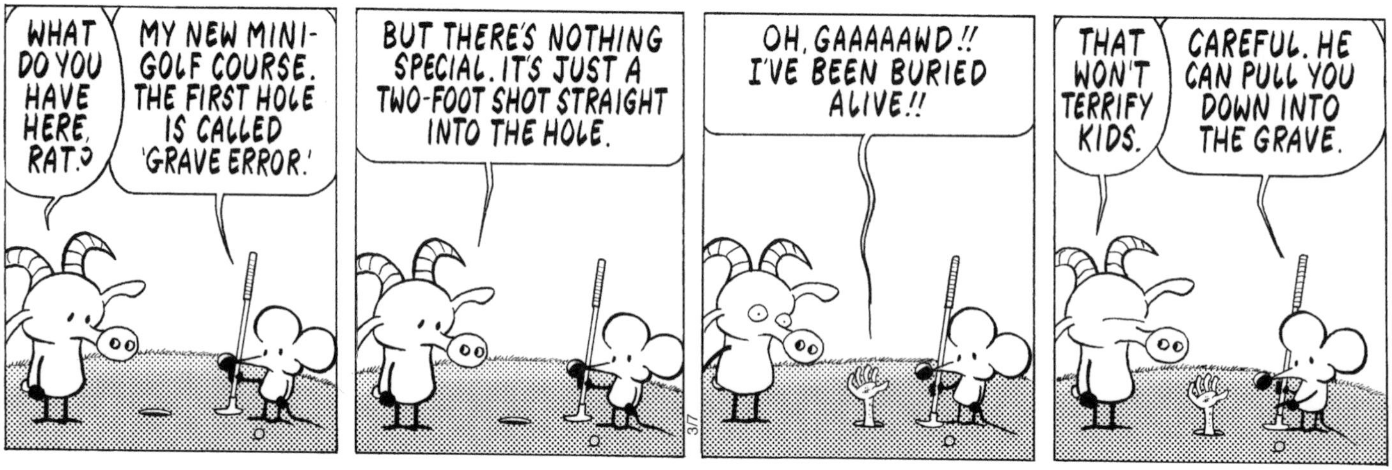
WHAT DO YOU HAVE HERE, RAT?
MY NEW MINI-GOLF COURSE. THE FIRST HOLE IS CALLED 'GRAVE ERROR.'
BUT THERE'S NOTHING SPECIAL. IT'S JUST A TWO-FOOT SHOT STRAIGHT INTO THE HOLE.
3/7
OH, GAAAAAWD!! I'VE BEEN BURIED ALIVE!!
THAT WON'T TERRIFY KIDS.
CAREFUL. HE CAN PULL YOU DOWN INTO THE GRAVE.

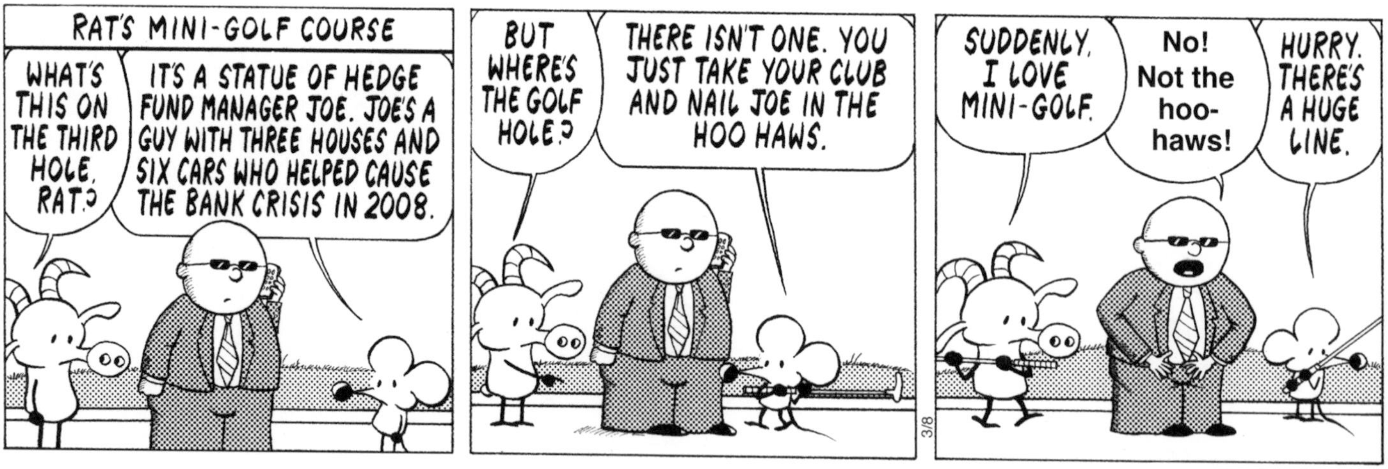
RAT'S MINI-GOLF COURSE
WHAT'S THIS ON THE THIRD HOLE, RAT?
IT'S A STATUE OF HEDGE FUND MANAGER JOE. JOE'S A GUY WITH THREE HOUSES AND SIX CARS WHO HELPED CAUSE THE BANK CRISIS IN 2008.
BUT WHERE'S THE GOLF HOLE?
THERE ISN'T ONE. YOU JUST TAKE YOUR CLUB AND NAIL JOE IN THE HOO HAWS.
3/8
SUDDENLY, I LOVE MINI-GOLF.
No! Not the hoo-haws!
HURRY. THERE'S A HUGE LINE.

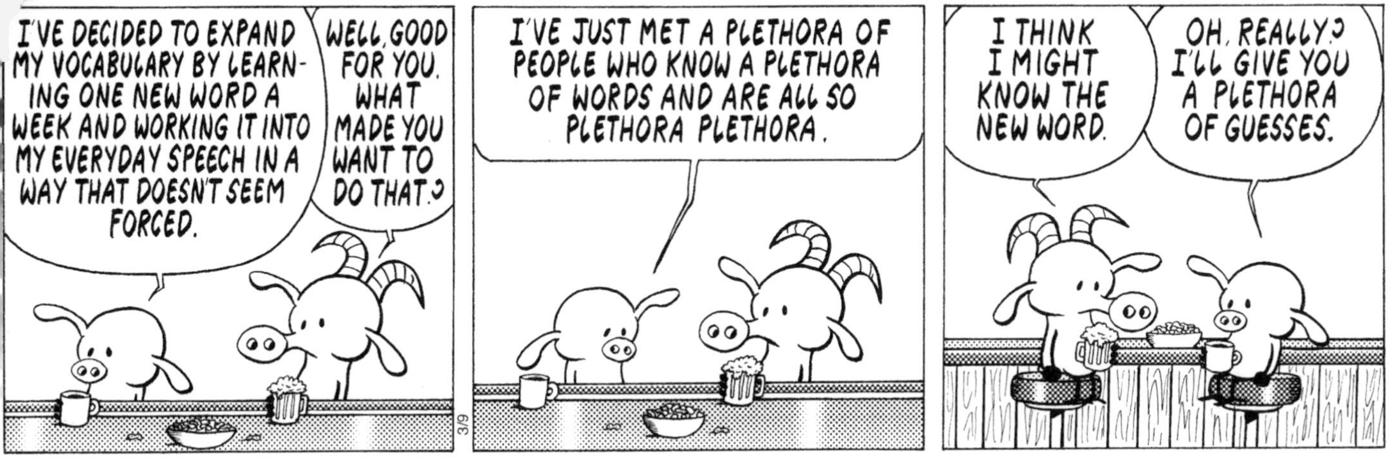
I'VE DECIDED TO EXPAND MY VOCABULARY BY LEARNING ONE NEW WORD A WEEK AND WORKING IT INTO MY EVERYDAY SPEECH IN A WAY THAT DOESN'T SEEM FORCED.
WELL, GOOD FOR YOU. WHAT MADE YOU WANT TO DO THAT?
3/9
I'VE JUST MET A PLETHORA OF PEOPLE WHO KNOW A PLETHORA OF WORDS AND ARE ALL SO PLETHORA PLETHORA.
I THINK I MIGHT KNOW THE NEW WORD.
OH, REALLY? I'LL GIVE YOU A PLETHORA OF GUESSES.

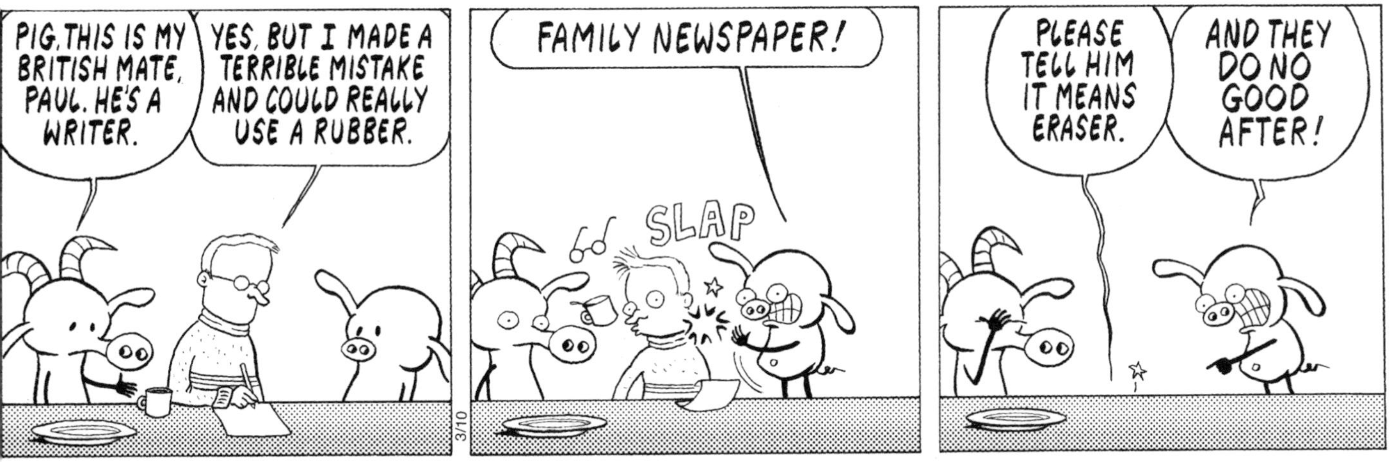
PIG, THIS IS MY BRITISH MATE, PAUL. HE'S A WRITER.
YES, BUT I MADE A TERRIBLE MISTAKE AND COULD REALLY USE A RUBBER.
3/10
FAMILY NEWSPAPER!
SLAP
PLEASE TELL HIM IT MEANS ERASER.
AND THEY DO NO GOOD AFTER!

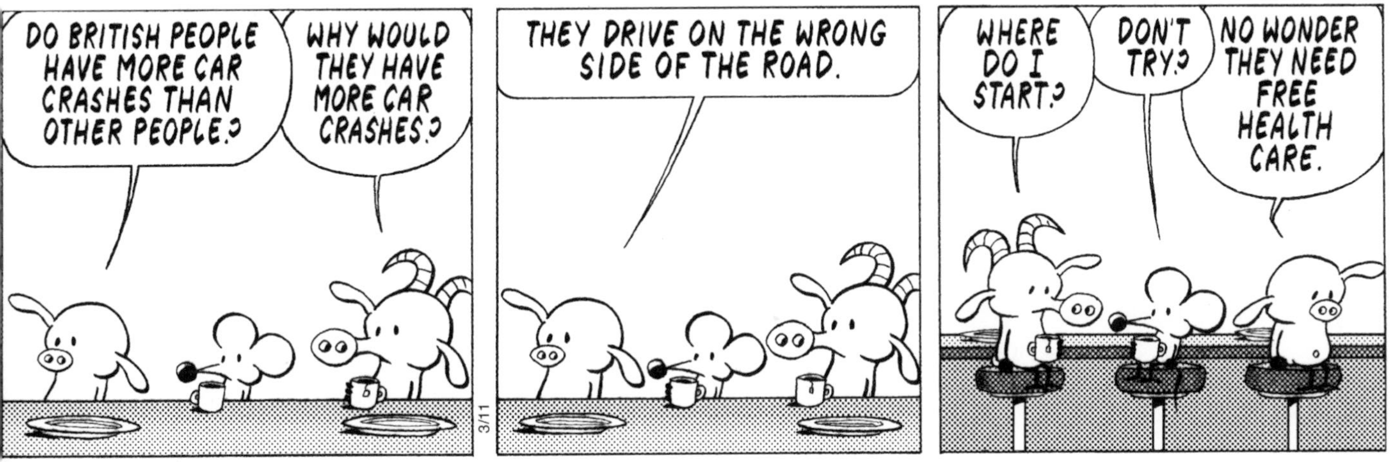
DO BRITISH PEOPLE HAVE MORE CAR CRASHES THAN OTHER PEOPLE?
WHY WOULD THEY HAVE MORE CAR CRASHES?
3/11
THEY DRIVE ON THE WRONG SIDE OF THE ROAD.
WHERE DO I START?
DON'T TRY?
NO WONDER THEY NEED FREE HEALTH CARE.

Pearls Before Swine is distributed internationally by Andrews McMeel Syndication.

Floundering Fathers copyright © 2018 by Stephan Pastis. All rights reserved. Printed in China. No part of this book may be used or reproduced in any manner whatsoever without written permission except in the case of reprints in the context of reviews.

Andrews McMeel Publishing
a division of Andrews McMeel Universal
1130 Walnut Street, Kansas City, Missouri 64106

www.andrewsmcmeel.com

18 19 20 21 22 SDB 10 9 8 7 6 5 4 3 2 1

ISBN: 978-1-4494-8934-2

Library of Congress Control Number: 2017947339

Pearls Before Swine can be viewed on the Internet at
www.pearlscomic.com

These strips appeared in newspapers from June 6, 2016 to March 11, 2017.